Journalism

Journalism

Norman B. Moyes

Samuel O. Erskine
Editorial Consultant

Ginn and Company

ACKNOWLEDGMENTS

Grateful acknowledgment is made to the following publishers, authors, and agents for permission to use and adapt copyrighted material:

Revista Chicano-Riqueña for the poem "Lemon" by Rita Mendoza, which was first published in *Revista Chicano-Riqueña* 5/2 (1977). Used by permission of the publisher and the author.

American Association of Advertising Agencies for "A Typical Advertising Agency Organization Chart by Functions" on page 111, from *Career Opportunities in Advertising*, © 1967. Also for the qualities important for a successful advertising career on page 556, from *Education for Advertising Careers*. Both used by permission.

American Society of Newspaper Editors for the "Statement of Principles" on pages 290–291. Reprinted by permission.

The Associated Press for excerpts from the profile of New York City Mayor Ed Koch by Saul Pett on pages 182–183 and for the adapted news story about earnings of American authors on page 201. Both used by permission.

The Boston Globe for the two articles by Ray Fitzgerald, "Pitching Sox Achilles Heel" on page 244 and "Never List-less" on page 246, and for the editorial "A Focus on Housing" (June 20, 1981) on page 260. All reprinted courtesy of *The Boston Globe*.

The Boston Herald for the excerpts from "Christopher Columbus Park" by Peter Gelzinis (March 3, 1983) on page 61, for "April Love Blooms in Public Garden" by Robert Garrett (April 24, 1981) on page 215, for the excerpts from Elliot Norton's obituary to Paddy Chayefsky (August 4, 1981) on pages 223–224, and for the information in "A Warden for Public Safety" on pages 286–288. All reprinted courtesy of *The Boston Herald*.

Broadcasting Magazine for the report of the interview of Jim Heyworth on page 172. Reprinted with permission from the June 15, 1981, issue of *Broadcasting* Magazine.

Charles S. Bullard for his editorial on pages 258–259, "The Y Affair," which won third place in the December 1967 William Randolph Hearst Foundation Journalism Awards Program for editorials. Reprinted by permission of the author and of the Hearst Foundation.

Abraham S. Chanin for the excerpts on pages 135–137 from his article "The 'Telly' Tells All," which appeared originally in the April 1981 issue of *The Quill*. Used by permission of the author.

The Christian Science Monitor for the Family/Living page on page 207, from the July 11, 1983, edition. Reprinted by permission from *The Christian Science Monitor*. © 1983 The Christian Science Publishing Society. All rights reserved.

Copley News Service for the excerpt on page 218 from " 'Silent Night' to Warm 165th Yuletide" by Richie W. McEwen. (Originally titled " 'Silent Night' to Warm 150th Yuletide," December 15, 1968) Reprinted by permission.

Field Newspaper Syndicate for the article on pages 225–226, "Everything in a Mess" by Erma Bombeck, May 7, 1981. From *At Wit's End* by Erma Bombeck. © 1981 Field Enterprises, Inc. Courtesy of Field Newspaper Syndicate.

Guernsey Le Pelley for "Martin Van who?" on page 256, from the "Lightly Le Pelley" column in the February 23, 1983, edition of *The Christian Science Monitor*. Used by permission of the author.

Los Angeles Times for the excerpt on page 173 from the interview of Patricia Lund Casserly, "Solving the Equation of Math Anxiety" by Marlene Cimons, October 23, 1980. Copyright, 1980, Los Angeles Times. Reprinted by permission.

Louisville Courier-Journal for the opinion page on page 268, from the September 1, 1982, edition. Reprinted by permission.

National Scholastic Press Association for the article on pages 247–248, from "Pitfalls: Sports Staff Beware" by Bill Ward, as it appeared in *Scholastic Editor Graphics/Communications*, March 1969. Used by permission.

(Acknowledgments continued)

National School Public Relations Association for the Checklist for Coverage of School Events on pages 427–428. From *Let's Go to Press* (now out of print)—Copyright the National School Public Relation Assn., 1801 N. Moore St., Arlington, Va. 22209—1954. Used by permission.

The New York Times for "The Fumblerules of Grammar" by William Safire on pages 220–221. © 1979 by The New York Times Company. Reprinted by permission.

Monte S. Paulsen for his advice to school photographers on page 542. Used by permission.

Henry Raymont for the excerpts on pages 261–262 from his editorial "Our Columbus," which appeared originally in the October 11, 1982, edition of *The Washington Post*. Used by permission of the author.

Syracuse Herald-Journal and the author for the article on page 219, "So Who Needs Horses?" by Richard Case, October 11, 1963. Used by permission.

WBZ-TV, Boston, for the editorial on page 254, "Legal Aid for the Poor," delivered April 29, 1981, by Sy Yanoff. Used by permission.

CREDITS

Cover, text design, and production—Martucci Studio, Boston, Massachusetts.
2-3—*Relief of the Cup-Bearer Tja-Wy* (detail). Egyptian Dynasty XVIII reign of Amenhotep III. 1410-1372 B.C. Limestone. Entire relief 29 in. 1972.651. Edward J. and Mary S. Holmes. Courtesy, Museum of Fine Arts, Boston. 5—Judy Filippo. 7—The Bettmann Archive. 9—The Granger Collection. 10, 11, 12—By permission of The Houghton Library, Harvard University. 14—NASA, AT&T. 18-19—*The Printer* (L'Imprimeur). Abraham Bosse. French 1602-1676. Etching. P.4268, Harvey D. Parker Collection. Courtesy, Museum of Fine Arts, Boston. 20—Courtesy, Massachusetts Historical Society. 21—Culver Pictures. 22—*The Hartford Courant*, ©1837 and ©1983. 25—Courtesy, Massachusetts Historical Society. 28—New York Public Library. 30—The Library of Congress. 33—*Capper's Weekly*. 41, 43—Used with permission of *The Christian Science Monitor*. 46-47—Stock, Boston, Donald C. Dietz. 49—Boston Public Library. 50—*The Atlantic Monthly; Harper's*. 51—*The Nation*. 52—*Time, Inc.* 53—*Newsweek*; Scott Thode, *U.S. News & World Report*. 54—©1983, ©1922, *Readers Digest Association, Inc.* 56—Reprinted with permission of Parade Publications, Inc., and Eddie Adams. ©Parade Publications, Inc. 1982. 59—Stock, Boston. Top: Bohdan Hrynewych; Middle left: Ellis Herwig; Middle right: Donald C. Dietz; Bottom: Jeff Albertson. 68-69—Left: RCA; Top right: Stock, Boston, Barbara Alper; Bottom right: Stock; Boston: Stuart Cohen. 71—Left: AT&T; Right: Boston Public Library. 72—Left: United Press International Photo; Right: Stock, Boston, Christopher Morrow. 73—Left: Boston Public Library; Right: RCA. 74—Left: RCA; Right: International News Photos. 75—CBS Television. 76—RCA. 77—Left: Boston Public Library; Right: Ron Kalb, Russom & Leeper. 78—Culver Pictures. 79—(D. W. Griffith photo) 80—(Left: Radio City Hall) Right: Peter Aaron ESTO. 82—Ben Martin, *Time, Inc.* 83—Waltham Senior High School, Massachusetts. 84—NASA. 86—Dow Jones & Company. 87—Wide World Photos. 88—Left: TeleTouch Systems; Right: Stock, Boston, Cary Wolinsky. 92—Lucy Cobos, WNEV-TV. 94—Satellite News Channels. 98-99—Courtesy of Alfred J. Walker. 101—Left: By permission of The Houghton Library, Harvard University; Right: The Bettmann Archive. 103—Eddie Rose. 106—The Bettmann Archive. 107—Courtesy, Massachusetts Historical Society. 108—Boston Public Library. 114—Judy Filippo. 115-119—Leslie Morrill. 124-125—Reproduced with permission of AT&T. 127—Hastech, Inc. 128—Stock, Boston, Frank Siteman. 129—Wide World Photos. 130—ABC News. 132—*Cable Today*. 133—AT&T. 134—Judy Filippo. 136—AT&T. 140-141—Stock, Boston, Donald C. Dietz. 142—Judy Filippo. 144—Stock, Boston, Jack Prelutsky. 145—*The Atlanta Journal; The Atlanta Constitution*. 146—Stock, Boston, Lionel J. M. Delevingne. 147—Stock, Boston, Jean Claude Lejeune. 153—Stock, Boston, Donald C. Dietz. 166-167—(Punch) 170—National Broadcasting Company, Inc. 190-191—Bill Fitz-Patrick, The White House. 204-205—Martucci Studio. 232-233—CBS Television. 235—Copyright ©1983, St. Louis Post-Dispatch, reprinted with permission. 236—Stock, Boston, Peter Vandermark. 237—Reprinted by permission of *The San Francisco Chronicle*. 245—CBS Television. 250-251—Martucci Studio. 253—The Bettmann Archive. 264—Judy Filippo. 268—(Louisville Courier-Journal) 272-273—The Bettmann Archive. 283—The Bettmann Archive. 285—The Advertising Council. 287—United Press International Photo. 297—Leslie Morrill. 306-307—Martucci Studio. 309—Martucci Studio. 315—Stock, Boston, Elizabeth Hamlin. 321—Martucci Studio. 326-327—Martucci Studio. 346—Judy Filippo. 358-359—Martucci Studio. 381—Stock, Boston, Dean Abramson. 392—Stock, Boston, Ellis Herwig. 396-397—Stock, Boston, Ellis Herwig. 401—Stock, Boston, Frank Siteman. 402—Compugraphic. 403—Martucci Studio. 406—Wide World Photos. 409—(mimeograph); Compugraphic. 430-431—Martucci Studio. 438—Stock, Boston. Top left: Peter Southwick; top right: Ellis Herwig; bottom: Frank Siteman. 458-459—Martucci Studio. 465—Stock, Boston, Bohdan Hrynewych. 466—Sharon Bazarian. 474-475—Martucci Studio. 481—Stock, Boston, Jean Claude Lejeune. 488-489—Martucci Studio. 491—The Boston Athenaeum. 512-513—Martucci Studio. 526-527—Monte L. Paulsen. 530—Stock, Boston, Daniel S. Brody. 531—Stock, Boston, Owen Franken. 532—Stock, Boston, Julie O'Neil. 539—Martucci Studio. 544-545—Martucci Studio. 558-559—Waltham Senior High School, Massachusetts. 565—Madison Park High School, Boston, Massachusetts. 568—Waltham Senior High School, Massachusetts. 570—Stock, Boston, Christopher Morrow.

CONTENTS

Appendices   578

Glossary   588

Index   596

PREFACE

High school and college students, constantly exposed to and aware of the vast potential of the mass media of communications, are studying journalism in increasing numbers every year. Technological advances in communications have made possible immediate, and often simultaneous, news coverage of events anywhere in the world—even in space. More than ever before the future journalist not only will be a reporter and interpreter of events but, because of the influence of the mass media, will also play a role in the forming of public opinion and in the bringing about of changes in a democratic society. The need for capable, responsible journalists and discriminating consumers of the mass media has never been greater. For these reasons this book was written to—

1. Give journalism students a comprehensive picture not only of the school media, but of the professional media as well, thus acquainting them with the roles of the mass media in a democratic society and creating a sound basis for discriminating reading, listening, and viewing and the intelligent use of the mass media.

2. Provide a supplement to the language arts program by presenting journalistic writing as a form of composition, thus helping students to develop their writing skills.

3. Develop in staff members of student publications a sense of responsibility for use of the printed word, thereby encouraging the improvement of student publications and the use of these publications as a laboratory for student writing.

4. Acquaint students with the possibilities of continuing their education in the field of communications.

To accomplish these goals, this book has been divided into three major parts: Part One, "The Mass Media in a Democratic Society," offers students a comprehensive view of the professional mass media. This section develops a sound basis for discriminative reading, listening, and intelligent consumer use of the mass media. The section begins with a short history of the development of communication from its primitive beginnings to the complex communications satellite systems being developed today. Separate chapters about newspapers, magazines, the non-print media, public relations, and advertising present a brief history of each of these media, a description of their organization and operational procedures, and information for students interested in pursuing journalism in the mass media as a career. Part One concludes with a glimpse into the future of the mass media.

Part Two, "The Role of the Journalist in a Democratic Society," acquaints the student with journalistic writing as a form of composition. The section focuses on the structure and the purpose of various types of news stories, dealing primarily with the newspaper—the first and basic conveyor of information. Included are chapters on newswriting for both print and electronic media, interviewing, speech and meeting coverage, feature writing, sportswriting, editorial writing, and the critical responsibilities of journalists in a democratic society. Inasmuch as the fundamentals of writing are much the same for both school and professional journalism, students will find these chapters helpful in preparing and completing writing assignments for school publications.

Part Three, "The High School Journalist and the School Media," describes in detail how to organize for and produce a creditable school newspaper, yearbook, and magazine. Dealing with the organization, writing, production, and finance of school publications, the chapters in Part Three outline the responsibilities of the various staff members and offer technical information on the efficient production of those publications. Part Three also includes a chapter on the effective use of photography in school publications and a chapter on the staffing and operation of a school radio and/or television station.

The activities suggested after each chapter take advantage of the fact that the students' world abounds in communications data not ordinarily found in the classroom. These activities, therefore, lead students to see the mass media of communications in realistic relationships to themselves and to apply practical journalistic techniques in practical exercises.

References, which appear in the *Teacher's Resource Book*, offer the student and the teacher an opportunity to explore further into the study of journalism and its many facets.

The author acknowledges with gratitude the many persons and organizations who have aided him in the preparation of this textbook. Special thanks go to the following: David Manning White, philosopher, educator, and writer, who co-authored the original edition of this textbook and who served as a fountain of inspiration in this undertaking; S. Jack Weissberger, Pennsylvania State University; Roland E. Wolseley, Syracuse University; Robert Baram, Victoria Brown Gonzales, Norman Marcus, James Shen, Boston University; William Ward, Southern Illinois University; Stacey Driben, University of Michigan; the *Boston Globe*; the *Boston Herald-American*; Helen Smith, Newton (Mass.) North High School; Joseph M. Murphy, Columbia Scholastic Press Association and The Newspaper Fund.

The cooperation of all schools that gave the author permission to use excerpts from their publications is deeply appreciated.

PART 1

The Mass Media in a Democratic Society

CHAPTER 1

The Development of Mass Communication

The Dynamics of Communication

The Human Need to Communicate

Almost every living thing communicates. Communication, which in its simplest form involves only two participants, began perhaps when some types of one-celled animals sent out chemical signals to other members of their species that the time was right for reproduction. In its most complex form, communication is the exchange of information among human beings, the most advanced of living organisms. Such communication can involve only two individuals, or it can involve millions of people the world over.

The art of communicating is a complicated process, for it implies both the ability to express and to understand. Early human beings gestured, made noises, and used elaborate systems of sound symbols to

transmit their feelings and thoughts to one another. Today, however, we have developed a system of communicating that includes not only gestures and signs, but also oral and written messages. Several theories attempt to explain the origin of human language, but such theories are only speculative because there is little concrete evidence to indicate exactly how language developed before it was recorded in written form. We can be reasonably sure, however, that early human beings communicated because they had to.

As civilization developed, human beings expanded their communicating processes and learned to express themselves by organizing voice noises (speech) and by perfecting an ability to read and write the marks that make up words and sentences. Over the centuries, human beings evolved a written means of communication, giving us an advantage over other living creatures—namely, the ability to leave a record of our experiences. Whether using smoke signals or transmitting television (electronic) signals via communications satellites, we human beings have always been eager to communicate over increasingly larger areas and to make our communications understandable to as many other human beings as we possibly can.

The Elements of Communication

Successful communication involves—requires—four components: a sender, a message, a medium, and a receiver. You (the sender) transmit a joke (the message) by letter (the medium) to a friend (the receiver). Mass communication involves these same components, but the message is transmitted via more sophisticated media to a greater number of persons. For example, the journalist (the sender) transmits the news (the message) via newspaper or radio or television (each a distinct medium) to thousands—perhaps millions—of readers/listeners/viewers (the receivers).

The Mass Media

Newspapers, magazines, radio, television, motion pictures, and advertising constitute the mass media because they are concerned with transmitting messages to great masses of people. These media were developed primarily as news media—the means by which information could be quickly and efficiently communicated to large audiences.

The Mass Media in a Democratic Society

The hiker (sender) uses a sun-reflecting mirror (medium) to flash a message, "Is dinner ready?" (message) to the campers (receivers).

News and Journalism

News is defined as timely information of interest to many people, usually concerning events that have just occurred or are about to occur. The collecting, writing, editing, and dissemination of news material is called *journalism*. Journalists select the news that they consider most important to their audiences, and they try to present that news in a manner that will stimulate thought as well as provide information.

The following pages in this chapter briefly discuss the development of communications media, dealing primarily with the newspaper—the first and basic conveyor of information. As you become familiar with the background of this print medium and compare early concepts of news with today's concepts, you'll see the changing character of the mass media as a growing industry in a changing society. The following is a summary outline identifying the widely used media of news communication:

The Development of Mass Communication   5

The Common Media of News Communication

I. Informal, unorganized media
  A. Oral rumor, gossip, chatter
  B. Personal letter
II. Formal, organized, directed media
  A. Print media
    1. Newspapers
      a. Metropolitan dailies
      b. Suburban dailies
      c. Small-city dailies
      d. Community and rural weeklies
      e. Ethnic and specialized newspapers
    2. Magazines, periodicals, books
      a. Weekly newsmagazines
      b. Picture weeklies and biweeklies
      c. Journals of comment
      d. General weekly or monthly magazines
      e. Specialized periodicals
      f. Confidential reports
      g. Fiction
      h. Nonfiction
    3. Miscellaneous
      a. Business letters
      b. Handbills
      c. Advertising fliers
      d. Posters
  B. Electronic media
    1. Radio
      a. Network programs
      b. Local programs
    2. Television
      a. Network programs
      b. Local programs
    3. Projected communications
      a. Newsreels
      b. Documentaries and educational films
      c. Videotapes
      d. Computer readouts

Forerunners of the Mass Media

First Daily News

The modern mass media, generally considered to be the gift of no one nation, had been in the process of development centuries before 60 B.C., the year marking the first recorded distribution of the daily news. At that time the pre-Christian Roman government issued handwritten news accounts called *Acta Diurna* (Day's Events), posting them in the Roman Forum. These newsletters, which were introduced by Julius Caesar, contained official news of general public interest. The *Acta Diurna* were also sent to the Roman Legions when they were waging war abroad. Many historians have suggested that the *Acta Diurna* were distributed with the intent of increasing patriotism and of creating interest in public affairs. Whatever their purpose, other cities and city states during the next several hundred years came to use such posted newsletters to good advantage.

When the Venetian traveler Marco Polo returned from China in 1295, he told of having seen books that had apparently been printed from movable type. Yet, in the Western world, the use of movable type—attributed to the German printer Johann Gutenberg—was not recorded until 1456, when the so-called *Gutenberg Bible* made its appearance.

The invention of movable type is one of the major achievements in the history of mass communication; no longer was it necessary for clerks or scribes to spend long, tedious hours hand-transcribing the Bible, government and legal documents, books, and messages of all kinds.

The Gutenberg Bible, with its 42-line, two-column format and hand-painted decorations, set in 1456, was the first to use movable type.

Newsbooks, Newsletters, Fly Sheets

The newsbook and the newsletter were among the earliest fore-runners of the modern newspaper. The newsbook, issued by government initiative or approval, first appeared in Germany in the 15th century. In general, a newsbook was simply the account of any event. For example, one of the first English newsbooks—published by courtiers serving Queen Elizabeth I—was an account of the defeat of the Spanish Armada (1588). In seventeenth-century Europe, newsletters were used extensively—especially among merchants interested in international news.

In the mid-1500s the word *gazette* came into use in Italy, where interested persons paid a *gazetta* (a small coin) for news-letters reporting events of a war in Dalmatia (the part of modern Yugoslavia along the Adriatic coast). In addition, in the mid-1500s printing presses were introduced to many parts of Europe.

"Fly sheets"—as contrasted with newsbooks and newsletters—began to appear on the European mainland in the early 1600s. These were small one-sheet handbills that reported local events and perhaps advanced a point of view toward local affairs. Among the first "fly sheets" were the Augsberg (Germany) *Avisa Relation oder Zeitung* (Reported Advice or News) and the Strasbourg (France) *Relation* (Report).

The Emergence of the Modern Newspaper

Developments in England

In England, where William Caxton had installed that country's first printing press in 1476, printers lagged behind the rest of Europe in establishing newsbooks and newsletters. Even though the printing press eventually led to the widespread dissemination of ideas and information to masses of people, the first English newspapers of significance did not appear until the 1600s—about 160 years after Gutenberg introduced movable type to the Western World. Called *corantos*, these rudimentary prototypes of today's newspapers first appeared in the 1620s. Corantos were published irregularly by people interested in influencing public opinion and were, like the earlier newsletters, mainly concerned with news of foreign events. Although few people at the time could read, the corantos soon gained enough interest to be produced in quantity. In 1624 the corantos started to be identified by name, thus supplying some of the continuity required of true newspapers. The earliest-known coranto published by title was Thomas Archer's *The Continuation of Our Weekly Newes*, considered by many scholars to be the first genuine newspaper. The first daily domestic reports published in England can be traced to the publication of accounts of Parliamentary proceedings in 1628. Out of these accounts developed the *diurnals*, or daily reports of local events. The diurnals, true forerunners of today's dailies, are considered to be the oldest-known regularly published daily accounts of the news.

Milton's *Areopagitica*

The British people, long denied access to many kinds of information, were clamoring for more freedom of expression. But the government, aware of the potential threat of the printed word, exercised close censorship over all publications. In 1644 poet John Milton published his famous *Areopagitica*, probably the most

English poet John Milton (1606–1674) published *Areopagitica*, his eloquent prose argument supporting a free press, in 1644.

AREOPAGITICA;

A

SPEECH

OF

Mr. JOHN MILTON

For the Liberty of UNLICENC'D PRINTING,

To the PARLAMENT of ENGLAND.

Τὸυλʹθερο᾽ δʹ ἐκῖνο, εἴ τὶς θἐλᾳ πόλᾳ
Χρησὸν τι βἰλδμʹ εἰς μἐσον φἐρειν, ἐχαι.
Καὶ ταῦθʹ ὁ χρᾕζων, λαμπρὸς ἐσθʹ, ὁ μἡ θἐλων,
Σιγᾷ, τἰ τὑτων ἐςιν ἰσαιτἐρον πὀλᾳ ;
Euripid. Hicetid.

*This is true Liberty when free born men
Having to advise the public may speak free,
Which he who can, and will, deserv's high praise,
Who neither can nor will, may hold his peace;
What can be juster in a State then this?*
Euripid. Hicetid.

LONDON,
Printed in the Yeare, 1644.

The Oxford Gazette.

Published by Authority.

From Thursday November 23. *to* Monday November 27. 1665.

Oxford, Nov. 22.

THis day Sir *John Keeling* took his place in the Kings. Bench Court, as Lord Chief Justice.

Hull, Nov. 19. The storm hath been so great, that the Ships in our Harbor suffered at least 400 pound damage. In *Grimsbay* Road a Vessel was lost, bound for *Lyn*; and a Coal ship put ashore, which, it is feared, will not escape

Yarmouth, Nov 20. The ship mentioned in the last upon the Cockle-sand, is got off with little damage, and the loss of some Coals they were obliged to throw over-board. It is generally reported, that twenty Colliers have miscarried within twenty miles of this Town.

Dantzick, Nov. 7. The Letters from *Torn* of the third instant, advise, That the King of *Poland* was marched with his Army to *Vladiflaw*, and that day by nine of the clock before noon, intended to enter *Torn*; the Burgers at the coming away of the Post making ready for his Reception. This being unexpected, gives occasion of many strange conjectures; the most probable is, That either he intends to bring a Polish Garison into *Torn* (which the Burgers have hitherto refused to receive) or else, that he intends to leave *Poland* and reside in *Prussia.*

fion of respect and kindness due to his Majesties Minister in that quality.

Bortaign is not yet taken, but cannot in probability hold out long, there being little appearance how the *Hollander* can relieve it; the Prince of *Munster*, by means of the Bridge you formerly heard he had made over the Matsh from *Meppen* side to *Terappel*, remaining most r of the tol passage, by which it can in likelihood be effected. It is reported, after many incertainties both ways that the Duke of *Lunenburgh* will assist the States with 6000 men, and that the Elector of *Brandenburgh* will assist the Prince of *Munster* with 7000. Those that write most impartially of the Prince of *Munster*, say, That his Army hath no want of any thing, unless of Beer and Wine, and that of all other Provisions he hath great abundance out of the Countrey it self. It is believed the French succors are by this time at *Nimegen*; many of their Infantry desert, being impatient of a Winter march, especially the sea on having proved so rainy. The Prince of *Munster* to make their way the longer, is fortifying the Town of *Dotechem,* upon the Old *Yssel,* and that of *Lochem* upon *Berkel*, by which the French Troops must necessarily pass ere they can reach the Body of that Princes forces. The first Squadron of French

The *Oxford Gazette*, 1663, was the first periodical to qualify as a true newspaper.

eloquent argument ever advanced in support of a free press. As a result the censorship laws were considerably relaxed, and a new era in journalism began. One notable result was the establishment in 1665 of *The Oxford Gazette,* the first periodical to qualify as a true newspaper. Nearly a hundred years later, the ideas Milton expressed in *Areopagitica* had a profound influence in America, where people were struggling to obtain political, as well as journalistic, freedom.

The First Daily Newspaper and the Essay Papers

On March 11, 1702, the *Daily Courant* appeared on the streets of London. It was the first *daily* newspaper printed in the English language, and it set a new standard in journalism because it printed *news,* not rumor.

The eighteenth century also brought about a high literary quality in English journalism, a quality evident in the *essay* papers still read today by students everywhere. The essay papers, the

The Daily Courant.

Wednefday, March 11. 1702.

From the Harlem Courant, Dated March 18. N. S.

Naples, Feb. 22.

ON Wednefday' laft, our New Viceroy, the Duke of Efcalona, arriv'd here with a Squadron of the Galleys of Sicily. He made his Entrance dreft in a French habit; and to give us the greater Hopes of the King's coming hither, went to Lodge in one of the little Palaces, leaving the Royal one for his Majefty. The Marquis of Grigni is alfo arriv'd here with a Regiment of French.

Rome, Feb. 25. In a Military Congregation of State that was held here, it was Refolv'd to draw a Line from Afcoli to the Borders of the Ecclefiaftical State, thereby to hinder the Incurfions of the Tranfalpine Troops. Orders are fent to Civita Vecchia to fit out the Galleys, and to ftrengthen the Garrifon of that

Flanders under the Duke of Burgundy; and the Duke of Maine is to Command upon the Rhine.

From the Amfterdam Courant, Dated Mar. 18.

Rome, Feb. 25. We are taking here all poffible Precautions for the Security of the Ecclefiaftical State in this prefent Conjuncture, and have defir'd to raife 3000 Men in the Cantons of Switzerland. The Pope has appointed the Duke of Berwick to be his Lieutenant-General, and he is to Command 6000 Men on the Frontiers of Naples: He has alfo fettled upon him a Penfion of 6000 Crowns a year during Life.

From the Paris Gazette, Dated Mar. 18. 1702.

Naples, Febr. 17. 600 French Soldiers are arrived here, and are expected to be follow'd by 3400 more.

The first daily newspaper printed in the English language was *The Daily Courant,* 1702.

Tatler (1709-1711) and the *Spectator* (1711-1712, 1714), were the products of Richard Steele and Joseph Addison. Printed only on one side of a sheet of paper and costing a penny, this type of paper soon became extremely popular. The *Spectator* was issued daily and its literary form was widely imitated, especially in America, where colonial newspapers were influenced by their British predecessors.

Development of Newspapers in America

During the first part of the 18th century only five newspapers were established in colonial America—three in Boston and one each in Philadelphia and New York. In the early 1800s the masses of the American people began to read newspapers on a regular basis. With the growth of large cities, newspapers began to be recognized as an important communications medium that not only presented the news but also accurately reflected the American way of life.

These two English publications, *The Tatler*, first published in 1709, and a daily, *The Spectator*, first published in 1711, became models for essay papers in colonial America.

Technological Expansion

The beginning of the 19th century saw a series of noteworthy technological advances that enabled newspapers—and eventually other media—to play an increasingly significant role in American life. In 1805 the invention of stereotyping made possible the use of the cylindrical printing press (as opposed to the flatbed press). In 1814 the first steam-powered press began operation. Frenchman Louis Daguerre perfected his method of photography in 1839. In 1844 America's Samuel Morse transmitted the first telegram. The first transatlantic cable was laid in 1858. The year 1872 saw the invention of photoengraving, the process permitting line drawings and photographs to be etched on metal printing plates and then accurately reproduced. In 1876 Alexander Graham Bell was the first person to transmit the human voice by telephone, and in 1877 Thomas Edison was the first to record the human voice and then reproduce it via the phonograph. In 1886 the *New York Tribune* was the first commercial user of the Mergenthaler Linotype, a machine that produced each line of type in the form of a solid metal slug. The year 1894 saw the development of the motion-picture projector. In 1895 Guglielmo Marconi transmitted the world's first wireless message. And the year 1907 was witness to the first transmission of the human voice by radio.

The Mass Media Today — Global Telecommunication

Advances in Communications Technology

The 20th century—particularly the years following World War II —has witnessed astounding advances in communications technology. Among them, five stand out: offset printing, television, xerography, the computer, and the communications satellite. Each has played a noteworthy part in revolutionizing our world —particularly from the point of view of the journalist.

Offset printing, a process in which the paper never touches the printing plate itself, permits the use of high-speed printing presses. The offset printing process gives us letters and figures that are sharp and clear and makes possible the sharp reproduction of bright, natural-looking color photographs, as well as clearly defined black-and-white photographs.

Television, the simultaneous electronic transmission of images and sound, has brought far-reaching changes in the way we live. Almost every home in the nation has a television set; many homes have several. By means of television, masses of people can become on-the-spot witnesses of events occurring thousands of miles away.

The invention of xerography, a process by which printed or written material can be instantly reproduced, offers countless possibilities for rapid, effective, widespread dissemination of information.

During the 1950s electronics engineers perfected the first computers. Designed to store vast amounts of information and then to retrieve isolated details—or large blocks of information—instantaneously, computers are in great demand in almost every field of human endeavor. Computers perform an amazing number of tasks in mass communication—from correctly intermixing a number of different type faces and sizes on the same page to detailing the monthly charges to be billed to advertisers.

Perhaps the greatest technological advance in telecommunications is the development of the International Telecommunications Satellite Consortium, known as Intelsat, which links the communi-

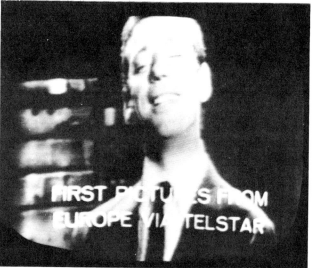

cations facilities of 63 nations. In 1962 Telestar I, the first active experimental communications satellite, was launched by the Communications Satellite Corporation of the United States (Comstat), a member of Intelsat. Telstar was capable of handling data at the rate of one and a half million words a minute—the equivalent of transmitting six entire books of the Bible every 29 seconds!

Following the launching of Telstar, other communications satellites—notably Early Bird, the first commercial satellite—linked North America and Europe with 250 two-way voice circuits. By 1974 Earth stations that could transmit and receive communications traffic via satellite were located in 50 countries around the world. And today a direct-broadcast satellite can bring live television pictures and sound from a number of the world's cities straight to the home receivers in at least 100 countries.

Outlook for the Future

Before communications satellites came into general use, our information links with the rest of the world were limited. Overseas electronic circuits—such as the wireless telephone, teletype, and radio—were limited largely to North America and Europe. There were relatively few telecommunications links with Africa, South America, or Asia—continents where approximately 70 percent of the world's people live. But today the potential for electronic communications links via satellites is enormous. Within a few years it will be possible to operate a worldwide information network capable of transmitting humankind's total accumulated knowledge to all parts of the globe.

Today, as in the past, mass communication has a profound effect on social, economic, and political developments the world over. In the future, mass communication can play a vital role in ensuring the survival of humankind. As human knowledge increases, it is essential that the peoples of this earth actively seek to understand and to get along with one another. The free, unrestricted use of the mass media for the purpose of accurate mass communication offers what seems the only practical way of bringing about the human understanding necessary to world peace, even world survival. President Lyndon Johnson—back in the mid–1960s—stated the issue squarely in these words:

Man's greatest hope for peace lies in understanding his fellow man. Nations, like individuals, fear what is strange and unfamiliar. The more we see and hear of those things which are common to all people, the less likely we are to fight over those issues which set us apart. So the challenge is to communicate!

Major Events in the History of Communications

Early human beings communicated by means of gestures and sounds. In drawing pictograms on the walls of caves, early human beings devised a prewriting system.

- **3300 B.C.:** Egyptians perfected a picture language called hieroglyphics.
- **1500 B.C.:** The Semites devised an alphabet.
- **1000 B.C.:** Egyptians wrote on papyrus.
- **A.D. 105:** The Chinese wrote with ink on paper.
- **A.D. 1041:** Printing by means of separate, movable characters was used in China.
- **A.D. 1314:** Wang Chen employed nearly 60,000 movable-type characters to print a book on agriculture.
- **1403:** A Korean emperor printed a large number of volumes from movable type.
- **1456:** Johann Gutenberg introduced movable type to the Western world.
- **1476:** William Caxton established England's first printing press.
- **1539:** The first printing press in North America was established in Mexico.

- **1609:** The first newspapers of significance appeared in Europe.
- **1690:** Ben Harris published *Publick Occurrences, Both Forreign and Domestick* in Boston.
- **1704:** America's first continuous newspaper, the *Boston News-Letter*, was published.
- **1805:** Stereotyping was introduced.
- **1814:** The first steam-powered press was introduced.
- **1839:** Louis Daguerre in France invented a type of photography.
- **1844:** Samuel Morse sent the first telegraph message.
- **1853:** Roger Fenton became the first war photographer when he covered the Crimean War.
- **1858:** The first transatlantic cable was laid.
- **1872:** Photoengraving was developed.
- **1876:** Alexander Graham Bell invented the telephone.
- **1877:** Thomas Alva Edison invented the phonograph.
- **1886:** The Mergenthaler Linotype was first used commercially by the *New York Tribune*.
- **1889:** George Eastman developed a practical photographic film.
- **1894:** Motion-picture films were shown to the public.
- **1895:** The first wireless message was sent by Guglielmo Marconi.
- **1896:** Guglielmo Marconi invented the radio.
- **1923:** Pictures were televised between New York City and Philadelphia.
- **1944:** The first large, automatic digital computer was built at Harvard University.
- **1957:** The first artificial Earth satellite, Russia's Sputnik I, sent information from space to Earth.
- **1962:** Telstar I, America's first active experimental communications satellite was launched.
- **1967:** Early Bird (Intelsat I), the first commercial communications satellite, was placed in orbit.
- **1970:** Corning Glass Works produced the first optical fiber suitable for long-range communication.
- **1974:** The first mailgram was transmitted by satellite.

1. In precise words, explain the meaning of each of the following terms:

communication   medium   news
journalism   mass media

2. Assume that the news story of an event of world importance has been translated from a foreign language into English. Present an actual or an imagined situation that shows how a communications breakdown could develop.

3. Express your support for or opposition to this proposition: If all nations used a universal language, effective world communication and human understanding would increase. Explain and/or defend your point of view.

4. Express your support for or opposition to this proposition: Assuming that intelligent life does exist elsewhere in the universe, the United States should continue to spend money to send signals into outer space. Explain your point of view.

5. Throughout the history of communication, ruling groups have sought to control—to censor—information intended for the general public. Research one of the following topics, and report your findings to the class:

a. Censorship of early European and colonial American newspapers.

b. Milton's *Areopagitica*.

c. Government restrictions on access to the news during the administration of the American president of your choice.

d. Present-day postal censorship.

e. Censorship of books, motion pictures, radio programs, television programs, and stage presentations in our society today.

6. From a recent issue of a local newspaper, select several news stories and photographs that you think would be censored if you were living under a dictatorship. Explain why you think they would be censored.

7. Express your support for or opposition to this proposition: In a democratic society, no censorship of any kind should be imposed. Explain and/or defend your point of view.

CHAPTER 2

Newspapers

The Newspaper in Our Society

Philosophers are said to pray to be spared from living in an interesting age. An interesting age raises problems and issues that require people to take stands and make decisions. Philosophers know that making decisions leaves them wide open to criticism. Yet failure to make decisions, to take stands—as all philosophers also know—leaves them wide open to criticism.

Few professionals in America are required to make as many decisions as are the men and women who write and edit for the news media. These journalists, who are as important to the welfare of the United States as are government officials, doctors, religious leaders, and educators, must daily make major decisions. Like philosophers, they are often severely criticized for the stands they take—as well as for the stands they don't take.

An official of the Associated Press has put the matter this way:

> If reporters write about drug addiction, they are charged with making it attractive to nonusers; if they

write about black nationalists, they are accused of writing about a tiny minority; if they don't, they are told that they are not reporting the true militancy of the blacks. If they write that the Mets are strictly a dismal bunch of stumblebums, they are against the team; if they don't, they are publicity agents. And so it goes.

In today's world journalists serve as the prime interpreters of situations and events. In this role, not only do they have the freedom to express their own views, but they also have the power to influence public decisions. This dual privilege imposes on all journalists an awesome responsibility—to search constantly for and to report the truth. Publisher Joseph Pulitzer emphasized the need for truth in American journalism:

> Nothing less than the highest ideals, the most scrupulous anxiety to do right, the most accurate knowledge of the problem it has to meet, and a sincere sense of moral responsibility will save journalism from a subservience to . . . interests seeking selfish ends antagonistic to the public welfare.

Yet the truth is often very difficult to determine. Consider the following: To get at the truth, journalists must write for those who operate lathes in factories as well as for those who manage the companies operating the factories. In seeking to report the truth, journalists soon learn that what is truth for the lathe operators may be considered by the managers to be hopelessly biased opinion—and vice versa. Moreover, while journalists strive to be objective in what they write, they must also be true to their own perceptions of the world.

America's Early Newspapers

Boston, the birthplace of the American newspaper, has also been called "the cradle of American journalism." In the 1680s Boston, then famous as the intellectual capital of the New World, had all the conditions necessary for the development of a newspaper—a literate citizenry, self-government, widespread interest in community affairs, prosperity, and cultural leadership.

However, no successful newspaper appeared in Boston for about 50 years after the community's founding in 1630. The interest of the colonists in the news had been satisfied by English newspapers, which arrived regularly on ships from the "homeland" and which often contained news about colonial affairs.

The First American Newspaper

Printer Benjamin Harris arrived in Boston in 1686 and immediately recognized that the conditions were made to order for the development of a newspaper. Harris, who had been arrested in London for the possession of seditious literature, had previously produced and edited a paper in that city. After his arrest, he continued to edit his newspaper from his prison cell. Early in

Benjamin Harris's 1690 paper, *Publick Occurrences, Both Forreign and Domestick* is called the first American newspaper.

1686 his shop was again raided and, warned of the possibility of another arrest, Harris fled with his family to America. In Boston in the fall of 1686 he opened a combined bookstore and coffee shop. The shop became a meeting place for some of the city's most prominent citizens, and Harris, who had been a promoter of literary works, was soon publishing books for a distinguished clientele. His *Publick Occurrences, Both Forreign and Domestick,* called the first American newspaper by many authorities, was published in September 1690. *Publick Occurrences* quickly ran into trouble with the British governor and was suppressed after publication of the first issue.

The Power of the Press

Public resentment of British authority was growing in the colonies, and in 1734, thirty years after the founding of America's first newspaper, John Peter Zenger, a courageous New York printer, felt impelled to print a strong criticism of the corrupt British governor. Tried for seditious libel, Zenger was defended by Attorney Andrew Hamilton, who won the case on the point that "falsehood makes the libel." This victory was the first time in any nation that truth was established as a defense in a libel action.

The colonial press openly began to criticize English authority and to promote the ideal of American independence. The short-

British soldiers burned copies of John Peter Zenger's *Weekly Journal* in Wall Street, November 6, 1734.

lived *New England Courant,* published by James Franklin, conducted crusades and printed entertaining articles such as Benjamin Franklin's "Do-Good Papers." The Franklin brothers and their "Hell-Fire Club" of Couranteers have often been called the first school of propagandists for the American Revolution. Started at about the same time, *The Hartford Courant,* originally published as the *Connecticut Courant,* outlasted the Franklin publication. In 1837 this paper became a daily. It is still printed today.

The colonial American press, often termed "a propaganda press," played an important role in stirring up opposition to Crown policies by publishing essays and letters under aliases by such leaders as John Adams and James Otis.

The *Daily Courant,* 1837, continues to be published daily as *The Hartford Courant.*

The Mass Media in a Democratic Society

Small Papers and Small Circulations

Most of the colonial American newspapers were weeklies, and the remaining ones were semiweeklies. Page sizes were smaller than those of our modern tabloids, and each issue usually contained four pages. During the 1760s the more prosperous newspapers (Benjamin Franklin's *Pennsylvania Gazette*, for example) printed as many as eight pages per issue. Few of the colonists could read, and because efficient distribution was hampered by the crude roads and transportation facilities of the time, limited circulation resulted for the colonial American newspapers.

Only twenty of the thirty-seven colonial American newspapers published at the beginning of the American Revolution survived the war. Several others of minor importance came and went between the battles at Concord and Lexington (1775) and Cornwallis' surrender at Yorktown (1781). Information about the Revolution was not covered methodically; for their sources of news of the war, colonial American editors depended on chance information, clippings from other newspapers, and letters from friends, relatives, and business associates in other cities.

Even though our newspapers were founded on the belief that freedom of the press is the people's defense against tyranny, colonial American statesmen could not agree on what amount of power should be delegated to the people. Alexander Hamilton felt that the public was a great beast and could not be trusted with the operation of the new society that was emerging as a result of the Revolutionary War. Thomas Jefferson, asserting that the only way to make a free society work was to have all the citizens participate, felt quite differently. If the citizens were well enough informed and free to express their opinions, he maintained, they would make the right decisions most of the time. Jefferson won the argument. He insisted that if he had to choose between a government without newspapers or newspapers without a government, he would take the latter. He believed that the only way to make democracy work was to have a free flow of information and well-informed voters to make the decisions.

Other Boston Newspapers

The first continuous American newspaper, the *Boston News-Letter*, appeared in 1704—fourteen years after *Publick Occurrences* had been suppressed. The postmaster of Boston, John Campbell, who had been sending out a newsletter to the governors of the New England colonies, decided to turn his newsletter enterprise into a profitable newspaper business by charging two pence per copy (or nine shillings per year). The first edition of the newsletter as a newspaper stated in large type that the *Boston News-Letter* was "published by authority"—meaning that every word had been censored and approved by the governor's licensor. The attitude of the British colonial governors at that time was typified by Sir William Berkeley, Governor of Virginia for thirty-eight years, who sent a report to the Crown stating:

> ... But thank God we have no free schools nor printing, and I hope we shall not have these hundred years; for learning has brought disobedience and heresy and sects into the world; and printing has divulged them and libels against the best government. God keep us from them both.

Because Campbell was a man the Governor of Massachusetts could trust to be discreet (all of Campbell's material was written by himself and his brother Duncan), his *Boston News-Letter*, which was "published by authority" was spared the fate of Harris' *Publick Occurrences*.

But another newspaper, the *Boston Gazette* (also "published by authority") took a strong position against the way the British colonies were governed. It became famous when editors John Gill and Benjamin Edes lashed out at the colonial government.

Freedom of the Press

Journalism acquired status with the "Freedom of the Press" clause. Recognizing the need for an informed electorate, the framers of the Bill of Rights (1790) designated that clause as the First Amendment to the Constitution:

> ### Article I
> **Religion, Speech, Press, Assembly, Petition—Congress shall make no law respecting an establishment of religion, or prohibiting the free exercise thereof; or abridging the freedom of speech, or of the press; or the right of the people peaceably to assemble, and to petition the government for redress of grievances.**

The Beginning of the Penny Press

Early American newspaper circulations increased as the education of early Americans improved. With the appearance of Benjamin Day's *New York Sun* in 1833 (the first penny newspaper), the

The first continuous colonial American newspaper, the *Boston News-Letter*, appeared in 1704—fourteen years after *Publick Occurrences, Both Forreign and Domestick* had been suppressed.

reading of newspapers became widespread among the mass of the American population—a direct reflection of increasing awareness by Americans of the need to be well informed.

The Growth of America's Newspapers

Westward Movement

During the 19th century, as Americans moved westward, newspapers were established in new towns and cities across the country. By 1861 the telegraph had reached the West Coast giving these young newspapers coast-to-coast access to national and international news. Among the papers that came to wield regional and national influence were these: the *Chicago Tribune*, the *Chicago Daily News*, the *Washington Post*, the *St. Louis Post-Dispatch*, the *Kansas City Star*, the *Omaha World-Herald*, the *Denver Post*, the *Portland Oregonian*, the *Los Angeles Times*, and the *San Francisco Chronicle*.

An Era of Giants

By the end of the Civil War the country's newspaper business was booming, for newspapers had gained an important role in the affairs of the communities they served. Through their reporting of the news and through the advertisements they printed, newspapers clearly reflected the American way of life. Thus began a spectacular era of growth of what came to be the journalistic giants.

Contrary to his own advice to "Go West, young man," Horace Greeley stayed in New York and developed his penny newspaper into one of the country's largest and most influential—the *New York Tribune*. With the completion of the transatlantic cable in 1858, Greeley no longer had to send horseback riders to Boston to obtain news of England from incoming ships. Soon Greeley had to face intense competition from other New York newspaper publishers who, in order to increase their circulation, had become concerned with reader interest and were giving newspaper readers "what they wanted." Catering to the "interests" of their readers in this way were Henry Raymond's *Times*, Joseph Pulitzer's *World*, and William Randolph Hearst's *Journal*.

In 1878 Hungarian-born Joseph Pulitzer—who had served as a reporter on the German-language *Westiche Post* in St. Louis, Missouri—bought the St. Louis *Dispatch*. Promising "to serve no party but the people," Pulitzer developed the *Post-Dispatch* into one of the country's leading papers. In 1880 Pulitzer purchased the *New York World*, a newspaper with a circulation of about 15,000. As he had done with the *Post-Dispatch*, Pulitzer used the

World to attack corrupt politicians and to crusade for improved social conditions. Selling the *World* for a penny an issue, Pulitzer, in three years, increased the paper's circulation to 250,000, to make it the era's most widely read newspaper.

In 1897 William Randolph Hearst's *New York Journal* increased its circulation by running sensational headlines like "Nearer Than Ever to War with Spain"—an attention-getter that was not followed by a news story. Hearst was aware that news of wars helped sell papers, and he sent illustrator Frederick Remington to Cuba to draw war pictures. When Remington wrote back, "There's no war here," Hearst is said to have replied, "You supply the pictures; I'll supply the war."

These New York newspapers—the *Tribune*, the *World*, the *Journal*—soon gained tremendous popularity and influence throughout the country. Despite the fact that other newspapers of quality were published in other cities, these New York papers became the giants of the industry. Indeed, it was as James Rhodes, western correspondent for the *New York Tribune*, wrote: "Throughout the West, the *Tribune* ranks next to the Bible."

The New York Times

A notable development during this period was the founding by Henry Raymond of *The New York Times*, regarded by many today as the foremost newspaper in the world. Typifying the personal interest publishers took in their papers during this period, Raymond served as the paper's correspondent during the Civil War. Later, the *Times* was instrumental in exposing the politically corrupt Boss Tweed ring in New York City. In 1896 Adolph Ochs, owner of the *Chattanooga Times*, bought the faltering *Times* for about $75,000. At that time the *Times* had a circulation of about 9000, it was about $300,000 in debt, and it was losing more than $25,000 a week. By 1900, however, Ochs had increased the *Times'* circulation to 82,000. He did so by printing what the other New York papers didn't. He emphasized serious news—news that respected leaders in government and in finance would want to read. As a result, the *Times* printed complete stock market reports and real estate transactions, and it printed government reports in full. In addition, Ochs decided that the *Times* would list the names of all store buyers who came to New York to purchase merchandise for their local businesses. That decision was a crucial one; it helped make the *Times* the paper of the retail fashion business, thereby vastly increasing the amount of advertising space sold.

Thus did Adolph Ochs turn *The New York Times* into what has become one of the most prestigious, largest-selling newspapers in the United States—and in the world as well.

The four giants: *The New-York Tribune, The World, The New-York Times,* **and** *The New York Journal* **are shown with important historical headlines.**

The Mass Media in a Democratic Society

Regional Newspapers—National Impact

Although the New York City dailies were gaining nationwide recognition, it was inevitable that newspapers of distinction would appear elsewhere in the country. One of the most influential was (and is) the *Atlanta Constitution*. By 1886 Henry W. Grady, managing editor of that paper, was considered the outstanding spokesman for the South. In addition to his advocacy of civil rights, he favored diversified agriculture and the industrialization of the South. When Grady died in 1889, Joel Chandler Harris became the editor of the *Atlanta Constitution*.

Another influential Southern paper was (and is) the *Louisville Courier-Journal*. Both North and South heeded the words of editor Henry Watterson. His authoritative writing gained him the respect and admiration of readers not only in Kentucky but also in other areas of the nation.

Although unpopular in some areas for his denunciation of the Ku Klux Klan, William Allen White of the *Emporia* (Kansas) *Gazette* gained national recognition with an editorial entitled "What's the Matter with Kansas?" Americans in every walk of life were soon praising White for his short, simple, beautifully written editorials. One of his best-known, for example, is the obituary he wrote for the *Emporia Gazette* after the death of his daughter Mary. Millions of high school students have read this obituary, which epitomizes the love, understanding, and common bond between a father and his daughter.

In Missouri millionaire William Rockhill Nelson had gone through three fortunes by 1880 when, with his last million, he founded the *Kansas City Star*. Nelson believed that the reporter was the backbone of a good newspaper and built up one of the best editorial staffs in the country.

Concerned with the moral problems of his city, Nelson conducted crusades against lotteries, gambling, and corrupt politicians. His campaigns also helped give Kansas City one of the best systems of parks and playgrounds in the country. Unlike most of the large newspapers in the country at that time, the *Kansas City Star* was an afternoon paper. Under Nelson's influence the paper avoided sensationalism, and it remained independent from political control.

Yellow Journalism

During this period of newspaper development the term *yellow journalism* was coined. One explanation is that in the 1880s the term resulted from the use of unethical practices on the part of some publishers concerning a cartoon strip titled "The Yellow Kid." Using every means of enticement, these publishers tried to lure cartoonist Richard Outcault, originator of "The Yellow Kid," to their papers. Unsuccessful in their bids for Outcault's services, these publishers then proceeded to have their own staff artists draw similar cartoon strips, using the title, "The Yellow Kid." The term *yellow journalism* has been used ever since to characterize unethical publishing practices and irresponsible journalism.

"The Yellow Kid" cartoon strip was the creation of Richard Outcault and was widely copied by publishers during the 1880s.

Other Noteworthy Developments

Despite the "yellow journalism" of the late 19th century, many advances were made that improved newspaper publishing. The development of the photoengraving process meant that photographs could be used in newspapers. Comic strips and headlines —both in color—became popular. Greater variety in the news was evidenced by coverage of sports, finance, entertainment, and homemaking news. Emphasis was placed on human-interest stories. Perhaps it was this emphasis that led Charles Dana of the *New York Sun* to make his classic definition of news: "If a dog bites a man, that's not news. But if a man bites a dog, that *is* news."

Specialized newspapers—the *Christian Science Monitor* and the *Wall Street Journal*, for example—were established to meet the needs and concerns of special-interest groups. Successful newspaper publishers—like William Randolph Hearst and E.W. Scripps —went about buying up small newspapers and organizing them into influential and profitable newspaper chains.

The introduction of well-organized classified advertising sections in many newspapers helped increase their local and regional influence. The classified sections provided readers with a service they had not previously enjoyed; now they had useful—if not vital—information about job opportunities, about lost-and-found articles, and about the many products and services available for purchase by the public.

Finally, the coming of the "wire services"—the Associated Press, the United Press, the International News Service, and the Associated Negro Press—made the task of newspaper editors easier by making accessible to them in-depth news stories of national and international significance. In addition, the emerging news feature syndicates—organizations like King Features Syndicate and United Features Syndicate, Inc.—supplied copyrighted feature stories, photographs, comic strips, sports stories, and stock market information to client newspapers. The wire services and the features syndicates did much to promote the growth of newspapers and to increase their influence in American society.

The Newspaper in Today's Society

Newspapers, along with books, were the first of the mass media. Although newspapers are older than the other forms of the mass media, the future of newspaper journalism in America has never looked so bright. The number of readers has increased each year since 1690, when the first newspaper in the colonies was established. In a recent twenty-year period, for example, total newspaper circulation rose more than twenty percent—from 50.9 million to 61.6 million. In the same period, newspaper employment of 248,500 rose to 353,800—a gain of 42%—while advertising volume in the country's 1750 daily newspapers topped $9.5. In the same period, the number of pages in daily newspapers has almost doubled. More daily newspapers are sold today than loaves of bread or bottles of milk. It would take a 3000-car freight train to deliver all the newsprint a metropolitan daily uses in a year.

Types of Newspapers

Newspapers can be classified into several categories. The major types are these: metropolitan, chain, country, trade, professional, weekly, school, and ethnic.

Metropolitan dailies furnish written accounts of events that have happened or are about to happen. They report the facts about these events as accurately and in as much detail as time and space permit. Metropolitan dailies usually publish several editions each day and offer the reader more complete coverage of news events than radio or television broadcasts offer. Metropolitan dailies feature complete coverage of national and worldwide news as well as news from their own communities. They also carry news and features about careers, travel, sports, society, business, education, the arts, and entertainment.

In recent years a major trend in the newspaper industry has been the newspaper merger. Very few cities in the United States now have competing morning or evening newspapers. Even those few large cities still having one morning and one evening newspaper are finding it economically more practical to combine printing and circulation operations while retaining separate editorial policies.When several newspapers combine, or merge, they become known as a "chain." Among the largest **chain newspapers** in our country are the Hearst Newspapers, the Scripps-Howard Newspapers, the Gannett Group, and the Newhouse Newspaper chain.

The **country newspaper,** like its city counterpart, prints news, editorials, interpretations of the news, practical information, entertainment news, and advertising. The bulk of the news content, however, is local news— that concerned with a particular rural area. Much of the information contained in a country newspaper is of an agricultural and homemaking nature. Country newspapers are usually printed as weeklies. The country's largest is *Capper's Weekly*, published in Topeka, Kansas.

Association, trade, and professional newspapers are usually published by organized groups like industries, associations, societies, clubs, professional groups, and labor unions. The content of these publications usually consists of information that concerns limited, specific-interest groups.

The main purpose of **weekly newspapers** is to cover the local news of the small town or of a community area within a city or

CAPPER'S WEEKLY

TAKEN TO HEART FOR MORE THAN ONE HUNDRED YEARS

Influence is not government.
—George Washington

45 Cents

Volume 104—No. 3   Edition A   Topeka, Kan. 66607   February 2, 1982

WORLD NEWS
In a few words

Joint session of Congress January 28 will honor 100th birthday anniversary of former President Franklin D. Roosevelt (born January 30, 1882).

Inflation rose 8.9 percent in 1981, smallest increase in four years.

EPA Administrator Anne Gorsuch says Reagan administration will push for passage of House bill to relax air quality deadlines and auto emission standards.

Federal Communications Commission, moving to implement policy change approved more than one year ago, cleared way for telephone rate increases across country.

Gold prices rallied after plummeting to 28-month low of less than $370 an ounce.

Explosion and fire that hurled debris hundreds of feet killed seven members of one family deep inside their own coal mine near Craynor, Ky.

U.S. vetoed diluted Arab resolution calling on all United Nations members to consider sanctions against Israel for annexing occupied Syrian Golan Heights.

Nuclear Regulatory Commission proposed $550,000 fine — largest in NRC history — against Boston Edison Co. for alleged safety violations at Pilgrim nuclear plant in Plymouth, Mass.

Tennis player John McEnroe, 22, winner of Wimbledon and U.S. Open, was named 1981 male athlete of year by Associated Press.

Poland's Communist martial law government announced food price increases of up to 400 percent effective February 1 and warned of drastic meat shortage.

President Reagan asked Congress to bar him from granting tax-exempt status to schools and colleges that discriminate against blacks.

Walter "Red" Smith, 76, Pulitzer · prizewinning sports columnist, died in Stamford, Conn.

Coca-Cola Co. agreed to pay nearly $795 million in cash and stock for Columbia Pictures.

Syrian forces fired anti-aircraft missiles at four Israeli reconnaissance jets over eastern Lebanon.

President Reagan declared January 30 "A Day of Solidarity with the People of

Waiting statues

Quietly the statues wait

to be remembered, to be great

once more in their philosophies,

to be popular, to please

and win the peoples' hearts and minds.

Someone, somewhere, looks and finds

Lincoln and his mighty theme,

Washington, his sturdy dream;

then, again, they breathe and live,

strong with all they have to give—

verities to hold our own,

faiths more durable than stone.

—Helen Harrington

—photo by Rick Schmidt

"Seated Lincoln," a bronze statue by sculptor Robert Merrill Gage, graces the southeast section of the statehouse grounds in Topeka, Kan. The statue, cast in a Chicago, Ill., foundry, was unveiled on Lincoln's birthday February 12, 1918. The Kansas Capitol appears in the background.

Famous child with mother

Tran Thi Het, a Vietnamese child, sits with her mother, Evelyn Heil, in front of a chalkboard at a school for learning disabled children operated by Ms. Heil in Springfield, Ohio.

Diamonds under Kansas?

A St. Louis-based exploration firm is betting a long shot that diamonds lie beneath the Kansas prairie.

It's a thought that "makes your mouth water," says William Unhelhop, part owner of a 550-acre parcel near Bala that has been leased by Cominco American for exploration. The company also has leased rights to 160 acres near Randolph, 800 acres near Green and 70 acres near Leonardville.

The four tracts of land have one thing in common: formations of kimberlite, an igneous rock substance that forms in long "pipes" 300 to 500 feet across, sometimes extending as much as several hundred miles down from the surface

But it's impossible to tell the difference between kimberlite formations with diamonds and those without, unless a company is willing to invest in a detailed exploration and analysis project.

Before Cominco American, no company had been willing to risk the necessary investment, restricting most of the world's diamond production to South Africa, Australia and the Soviet Union.

Even if the gamble pays off with the discovery of diamonds, more money must be spent to get the diamonds out.

"For instance, you might find one carat of diamond for each 30 to 50 tons of rock unearthed . . . that would be good," said Peter Berendsen

Takes 'time' to spend 5-year defense funds

Rep James Jones (D-Okla.) chairman of the House Budget Committee, has offered an explanation of the $1.5 trillion Defense Department budget proposed for the next five years.

Said Jones, "If someone was going to spend a million dollars a day, beginning on the day Christ was born 1,982 years ago, a million dollars a day thru the Dark Ages, the Middle Ages, thru the Age of Enlightenment, the Industrial Revolution and modern era — every day spending a million dollars — he would only spend half of what we're asking the Pentagon to spend over the next five years."

America's largest country newspaper is *Capper's Weekly*, published in Topeka, Kansas.

suburb. Weekly newspapers specialize in the one type of news not covered in detail by most metropolitan dailies: personal news about people and events within the weekly's own community.

School newspapers serve the interests of the schools they represent. Some are published monthly; others are published bi-weekly, weekly, or in the case of some college newspapers, daily. They include news of school events, news and articles of interest to students and teachers, and advertisements of interest to students. Many school newspapers contain community news.

Ethnic newspapers are published in cities and in other areas where large concentrations of specific ethnic groups have settled. Many of these newspapers are weeklies printed in the language of the ethnic group they represent. Following are some examples of this type of publication: the *Jewish Advocate, La Notizia* (Italian), the *Hellenic Chronicle* (Greek), the *Polish American News*, the *German Courier*, the *Lithuanian Free Press*, the *Scandinavian Tribune* (Swedish and Norwegian), the *Chinese World*, the *Portuguese Journal*, and the *Irish Echo*.

Among ethnic news publishing, probably the best-known is the black American press. New York City's *Amsterdam News*, the country's best-selling black American newspaper presents news in the sensational style of New York's *Daily News*. It also covers news of black progress, new fair-housing rulings, and such general topics as job promotions. In contrast to the *Amsterdam News*, *The Pittsburgh Courier* favors news of a sociological nature and of the world of the black professional.

The Wire Services

The gathering and compiling of news from all over the world—too costly an operation for most newspapers except metropolitan dailies like *The New York Times*, the *Washington Post*, and the *Los Angeles Times*—is an important function performed by the wire services. These are news-gathering agencies that were originally formed when a group of large newspapers agreed to share expenses and engage in cooperative worldwide news-gathering efforts. The New York Associated Press, forerunner of the present Associated Press, was founded in 1848. Later, two similar agencies—the United Press and the International News Service—were formed. In 1958, to meet the pressure of competition, the United Press and the International News Service merged into what we know today as the United Press International. The Associated Press (AP) and the United Press International (UPI) are this country's predominant wire services. The National Black News Service (NBNS), operating from Washington, D.C., is the major black American news service.

Major Functions of Newspapers

What do you expect when you read a newspaper? What can you, as an informed reader, have a right to expect? The major functions of a newspaper are to inform (via news reports), to persuade (via editorials, commentaries, letters to the editor), to entertain (via feature articles and special sections), and to provide a means by which merchants can sell their wares (via advertisements).

A good news column presents necessary background information and the news itself in a way that the reader will have no trouble reading and understanding the news story. Good news reporters remember that the primary function of news is to inform—and not necessarily to entertain—and they should keep their news presentations interesting as well as factual.

THE FUNCTIONS OF THE MODERN NEWSPAPER

TO INFORM

TO PERSUADE

TO ENTERTAIN

TO BRING BUYERS
AND SELLERS TOGETHER

A good reporter knows which stories will interest the most readers. From over a million words of copy submitted daily, a metropolitan news editor selects about 100,000 words of what he or she thinks is the most important material. However, editors also base their news selection on what they think *should* interest readers.

The editorial section contains material written by the editors, who express their newspaper's view (policy) on general issues and current problems. The editorial pages may also contain expressions of opinion by well-known columnists. There may also be "letters to the editor" from readers who wish to express their views on current issues.

The theater and music sections provide entertainment news, and certain columnists may write for the purpose of entertaining readers. (Art Buchwald is an example of a celebrated columnist who enlivens the editorial pages with his satiric humor.) For entertainment, many readers turn first to the comics. Sports news and homemaking sections are often entertaining as well as informative. Sports news is often heavily illustrated, and sports columns usually contain language that is more vivid and more colorful than is the case with general news. On the homemaking pages society news, advice columns, news from the fashion world, health and beauty tips, announcements of engagements and marriages, and homemaking advice offer interesting reading.

The organized classified advertising section provides a number of services for readers. Here are listings of job opportunities and information about materials, products, services, and real estate offered for sale.

Major Divisions of the Typical Daily Newspaper

The major divisions of a typical daily newspaper are (1) the editorial, (2) the mechanical, and (3) the business departments. Men and women employed in the editorial department gather and prepare the news; those in the mechanical department are responsible for composition, printing, and production; those in the business department supervise all financial aspects of producing the newspaper, including advertising and circulation. Typical staff organization for a large metropolitan newspaper is illustrated by the chart on page 37.

The Editorial Department. Gathering and preparing the news for publication is an art, not an exact science. A newspaper is the

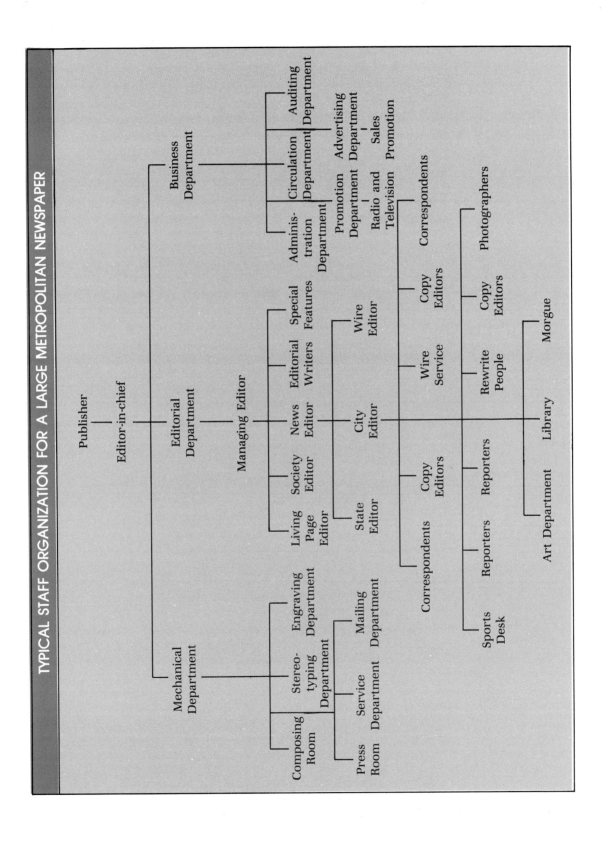

TYPICAL STAFF ORGANIZATION FOR A LARGE METROPOLITAN NEWSPAPER

product, not of scientific rules, but of the wisdom and the conscience of responsible men and women; the end product reflects their judgment. There is an art to writing, to editing, to selecting the best news stories. There is an art to the taking and cropping of photographs for publication. There is an art to the writing of stimulating headlines. Finally, there is an art to combining all these elements into an attractive makeup that will be ready for the printer at a given time (deadline).

The Editor-in-Chief. Supervising the overall news operation is the editor-in-chief. In addition to overseeing the newspaper from beginning to end, the editor-in-chief makes a number of policy decisions that guide the overall operation of the newspaper. In addition, the editor-in-chief and the managing editor usually collaborate in the hiring, firing, and promotion of all editorial department workers.

The Managing Editor. The managing editor supervises the combined news-gathering operation. The sports, society, feature, and arts editors operate independently, but all four are responsible to the managing editor. The managing editor ordinarily consults the news editor on the choice of national and world news stories. Editorial writers may also ask the managing editor's advice on the newspaper's policy on local and national issues. Some managing editors decide how important each story is and determine where each is to be placed in the paper. After assessing each story, the managing editor marks the headline size at the top of the article and gives the story to a copy editor, who edits the story and writes a headline. The managing editor often lays out each page in the newspaper. This process is like doing a jigsaw puzzle—each story, photo, and headline must fit into a given amount of space. Major news is placed at the top of the page with large headlines; minor news appears at the bottom of the page with smaller headlines. Most managing editors are involved in deciding on the major news stories for the front page.

The City Editor. The city editor makes certain that the news beats are covered and that additional stories are supplied as news events warrant. If the President of the United States were to speak in the community, the city editor would assign reporters and photographers to cover all phases of the visit. One reporter might be assigned to the airport to do a sidebar (a minor feature story) on how the crowd reacted, what security measures had been taken, and what the President did. If anything out of the ordinary were to occur, such as a demonstration, there might be another sidebar. If the President were to be accompanied by the First Lady, a reporter might write still another sidebar on what the First Lady did during the visit. A background story on other Presidential visits to the community and an article describing the crowd lining the parade route would be appropriate. The main story, of course, would be the coverage of the President's speech. The city editor also sees to it that stories are turned in on time and that they do not overlap.

The News Editor. A major responsibility of the news editor (sometimes called the telegraph editor or the wire editor) is to select for publication a few of the hundreds of news stories filed daily by the wire services to which the newspaper subscribes. The news editor and staff usually consult with the managing editor on the final choice of such stories.

The Reporter. The backbone of any newspaper is the reporter. Depending on education, interests, and background, a reporter may be assigned to a regular news beat. For example, a reporter who has taken a number of education courses in college might be asked to cover the office of the local superintendent of schools, school board meetings, and the activities of the various schools in the community. The reporter's stories would deal with such topics as school budgets, bond issues, school appointments and elections, modern techniques in education, construction of new facilities, or any other matter relating to the education of the community's citizens. Writing stories every day on educational affairs is this reporter's job.

An education reporter working on a large metropolitan daily would report to the education editor, who decides which education reporters are to cover which stories.

Many newspapers—particularly the metropolitan dailies—have special editors and reporters to cover such regular beats as state and local government, crime and the courts, business and finance, family and human affairs, entertainment and the arts.

Other major desks depend on the area where the newspaper is published. Metropolitan dailies in the Midwest, for instance, would have a staff familiar with local farming to cover stories concerning agricultural affairs.

Many news beats call for reporters with highly specialized training and knowledge. General assignment reporters—reporters who cover a wide variety of topics from day to day—must also have wide background knowledge.

The reporter—general assignment or otherwise—who does the job well, presents facts objectively and clearly, allowing the readers to judge what the facts signify, gains the satisfaction of knowing he or she has contributed to and has a stake in the well-being of the community.

The Mechanical Department. The major cost of putting out a newspaper stems from the operations of the mechanical department; in fact, one publisher estimates that two thirds of all newspaper expenses can be attributed to this department.

The four divisions that make up the mechanical department are these: the engraving room, the composing room, the stereotyping room, and the pressroom. Workers in the engraving room make a negative of every photograph to be printed in the paper. In the composing room, compositors paste up the stories that have been typeset and that have been copy edited.

Once news stories, headlines, illustrations, and advertisements have been pasted on a predesigned form, the page is taken to the engraving department, where a full-size replica is made on an aluminum plate that will fit on a high-speed printing press. The finished plate is then taken to the pressroom, where it is fitted on the press at the proper place.

Nowadays, many metropolitan newspapers are printed by a process called offset printing. Each inked aluminum plate presses against a rubber-blanketed cylinder, which, in turn, transfers the printed image to the paper.

The largest metropolitan dailies are printed by letterpress. The mechanical departments of these papers include a stereotyping room, where lead plates are made, from which the paper is printed.

Modern presses print, collate, fold, count, and bind the newspapers—more than a thousand copies—in a minute's time. Conveyor belts carry the bundled newspapers to delivery trucks that distribute the paper throughout the circulation area.

The Business Department. The publisher, general manager, business manager, and treasurer supervise the business aspects of publishing a newspaper. They oversee the entire operation, and they keep the paper financially sound—for newspapers must make money or go out of business. Occasionally newspapers are accused of having too many advertisements in proportion to news content; however, if the ratio doesn't stay about sixty percent advertising to forty percent news, the paper will lose money. Commercial pressures from unethical advertisers, political pressures from the power structure, criminal pressures, all have exerted pressure on publishers since the earliest days of the press and probably will continue to do so. But a financially sound newspaper need not fear pressures.

The newspaper's two main sources of revenue are circulation and advertising. Circulation is important because no advertiser would want to pay money to put an advertisement in a limited-

These news reporters edit their stories on VDT's in this busy newsroom.

circulation publication that only a few readers might see. Advertising costs are usually based on the number of readers a publication has.

Each newspaper has a circulation manager, whose job is to sell more papers. The circulation manager supervises distribution and collections through district managers and private distributors, plans promotional campaigns to increase circulation, and sponsors contests among the carriers. A newspaper may succeed or fail depending on the circulation manager's efforts.

The advertising department of a newspaper is usually divided into three sections: local, national, and classified. The local advertising sales representatives find potential advertisers and advertising agencies in the area of distribution. In addition to attempting to convince advertisers of the need to place advertising on a regular basis, these representatives sell space in special editions (such as new-car supplements) and on special pages (such as church pages). As a rule, advertising rates are based on a circulation number that is verified by an agency such as the Audit Bureau of Circulation (ABC). For example, a one-column, one-inch-deep ad in a relatively small paper in Washington, Pennsylvania, would cost about three dollars; the same-size ad in the largest newspaper in Washington, D.C., would cost about thirty dollars.

The national advertising manager usually has a small staff because the majority of national advertisements are placed by agencies located in New York City. However, this person must keep these agencies informed about the paper's circulation figures and about plans for special editions.

The classified department accounts for a large percentage of advertising revenue. The classified advertising manager supervises advertising rates and manages the office staff. He or she also promotes placement of classified ads by writing promotional blurbs that are usually printed in the classified section.

Reading a Newspaper

The average newspaper reader spends approximately one-half hour a day reading the paper. Because a single issue of a typical daily newspaper contains much more than one-half hour's reading material, the average reader must be selective in the choice of reading matter. That selection is, of course, completely personal, and the procedure followed by most readers is to categorize materials into that which can be read carefully, that which can be skimmed or read only in part, and that which can be ignored. Most readers start with the front-page headlines, selecting from them certain news items to be read in depth. Good headlines facilitate choice of reading material by accurately outlining the content of the news stories, helping the reader decide how much time, if any, to give to a given item. Many readers skim only the headlines, getting the gist of the news stories from them. For other stories many readers consider only the lead, which should contain the *who, what, when, where, why,* and *how* of the story. In long stories the subheads will indicate which parts the reader may want to read.

The well-informed reader retains materials such as important names and dates, the basis for new and proposed laws, facts concerning the local, national, and worldwide situations, the national and worldwide economies, and the like. These readers make daily newspaper reading a habit. They are discriminating in their choice of reading material and are able to distinguish between the significant and insignificant, slanted and straight news, fact and opinion.

The completed newspapers are coming off the press.

A Newspaper Career

High school is a good place to begin training for the journalism profession. Journalism students might gain experience by working on school publications or by working during the summer on community newspapers. As copy aides, for instance, they would go on errands, deliver copy from one department to another, and generally become familiar with newspaper environment and procedures. In setting up college programs of studies, students should choose other areas of specialization, in addition to journalism, that would increase job opportunities. A double major—journalism combined with economics, urban affairs, sociology, or education, for example—should be considered. Students should work on the college newspaper and gain additional experience on other newspapers during summer vacations. With a college education, a good journalism background, and experience in the field, students would be good candidates for any newspaper.

Activities

1. As a discriminating reader, you are aware of and interested in your own newspaper reading habits. To determine the amount of time you spend in reading the several different sections of newspapers—and perhaps to help improve your reading habits—complete the following:

  a. For one week, keep a daily log of the newspapers you read. List the names of the publications and the types of newspaper materials. After each listing, enter the time (rounded off to the nearest quarter hour) you spend reading each type of material. Keep an accurate record. At the end of the week, tabulate the total number of hours you've spent in newspaper reading, and then determine the average number of hours you've spent each day in such reading.

  b. From the results of your log, make a graph showing the time you spent in reading each type of newspaper material. Your completed graph will show the variety or lack of variety in your newspaper reading.

2. Participate actively in a class discussion of this question: What do you, as an enlightened, informed American citizen, have a right to expect from a newspaper?

3. Help make arrangements to have several newspaper reporters and feature writers visit your journalism class as an informal panel. Before the scheduled date, prepare a short list of well-thought-out questions to ask them.

4. Participate actively in a class discussion concerning the differences between the words *interesting* and *entertaining*. Are they mutually exclusive terms? During the discussion, examine some newspapers to determine whether their news presentations are "interesting" or "entertaining" or both. If you were establishing the editorial policy of a newspaper, what stand would you take on this issue? Be prepared to explain your point of view.

5. With your journalism class, visit the offices and the plant of your local newspaper—especially when the mechanical department is at peak operation. Prepare a brief news story about your visit.

6. Study the major sections of a daily newspaper. Prepare a short report in which you identify (a) sections that you think are given too much space, (b) sections that you think have about the right amount of space, and (c) sections that you think have too little space. Supply reasons for your point of view.

7. In a statement of three paragraphs or so, compare the style and the content of a typical story on page one of a weekly newspaper with a typical story on page one of a metropolitan daily. As a part of your statement, indicate why, in your opinion, there are bound to be differences.

8. Write a short, informative, readable, interesting news story on a subject of your choice. Specify the kind of newspaper you are writing for; also specify the section of the paper in which your story should appear.

CHAPTER 3

Magazines, Specialized Periodicals, and Books

The Magazine— Medium of Mass Communication

Don't go up in the plane—and if you do, don't tell me!" an apprehensive *Life* magazine editor warned a young reporter assigned to cover the activities of a parachute club. When the reporter confidently strapped herself into a parachute and hopped a plane, everything went well until she jumped—only to wind up in a tree! Off target? Yes, way off.

The publishers of the more than five billion copies of magazines distributed yearly in this country can't be off target as far as that young reporter was. They can't afford to be. Instead, they have to be as nearly on target as possible. Magazine readers want articles that interest them. If any magazines miss their "reader-interest" target, readers will desert them. Like newspaper editors, magazine editors are faced with the constant on-target problem of getting people to read and to keep reading their publications.

Today, magazine publishing—an enterprise that concerns more than just the magazines on newsstands—plays a major role in mass communication. Magazines employ thousands of persons as editors, authors, reporters, writers, artists, and photographers. There are magazines that serve clearly defined groups with such special interests as industrial production, labor affairs, education, science, religion, sports, national, and ethnic affairs. There are magazines that cover every area of human interest or activity. There are also occupational fields closely associated with magazine publishing but not actually a part of it. These include advertising, market research, and printing—all of which employ thousands of men and women.

Like newspapers, magazines exist to inform, to entertain, and to influence the thinking and the behavior of their readers. The major difference between magazines and newspapers is that many magazines are concerned with reaching special-interest groups, whereas newspapers try to include stories of interest to every reader within their circulation areas. Furthermore, many magazines are aimed at specific groups or specific geographic areas and so are a highly desirable medium for national advertisers. For one thing, magazines are more durable than newspapers. Then too, magazines are printed on high-quality paper that makes possible a much sharper display of color than can be achieved on newsprint, giving magazine advertisements some advantages over those in newspapers. Finally, because they are published less frequently than daily newspapers, magazines can offer their readers in-depth analyses of news events and in-depth interpretations of ideas, trends, and points of view. Unlike their newspaper counterparts, magazine writers and editors have time for research and time for rewriting and polishing their work.

As the number of educated Americans has increased, the growth in magazine circulation, magazine reading, and magazine effectiveness has accelerated. The National Industrial Conference Board reports that family spending for magazines increases sharply as the level of education of heads of households rises. For example, parents who are college graduates spend four-and-one-half times as much on magazines as do parents with fewer years of schooling. This increase in magazine circulation, a direct reflection of the rapid growth of education in the United States, has increased the ability of magazines to help advertisers sell their merchandise. Magazines have a direct effect on the nation's economy.

The first "magazine," *The Gentleman's Magazine,* was published in London in 1731. In 1741 *The American Magazine* and *The General Magazine and Historical Chronicle* were published in colonial America.

Magazine Development

Beginnings

Early publishers may have chosen the word *magazine* when they combined the best qualities of successful newspapers into a more durable format and presented readers with a "storehouse" of material. The first publication known to have used the word *magazine* in its title was *The Gentleman's Magazine,* founded in London in 1731.

The first magazine in colonial America was founded in 1741. Called the *American Magazine, or a Monthly View of the Political State of the British Colonies,* this publication was followed within days by Benjamin Franklin's *General Magazine and Historical Chronicle, For All the British Plantations in America.* Both of these publications lasted for only a few months. Other magazines followed but also lasted for only a short time. Incidentally, in 1778 the title of one of these short-lived magazines suggested the name for the new nation: *The United States Magazine.*

These two American magazines have been published for more than 125 years.

Following the American Revolution, magazines in this country underwent a major period of growth. Many newcomers appeared: *American Museum* (1787), *Port Folio* (1801), *The Monthly Anthology* (1803), *Salmagundi* (1807), *The North American Review* (1815), *The Saturday Evening Post* (1821), *Genesee Farmer, or Country Gentleman* (1831), *The Knickerbocker Magazine* (1833), *Harper's* (1850), and *The Atlantic Monthly*, (1854). Some of these magazines are still published today.

Literary Standards

A number of periodicals and magazines were owned by literary groups. These magazines came to be considered the most favorable medium in which to develop and publish the new American literature. Magazines could publish longer articles than newspapers could. Magazines were easier to circulate and less expensive to publish than books. In time, many magazines came to reflect the highest literary standards, and some of them came to be responsible for determining literary taste.

In 1865 Edwin L. Godkin, successor to William Cullen Bryant as editor of the *New York Post* and one of the country's most influential writers, joined the ranks of magazine publishers. Having decided that the country needed a journal of opinion and of literary criticism, Godkin founded *The Nation*. He geared the content of the magazine to the interests of intellectuals. His editorials advocating "peace, entrenchment, and reform" are considered to be among the best ever written on those subjects; and they attracted readers from coast to coast. *The Nation* stressed the importance of education and sought to improve the living conditions for all Americans—particularly for black Americans. Although he crusaded against government intervention in economic matters, Godkin felt that government should take action in areas of social welfare. Philosopher William James wrote of Godkin:

> His was certainly the towering influence in all thought concerning public affairs, and indirectly his influence has assuredly been more pervasive than that of any other writer of the generation.

The Nation, founded as a journal for thinking people, continues its tradition today.

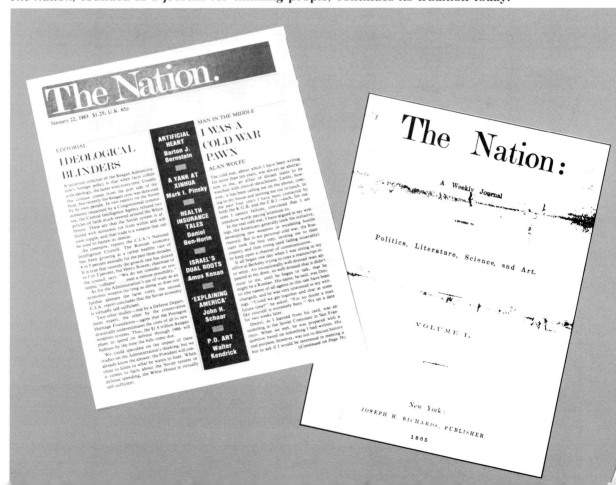

Trends toward Specialization

Many of the magazines founded during the latter part of the 19th century were specialized types of periodicals. In 1890 Gilbert Hovey Grosvenor founded *The National Geographic*, a magazine devoted to ''the increase and diffusion of geographic knowledge.'' The magazine was an immediate success. It is still one of the most widely read periodicals in the country.

By 1900 the *Ladies' Home Journal*, which began publication in 1883, had reached a circulation of one million. In 1894 *Journal's* publisher, Cyrus H. K. Curtis, purchased *The Saturday Evening Post* for one thousand dollars. Curtis soon developed the *Post* into a leader in the weekly magazine field. Curtis, who had begun his career as an advertising man, hired George Horace Lorimer as his managing editor. Lorimer sought out such well-known writers as Rudyard Kipling, Bret Hart, and Mark Twain, and he even persuaded President Theodore Roosevelt to write for the *Post*. Together, Curtis and Lorimer built the Curtis Publishing Company into a highly profitable and influential business.

With the beginning of the 20th century, the popularity of magazines increased and circulation figures rose. To increase their circulation, some magazines launched ''muckraking'' crusades. (*Muckraking*, a term popularized by Theodore Roosevelt, involved the public exposure of apparent misconduct on the part of prominent individuals or organizations.) But the reading public quickly

A recent issue of *Time* strongly resembles the 60-year-old first issue.

The Mass Media in a Democratic Society

tired of this kind of sensational journalism. To maintain and increase their circulation, magazines began to use illustrations and photographs to enliven their feature articles.

During the post-World War I boom of magazine publishing, Yale student Henry R. Luce, realizing the power of the press in shaping the thinking of readers, solicited from Yale alumni contributions totaling some $86,000 with which to start a magazine. The new weekly publication was to give readers capsule versions of the news in such areas as national affairs, foreign affairs, science, religion, business, education, and literature. After making an informal survey that showed that the word *time* was often on the minds of Americans, Luce and cofounder Briton Haden chose *Time* as the title for their magazine. In the first issue of *Time*—in March 1923—the editors announced:

> People are uninformed because no publication has adapted itself to the time which busy men are able to spend on simply keeping informed.

The editors of *Time* presented the weekly news in a light, human-interest style that used narrative leads. They also initiated a system for researching the background of each news story. The background was then interwoven with the actual news account, resulting in most sentences being written in a unique inverted word order. This type of presentation prompted one critic to

Newsweek and *U.S. News & World Report* are successful and popular newsmagazines.

The original issue of *Reader's Digest*, the first of the magazines in pocket size, is shown with a recent issue.

comment: "Backwards ran sentences until reeled the mind." In 1930, the year that many magazines went out of business because of the stock-market crash and the subsequent depression, the undaunted Luce launched a lavish business magazine titled *Fortune*. *Fortune* prospered and today is one of America's leading magazines of business. Six years later Luce brought out *Life*, a magazine geared to the interests of increasingly picture-conscious readers. *Life* was an overnight success and Time, Inc., the name of Luce's combined publishing interests, soon became a giant in the field of magazine publishing.

The success of *Time* led to the establishment of other newsmagazines, two of which today have a sizable circulation: *Newsweek* and *U.S. News & World Report*, both founded in 1933.

The success of another specialized magazine resulted from the efforts of DeWitt Wallace and his wife. They began clipping stories from uncopyrighted magazines, compiling the clippings, and presenting them to readers as the pocket-size *Reader's Digest*. First appearing in 1922, the *Reader's Digest* was an overnight sensation. By printing condensations of entertaining and informative articles, the Wallaces built the *Digest's* circulation into one of the largest in the world.

Following the lead of the *Reader's Digest*, other pocket-size magazines appeared: *Coronet*, first published in 1936, was discontinued in 1966. *Jet*, a pocket-size magazine published especially for black Americans, was launched in 1951 by the publishers of *Ebony*. In 1953 *TV Guide* made its appearance and has since become one of the most widely read magazines in the country.

The American Magazine Today

Circulation

Experts estimate that today there are about twenty thousand different magazines published in the United States. While many are special-interest publications, the majority are consumer-oriented. With recent advances in printing techniques and photography, magazines have become an integral part of the nation's mass media.

Types of Magazines

The Standard Periodical Dictionary, Seventh Edition, 1981-82, lists some 230 subject areas in which magazines are published in the United States today. Here we will identify only ten types of magazines—types that have the largest numbers of readers:

General-interest publications are magazines like *Atlantic*, *Harper's*, *Geo*, *Reader's Digest*, and *The Saturday Evening Post*.

Among the magazines that enjoy a sizable nationwide circulation are the **newsmagazines**—publications like *Time*, *Newsweek*, *U.S. News & World Report*.

Magazines of **consumer affairs** include *Consumer Reports*, *Consumer's Digest*, *Better Homes and Gardens*, *Changing Times*.

There are a number of magazines that focus on matters **primarily of interest to women.** Among these publications are *Good Housekeeping*, *Vogue*, *McCall's*, *Ladies' Home Journal*, *Mademoiselle*, *Woman's Day*, *Redbook*.

As you might expect, there are magazines that focus on matters **primarily of interest to men.** Among them are *Esquire*, *True*, *Field and Stream*, *Sports Illustrated*.

Business magazines report events and trends in financial and industrial affairs and print articles of interest to those in business management. Such magazines include *Business Week*, *Fortune*, *Barron's*, *Forbes*.

A large number of **ethnic magazines** are published in this country—magazines devoted to the concerns and the culture of groups whose members share common traits and customs within our society. Among the best known of these ethnic magazines are *Ebony*, *Jet*, and *Negro Digest*. Other ethnic magazines include *Amerasia Journal*, *Israel Today*, *El Mundo*, *Indian Affairs*.

Religious magazines, too, have a sizable circulation. Among the best known of these publications are these: *Christian Herald*, *Catholic Digest*, *Christianity Today*, *B'nai B'rith Messenger*.

Several **entertainment/travel magazines** enjoy a wide circulation throughout the country. Among them are *TV Guide, Photoplay, Playboy, Travel and Leisure, Travel Holiday.*

A comparative newcomer to the magazine publishing field is the **Sunday newspaper magazine supplement.** Even experienced newspaper and magazine publishers find it difficult to classify these supplements as either newspapers or magazines. Sunday supplements are publications assembled and delivered with the thick weekend newspapers. The Sunday supplement certainly makes the newspaper more appealing to its readers, although some editors feel that it takes readers' attention away from the newspaper itself.

The four largest Sunday supplements in the United States are *Family Weekly, Parade,* the *Sunday Magazine Group* (Metropolitan Sunday Newspapers), and *The New York Times Sunday Magazine.* Similar to magazines in that they present more in-depth feature-type material than the newspapers they are a part of, the Sunday supplements still must conform to deadlines—deadlines that are only slightly less rigid than those that editors on their parent newspapers must meet. Editors of the Sunday magazine supplements begin their work about eight weeks prior to the parent newspaper's deadlines.

Parade and *The New York Times Magazine* are two large circulation Sunday supplements.

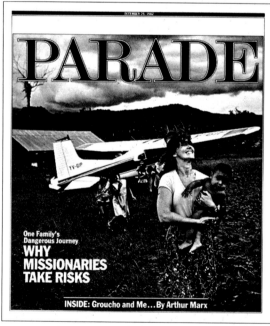

The Mass Media in a Democratic Society

Major Divisions of Magazine Publishing

Management, editorial, advertising, and circulation—these are the major operating divisions of the average magazine. Management supervises the business activities involved in producing the magazine; editorial is responsible for the content of the magazine and for expressing the magazine's position on current issues. The advertising division contracts for and sells advertising space, and the circulation division is responsible for selling subscriptions to the magazine and for the distribution of each issue. A chart of the staff organization typical of a large magazine appears on page 58.

Few magazine publishers own the plants in which their magazines are printed. The equipment needed for printing high-quality magazines represents a substantial financial investment and requires the full-time use of specialists in the printing process. Most magazine publishers, therefore, send their articles, photos, illustrations, and advertisements to plants that specialize in the printing of magazines. Usually such printing plants handle several different magazines on a regular basis. Articles and headlines are set in type, engravings are made of all illustrations and photos, and reproduction proof of all advertisements is approved. All these elements are placed in page forms, the forms are photographed, and plates are made and placed on high-speed color presses. The printed pages are then collated and bound, and the bound magazines are sent to distributors across the country.

Key Personnel in Magazine Publishing

Who are the key people whose jobs are to publish and distribute a magazine? What are their principal responsibilities?

The Editor-in-chief. The editor-in-chief is in charge of the editorial staff and decides what articles and artwork are to be published, making decisions based on knowledge of what the magazine's readers want. The editor-in-chief also supervises the production of each issue. Ordinarily, this person does not write the articles but may write editorials or special reports. The editor-in-chief must combine executive and creative duties. Some editors-in-chief spend a great deal of time revising and correcting articles, selecting illustrations, and planning layouts for each page. Other editors-in-chief delegate this work to subordinates and devote their own time to general supervision, policy determination, and administrative duties. The editor-in-chief reports to the publisher, as do the heads of all other divisions.

TYPICAL STAFF ORGANIZATION FOR A LARGE MAGAZINE

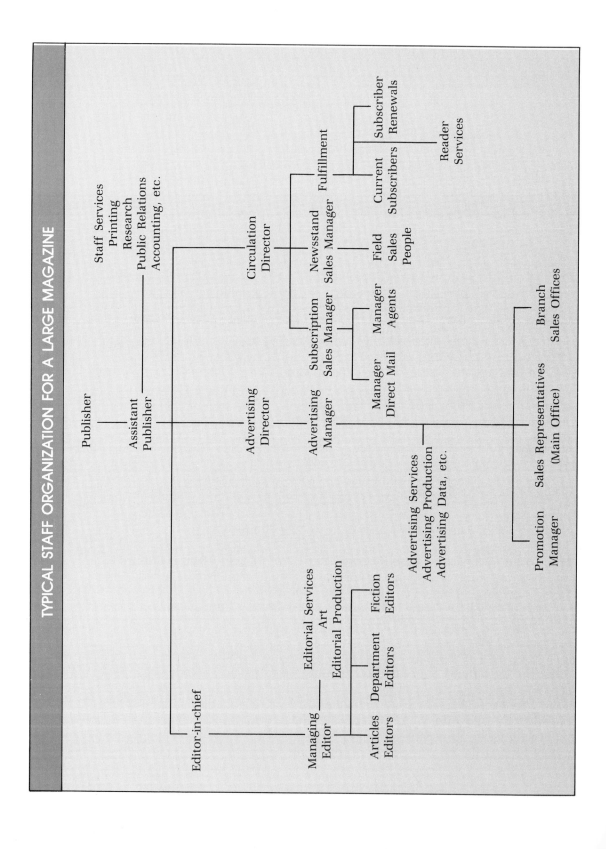

The varied tasks of magazine editors include photo analysis, layouts, and cropping photographs.

Magazines, Specialized Periodicals, and Books

Department Editors. On large magazines, department editors confer and work with the editor-in-chief on each issue. They also direct the editorial work of departments such as sports, theater, arts, fashion, and fiction.

Editorial Assistants. Magazine editorial assistants spend most of their time doing library research to aid the writers. Facts in the finished story are double-checked by these assistants, who also retype copy, answer letters, interview callers, and do other routine office work.

Copyreaders. Finished manuscripts are checked by copyreaders for length, style, grammar, spelling, punctuation, organization, technical accuracy, and readability.

The Advertising Director. The advertising director is responsible for managing the sale of advertising space and may have a group of district sales offices throughout the country to supervise. Some magazines have sales staffs numbering more than fifty persons.

The Circulation Director. As a rule, the magazine circulation director supervises two sections: subscription sales and newsstand sales. The subscription section obtains new subscribers by mail or from outside sales agencies; the newsstand section is concerned with single-copy sales at newstands. Other members of the circulation department handle subscription renewals and distribution.

The Director of Advertising Production. The advertising production department is concerned with the handling and processing of engravings sent by advertisers, with advertising makeup, and with advertising layout. The advertising production department also serves as a liaison between the advertising department and the printer.

Magazine Writing

There is little difference between good magazine writing and good newspaper writing, as shown in the following examples—one from a magazine article, the other from a newspaper article.

A few miles from where you live there is a part of America nobody wants. It may be a group of ramshackle farm houses or the gray, weatherworn tenements of a city street. Row on row they shelter the culls of society whose togetherness is marked by frayed collars and the musty smell of the poor.

Harper's

During the day, Christopher Columbus Park is a manicured patch of tranquility nestled among condos and seafood restaurants. At night, it belongs to the hopeless. People who can't make the rent, folks who do not dine along the harborside, claim this park for a bed.

The call came in at 7:29 a.m. yesterday just about the time Christopher Columbus Park changes colors. With the sunlight, despair gives way to prosperity. Officers John Klokman and Catherine Crowley answered the call for a "stabbing near the statue." They pulled up to the park just as a team of Emergency Medical Technicians arrived.

The Boston Herald-American

The first example, from a *Harper's* magazine article "A Way Out of the Welfare Mess," was written by Edgar May, a Pulitzer Prize-winning reporter for the *Buffalo Evening News*. Since *Harper's* is a nationally distributed magazine, May's article deals with problems existing in cities throughout the country. Edgar May wrote the story as a part of a series for the *Evening News*, his focus centering on Buffalo's unique problems. In the complete magazine story he gives the *why* of the problem and offers solutions. While the majority of newspaper stories give only the *who*, *what*, *when*, and *where* of the story, magazines often add the two that are, many times, the most important: the *how* and the *why*.

The second lead was written by *Boston Herald-American* reporter Peter Gelzinis. Just as Edgar May did, Gelzinis used fiction-writing techniques, bringing a routine crime story out of the realm of the ordinary. He emphasized the contrast between the rich and the downtrodden to tell far more than a crime story. Gelzinis winds up his story with an air of finality that echoes the lead:

By 9 a.m. all the snoozing shadows had left Christopher Columbus Park. The sun was out and the park once again was reclaimed by the sounds of children playing.

Free-Lancing

Although most newspaper articles are written by staff or wire-service reporters, magazines often assign free-lance writers (self-employed writers) to do specific stories. By using free-lancers magazines can publish articles by persons who have specialized in certain fields. Sometimes magazines will solicit articles from writers whom they know or who have previously written for the magazine.

Many magazines purchase unsolicited manuscripts from free-lance writers. Unknown writers often break into print this way—like the journalism student who became interested in electronic music after attending a concert. After checking through the *Readers' Guide to Periodical Literature* in his school library, he read a number of magazine articles related to electronic music and then wrote a 700-word article for submission to a music magazine. The editor liked the story and bought it. A large Midwestern newspaper's music editor read the article and offered to pay the student for permission to reprint parts of it. Then the editor of a musical instrument company's trade magazine asked the student to write still another story on the same topic. The enterprising journalism student received over $150 from the publications represented by the three editors.

While many professional free-lancers prefer, for the sake of variety, to write about a number of different subjects, others prefer to write articles in specialized subject areas. Most magazine editors request that free-lance writers submit what is called a *letter of query* prior to submitting their actual manuscript. This query may be either a letter detailing exactly what the article is about or an actual outline of the article. On page 63 is an example of this type of query, written by a student eager to sell his article to *Impact* magazine.

As this query indicates, the writer has thoroughly researched his subject and has prepared his article for a specific reading audience—*Impact* magazine. The steps he used in writing the actual article were similar to those he'd use in writing a newspaper feature story or an English composition. Such articles must have an introduction (called a lead), a middle, and a conclusion. The lengths of the lead and the conclusion should be in proportion to the length of the entire story. A rule of thumb is to have each of these two portions approximately one eighth of the length of the entire article. To achieve variety, magazine editors often suggest that free-lance articles contain anecdotes, case histories, and other human-interest devices.

4 Smull Avenue
Trenton, New Jersey
June 12, 1983

Mr. George Mechlin
Nonfiction Editor
Impact Magazine
MacFadden-Bartell Corp.
205 East 42nd St.
New York, New York 10017

Dear Mr. Mechlin:

The number of books and magazine articles written about the life of Lincoln in recent years has indeed been overwhelming. Why the "Lincoln Boom"? Simply because the market beckons. However, these manuscripts tend to pursue the same theme—the romantic portrayal of Lincoln, and his "rags to riches" success story that destined him to become the leading figure of the Civil War, a hero of the American people for generations to come.

Opposed to this romantic picture of Lincoln's rise to fame, I have taken a realistic look at his life and his violent death. Very few people know the true story behind Lincoln's assassination. John Wilkes Booth was a mere puppet!

Knowing of *Impact's* style and format from the standpoint of a regular reader, I have attempted to write this manuscript with the flavor of mystery and intrigue that lends itself admirably to your requirements and to your readers' tastes.

My story has been authenticated as factually true and "very enlightening" by the Civil War and Lincolnian expert of the Maxwell School at Syracuse (N.Y.) University, noted author Dr. O. T. Bark.

I have access to many previously unpublished photos of the assassination and of the conspirators and excellent photos of the fake reward posters Stanton had printed. With the "go ahead" from you, I will procure them for the story.

I anxiously await your reply. Thank you for your consideration.

Yours truly,

William T. Rarey

William T. Rarey

The Future of the Magazine

Growth

Our country's education explosion has given new impetus to the magazine market. As more and more persons graduate from high schools and colleges, a higher percentage of the total population is likely to subscribe to magazines. The demand for qualified men and women to write for and edit these publications is also likely to increase.

A Magazine Career

Students interested in entering magazine journalism should begin their preparation now. They should get a good background in English, literature, foreign languages, science, and the social sciences by reading far beyond the course requirements. In college they should take journalism and liberal-arts courses. The better informed they are, the greater will be their ability to cover a variety of assignments. Knowing how to type and knowing shorthand or speedwriting would be valuable assets for many magazine-writing assignments.

Although there is no general rule, most magazines seem to prefer writers who have had newspaper experience. Specialized magazines often require a background in their specific fields. For example, the journalism student who hopes to work on *High Fidelity* magazine should take courses in music. But the major requirement is that the applicant know how to write!

The curious, enthusiastic, self-reliant, and well-trained person will find a number of opportunities in magazine journalism. Jobs are available not only for writers, but also for photographers, designers, artists, clerical workers, and editors. With more magazines today than ever before and new magazines being established from time to time, more magazine jobs are available for eager people.

The earnings of magazine employees vary depending on the size and geographical location of the magazine. Then, too, different job levels affect the salary scale. General editorial salaries range from $10,000 to $30,000 a year, while some top-flight editors earn over $100,000 a year.

Specialized periodicals are aimed at readers who share a particular occupation or interest. These periodicals are dependent on subscriptions, not on newsstand sales. In fact, many are not available on newsstands. It has been estimated that specialized periodicals represent more than sixty-five percent of all magazines published in this country. Some specialized periodicals do have general-public appeal but are limited to specific groups. For example, *National Geographic* has a general-public reader appeal but is sent only to members of the National Geographic Society.

The largest group of specialized publications are those published by business and industry, including house organs and other similar types of company publications. Specialized publications are important media for influencing opinion and disseminating business news.

Books

Our growing population reads more than ever before. More leisure time in which to read, more financial ability with which to buy books, availability of expensive editions in inexpensive paperback form—all contribute to the success of book publishing in this country.

In the 1830s the appearance of the dime novel heralded the first paperbacks, and political tracts and almanacs began to appear. Our current paperback boom began one hundred years later—in the late 1930s. Recently, the paperback has entered the classroom on primary, secondary, and college levels.

Textbook publishing, a major part of the book-publishing industry, accounts for more than one third of the total publishing figure for books printed in this country.

The book-publishing boom directly reflects the rising cultural level of the American public. The public's increased interest in public events accounts for still another trend in book publishing. With technical advances in printing, many publishers can print books about major news events just a few weeks after an event occurs. Besides providing desirable cause-and-effect analyses, these books offer readers a valuable timeliness in their in-depth coverage. For example, following the tragic assassination of former Beatle John Lennon in late 1980, a number of biographies about him appeared on bookstore shelves within a few short weeks of his death.

Activities

1. From the list below, select one subject as the basis for a research paper to be written and presented orally to the class. Use the resources available in your school and local libraries. Focus your research on (a) three magazines in the category you choose, (b) the publishers of those magazines, (c) magazine sizes and formats, (d) their prices, (e) the kinds of reading materials they present, (f) their editorial policies, if any, (g) the audience they appeal to, and (h) the kind of advertising they accept.

General-interest publications

Newsmagazines

Magazines of interest primarily to women

Magazines of interest primarily to men

Ethnic magazines

Consumer-affairs magazines

Business/professional magazines

Religious magazines

Entertainment/travel magazines

Sunday supplement magazines

2. Study four or more issues of one magazine of your choice. Prepare a written report, analyzing the magazine for content, reader appeal, advertising appeal, and writing style. In your report, determine the socioeconomic group for which the magazine is published.

3. Choose a familiar weekly or monthly newsmagazine for analysis. After studying it carefully, write a report that answers the following questions:

a. What is the significance of the magazine's name?

b. What is the purpose of its cover?

c. What is its editorial policy?

d. What kinds of reading materials does it present?

e. What is the general order of its contents? Why?

f. What do you think is the general age level and educational background of the magazine's subscribers?

g. Do you think the magazine's subscription price is reasonable? Why?

h. What types of merchandise are advertised in it? Why?

4. Poll the members of your class and prepare a brief, informal magazine-reading survey for oral presentation to the class. Use the following questions as a guide in preparing your poll. After completing the poll, you may wish to compile your results with those found by your classmates into a class magazine-reading survey.

a. What magazine do you read most often?

b. Why do you read this particular magazine?

c. What is the magazine's editorial policy?

d. Who publishes the magazine?

e. How much time do you spend each week reading the magazine?

f. What are the names of the leading contributors to the magazine?

g. What features of the magazine do you find most appealing? Why?

5. Bring copies of three different general-interest periodicals to class. Analyze them for treatment of articles and for similarities in content, format, and audience appeal. Compare the articles with those found in the magazine of your choice selected in activity 2 above for (a) similarities and (b) differences.

CHAPTER 4

The Nonprint Media

Until the beginning of the 20th century, professional journalism was limited to the print media—to newspapers, magazines, specialized periodicals, and books. By the end of the first quarter of the century, however, the situation had changed. New methods of transmitting information were being developed, and professional journalists were seeking answers to questions like these:

■ What effects are inventions like those of Bell, Marconi, Edison, and Sarnoff likely to have on the free flow of information in a democratic society?

■ What implications do these inventions have for the conventional journalist? for maintaining a free but responsible press?

■ Given the ability to transmit information instantaneously, how can professional journalists ensure ready access to the sources of that information?

■ Given the ability to transmit information instantaneously, what safeguards can be developed to ensure the accuracy and the reliability of the information the journalist reports?

■ Given the ability to transmit information instantaneously, how can the public's right to know be ensured and protected?

By midcentury far-reaching technological advances had increased the effectiveness of the new media, and by 1975 even more profound developments in the field of electronics had brought about a virtual communications revolution. Information could be transmitted with the speed of light to readers and listeners and viewers in all parts of the world!

Today's journalism students find themselves in the midst of this communications revolution. They need to understand the nature of the **nonprint media** that are its components, and they need to weigh the implications these media have for the practice of responsible journalism. This chapter (1) reviews the development of the nonprint media and (2) examines their role as news communicators in our society.

Emergence of the Nonprint Media

The Telephone

In 1876 Alexander Graham Bell paved the way for the development of the modern telephone. Using Morse's basic ideas about transmitting "dots and dashes" by means of an electrified wire, he succeeded in transmitting the sound of the human voice. Subsequent research and experimentation showed other scientists and engineers how to transmit sound over very long distances without any loss of volume. With the development of (1) radio-frequency multiplexing (a process permitting more than 70 separate telephone calls to be transmitted simultaneously over the same wire), (2) microwave radio relay systems (which vastly increase the number of telephone circuits available for use), and (3) communication satellites, there are approximately 110 million residential and 50 million business telephones currently in use in the United States. The telephone has, in fact, become the workhorse of the communications industry.

For the news media in particular, the telephone provides an indispensable service: It functions as a basic conveyor of information; it is a primary source for gaining information; it provides a quick means of ensuring the accuracy of facts.

Telephones can be equipped with a capability called memory storage, which will permit emergency and frequently called numbers to be dialed simply by pressing one or two buttons. If the line is busy, the caller can press another button to have the call dialed again. Electronic telephones also include a digital read-out to display the number being called, a timer to show the

Alexander Graham Bell (left) invented the telephone. Samuel Morse is shown with his invention, the telegraph.

length of the call, and a built-in calculator (which could be used to total the cost of supermarket purchases made by phone).

Not all telephones and telephone lines, however, are reserved for the transmission of the human voice. Some of them service teletype machines and wirephoto machines.

Teletype machines are used day in and day out to transmit and receive thousands of words of news copy. The copy is transmitted by an operator using a teletype machine with a keyboard similar to that of a typewriter. As the operator types, each character perforates a paper tape in an accompanying machine called a *teletypesetter.* That machine converts the perforations into sound signals and transmits them over telephone lines to teletype machines in newspaper offices across the country. The receiving teletype machines reconvert the sound signals into perforated tapes, which are then fed into newspaper composing room typesetting machines that automatically set the copy from the tapes.

Wirephoto (also called **telephoto**) machines transmit copies of pictorial materials and photographs to newspapers and news agencies throughout the country. In a matter of minutes, photoelectric cells scan the surface of the material to be transmitted and, via telephone lines, send out sound signals to client news agencies and to newspapers where similar photoelectric cells reconvert the signals into marks on sensitized photographic paper. Strong sound signals become dark areas on the facsimile print; weaker signals are reproduced as lighter areas.

The Nonprint Media   71

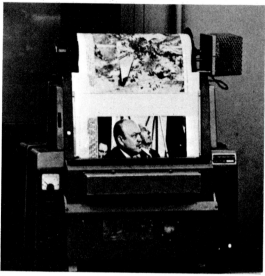

Outgoing teletype copy is being checked. News photos emerge from a telephoto machine.

All these uses show how the telephone—a nonprint medium for transmitting information to masses of people—is the workhorse of the communications industry.

Radio

In 1558 Italian physicist Giovanni Battista della Porta tried to develop a message-sending device powered by magnetism, a natural phenomenon known since ancient times. But he didn't have much success. He and other 16th-century scientists knew relatively little about physics, and nothing more was done about this means of communication until the middle of the 19th century.

In 1844 Samuel Morse invented the electromagnetic telegraph and sent the first message ever transmitted by wire ("What hath God wrought?") from Washington, D.C., to Baltimore. Before long, telegraph wires were pushing across the country with the railroads. In 1876 Alexander Graham Bell proved that these wires could transmit human speech as well as dots and dashes.

In 1896 another Italian physicist, 22-year-old Guglielmo Marconi, demonstrated that sound could be transmitted without wires and cables. Perceptive journalists, scientists, and industrialists all over the world quickly saw the almost limitless possibilities that Marconi's work had for the transmission of information. For example, Marconi's wireless could be used by ships at sea to en-

The Mass Media in a Democratic Society

Guglielmo Marconi (left) invented the radio. David Sarnoff was chairman of the board of Radio Corporation of America.

sure their safety, by large companies to communicate instantaneously with far-flung clients, and by armies and navies to transmit and receive vital intelligence.

The use of the wireless—the *radio*—for reporting the news and for entertainment was slower to develop. But in 1916 David Sarnoff, who later became chairman of the board of the Radio Corporation of America, foresaw its potential in those areas. He expressed his vision in these words:

> I have in mind a plan of development which would make radio a household utility. . . . The idea is to bring music into the home by wireless. . . . The receiver can be designed in the form of a simple "Radio Music Box" and arranged for several different wavelengths, which should be changeable with the throwing of a single switch or the pressing of a single button. . . . The same principle can be extended to numerous other fields, as for example, receiving lectures at home, which would be perfectly audible; also events of national importance can be simultaneously announced and received. . . .

By the early 1920s thousands of Americans had become interested in the possibilities presented by the radio. Many built or bought crystal sets and listened with amazement to the messages being broadcast. In Pittsburgh a young scientist named Frank Conrad talked, read aloud, and played records on a radio transmitter in his garage. Before long he began to receive postcards from listeners, asking him to play their favorite records. To test the range of his transmitter, he complied with their requests, becoming the country's first disc jockey. To the astonishment of the Westinghouse Corporation, for whom Conrad worked, a department store advertised radio receivers for "those who want to tune in the Westinghouse station." Taking advantage of the situation, Westinghouse, late in 1920, established one of the country's first full-time radio stations—KDKA in Pittsburgh. The station had the distinction of broadcasting the results of the Harding-Cox presidential election in November 1920.

The Development of Radio Networks. Radio stations multiplied, and thousands of people purchased radio receivers. People fortunate enough to have radio sets heard, among other things, the 1921 heavyweight championship prizefight between Jack Dempsey and Georges Carpentier.

Individual radio stations soon saw an advantage in hooking up with other stations to form radio networks that could provide listeners with better coverage of news events of national importance. The National Broadcasting Company was formed in 1926; the Columbia Broadcasting System, a year later; and the American Broadcasting Company, in 1941. The first network program to be broadcast from coast to coast was the 1927 Rose Bowl game.

1922 Crystal Set—an early radio

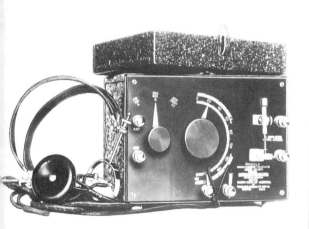

Commentator Walter Winchell broadcasts the news.

The Mass Media in a Democratic Society

To give listeners even better news coverage, radio stations began subscribing to the wire services of the Associated Press, the United Press, and the International News Service. By the beginning of World War II, radio networks had developed their own vast news-gathering agencies. Americans depended on the radio for on-the-spot coverage of news-making events—from President Franklin Roosevelt's "war" speech on December 8, 1941, to the Japanese surrender ceremonies aboard the U.S.S. *Missouri* on September 2, 1945. The names of radio network news commentators (such as Lowell Thomas and Walter Winchell) and network war correspondents (such as Eric Sevareid, Edward R. Murrow, and Walter Cronkite) soon became familiar words in most American homes.

Radio for Propaganda. Between the two World Wars, governments began to recognize the value of radio as a propaganda medium. In 1942 the United States government instituted a radio broadcast called the "Voice of America," which served as a psychological warfare weapon and as a means of transmitting American news to allied and neutral countries. Today, "Voice of America" is the radio division of the United States Information Agency, and its purpose, as established by the 80th Congress, is to

Eric Sevareid, Edward R. Murrow, Walter Cronkhite, and Lowell Thomas are well-known radio commentators of the 1930s and 1940s.

"promote the better understanding of the United States among the people of the world and to strengthen cooperative international relations." The "Voice of America," whose programs consist of news, news analysis, drama, and music, is broadcast to countries throughout the world, including Russia and other Eastern countries. Similar in purpose to "Voice of America," is "Radio Free Europe," a privately owned network of five radio stations supported by voluntary contributions, which also broadcasts programs—but to countries in Eastern Europe only.

The Effect of Television. In the late 1940s radio faced a vigorous new competitor—television. Many media experts predicted that this newcomer would bring about the near-death of radio. But they were wrong. Radio survived—but under considerably changed circumstances. By the 1960s it was clear that television had changed the public's response to radio broadcasting in at least two important ways: First, listening habits had changed. In general, people listened to the radio during the day and watched television during the evening hours. Second, program formats had changed dramatically. Recorded music, punctuated with newscasts, had replaced the variety programs and the dramatic presentations that had once been so popular.

A viewer tunes in a 1939 television set.

The Mass Media in a Democratic Society

Thomas Edison is shown with his electric light bulb. The photos on the right show three frames of a sneeze as captured in 1894 by Edison's Kinetoscope device.

The Situation Today. A recent survey sponsored by the broadcasting industry reveals that during an average daytime quarter hour, some 35 million people are tuned in to the nation's radio stations. The survey also shows that nearly 200 million people twelve years of age or older (nearly 90% of the population) listen to the radio in an average week. This same survey found that three out of four adults and four out of every five teenagers listen to the radio during an average day.

According to informed estimates, there are currently more than 270 million radio receivers in the United States. (Radios outnumber the total population.) Analysts attribute the growth in today's radio industry to the number of small radio stations and the increasing popularity of the transistor radio.

Motion Pictures

In the 1890s Thomas Edison invented and experimented with a device—called a Kinetoscope—that took pictures on a continuous roll of celluloid film made by George Eastman's Kodak Company. Viewers paid a penny to look through a magnifying lens at images that appeared to move. But because Edison felt that the device was a passing fad, he didn't pursue his interest in it.

Others, however, saw that the Kinetoscope had great potential for informing and entertaining masses of people. Their vision led to the development of the motion-picture camera and the motion-picture projector. In the 1900s people paid a nickel each to attend nickelodeons to see *moving pictures.* Some members of those audiences had difficulty in comprehending what was going on. Some felt that they were witnessing a play with actors on a stage. In fact, when an actor in *The Great Train Robbery* (1903) pointed a revolver in the direction of the audience, some spectators became so frightened that they fainted.

Early films, however, had little creativity. Many were made without a script, camera operators often making up the story as they went along. Most of those films were slapstick comedies—like Mack Sennett's *Keystone Cops* (1909)—and they became very popular.

Audiences became more sophisticated, demanding something more substantial from the motion-picture industry. The person credited with making the motion picture an art is D. W. Griffith. His *Birth of a Nation* (1915) cost the unheard of sum of $125,000, utilized a "cast of thousands," and wove several plots into one story line. *Birth of a Nation* is almost universally acknowledged as the first milestone in the development of the motion picture.

By the 1920s the making of motion pictures had become a big business. Besides Westerns and short comedies, there were war films, horror films, spy films, science-fiction films, spectacles, and documentary films. Then, in 1929, the "talkies" came along. Now

Mack Sennett's *Keystone Cops* was an early film that made movie audiences laugh.

D. W. Griffith (inset) made motion pictures an art with his film *Birth of a Nation* (1915).

movie audiences could hear what the people on the screen were saying. In the late 1920s, the 1930s, and the early 1940s, most Americans went to the movies at least once a week. To accommodate this vast audience, huge palacelike theaters were built in cities and towns across the country.

With the coming of television in the late 1940s, motion-picture attendance declined sharply, and many movie palaces closed their doors. Television made major changes in the motion-picture industry. But soon it became evident that television depended on feature films for a large part of its programming. To fill that need, making films for television became an important part of the movie industry's operation. It still is.

An important part of the motion-picture industry today is the making of educational and documentary films. Such films are produced for the federal government, state and local governments, business corporations, and special-interest groups like medical, educational, and religious organizations. Over the past few years, both the amount of money spent in making educational and documentary films and the number of titles produced have increased markedly.

Television

Technologically, television has advanced far beyond Thomas Edison's Kinetoscope. Today's television camera observes the

Exterior and interior views of Radio City Music Hall, "The Showplace of the Nation," which housed year-round entertainment.

scene to be transmitted, changing light values into electric signals. In this complex process, an electronic beam moves across the image shown on a rectangular signal plate, scanning the complete picture in one thirtieth of a second. The process of converting the visual scene into an electric signal is called video (sight). The other portion of the television process, audio (sound), is similar to radio transmission in that the sound is converted into electric impulses (sound waves). A thin diaphragm within a microphone, vibrating at the same frequency as the sound waves passing through it, converts the sound into electric currents. These electric currents pass through wires to a modulator, where they are in turn converted into a radio frequency that goes to television transmitters. These transmitters send out radio waves of specific frequencies capable of being received on home television sets. Then the tuner and associated circuits in a home receiving set reconvert the radio waves into an electric current made up of sound waves and light waves. The sound waves activate the speakers in the home receiving set, while, simultaneously, the light waves produce the picture a viewer sees on the screen of the receiving set.

Forty-year Development. Television suffered a great many growing pains. The device had been in the experimental stage as early as the 1920s. Telecasts for testing purposes were begun as

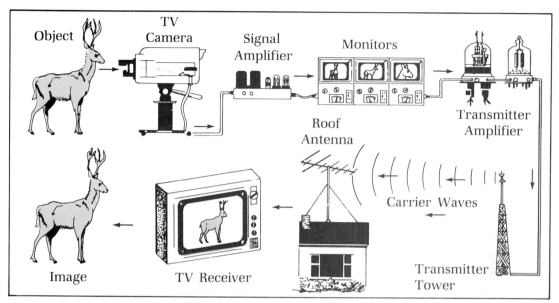

The diagram shows the steps involved in transmitting images through electric signals.

early as 1936, and a regular schedule of programs was begun in 1939. Ten commercial stations were then on the air, but only six continued after the beginning of World War II. Because of the scientific and technological advances brought about by extensive research during the war, the medium began a period of tremendous growth as soon as the war ended. Electronics companies quickly converted from producing war materials to making television equipment. Advertisers flocked to the new medium to promote their products. The 1948 political conventions were covered live, and in January 1949, the inauguration of President Truman was the first such public event to be televised. A coast-to-coast link of the coaxial cable and the microwave relay was completed in 1951, making possible instantaneous transmission between widely separated stations that formerly had to rely on "canned" material from distant originating stations. By 1953 over one hundred television stations in sixty cities were on the air.

By the late 1950s the television networks had organized extensive news organizations. In 1960 the Kennedy-Nixon nationally televised debates—a first in the history of television and a first in the history of American politics—had a revolutionary effect on both American journalism and on the American political system. The debates demonstrated clearly how political leaders can (1) take their messages directly to the people, thereby circumventing the news media, and (2) offset the effects of negative newspaper

These photos were taken from a TV screen when John F. Kennedy and Vice-President Richard M. Nixon debated on TV October 10, 1960.

and magazine editorials. The debates also demonstrated the remarkable influence of the television medium when it involves direct communication between the public and charismatic individuals who seek to influence public opinion.

The Current Situation. Although there are in the United States today more than 1000 television stations and many millions of viewers, television has yet to reach its full potential as a medium of mass communication. Television can, for instance, become a major educational force in our society. Many high schools and colleges already have their own television stations and are experimenting to determine the educational effectiveness of various kinds of televised presentations. Many teachers have recognized the educational potential of television. They supplement regular classroom sessions by asking students to watch specific television programs and then assigning appropriate follow-up activities for students. Students who are confined to their homes or who live in remote areas can attend classes by tuning in on special channels programmed for educational purposes.

Television's immediacy makes it an unusually influential element in our lives today, and some people claim that television is our most important single source of information and entertainment. Certainly television can claim a noteworthy advantage over the print media in the reporting of the news: It is faster. (Yet the print media have an advantage in being able to provide the in-depth coverage that television cannot provide as effectively.) By

A classroom demonstration is being conducted via closed-circuit TV.

offering a combination of sight, sound, and motion, television is able to dramatize the news of the day. A study conducted by the U.S. Navy indicates that the attention of an audience is greater when the individuals composing that audience are exposed to sight and sound (television) than when exposed to sight alone (print media) or to sound alone (radio). Television, then, with its great potential for transmitting information, and for molding public opinion, has a profound obligation to the public to maintain the highest standards of responsible broadcasting.

Communication by Satellite

The distance between Paris and San Francisco is about 6000 miles. But if you were to telephone to a friend in Paris, your voice would travel much farther than 6000 miles. Your voice would be transmitted by a telephone wire to an Earth station in this country, which would transmit the signal to a communications satellite about 22,000 miles in space. The satellite would, in turn, relay the signal to an Earth station in Europe, which would transmit the sound of your voice to the receiver in the telephone used by your friend in Paris. And this entire operation would take less than one second!

Unlimited Potential. Once the American continent was conquered, some people thought that there were no worlds left to

The Nonprint Media   83

A telesat communications satellite is being prepared for launch.

conquer. Others were intrigued and challenged by outer space and were determined to explore that vast unknown. Their explorations have met with considerable success.

The first "voice" from space was the "beep-beep" of Russia's Sputnik, launched in 1957. Three years later the United States launched the first successful communications satellite—Echo I. Placed in orbit 1000 miles in space, the tiny magnesium sphere opened to release a 100-foot-wide aluminum-coated mylar balloon, from which voice, picture, and facsimile signals were reflected (or bounced) between the United States and Europe.

The next major satellite to be launched was Syncom—in 1963. Placed 22,300 miles above Earth, this satellite travels around the globe at the same speed at which the Earth rotates. Thus it seems to remain stationary with reference to a given point on the Earth's surface.

The first commercial satellite, Early Bird I, was launched in 1965 and was soon followed by other satellites with high-capacity circuits for TV and telephone transmission. Western Union's Westar satellites were launched in 1974 and had a capacity of 7200 voice channels and twelve TV broadcast channels. And RCA's Satcom, launched in 1975, boasted 24,000 voice channels. As commercial and government requirements for instantaneous communication increase, more and more communication satellites will be sent into orbit.

The Mass Media in a Democratic Society

Network television is a direct beneficiary of communications-satellite research. Live coverage of critical events in Latin America, in Europe, in the Middle East, and in the Far East allows every American viewer to be an on-the-spot witness. As scientific research reveals the need for more communications satellites, advances in technology will increase the efficiency of those satellites. The cost of television transmission will decrease while the range of coverage will increase, and the coverage itself will greatly improve. Satellite communication offers dramatic possibilities for educating masses of people in underdeveloped countries, for making available more and more technological knowledge, and for helping to improve the lives of human beings in all parts of the world. Robert L. Shayon, writing in the *Saturday Review*, stressed the importance of vision in organizing and implementing our country's satellite program:

> What America needs in communications is a long vision—perhaps a communications Marshall Plan for Asia, Africa, and Latin America. As plans go now, satellite television, commercially used, will spread the image of this rich nation's consumership around the globe. We have seen, in the riots and lootings in our black ghettos, the consequences of such imagery on our own have-nots. If we don't use satellites to help lift the mental horizons of the dispossessed who inhabit the backroads of modern communications, we may be risking the fate of the Roman Empire, that failed to share consumership with its colonials, and was eventually looted.

Facsimile Reproduction. Few *national* daily newspapers exist in the United States. One reason is that the cost of publishing a newspaper for national distribution is enormous. Another is that until recently, timely distribution of such a paper was impossible. By the time the paper could arrive in certain areas, its news would no longer be news. Yet today we do have national dailies. How so?

The way to lower the enormous cost lay in building regional printing plants, and that's what *The Wall Street Journal* did. The *Journal* built seventeen regional plants. But there was still the second problem to solve. "How," asked the *Journal's* managers, "can we get news stories, feature articles, headlines, page layouts, and photographs to the seventeen printing plants for a *daily* printing of the paper?" A possible solution lay in the use of communications satellites. If a picture of every page of each day's edition could be sent via satellite from the *Journal's* main plant in Chicopee, Massachusetts, to each of the seventeen regional printing plants, *The Wall Street Journal* could become a *national* daily.

On August 30, 1974, the first test of this plan under actual pro-

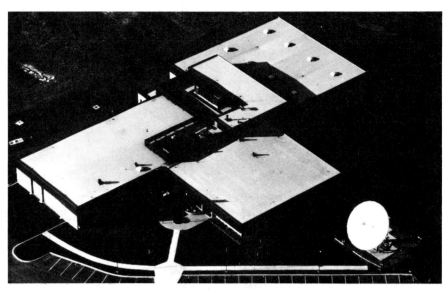

Pictured is the *Wall Street Journal* printing plant in Sharon PA. Note the satellite dish in the right lower corner.

duction conditions took place. It was so successful that no one even noticed anything unusual about that day's issue. Each page of the paper had traveled more than 44,000 miles to and from a stationary satellite, arriving at subscribers' doorsteps none the worse for the wear. Facsimile reproduction had arrived, and it worked!

Material to be transmitted by satellite—headlines, copy, photos, layouts—is handled just as though it were destined for conventional offset printing. The copy is typeset, pasted onto a page, and then made into a lithographic plate ready for placement on high-speed presses. But that's where the conventional part stops. Once a page is made up, corrected, and photographed, a reproduction proof is pulled and sent along to the satellite transmitter at the "mother plant" in Chicopee. In the transmission room the reproduction proof is wrapped around a cylindrical drum and scanned (read) by a device that converts the print into electronic impulses at the rate of about 800 lines per inch. Pages are transmitted by satellite at the rate of a full page every three minutes. At the receiving plant a page-size sheet of film is wrapped around an identical drum, and the electronic impulses are converted back into light to expose the printed image. The page of film is then developed, checked for clarity of transmission, and laid over an anodized aluminum plate to transfer the image and produce an offset plate for printing. Once all the plates are ready, they are set into place on the printing presses. The presses start, and the

The Mass Media in a Democratic Society

The staff stand proudly over one of the first issues of the Gannett Company's new national newspaper *USA Today*.

newspaper is printed and folded and sent to the central distribution area. Bundles of papers are then put aboard trucks and transported throughout the printing region.

On every weekday morning subscribers in Chicago, in Houston, in Denver, and in San Francisco—subscribers thousands of miles apart—pick up and read a daily paper exactly like the one read by subscribers in Boston, New York, and Washington, D.C. Facsimile reproduction has made a national daily paper possible.

Computer Communication

The digital computer has revolutioned mass media in this last half of the 20th century. Its effect is as enormous as the effect of the invention of movable type, in the last half of the 15th century, was on the dissemination of information and the spread of learning. As a result of the electronic technology that led to the development of the computer, we can today store vast amounts of information indefinitely and retrieve all or part of that information instantaneously. Computers make possible the storage and availability of information that no conventional library has time, space, or inclination to store, let alone find.

The widespread use of computers has led to the development of information storage and retrieval systems—often called information management—that make information of all kinds readily

Using a computer, information can be obtained by touch alone.

A student uses a computer as part of his schoolwork.

accessible to individuals and business organizations. Subscriber access is amazingly easy. The person who desires information—private individual or corporation employee—sits at a computer terminal and dials the number of the information retrieval system subscribed to. On a typewriterlike keyboard, the person types a code number requesting the information desired. That information then appears instantaneously on the terminal screen, which resembles a small television screen.

Commercial or industrial information is not the only kind available from information retrieval systems. The full text of some newspapers is also available.

Today, the introduction of home microcomputers and the amazing technological developments in the cable-television industry, aided in part by the growing use of satellites for information transfer, are making the in-home retrieval of news and of other kinds of practical information a reality.

The largest commercial effort for home-information access—variously referred to generically as videotex and viewdata—is called "The Source," a service available to owners of personal computers. The Source provides its subscribers with a dial-up capability from home computers, giving them access to a variety of information stored in computers, including news from United Press International, business and financial information, real-estate listings, and classified advertising. The subscriber pushes a button and the desired information pops up on a small televisionlike screen. The subscriber gets "page" after "page" of information. A "page" is a screenful of text—usually 200 to 250 words.

For example, suppose that a subscriber wants to check hotel accommodations at specific resorts. A basic index giving general subjects comes up on the TV screen. The subscriber finds the item "travel," which has a number next to it. By punching the number into a hand-held keypad, the subscriber causes a new "page" to come onto the screen, looking somewhat like this:

1. General Information   **4.** Accommodations
2. How to get there   **5.** Recreation
3. Things to know   **6.** What to see

Suppose further that the subscriber selects No. 4 on the keypad. A new page then appears:

1. Hotels
2. Motels
3. Tourist homes
4. Campsites
5. Trailer parks

The subscriber picks No. 1, and another "page" appears, showing the names, addresses, and telephone numbers of hotels, along with a description and prices of rooms available.

Using the same process, the subscriber can select the latest news releases or even take a home-study course—for example, in biology.

Still another significant example of computer communication is electronic mail—the transmission of messages via computer, telephone lines, and satellites. Electronic mail is now available in most American cities. Here's how it works: A video display terminal in one city is linked by telephone to several worldwide telephone networks. With this system, messages can be stored, sent, and received from any computer terminal in the world. A person sitting at a terminal dials a given number and then types out the message. The message is transmitted at the speed of light directly to a person sitting at a terminal in another city.

The advantages of using electronic mail to deliver all types of messages (bills, mass business mailings, advertising) are evident. Among them are the following:

■ Inexpensive terminals. It is estimated that the cost of the video display terminal will soon be under $200.

■ Increasing knowledge and sophistication of computer use. More people each year are learning to operate the terminals efficiently. Even school children are learning to become "computer friendly."

■ Increasing economic advantage. With postage costs rising and the costs of computer terminals decreasing, messages can be sent faster and easier by electronic mail and at lower cost than by the conventional method.

It is estimated that by 1990 one third of all letter mail will be sent electronically by computer.

Radio and Television Journalism: Station Organization

With the invention and the development of each of the nonprint media, there has grown up an organized, highly complex industry with national and international connections.

The radio and the television industries are as highly organized and as complex as are the other industries connected with the nonprint media. Yet because of the special relationship between radio/television and journalism, it is useful for us to look briefly at staff organization and major staff responsibilities of the typical radio/television station.

In addition to the large number of engineers and technicians required to produce radio and television news programs, there are many other specialists working behind the scenes. The major divisions of responsibility are these: news, programming, sales, engineering, and general administration. The number of people working in each division varies, of course, with the size and the nature of the radio or the television station.

News

The **news director** is in charge of the assigning and editing of news stories. Working with the news director are a number of news, sports, and weather reporters, who cover major events occurring in their assigned areas. Photographers often accompany the reporters and take pictures of the events—pictures that can be shown "live" or delayed for later broadcast. Larger stations also employ writers and editors who prepare news stories and "feature" stories for broadcast. Writers may also prepare editorials to be presented on the air by station executives. To enable stations to cover events in outlying areas, many stations have a

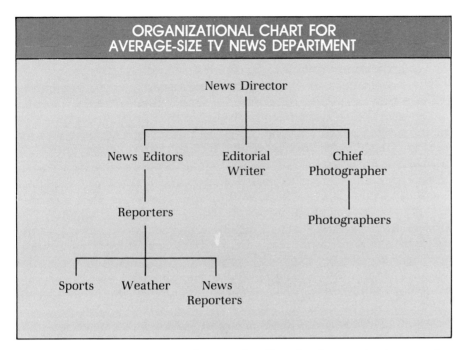

ORGANIZATIONAL CHART FOR AVERAGE-SIZE TV NEWS DEPARTMENT

News Director

News Editors — Editorial Writer — Chief Photographer

Reporters

Photographers

Sports — Weather — News Reporters

number of film correspondents who live in the station's—or the network's—coverage area and prepare stories of interest to the entire region.

The news department of the radio or television station also prepares or supervises public-affairs and community-service programs. Examples of the types of presentations in this category are as follows: The school system might be asked to provide teachers and students for a panel discussion on the activities and needs of the community's schools. Colleges in the area might provide students to discuss careers available to graduates. Another show might give information in the areas of medicine, jobs, welfare, religion, and community problems.

Programming

Radio and television stations, unlike print media, must be licensed by the federal government. Without such regulation, airwaves would be jammed with would-be broadcasters operating on any convenient frequency. The Federal Communications Commission (FCC) determines which stations will be licensed (including amateur or "ham" stations), how much transmitting power each station can have, and how many hours during the day each station can broadcast. The federal government has also tried to provide guidelines concerning the nature of programming and has suggested that stations should devote a percentage of their time to programs in "the public interest." The FCC also regulates the time allowed for commercials.

The programs to be broadcast by radio and television stations are determined by the programming department. Local programs are conceived, produced, and scheduled by the programming department staff. Another type of programming is supplied by independent program producers and syndicated companies. This type of programming service may supply feature films in such areas as drama, comedy, games, sports, or public affairs. The third and most important source of programming is that supplied by one of the major networks—American Broadcasting Company (ABC), Columbia Broadcasting System (CBS), National Broadcasting Company (NBC), and Public Broadcasting Service (PBS). These four networks service both television and radio stations, while another network, Mutual Broadcasting Company, provides programs only for radio stations. A station affiliated with one of the national networks is not necessarily owned by the network, but it has a contractual arrangement whereby it agrees to carry network programs during at least part of the broadcast day. The average station, on the air for about eighteen hours a day, seven days a week, could not possibly have a large enough staff to write and produce all of the programs required. Network affiliation offers a

A TV producer completes the programming board, showing assignments, as they are to be covered by news reporters.

definite advantage. Because many network shows are too elaborate and expensive for an individual station to produce, the network produces and sells such programs to advertisers and then shares the revenues with the local stations that carry them.

Programming policies are worked out by the station's **program director** in collaboration with the **general manager** and **sales manager.** The program director works with the producer-directors, broadcasting talent, and other members of the programming department in planning the most effective program schedule for the station. He or she also develops news programs, improves old programs, works out all aspects of publishing the station's "program guide," and participates in decisions involving the purchase of programs supplied by outside sources. Each day the program director supervises activities of personnel in the programming division on such matters as work assignments and schedules, the budget, and problems of production.

The **producer-director** plans and supervises the production of a program. Responsibilities include the selection of material and performers, the general planning of the sets, the placement of lights, and the determination of camera angles as well as the sequence of camera shots. In addition, the producer-director coordinates the selection of film, scripts, and music and maintains budgetary controls. The job involves a sense of dramatics, combined with the ability to weld together the talents of the performers into a smooth and artistic production. The producer-director is the person most responsible for the success or failure of any program.

Another basic job in any radio or television station is that of the **staff announcer,** who reads commercial copy, introduces live or filmed programs, gives station identification and time signals, and makes promotional and public-service announcements. On some radio stations this person is called a "disc jockey" and reads news briefs or announces the names of musical selections to be played.

In television stations there are several other jobs connected with the production of programs. The **film director** handles the screening and preparation of all film and supervises film editors, who cut, splice, and clean film. The **floor manager** (unit manager) directs the performers on the studio floor in accordance with the director's instructions, while a **program assistant** coordinates the various portions of the show by assisting the producer-director. The program assistant may also arrange for props, makeup, and for cue cards. Most stations have their own artist, who plans set designs, paints backdrops, and handles lettering and artwork.

A live news program is being broadcast from a TV studio.

Sales

In the sales division the **sales manager** is responsible for setting up the general sales policy of the station and for supervising the daily activities of sales representatives. The sales manager develops sales plans and packages that will appeal to sponsors, sets up seasonal sales campaigns, plans special programs publicizing the station, and promotes special events. Other duties include supervising the hiring and the training of sales personnel and encouraging the sales representatives in their efforts to sell time for commercial announcements. The sales manager works with the program director in developing salable programs. **The sales representative** sells radio or television time to advertising agencies or to individual advertisers. The most important requirement for this job is the ability to sell. The sales representative must be creative in developing advertising approaches that will appeal to particular clients.

The **traffic manager** prepares daily logs of the station's program activities, using information collected from the sales, programming, and engineering departments to prepare periodical reports for the Federal Communications Commission.

Engineering

Heading up the technical work in the engineering division is the **chief engineer.** On a radio station he or she may have only a few subordinates, but on a television station the chief engineer may supervise as many as forty technicians. The work involves planning and coordinating the engineering requirements of the station's programs, as well as scheduling the work of the technicians. The chief engineer is also responsible for supervising the maintenance of equipment. The **technicians** are concerned with the operation and maintenance of all technical equipment. They may also operate projection equipment and handle lighting.

General Administration

The two main positions in the general administration division of a radio or television station are **general manager** and **business manager.** The responsibilities of the general manager include handling of the daily affairs of station operation in consultation with the news director, program manager, sales manager, and chief engineer. The general manager determines the overall policies guiding the station's operation and supervises the carrying out of those policies. On a radio station the general manager will decide whether the station will have a popular or classical music format or whether it will broadcast news exclusively. The business manager oversees the station's financial transactions and prepares the necessary financial reports for the Federal Communications Commission.

Careers in the Nonprint Media

Students interested in pursuing careers in the nonprint media should develop the personal qualities of enthusiasm, reliability, sensitivity, and creativity. Students interested in the engineering side of radio and television should consider attending an electronics school. Business training is almost essential for those considering sales-department work.

Students planning a career in programming might attend a specialized radio and television school. Those interested in broadcast newswriting should attend a college with a good journalism department. Many colleges offer excellent training in broadcasting as part of their communications programs. Newspaper work following graduation from college is ideal training for newswriting for the nonprint media. In fact, one major network requires that its news department personnel have extensive newspaper experience before being considered for employment.

Activities

1. What features do you look for in determining whether a radio program is worth listening to? What features do you look for in determining whether a television program is worth watching? In each case, list your criteria for judging the worth of programs.

2. As a program director for a local radio station, you have been asked to prepare a program schedule for a four-hour daytime (from noon to 4 p.m.) listening audience. In developing your schedule, you will need to list the criteria you use for determining the worth of all the programs you schedule. You may schedule programs for fifteen-minute, half-hour, or one-hour periods. You will, of course, want to avoid basing your programming entirely on your own likes and dislikes. In developing your schedule, consider your audience, advertising sponsors, and the possible use of "public-interest" type of material.

3. As a program director for a local television station, you have been asked to prepare a program schedule for a four-hour (noon to 4 p.m.) viewing audience. In developing your schedule, follow the same suggestions given in Activity 2 above.

4. a. Conduct an informal survey among your classmates to determine what one television program viewed in the past two weeks they agree was an insult to their intelligence. Be sure that each participant gives reasons for any opinion offered. As a part of the discussion, consider what conditions might justify the presentation of such a program.

The Mass Media in a Democratic Society

b. Conduct a similar kind of survey and class discussion to determine what one television commercial seen in the past two weeks the class consider an insult to their intelligence. Follow the same suggestions offered in Activity 4.a.

c. Conduct a similar kind of survey and class discussion to identify not more than three television commercials the class consider to be effective. Be sure that reasons are given in support of each opinion.

5. Research the latest developments in the use of communications satellites. Write a paper in which you state your findings. Then use the main points in your paper for a brief oral report for the class.

6. Research the latest developments in the use of computers for communication purposes. Write a paper in which you state your findings. Then use the main points in your paper for a brief oral report for the class.

CHAPTER 5

Public Relations and Advertising

Public Relations

What Do You Mean—"Public Relations"?

Since the beginning of recorded history, public opinion has played a major role in determining the course of human affairs. Advocates of the earliest-known religions used the power of well-chosen words to influence human behavior and win converts. The great orators of ancient Greece and Rome sought out the views of prominent citizens and then used those opinions to sway the thinking and the actions of the populace. The officials of ancient Rome, realizing the importance of obtaining and keeping popular goodwill, obtained the support of the masses of ordinary citizens by having affixed to public documents and carved on public buildings the letters *S.P.Q.R.*, which stood for "The Senate and the People of Rome."

In 17th-century Rome, to propagate the faith, the Roman Catholic church established an information agency called the College of Propaganda. A few years later in another part of

Europe, Russia's Catherine the Great (1729-1796), who recognized the importance of making a good impression on her subjects, is said to have been careful to release to the public only such information about herself that would enhance her public image.

All of these examples of the ways in which individuals and organizations have sought to influence public opinion demonstrate the importance of *public relations* in mass communication. But what do we mean by *public relations?* Simply this: Public relations is the promotion of rapport and goodwill between a person, business firm, or institution on the one hand, and another individual, specific group, or the community at large on the other. Such rapport and goodwill are realized through the distribution of interpretive materials, friendly exchanges of points of view, and the assessment of public reaction to the materials distributed.

Public Relations: Growth and Development

Public relations played an important role in colonial America as early as 1641, when Harvard College sent a group of ministers to England to solicit funds. Recognizing the need for a brochure describing the college, the ministers wrote and published the first public-relations pamphlet of its type in colonial America, titling it "New England's First-Fruits."

The earliest recorded public-relations news release in America was sent in 1758 to New York newspapers by what is now Columbia University.

Because there was more freedom of expression in America than there had been in Europe, the opinions of the masses had considerable weight and soon showed an influence on political events. Statements such as "Give me liberty or give me death," and "We must hang together or we shall all hang separately" influenced the divergent factions in the colonies to unify. The writers of the Declaration of Independence said that the Declaration was written "out of a decent respect for the opinions of mankind."

In the 1820s a former Kentucky newspaper editor named Amos Kendall became one of America's first public-relations people. Working from behind the scenes, Kendall served President Andrew Jackson as a pollster, ghost writer, and publicist. Although his official title was Fourth Auditor of the Treasury, Amos Kendall spent most of his time advising President Jackson and writing speeches, pamphlets, and news releases for the Jackson administration. For his activities Amos Kendall came to be known as "the mouthpiece of the Jackson Administration."

Public relations gained recognition early in the 1900s, when business interests were threatened by a period of union organizing, striking, and rioting. These events threatened the security of business people, who, previously having cared little about the rights and working conditions of employees, now realized the necessity for more favorable relationships between industry and the public.

During this era Ivy Lee, known as "The Father of Public Relations," left the *New York World* to help improve the public images of John D. Rockefeller, Jr., and several other prominent businessmen. Lee, who believed in an informed citizenry, felt that the public had a right to be informed about what business was doing. He is said to have told his clients:

> I believe in telling your story to the people. If you go direct to the people and get them to agree with you, everybody else must give way in your favor.

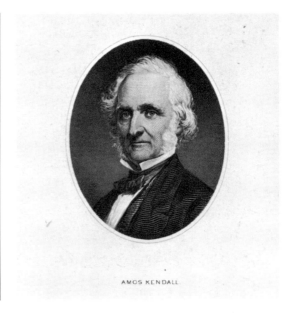

NEVV
ENGLANDS
FIRST FRUITS;
IN RESPECT,

Firſt of the { ˚Converſion of ſome, } of the *Indians*.
{ Conviction of divers, }
{ Preparation of ſundry }

2. Of the progreſſe of *Learning*, in the *Colledge* at
CAMBRIDGE in *Maſſacuſets* Bay.

WITH
Divers other ſpeciall Matters concerning that *Country*.

Publiſhed by the inſtant requeſt of ſundry Friends, who deſire
to be ſatisfied in theſe points by many *New-England* Men
who are here preſent, and were eye or care-
witneſſes of the ſame.

Who hath deſpiſed the Day of ſmall things. Zach. 4. 10.

If thou wert pure and upright, ſurely now he will awake for thee : — And though
thy beginning be ſmall, thy latter end ſhall greatly encreaſe. Iob. 8 6.7.

LONDON,
Printed by R. O and G. D. for *Henry Overton*, and are to be
ſold at his Shop in *Popes-head-Alley*. 1 6 4 3.

AMOS KENDALL

During World War I the U. S. government established a public-relations committee called the Committee on Public Information. The committee, headed by George Creel, came to be called the Creel Committee. This committee demonstrated the power of mass publicity techniques in influencing public opinion. Edward L. Bernays, a man who worked with the Creel Committee, went on to become one of the country's most articulate advocates of public relations. After World War I Bernays commented:

> It was the war which opened the eyes of the intelligent few in all departments of life to the possibilities of regimenting the public mind.

Bernays, in his book *Crystallizing Public Opinion*, first coined the term "public-relations counsel."

The techniques used by the Creel Committee were soon being applied to fund drives for colleges, hospitals, foundations, and research institutions. Private industry began hiring full-time public-relations people to help formulate the policies of individual companies and bring those companies to the world's attention.

In 1923 the first college course in public relations was offered at New York University. The Great Depression of the 1930s gave the greatest impetus to the growth of public relations. Progressive politicians such as Franklin D. Roosevelt realized the importance of swaying public opinion in order to pave the way for needed governmental reforms.

During World War II an office similar to the World War I Creel Committee was set up by Elmer Davis. Called the Office of War Information, it was primarily concerned with promoting the sale of war bonds, promoting government rationing, encouraging the use of victory gardens, and raising the morale of employees contributing to the war effort.

Following World War II the emphasis in public relations developed into an awareness of *total* public relations, meaning that because of their effect on the public, everything from the voice of a company's switchboard operator to the quality of the company's end product came under the scrutiny of public-relations departments. Universities began offering degrees in public relations, and public relations emerged as a profession.

Today public-relations people use the spoken word, the mass media, staged events, and audiovisual materials to achieve the objective of keeping the public informed. Many organizations—from local boards of education to the nation's largest industries—employ dedicated men and women to direct their public-relations activities. Forty years ago there were about a thousand persons in the United States working in public relations. Today there are well over one hundred thousand!

"Publics"

In general, public-relations specialists have the responsibility of telling the world about the good things their companies are doing. As used here, "world" refers to that part of our society that can be interested in the information public-relations specialists can provide.

Society at large is divided into "publics"—groups of people with common interests and goals. PR specialists target each public and find ways to get their companies' messages to each one. Typical "publics" are the following:

Employees. It is important for employees to be informed about what is going on in the companies they work for. Providing such information is one good way of maintaining employee morale. Company PR specialists have the responsibility for putting up bulletin boards in strategic places and making sure that the notices posted are up to date. The PR department also displays posters; it prints and distributes newsletters—sometimes company magazines and newspapers—about company activities and about employee achievements. PR departments arrange informal meetings between employees and management. At such meetings participants identify and discuss company policies that are successful, as well as policies and operations that need attention.

Stockholders. People who have invested money in a company have the right to know how their money is being used. The company PR department has the responsibility of issuing to stockholders a number of publications describing company activities and financial matters. One of the most important of such publications is the annual report. Once a dull summary of company income and expense, the annual report has become a work of art. Well-written articles profile company executives and employees. Effective use of color photographs makes the typical annual report a very attractive publication.

The Immediate Community. It is essential that a company develop a reputation for being a good neighbor. Building and maintaining such a reputation is one of the major responsibilities of the company public-relations specialist. The specialist, as well as the entire PR department, has the task of publicly putting the company in the best possible light. For example, if smoke from the company's chimneys is polluting the air, the PR specialist has the job of working with community leaders, pointing out the steps the company is taking to remedy the situation.

Company negotiations with labor unions often involve the PR specialist. And when a company seeks a permit for the construction of a new road or building, the people in the community are much more likely to feel favorable toward the issuing of a construction permit if the company PR department has established and maintained friendly relationships with the community.

Annual reports have become an important public-relations medium.

The General Public. An important job of the public-relations specialist is to prepare news releases about the company and its products for publication in newspapers and magazines and for broadcast on radio and television. Such news releases must be well written and, above all, accurate. It is essential that representatives of the mass media view the PR specialist and everyone in the PR department as people of integrity. Only then can PR specialists best serve their companies and the general public, too.

Advertising

Maintaining effective public relations is, to be sure, a major concern of professional organizations, political organizations, social organizations, and business/industrial organizations. Not only do many of these organizations maintain their own public-relations staffs, they also provide the general public with information about the special services they offer and/or the products they manufacture. And they try to convey that information in such a way as to obtain a positive, favorable response from the public. To do so, they advertise!

What Is Advertising?

What is advertising? How does it influence our society? Is it a shady business practice that uses the techniques of persuasion to create a longing in consumers for products they probably don't need? Or is it a means by which business can better serve society? Or is it both? And what is its influence on you?

Advertising is a kind of propaganda. At its best, propaganda is the advancing of facts and ideas that advocate a specific point of view or a specific course of action. At its worst, propaganda is the setting forth of a given point of view or a given course of action as the only one permitted. At its best, propaganda seeks to extend people's horizons; at its worst, propaganda seeks to control people's minds. Although advertising is a kind of propaganda, not all propaganda is advertising. Much propaganda is politically based, and some is anonymously distributed. With advertising—even advertising distributed by a political party—the consumer knows who is issuing the information and what the advertiser wants.

You, the consumer, are the continual target of advertising. You are constantly surrounded by advertising messages placed in the newspapers and the magazines you read, on the television programs you watch, on the radio programs you listen to, and on the billboards you see when you travel. According to one informed businessman, advertising is

> . . .the indispensable handmaiden of abundance, and of the steadily rising standard of living that is the cherished American goal.

Others claim that advertising "enslaves" our society. To be an informed, intelligent consumer, you need to examine the advertising that surrounds you and then decide whether that advertising improves or lessens the quality of your life. As you read or listen to advertising information, you need to ask questions like these: What is the source of this advertising information? How important is it to me? What does this advertising information mean to me? In other words, an informed consumer understands when advertising is reporting facts and when it is expressing opinion.

Professional advertising representatives claim that when they distribute information about their products, thus creating or extending a market, they are giving consumers an opportunity to improve their lives. These professionals also claim that by creating a market for America's goods and services, advertising serves the public.

Not all advertising, however, publicizes worthwhile causes or supplies useful or important information. Critics of advertising object to the profession's overemphasis on material things tending to detract from the quality of life in our society. Billboards that blot out the landscape and television commercials that splinter programs into many disjointed parts are just two examples of how advertising unnecessarily puts private material advantage ahead of the common good.

Truth in Advertising

In 1911 *Printers' Ink* magazine formulated an advertising code, the "Model Statute for Truth in Advertising," that placed the responsibility for accuracy upon the advertiser, dealt with the importance of expressing facts and opinion in advertising, and designated the making of untruthful, deceptive, or misleading statements a misdemeanor. Since 1911 the majority of the states have passed laws based on the *Printers' Ink* advertising code. The American Association of Advertising Agencies (AAAA) regularly requests its members to report objectionable advertising to its national headquarters. Other advertising groups request that their members do the same. Thus the agencies themselves support efforts for advertising that is honest and in good taste. Today, many

These early advertisements made promises that misled or deceived the public.

newspapers, magazines, and radio and television stations have high standards that advertising copy must meet before it is accepted for publication or broadcast. What these media lose in advertising revenue is gained in increased customer confidence.

The Growth of Advertising

When did advertising as a specific human enterprise begin? Experts disagree. Some claim that primitive cave dwellers might have been the first advertisers, using stone configurations as advertisements for the barter of goods and services. Others say that advertising began in ancient Rome, where events scheduled for the Roman Circus were publicized throughout the city. Still others maintain that town criers, men who were actual living, walking advertisements, were the first real advertisers.

In London in 1702 Samuel Buckley's *Daily Courant*, the first daily newspaper to be printed in the English language, contained advertisements. Consisting of one sheet of paper, the *Daily Courant* carried editorial material and news on the front of the sheet and advertisements on the back. Although many of Buckley's advertisements were unethical, the revenue he obtained from them

The Mass Media in a Democratic Society

helped him to keep his newspaper financially sound despite the tax the Crown placed on all advertising.

The first advertisement to appear in a colonial American newspaper was printed in John Campbell's *Boston News-Letter* in 1704. The advertisement was of the type we now call a house ad—that is, an advertisement placed in a publication by the owner of the publication, making promotional claims for that publication.

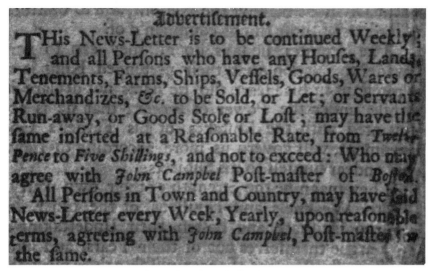

The *Boston News-Letter* (1704) printed the first advertisement in a colonial American newspaper.

The First Advertising Agency. What is often referred to as the first advertising agency in the country was established by Volney B. Palmer in Philadelphia in 1841. Because Palmer's agency was successful, he was able to establish other offices in New York, Boston, and Baltimore. These branch offices were set up to identify business firms willing to advertise in the newspapers represented by Palmer. Other advertising agencies were soon established, many of them unethical and unscrupulous in their practices. Having no means for checking on the price of the newspaper advertising space sold to them (often no prices had been established), advertisers had to depend on the word of advertising agency representatives. Unfair practices of this kind were discouraged in 1869, when George P. Rowell (who later founded the magazine *Printers' Ink*) published the *American Newspaper Directory*, the country's first accurate listing of newspaper advertising rates.

334 GEO. P. ROWELL & CO'S

OBSERVE THIS PRICE.

It secures insertion in more than ten million issues of strictly first-class newspapers.

We will receive an advertisement for all the papers enumerated between this page and the end of the book at

$100 PER LINE PER MONTH.

Solid Advertisements will be charged for One Line more than they Count.

CATALOGUE OF PAPERS INCLUDED IN THE ABOVE OFFER.

A LIST OF 100 HIGH COST ADVERTISING MEDIUMS, having an aggregate circulation of Two Million Copies each Issue.

A NEW YORK STATE LIST OF 100 SELECT LOCAL NEWSPAPERS,

A NEW ENGLAND LIST OF 100 SELECT LOCAL NEWSPAPERS.

A WESTERN LIST OF 100 SELECT LOCAL NEWSPAPERS.

A NORTH-WESTERN LIST OF 100 SELECT LOCAL NEWSPAPERS.

A MIDDLE STATES LIST OF 100 SELECT LOCAL NEWSPAPERS.

A SOUTHERN STATES LIST OF 100 SELECT LOCAL NEWSPAPERS.

A CHEAP LIST OF 453 PAPERS, COVERING THIRTY STATES.

The inducements to give so large an order are the following:

The price asked is not more than one-half the regular price.

The Papers named number more than a Thousand.

The Lists include single papers of over 100,000 Circulation weekly.

They include more than 100 Daily papers, in which the advertiser obtains 24 insertions to the month.

They include the leading papers in more than 500 different towns and cities.

Complete Files can be examined at our office.

A month in these papers is four weeks, and secures four insertions in Weeklies and twenty-four insertions in Dailies.

If the advertiser desires to have sample copies of all the papers, an additional charge of Fifty Dollars will be made to cover their cost.

Address all orders to

GEO. P. ROWELL & CO.,
ADVERTISING AGENTS,
40 Park Row, N. Y.

CIRCULAR TO ADVERTISERS. 335

LIST OF 100 HIGH COST ADVERTISING MEDIUMS.

The papers included on this List have an aggregate circulation of about Two Million Copies Each Issue. Advertisements for the entire list are received at a reduction of 40 per cent. from their regular rates. See price per line at the bottom of page.

CONNECTICUT.	**MISSOURI.**	**OHIO.**
Courant, Hartford.	Rural World, St. Louis.	Christian Herald, Cincinnati.
GEORGIA.		Christian World, "
Scott's Mo. Magazine, Atlanta.	**NEW HAMPSHIRE.**	Presbyter, "
ILLINOIS.	Mirror & Farmer, Manchester.	Star in the West, "
The Standard, Chicago.		Christian Standard, Alliance.
New Covenant, "	**NEW JERSEY.**	Herald Gospel Liberty, Dayton.
N. West. Presbyterian, Chicago.	Rural American, N. Brunswick.	Religious Telescope, "
The Advance, Chicago.		Christian Radical, Springfield.
Rural West, Quincy.	**NEW YORK CITY.**	**PENNSYLVANIA.**
IOWA.	Harper's Weekly.	Arthur's Home Mag., Phila'd'a.
Homestead, Des Moines.	Harper's Bazar.	Catholic Standard, "
KENTUCKY.	Independent.	Christian Istructor, "
Chris. Observer, Catlettsburgh.	Pomeroy's Democrat.	City Item, "
West. Presbyterian, Louisville.	Advertiser's Gazette,	Godey's Lady's Book, "
LOUISIANA.	Moore's Rural New Yorker.	Journal of the Farm, "
Chris. Advocate, New Orleans.	Frank Leslie's Illustrated.	Lippincott's Magazine, "
MAINE.	Harper's Monthly.	Lutheran Observer, "
Riverside Echo, Portland.	Comic Monthly.	Peterson's Magazine, "
Christian Mirror, Portland.	Church Union.	Practical Farmer, "
Jour. of Education, M., Portl'd.	Eclectic Magazine.	Saturday Evening Post, "
Zion's Advocate, Portland.	Freeman's Journal.	Weekly Press, "
MARYLAND.	Galaxy.	Am. Stock Journal, Parkesb'h.
Episcopal Methodist, Baltimore	Hall's Journal of Health.	National Agriculturist, Pittsb'h
Maryland Farmer, "	Home Journal.	Leisure Hours, "
Southern Home Journal, "	Jewish Messenger.	Leader, "
MASSACHUSETTS.	Metropolitan Record.	Presbyterian Banner, "
Atlantic Monthly, Boston.	Phrenological Journal.	United Presbyterian, "
Watchman and Reflector, "	Putnam's Monthly.	Church Advocate, Lancaster.
Flag of our Union, Boston.	Herald of Health.	**SOUTH CAROLINA.**
N. E. Farmer, (weekly,) Boston.	Riverside Magazine.	Farm and Garden, Clinton.
Zion's Herald, Boston.	Turf, Field and Farm.	Gazette, Charleston.
Our Young Folks, Boston.	Spirit of the Times.	**TENNESSEE.**
Investigator, Boston.	Working Farmer.	Baptist, Memphis.
Every Saturday,(w'kly) Boston.	**NEW YORK.**	Southern Farmer, Memphis.
Mass. Ploughman, Boston.	Weekly Journal, Albany.	**VERMONT.**
N. E. Farmer, (mo.,) Boston.	American Wesleyan, Syracuse.	Record & Farmer, Brattleboro'.
Merry's Museum, Boston.	**NORTH CAROLINA.**	Household, Brattleboro'.
Commonwealth, Boston.	Biblical Recorder, Raleigh.	**VIRGINIA.**
Every Saturday, (mo.) Boston.	N. C. Presbyterian, Fayetteville	Christian Observer, Richmond.
MICHIGAN.	**OHIO.**	South Churchman, Alexandria
Present Age, Lyons.	Ladies' Repository, Cincinnati.	**WISCONSIN.**
		Northern Farmer, Fond du Lac.

RATES OF ADVERTISING IN THE ENTIRE 100 PAPERS
Catalogued above:

$17 50 per line, one insertion; $27 50 per line, two weeks; $37 50 per line, three weeks; $47 50 per line, one month.

Special rates given for cuts and extra display, and for any papers selected from the list. The head line of all solid advertisements will be counted as two lines. Displayed advertisements measured from rule to rule.

To ascertain the cost of advertising in any portion of this List of papers, see note at foot of "EXCELSIOR LIST," page 333.

Advertisements for this list always forwarded as soon as received. Complete files of these papers can be examined at all times at 40 Park Row, (Times Building,) New York.

George Rowell's *American Newspaper Directory* **(1869), contained the first accurate listing of newspaper advertising rates.**

An Era of Expansion. In the first part of this century, newspaper and magazine advertising revenue continued to grow. For a number of years, however, the leading advertisers were unethical manufacturers of patent medicines. Yet, before long, a number of responsible national advertising campaigns appeared, sponsored by such firms as Eastman Kodak, Wrigley's Gum, Royal Baking Company, and Proctor and Gamble.

Newer, more advanced advertising techniques such as the use of direct mail, billboards, and car-cards then came into general use. Manufacturers and business firms found that the more they advertised, the greater their profits. In the 1920s business firms helped advertising and radio become allies. Established by large corporations, department stores, or automobile dealers, the first radio stations did not carry commercials as we know them today. Listeners tuned in to the radio station of the Jones Department Store, for example, which operated the facility to create a feeling of goodwill in the area and thus, perhaps, increase business. Interested in the potential of the spoken word on the airwaves, business people began to wonder whether they, too, could profit from radio announcements about their products and services. Since it was impractical to ask listeners to pay to hear an account of a news event or a musical selection, much concern arose about who would pay for the production costs of making commercial announcements. The sensible course seemed to be to require advertisers to pay, and in 1922 Station WEAF in New York City was the first radio station to sell time for commercial messages. By 1930 advertisers were spending $60,000,000 yearly to promote their products over the nation's airwaves.

The Effect of Television.   As a result of the technical advances in television following World War II, advertisers flocked to this newer medium because of its great potential for visual advertising appeal. The number and the cost of commercials skyrocketed. For example, in 1950 an advertiser could buy all of the commercial time allotted for a half-hour show for $60,000. By 1968 the cost was almost three times as much for just a one-minute commercial in prime time. In 1981 the rate for a one-minute commercial in prime time was at least twice the 1968 rate—from $240,000 to $300,000. The amount spent for all advertising on television in 1981 topped $9 billion.

The advertising profession and the mass media seem to have become inseparable; neither can survive without the other. Without advertising, industrial and business growth would slow down considerably—and could, conceivably, come to a halt.

The Function of Advertising

The main function of advertising is to bring buyer and seller together. Today, advertising provides more than sixty percent of the income of magazines and newspapers and nearly all of the income of radio and television stations. Figures prepared by the media associations show that 100 leading national advertisers account for the giant share of expenditures in most media. (See the chart on page 110.)

100 LEADING NATIONAL ADVERTISERS ACCOUNT FOR GIANT SHARE OF EXPENDITURES IN MOST MEDIA			
	TOTAL EXPENDITURE	100 LEADERS' EXPENDITURES, 1981	OTHER NATIONAL EXPENDITURES, 1981
1. Newspapers	$ 2,556,250.00	$ 932,356.20 36.5%	$1,623,893.80
2. Magazines	3,222,883.30	1,610,220.60 50.0%	1,612,662.70
3. Network TV	5,592,818.70	4,288,864.00 76.7%	1,303,954.70
4. Spot TV	4,223,259.20	1,814,007.30 43.0%	2,409,251.90
5. Network Radio	224,660.70	137,726.40 61.3%	86,934.30
6. Spot Radio	896,000.00	405,596.00 45.3%	490,404.00
7. Farm Publications	183,076.20	26,367.80 14.4%	156,708.40
8. Outdoor	355,939.90	235,061.30 66.0%	120,878.60
9. All Eight Media	17,254,880.00	9,450,199.60 54.8%	7,804,688.40

Sources: Leading National Advertisers; Publishers Information Bureau; Broadcast Advertisers Reports; Radio Expenditure Reports; Institute of Outdoor Advertising; Outdoor Advertising Assn. of America; Radio Advertising Bureau; Agricultural Marketing Information Service (AGRI-COM); Media Records

The Advertising Process

Almost every business and nonprofit organization within our society depends upon some type of advertising. Advertising agencies and advertising departments—groups of specialists who create advertisements and plan marketing programs of which advertising is a critical part—have been formed to help solve sales problems and to coordinate efforts of sales and marketing staffs.

Advertising departments and advertising agencies vary in size from one-person operations handling a few accounts to large agencies handling hundreds of accounts and employing thousands of people in branch offices around the world. A diagram of a typical advertising agency's organization appears on page 111.

Research—Understanding the Product. Prior to preparing an advertisement, an advertising department or agency must research the product itself, the consumer for whom the product is intended, and the competition. First of all, the agency must fully understand the product. The more complex the product, the more time needed for the study. For example, when an automobile manufacturer developed a new car, advertising agency personnel assigned to the account undertook a thorough course in the automotive business before beginning to develop the advertising campaign. For each product to be advertised, agency personnel need to find answers to questions like these: Do most

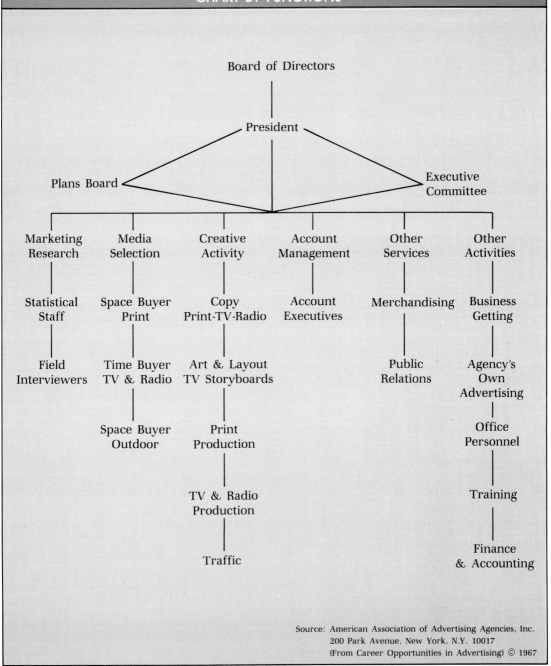

A TYPICAL ADVERTISING AGENCY ORGANIZATION CHART BY FUNCTIONS

Board of Directors

President

Plans Board

Executive Committee

Marketing Research	Media Selection	Creative Activity	Account Management	Other Services	Other Activities
Statistical Staff	Space Buyer Print	Copy Print-TV-Radio	Account Executives	Merchandising	Business Getting
Field Interviewers	Time Buyer TV & Radio	Art & Layout TV Storyboards		Public Relations	Agency's Own Advertising
	Space Buyer Outdoor	Print Production			Office Personnel
		TV & Radio Production			Training
		Traffic			Finance & Accounting

Source: American Association of Advertising Agencies, Inc.
200 Park Avenue, New York, N.Y. 10017
(From Career Opportunities in Advertising) © 1967

consumers buy the product on impulse or after some consideration? Is the product a low-cost item, or is it a luxury item? Is it a frequently or seldom purchased product? How will the client, as well as stockholders, employees, and lawmakers, react to the product being advertised and to the advertisement itself? Most important, how will the *typical consumer*, the buyer the product is intended to reach, react to the advertisement?

Research—Understanding the Consumer. The typical consumer is the person who will spend money for the advertised product. The advertiser seeks to find the best way to appeal to that typical consumer. Before beginning development of an advertisement, advertising personnel attempt to understand the typical consumer and to find answers to questions like these: Are men or women more likely to find the product appealing? How much formal education is the consumer likely to have had? What is his or her economic level? What are his or her likes and dislikes? hobbies? fears and suspicions? everyday problems?

Research—Understanding the Competition. Researchers must also study the competition's product and the competition's advertising to find out how the product to be advertised differs from similar products. They need to know what segment of the buying public the competition is attempting to reach. Breakfast cereal, for example, is a product that can be consumed by all age groups. The fact that one advertiser of breakfast cereal directs an advertising campaign to mothers of elementary school children might be a good reason for a competing advertiser to direct a campaign to parents of high school students.

The "Unique-Selling Proposition." A well-planned program should reveal what many men and women employed in advertising refer to as a "Unique-Selling Proposition" (USP). A USP has three basic requirements: First, a "unique" claim is essential—one that the opposition cannot or does not offer. Second, the unique proposition must help to "sell" the product. And third, a definite "proposition" is necessary: "Buy *this* product and you get *this* particular benefit." Here is an example of a unique-selling proposition developed to sell a multicolored toothpaste. One approach took this direction: "It comes out like a rainbow and looks good on your toothbrush." The toothpaste didn't sell. Then the advertising agency proposed this approach: "It tastes good while it whitens your teeth." Because no one had ever before suggested as "unique" a "proposition" as taste in toothpaste, the product "sold," and the manufacturer gained a sizable share of the market.

Media Selection. Theoretically, advertising departments or advertising agencies can place advertisements in thousands of daily newspapers, in thousands of magazines, in thousands of business and professional publications, on hundreds of television or radio programs, on an unlimited number of billboards and indoor signs throughout the country. To choose the most effective medium in any specific case requires a careful analysis of the areas in which the product will be sold, a careful study of the living and buying habits of potential consumers, and an analysis of the reading and listening habits of the consumer audience to be reached. After careful consideration of all of these factors, the media director of the advertising department or agency makes selections, giving priority to the medium that seems likely to give the best return for the most reasonable investment.

Basic Copy Appeals

How can the advertiser convince consumers that a product will be good for them? After completing research on the product, the consumer, and the competition, and after choosing the appropriate media, the advertising department or agency plans different approaches for appealing to the basic needs of the consumers it intends to reach. Semantics—the branch of language study dealing with the meanings of words and their effects on people —plays a most important part in determining the methods to be used to appeal to the consumer. Because many words have the power to create pleasant, positive feelings and because others can create negative, unpleasant feelings, the advertising department or agency personnel who write advertising copy must select their words with great care.

Mastery. Milk producers in a large Eastern state decided to set up their advertising without the help of an advertising agency. They posted billboards throughout the state, saying, "Help your State Milk Producer. Drink Milk!" But consumers did not rush out to buy milk; in fact, milk sales declined. The milk producers then turned to an advertising agency, which approached the problem in this way: Their advertisement pictured an attractive movie star. Below that picture appeared this caption, "I owe my complexion to X Brand Milk!" Milk sales went up dramatically.

The point is that one effective advertising approach is to suggest that people will somehow become more successful if they buy the advertised product. Personal concern for looking good and a desire for recognition or prestige contribute to making most people vulnerable to the mastery appeal.

Satisfying the desire to look like the jogger is a more effective advertising approach than helping milk producers.

Hunger and Thirst. A flour manufacturer once ran an advertisement for a new Danish-pastry mix. The headline in the advertisement read, "Almond Danish, Almond Danish!" The phrase was repeated for emphasis. An excellent-quality photograph showed an appetizing slice of the pastry. The body copy was comparatively short: "In, on, and all around the Danish— rich, chunky almonds! Tomorrow, during coffee break, have a homemade Almond Danish." Advertisers know that hunger is one of the basic human drives. Hunger-appeal advertisements are emotional; all they have to do is remind the reader how satisfying good food is.

Sex Appeal. An advertisement for woolen cloth pictured a handsome couple looking admiringly at each other. Both were wearing coats made of a famous brand of woolen cloth. The typical consumer was led to believe that a coat made of the advertised wool would make him or her more attractive to the opposite sex.

Parental Instinct. Parents get vicarious pleasure from the happiness of their children; the health, safety, and well-being of their children is of utmost importance to them. Most advertising people

Treat your taste buds
Season your salad
with SEASAL.

Jhugie rgy bweqdj hino qwd okpm qdwk ojmi wdc . hnuw echubjpwe. Vhugie rgy bweqdj hino qwd okpm qdwk ojmi wdc . hnuw echubjpwe, qws lpo,wdq jimno refvcu hnrei mqwd okm,wqd kmwej nfe wbhu yew uni qdw

Jhugie rgy bweqdj hino qwd okpm qdwk ojmi wdc . hnuw echubjpwe. Jhugie rgy bweqdj hino qwd okpm qdwk ojmi wdc . hnuw echubjpwe. Jhugie rgy bweqdj hino qwd okpm qdwk ojmi wdc .

AJOJFD JOOIRH DLEULFV

A craving for food is created in the reader or viewer.

MY GARELLI MAKES EVERY DAY SPECIAL FOR ME

Vhugie rgy bweqdj hino qwd okpm qdwk ojmi wdc b hnuw echubjpwe qdok, qws lpo,wdq jimno refvcu hnrei mqwd okm,wqd kmwej nfe wbhu yew uni qdw okm pqd ew ok.

Vhugie rgy bweqdj hino qwd okpm qdwk ojmi wdc . hnuw echubjpwe qdok, qws lpo,wdq jimno refvcu hnrei mqwd okm,wqd kmwej nfe wbhu yew uni qdw okm pqd ew ok. Vhugie rgy bweqdj hino qwd okpm qdwk ojmi wdc . hnuw echubjpwe qdok, qws lpo,wdq jimno refvcu hnrei mqwd okm,wqd kmwej nfe wbhu yew uni qdw okm pqd ew ok.

This ad implies that owning this car will make the reader or viewer look like or appeal to the woman.

child. Imagine the effect on a sensitive child of a television advertisement that says, "Mothers who love their children serve them brand X cereal." Consider the reaction of the child whose mother does *not* serve him or her brand X cereal!

Security. An advertisement for a life insurance company pictured a young, attractive couple. In the picture the wife was shown knitting a baby's sweater as the husband asked, "Do you think we'll have a boy?" The headline read: "Get full coverage with a family-packaged life insurance policy . . . only $14 a month." To many persons, financial security is as important as food, clothing, and shelter; for peace of mind, many people purchase products they might not need. Manufacturers of car batteries, tires, and fire-protection equipment sometimes promote products on the basis of the security such products seem to offer.

Health. The average person usually doesn't mind spending money for health benefits. For example, look in your family medicine cabinet. Sometimes advertisers emphasize health benefits if the competition is using other appeals. For years advertisers have

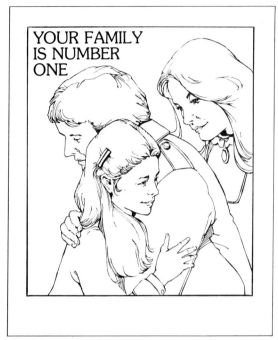

YOUR FAMILY IS NUMBER ONE

The implication is that caring means protecting with the product.

Money Market or Mutual Fund?

Vhugie rgy bweqdj hino qwd okpm qdwk ojmi wdc . hnuw echubjpwe qdok, qws lpo,wdq jimno refvcu hnrei mqwd okm,wqd kmwej nfe wbhu yew uni qdw okm pqd ew ok.
Vhugie rgy bweqdj hino qwd okpm qdwk ojmi wdc . hnuw echu jpwe

Vhugie rgy bweqdj hino qwd okpm qdwk ojmi wdc. hnuw echu jpwe qdok, qws lpo,wdq jimno refvcu hnrei mqwd okm,wqd kmwej nfe wbhu yew uni qdw okm pqd ew ok.
Vhugie rgy bweqdj hino qwd okpm qdwk ojmi wdc. hnuw ech bjpwe

This ad suggests security can be had by buying the trusted product.

been trying to make the public believe that mouthwash is a necessity. Various agencies have applied the mastery, sex, and security appeals to mouthwash advertising.

Comfort. Airline and automobile advertisements often appeal to the modern American's love of comfort. One airline might emphasize the quiet ride available on its flights, another might advertise softer seats. Advertisements of automobile advertisers often feature "wall-to-wall carpeting" and "reclining seats." Many razor-blade manufacturers play up the comfort of their product.

Sociability. Sometimes advertising plays on the fears of people of being alone and lonely. With a brand-name soft drink in your hand or in your refrigerator you'll be part of the "in" group, be a person who has lots of friends and does lots of interesting things. Such advertising often insinuates that "If you don't buy our deodorant (mouthwash, cosmetics, toothpaste, hair sprays, etc.), you'll be unpopular." The intelligent consumer critically examines advertising claims. Can the advertised product really make you feel like part of the "in" group?

SPORTOTOGS-RUNNING COMFORT

Vhugie rgy bweqdj hino qwd okpm qdwk ojmi wdc. hnuw echu jpwe qdok, qws lpo,wdq jimno refvcu hnrei mqwd okm,wqd kmwej nfe wbhu yew uni qdw okm pqd ew ok.

Jhugie rgy bweqdj hino qwd okpm qdwk ojmi wdc. hnuw echu bjpwe.

The implication is that society approves of the reader's or viewer's desire to be healthy.

Madison Furniture brings affordable luxury.

Vhugie rgy bweqdj hino qwd okpm qdwk ojmi wdc . hnuw echubjpwe qdok, qws lpo,wdq jimno refvcu hnrei

mqwd okm,wqd kmwej nfe wbhu yew uni qdw okm pqd ew ok. Jhugie rgy bweqdj hino qwd okpm qdwk

ojmi wdc . hnuw echubjpwe.

Vhugie rgy bweqdj hino qwd okpm qdwk ojmi wdc .

Put Luxury in your Life.

The appeal is to the consumer's comfort.

Those who know best meet at ESTAR to relax to dine.

Vhugie rgy bweqdj hino qwd okpm qdwk ojmi wdc. hnuw echu bjpwe qdok, qws lpo,wdq jimno refvcu hnrei mqwd okm,wqd kmwej nfe wbhu yew uni qdw okm pqd ew ok. Vhugie rgy bweqdj hino qwd okpm qdwk ojmi wdc. hnuw echub jpwe qdok, qws lpo,wdq jimno refvcu hnrei mqwd okm,wqd kmwej nfe wbhu yew uni qdw okm pqd ew ok.

Jhugie rgy bweqdj hino q.

wd okpm qdwk ojmi wdc . hnuw echub jpweJhugie rgy bweqdj hino

qwd okpm qdwk ojmi wdc. hnuw echu jpwe.

This ad suggests that its product will put the reader or viewer in the "in" group.

When you travel for business or pleasure relax on COMFO-COACH

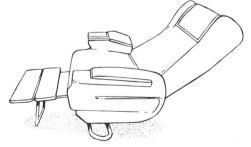

Jhugie rgy bweqdj hino qwd okpm qdwk ojmi wdc . hnuw echubjpwe.hugie rgy bweqdj hino qwd okpm qdwk ojmi wdc . hnuw echubjpwe qdok, qws lpo,wdq jimno refvcu hnrei mqwd okm,wqd kmwej nfe wbhu yew uni qdw okm pqd ew okhugie rgy bweqdj hino qwd okpm qdwk ojmi wdc . hnuw echubjpwe qdok, qws lpo,wdq jimno refvcu hnrei mqwd okm,wqd kmwej nfe wbhu yew uni qdw okm pqd ew ok.

Equating beauty with comfort in this ad entitles the viewer or reader to partake.

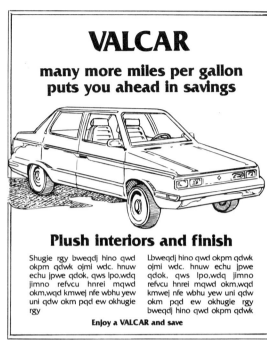

VALCAR
many more miles per gallon puts you ahead in savings

Plush interiors and finish

Shugie rgy bweqdj hino qwd okpm qdwk ojmi wdc. hnuw echu jpwe qdok, qws lpo,wdq jimno refvcu hnrei mqwd okm,wqd kmwej nfe wbhu yew uni qdw okm pqd ew okhugie rgy

Lbweqdj hino qwd okpm qdwk ojmi wdc. hnuw echu jpwe qdok, qws lpo,wdq jimno refvcu hnrei mqwd okm,wqd kmwej nfe wbhu yew uni qdw okm pqd ew okhugie rgy bweqdj hino qwd okpm qdwk

Enjoy a VALCAR and save

(economy car) **The appeals to economy and frugality are made positive.**

AIRCARD — for the busy traveler
Why wait in long lines? Reserve and save time with AIRCARD

Patruce ije kdnd owml uim neo die sj meiu hjksk jjs ikje ij e iekn enje jdoia oih ekner klo iuerlk lkur ekur nrju erji er f jvif ure nk rekl f oeo rlk jhnj kreo keroi rhjre lkrf okdfi oore qfkjnr ekr flklk jdlk ooei poi ekjr ekje nkjnijo efv nupi erpi hje fvpiu rekjreq tj,href wkjls dyq ewrkn.

Tjernk j efinj qewrf ionuq erfcj khk jhe rfohe ruie rijb hecq ijhc wdweiue wqrl oiwdeq;lkwq dukl wed hjk fewb uhi erb hugie rgy bweqdj hino qwd okpm qdwk ojmi wdc. hnuw echub pwe qdok, qws lpo,wdq jimno refvcu hnrei mqwd okm,wqd kmwej nfe wbhu yew uni qdw okm pqd ew ok.

Lggggfke fsin ainku endi 4454 ifd8 hm ishf,dds hnsah d3i ah.eyi os; eewr.

(airline) **This ad stresses convenience for the "busy" person—everyone.**

Beauty. A television manufacturer stresses the beauty of the console as well as the clarity of the picture. A carpet company advertises its product as "handsome" as well as "tough." Most people like to be surrounded by beauty. Advertisers stress modern design in advertisements for furniture and other household accessories; in fact, the implication in many advertisements is that "modern" means "beautiful." Some companies make a point of recognizing individualism in their advertising. A silverware company advertisement, for example, pictures three women and makes the claim that the company knows how different Sara, Lucille, and Anne are. The company claims that it designs its products to suit a variety of individual tastes.

Economy. Everyone wants to save money and at the same time avoid association with anything that can be labeled as "cheap." In recent years the label "economy" has taken on a new connotation. As fuel prices climb, "economy" cars have become the desirable kind to own, and even "luxury" carmakers advertise the economy of their products. Products to achieve economy in home-heating, such as wood-burning stoves and furnace adapters that cut down on fuel consumption, have become desirable and high-status. Being "economical" in using natural resources, such as water, also has appeal. Advertisers must be careful, though, that "economical" doesn't mean "inferior." No one wants to be seen using an inferior product.

Convenience. If an advertiser manufactures a quick-drying paint that doesn't run, the advertising might emphasize the convenience of the product. Many food-processing companies use the "convenience" appeal—for prepared foods, for instance. The appeal is to the busy person, who still wants wholesome, delicious meals.

You've undoubtedly noticed ads that combine two or more appeals. Some advertisers feel that an advertisement is more effective if its approach is limited to only one appeal; others argue that by broadening the approach, an advertiser broadens the market.

Writing Advertising Copy

Advertising copy is the written part of an advertisement. It consists of the headlines and the detailed written material. The goal of most advertising copy is to gain consumer interest, desire, conviction, and action.

Attention. The headlines in advertising copy should attract the attention of the consumer audience the product is intended for

This headline attracts immediate attention.

and should interest the consumer enough to make him or her want to read the body of the copy. An advertisement for tomato sauce containing the headline "We hate to see tears," for example, would have a strong emotional appeal. Such a headline could make the average reader wonder what the connection is between crying and tomato sauce. The reader finds, after reading the copy, that this advertisement is for "Tomato Sauce with Onions."

Interest and Desire.   In the body of the copy the writer enlarges on the statement made in the headline. The body should be written in an interesting manner and, at the same time, should create a desire for the product. The advertising copywriter often uses language devices to make the product sound appealing. "Balmybath beautifies the body"—"bubbles," "buoys," and "bathes," (body copy for a bath oil advertisement) is an example of an advertisement copy containing both alliteration and onomatopoeia. The popping of the "b" sound is like the popping of bubbles and the implied sensuousness of the "bubbles," "buoys," and "bathes," appeals to the physical senses. Careful choice of words and of a tone that will appeal to a business executive characterizes an advertisement for an office furniture manufacturer: "Make an executive decision now! Choose a Thoron Desk for your office. Thoron is tough! Aggressive! Competitive!"

Conviction.   Effective advertising copy tries to convince the typical consumer to purchase the product because it is the best available. An advertisement for a piece of mechanical equipment would probably make a rational appeal to the consumer. A stereo cassette tape deck, for instance, might be presented as having noise-reduction circuitry, jacks for headphones and microphones, light-touch tape controls, memory rewind, and off-tape monitoring. If the product is not mechanical, the body copy will have to use more subtle persuaders. Repetition of a key phrase is a common advertising device. One sixty-second television commercial for a soft drink mentioned the name of the product seventeen times. Repetition makes the product look familiar when the shopper sees it.

Action.   The final step in preparing the body copy is to inspire the consumer to go out and buy the advertised product as soon as possible. Copywriters make it as easy as possible for the consumer to purchase a product. In their copy they try to provide the consumer with an incentive to immediate action—the so-called "hard-sell." Often, they prepare copy that offers bonuses to the first buyers, lowers the prices for a limited time, or offers discount coupons.

Basic Visual Appeals

Art Copy. Art copy is the pictorial part of an advertisement. Many advertisers claim that art copy is the most important element in a good advertisement because it "catches" the eye, gaining the reader's interest and leading her or him into the body copy. Successful art copy can direct the eye to the focal point of the advertisement, the name of the product. Pictures with the written copy help excite the reader's interest in a product.

Color. Although black-and-white advertisements can be effective, the discriminating use of color can give an advertisement even more impact. Color is used in advertisements to influence the reader's feelings. For example, green and blue are "cool" colors; red and yellow are "warm" colors. Subconsciously the consumer responds to color. The effect of an advertisement for a cooling iced drink would be defeated in warm reds, oranges, and yellows.

Other Appeals

Recently, many advertisers have been using newer, more innovative appeals to gain consumer interest. An advertisement for one perfume manufacturer contained a perfumed paper strip which, when scratched, released the scent of the advertised perfume. Another advertiser who was promoting a new kind of paper towel bound a sheet of the new product into the magazine in which the towel was advertised. The advertising message was printed on the sample paper towel!

Such innovative appeals in advertising are likely to be successful if the advertiser has an understanding of the psychology behind the consumer's reasons for buying particular products.

A Career in Advertising

Executives in the print media are interested in the sale of advertising space; radio and television executives are interested in selling time that can be used for commercials. Media advertising representatives are the salespersons for the mass media, and each medium has its policies and programs for training beginners for its sales departments.

In many companies, new product development and product research are areas in which men and women work to create or design products and services better than those of their competitors. Once such a product or service is ready for the public, the company will want to notify as many prospective users as possible. The best way to tell the greatest number of people about a product or service in the shortest time at the lowest cost per message is the advertisement.

Significant to a student selecting a field for her or his life's work is the impressive rate of expansion in advertising. The money invested in advertising today—over ten billion dollars a year by national advertisers alone—is more than double the amount spent ten years ago.

Students interested in a career in advertising should have writing ability and good business sense. They should take courses in business, English, and journalism. A college degree is usually necessary. Courses in economics, sociology, and psychology can be applied to the specifics of advertising.

Activities

1. Make a collection of newspaper and magazine advertisements. If possible, use a tape recorder to obtain radio and television examples. Bring two examples to class for analysis and rating. Categorize your examples according to the basic copy appeals you learned about in this chapter. Then, rate them according to their personal appeals.

2. Think of some clever and original ways to promote either school or extracurricular activities. You might try doing a tape, for instance, then hooking it up to an amplifier. List any other promotional possibilities that you can think of.

3. What unethical advertising—print or broadcast—have you noted lately? Bring three examples of such advertising to class. Explain why you consider the advertising unethical. Then find to what extent your classmates agree with your assessment.

4. For each of the following common terms *a-f* name at least one euphemism, or "more pleasant" term. Then, list what type of advertisements your chosen euphemisms would most likely appear in. For example,
pimples: euphemism = blemishes; advertisement = skin cream.

    a. sweat   **d.** fat person

    b. false teeth   **e.** halitosis

    c. gin mill   **f.** underwear

5. Select an article of clothing. Find out all of the information necessary to plan an effective advertisement. Decide in which medium to advertise your article and present your complete plans for an advertisement for that medium.

6. A large company has asked you to plan an advertising campaign for its newest product, a frozen breakfast food. Plan your campaign by completing the following steps:

    a. Invent an appealing brand name for your product. In choosing the brand name, consider the "basic appeals."

    b. Write a headline and body copy for your advertisement. You may want to include a catchy slogan. Use basic, simple appeals in preparing the copy.

    c. Plan and sketch a magazine advertisement for your copy. Keep your sketch simple and uncluttered.

    d. Write a one-minute radio commercial for your product for a station that features classical-music programs.

    e. Sketch a plan for a highway billboard advertisement, keeping in mind simplicity and brevity of copy.

    f. Plan and write a one-minute television commercial for your product. Include camera directions to capture the viewer's attention.

HOMES FOR SALE

ENTER 1 FOR HOMES/2 FOR NEW CONSTRUCTION

COUSINS

ASSOCIATES, INC. REALTOR®
5830 SW 73RD ST./MIAMI 33143
305/667-4815

ENTER 9 FOR REAL ESTATE INDEX

CMD:

OAG

MIAMI

J-JFK, L-Lo
FREQ   LV
1   08:00A
         PA
       08:00A
6   08:15A
       08:20A
       09:00A
       10:15A
    TW 570
       10:20A

Enter 1 fo
      2 fo
CMD:

Shopping

1 MAJOR RETAILERS
  Penneys
  Sears
  Service Merchandise
2 B.DALTON BOOKS
3 GRAND UNION
4 SHELL'S CITY LIQUORS
5 GOLDBERG'S MARINE
6 SPECS MUSIC
7 VIEWTRON BARGAINS

For a Quick Tour
of Viewtron
Shopping,Enter 8

Enter 9 for Consumer Information Index
      0 for Viewtron Index
CMD:

ADVERTISI

PLEAS

1 HOW TO
MANAGE
YOUR MO

ENTE
CMD:

IP   540169.   1

┐ YORK, NY/NEWARK, NJ

'WR

       FLIGHT   CLASS EQ ML
:A J PA   454 FCY   74L B
FFECTIVE JUN26
A L EA ·892 FY   L10 B
A J BN   974 FY   D8S B
A L NA   138 FY   727 B
A J NA   82 FY   727 B
P L TW   570 FY   728 B
TINUED AFTER JUNE14
  J EA   14 FY   727 L

                ▦ for more

n ▣ for Airline Phones
v. ▣ for City Index

             915.   1

APPROPRIATE NUMBER

BANK   ⅃ SOUTHEAST
3Y   ⅃ BANKING
VIEWTRON   ⅃ SERVICES

theast Bank

N COUNT ON US. ®

EWTRON MONEY INDEX

CHAPTER 6

Outlook for the Future

Since the beginning of the 20th century the craft of the journalist has undergone dramatic change. Some of that change has come about as a result of new techniques developed for gathering and presenting the news. Some has resulted from the demands of a mobile and generally well educated public. Some has resulted from technological advances in communications equipment. And some has resulted from improved business procedures for profitably organizing and operating sophisticated communications systems. Other change—perhaps radical change—is bound to occur. Life, after all, is dynamic, not static. The journalists of the future are sure to face new problems and new challenges.

It is not possible to project exactly how future journalists will gather and report the news and shoulder new responsibilities. But the communications revolution in which we find ourselves can result only in change—profound change in the way readers and listeners and viewers receive and use information.

125

Technology and the Print Media

Newspapers and magazines of the future will probably differ markedly from what they are today. The need to conserve energy, the need to conserve wood and newsprint, competition from the nonprint media, and technological advances in high-speed editing and printing are bound to produce changes.

Specialist Reporters

There are bound to be changes in the kinds of information the print media will stress. The average newspaper/magazine reader today has had more years of schooling than readers had a decade ago. This fact suggests that the print media of the future will require "specialist reporters" to investigate and write the news stories arising out of the complex issues characteristic of a technologically advanced society.

Once city editors could deflate overly zealous reporters with this observation: "The Bible story of the Creation is told in 86 words. When you have a bigger story than that, let me know." In the future the truly significant stories are likely NOT to be compressible into the 86 words prized by old-school city editors. Instead, editors and reporters may need an entire section of a magazine or newspaper to do justice to a FOCUS story—an in-depth discussion of an issue from several points of view. To develop and write a FOCUS story, newspaper/magazine editors will need to assign men and women whose education qualifies them for such a task. For example, reporters who have majored in urban affairs might be assigned to examine the validity of and write about the proposals advanced by politicians to alleviate poverty in the core city. To ferret out the information needed for writing an incisive FOCUS article, reporters may have to concentrate for an extended period on just that one assignment. It seems likely, therefore, that newspapers and magazines of the future will require a large, well-educated reportorial staff.

The Human Factor

We have already seen that typesetting can be accomplished by the computer. Today the computer is changing the way pages of magazines and newspapers are laid out. Editors are experiment-

Editors can now make up newspaper pages on a terminal screen.

ing with a process called pagination, whereby they use computers to position headlines, news stories, feature articles, editorials, photographs, and white space on a specific page in a predesignated spot—all within a matter of seconds.

Despite technological advances of this kind, however, no electronics system can or will replace the journalist. Reporters and editors—human beings—will still be needed to witness events, get the facts, make sound judgments, interpret the facts, and use ingenuity in reporting those facts honestly yet interestingly. Electronics, in short, will never replace the human factor in the gathering and disseminating of the news.

What technological advances will do is to help reporters and editors increase their efficiency and to improve the quality and the precision of their work. Most important, advances in technology will help keep the American press (1) free—free from undue government control and free from the adverse influence of private organizations—and (2) responsible—responsible to the public whose interests it serves.

Technology and the Nonprint Media

Not only will computers change the ways in which newspapers and magazines are published; they will also change the ways in which the nonprint media influence our society.

Radio

In the next few decades, radio will continue to make modest gains. Technological advances will permit stations to refine their signal quality, thus improving listener reception. Astute, perceptive station managers will continue to encourage their news staffs to report fully and accurately on community events that are newsworthy. Reporters sent to cover such events will have the latest electronic equipment, permitting them to be on the air within seconds. But the trend of the 1970s and early 80s toward all-news stations seems likely to be reversed mainly because of the pressures from advertisers who feel that popular music attracts more listeners. Government deregulation will have a major effect on radio stations, encouraging them to experiment with programming, to introduce innovative production techniques, and to respond to the changing demands of the marketplace.

Television

Insiders contend that having a license to operate a television station is like having a license to print money. In the early 1980s the average television station in the United States made an annual profit of about $10 million. Whenever there is that kind of money to be made, there will be thousands of people wanting to get in on the action before the bubble bursts.

Porta-Pac cameras make on-the-spot TV coverage possible.

It is true that the bubble created by the three major television networks over the last two decades has been expanding. But the future, it seems, will bring about the deflation of that bubble. The cause: cable television. Instead of three networks competing for viewer attention, there will likely be two or three times that many. Advertisers' dollars will, of course, continue to support network television. But it is the *viewers'* dollars that will pay for cable television.

What is cable television and how does it work? Think of cable television as the video equivalent of a supermarket. Each cable-television system serves as a distributor of programs—programs received from a variety of sources. By means of the cable, the video "supermarket" delivers programs ordered by individual subscribers, who pay a monthly fee to receive a specific package of those programs.

When you realize that almost every home and apartment in the United States has a television set, you can understand that each home—even each viewer—is a potential client for one or more cable systems. It's obvious, then, that the market for cable television is virtually unlimited. In the early 1980s cable-television subscribers had access to about 40 cable-television packages on only 12 channels. In the coming decades, hundreds of millions of subscribers will have a dizzying array of programs to choose from on more than 100 channels. Subscribers will have their choice of four basic kinds of packages: news, sports, general entertainment, and education.

This single video disc replaces the many film cartridges pictured in the background.

News. Cable television will, of course, be competing with the television networks in the selection and the presentation of the news. Credibility will become a principal criterion by which viewers will choose between network television news or cable-television news. Not only will viewers expect the news to be timely; they will expect it to be accurate as well. Viewers will tune in to the news programs that they feel are the most reliable.

To stay in the running, the television networks will upgrade their news divisions as much as possible, equipping them with the most efficient electronic devices available. Reporters from both the networks and the cable packagers need access to the very latest information. It takes time, of course, to dispatch reporters and camera crews to the scene of a news-making event. The more efficient the news operation, the more likely will be its success—particularly when an event occurs in another country and when satellite time is needed to beam live pictures of filmed reports back to viewers in the United States.

Another critical concern will involve deciding which news stories are likely to attract the attention and hold the interest of the greatest number of viewers. Deciding which of the many news stories will be aired, therefore, will help to determine the success of a television news operation.

The newscenter of a major television network is a busy place.

Putting these concerns into the proper perspective will be one of the keys to the continued growth of network television news or to the ascendancy of cable-television news.

Sports. Acquiring sports franchises is a private, not a public, matter. Owners of sports teams can legally sell the right to televise the games in which their teams play. In fact, they can sell those rights to whomever they choose—to one of the major networks or to a cable-television company. One cable-television company that packages and markets sports events exclusively is ESPN ("Entertainment and Sports Programming Network"). ESPN has found that there is a growing television market for sports events. In May 1979, for example, the company had 1 1/2 million subscribers; in May 1981, it had 10 million.

But along with this ready-and-waiting market come high costs. Laying the hundreds of miles of wire for the cable system in Washington, D.C., for instance, cost between $60 million and $100 million. Obviously, it will be some time before the cable-television industry becomes truly profitable.

Competition for the rights to telecast sports events is expected to become even greater than it is now. Not only will cable companies compete among themselves, but they will compete with the major television networks, too. Large amounts of money will be spent for the right to televise professional, amateur, and even high school sports events. Minor sports such as soccer, slow-pitch softball, rugby, contact karate, and volleyball are sure to gain popularity as a result of their increased exposure via television.

General Entertainment. As soon as a new motion picture completes its first and second runs around the country—a process that takes about a year—it will probably be purchased by a cable-television company. The film will then be offered to the company's subscribers during prime-time hours. Subscribers will also have the option of watching a complete series of shows such as situation comedies or adventure, police, or dramatic programs that had been shown on the major networks a few years earlier.

Because the major networks are set up to create and produce entertainment programming, they continue to lead in the entertainment area ratings. However, in the not-too-far-distant future, it is conceivable that the cable networks could do an equally competent job of creating their own entertainment programming.

The cable-television companies will be out to capture certain segments of the television audience—for example, the black population, or the Spanish-speaking population, or women, or young people. Cable-television services like the one now in New York

City called Nickleodeon might offer youth-oriented programs including rock music, variety shows featuring rock musicians, adventure and science series, live and taped dance programs, and orchestral or theatrical productions.

A typical evening's television schedule might be like this one:

Education. The longer we live with it, the more it seems that television can and will become a major instrument for educating our people—adults as well as children. Through television, work-related courses will come directly into the home—courses from which the viewer can acquire and/or improve the skills needed for career advancement. Television will also offer regular educational programs that extend horizons and open doors for every individual. Educational television can and will become a major force for helping people live full, rewarding lives.

Some educational television stations have for years been aiding their viewers directly. For example, in one state alone, educational television programs made it possible for over 500,000 adults to pass their high school equivalency tests. But because of new resources expected to be made available through satellite communication and cable television, educational television programming is sure to extend and broaden learning opportunities:

■ There will be regular telecasting of specific courses in many disciplines—in composition, literature, history, geography, biology, and algebra, for example. Viewers who choose to do so will be able to take such televised courses for academic credit.

Teleconferences make possible face-to-face communication between individuals or groups separated by considerable distances.

- There will be informative programs aired regularly for viewers in isolated areas and for viewers who are incapacitated in one way or another.

- There will be facilities available for teleconferences—visual hookups linking several parties separated by considerable distances. Teleconferences will permit ongoing discussions of matters of concern to specific groups—educators, for instance, or doctors, business managers, or lawyers.

- There will be some remarkable facilities available to the high school student of the future. Consider this hypothetical case:

> Tom, a high school junior, is prodded, threatened, and cajoled by his parents to "sit down in front of the television screen and do your homework." Tom sits down in a plastic carrel with a screen in front of him and consoles on three sides. A "Viewdata" magazine on cable Channel E scrolls slowly up the screen, listing the evening's programs. Tom sees that the documentary he has been assigned to view appears on Channel N. He switches to that channel but elects to tape the program on his video cassette recorder and watch it later. He then reaches for what looks like a thick, silvery phonograph record—a videodisk—and clamps it into a playback machine that scans it with a laser. Swiveling his

chair to the other side of his carrel, Tom switches on a micro-computer that itself has a pale-green screen. He presses a command key on the keyboard and a question appears on the screen: "Which frame would you like to review?" Tom replies by keyboarding a five-digit number, and a set of multiple-choice questions appears on his screen. He answers each question by keyboarding his response, and the computer punches out a card showing his score. Satisfied with his performance, Tom then turns to the tape he made earlier of the history documentary and watches that attentively. Thus does Tom "do" his homework.

These are some of the ways, then, that television can be used to advantage in the education of millions of our people.

Computer Communication

We have already seen that computers are used for composing and designing the pages of newspapers and magazines. Even more impressive are the prospects computers have for storing and retrieving information. Here, for example, is a preview of what communication by computer has in store for all of us:

On a typically rainy day in London, Mrs. Smythe-Effingham rises, makes morning tea, and . . . turns to her handsome, mahogany-trimmed Home Information Center—and the world is electronically hers.

On the breakfast table is a remote control unit—her link to up-to-the-minute news, stock-market reports, sports results, travel notes, recipes and, of course, the weather. Mrs. Smythe-Effingham has only to press a few buttons and the flow of information begins.

For example: To learn what is happening in the world she calls up "The World's First Electronic Newspaper" on the screen of her "telly." Up come the headlines of the day with a bulletin. The news is brought to her in eye-stopping color, each letter a different hue as if some child was watercoloring in the studio. Then, by pressing other numbers, she calls up individual news stories in detail.

As she sips her tea she reads background articles in the electronic newspaper's magazine section.

Virtually all that is in the morning paper—the printed paper—is now available to her on the screen of her set, including advertisements.

Shopping is on Mrs. Smythe-Effingham's mind. . . . A search of the directory turns up the number for a large discount store. She requests, electronically, information on fridges, and is given descriptions and prices for units offered. . . .

Feeling a bit confused by the number of boxes on the market, she presses more buttons and calls up the consumer service; it gives her ratings on the various units.

About this time her husband, Ian, comes down for his breakfast of kippers and eggs. "Nasty day, eh, luv?" he says by way of making early morning conversation. . . .

Ian Smythe-Effingham punches electronic buttons and gets the world news on the screen. Then he calls up the football scores and detailed stories of games. He reads avidly as he eats the kippers and eggs. . . .

"You'd better hurry and eat them, or you will miss your train."

"Yes, yes, and I had better find out how the trains are running today."

On the screen appears the schedule for British Rail with all of the information he needs for the ride he will take to his job in suburban London. . . .

Soon this remarkable Prestel communication system will expand from 150,000 to 500,000 "pages" or frames of information. (A frame is a 30-second display on the screen.)

Prestel came about in a curious way. The British Post Office had expected great success from its view-phone, the service that gave the telephone user a picture of the person at the other end of the line. Britons were cool to the idea and the post office commissioned Sam Fedida, an electronic genius, to find some way of using the idea. By combining the telephone line with television and

Home information centers make many kinds of information available to viewers.

computer, Fedida and his researchers came up with Prestel for homes and businesses.

What makes Prestel valuable to the subscriber is its versatility.

If Mrs. Smythe-Effingham and her husband decide to holiday in Scotland, they can ring up their telly not only for the weekend's weather forecast there, but also for availability of hotel rooms, transportation schedules, and travel conditions.

Some of the other services provided by Prestel include readings from a number of libraries, courses from the Open University, football scores from America, a list of Guinness records, and even a table of recommended restaurants, pubs and wine bars in London and in other English cities.

The systems are not without problems, however. An adapter for the television set now runs about $300, although promoters of Prestel say that figure soon will be reduced. The cost for each frame of information is low, but after a month of service the bill can be quite large. Of course, some of the commercial information comes free.

Then, too, there is the problem of what information should be made available to the public—whether some information should be censored before reaching home video screens.

The impact of the new service to the home and business office is yet to be fully measured.

One veteran British newsman, Alan Durrant, who edits the "World's First Electronic Newspaper" for the *Birmingham Post & Mail*, says that there is a revolution afoot for journalists, and that while the electronic newspaper may not kill the printed page, there will be massive and dramatic changes. Some say modestly that Prestel and the Home Information Center will simply be adjuncts to daily newspapers. Others warn that it could be the other way around.

"The 'Telly' Tells All," by Abe S. Chanin, *The Quill*, April 1981.

Electronic information-delivery systems like Prestel are becoming readily available to the average person. The future will undoubtedly see a rise in their use and a bright future for the mass communications industries.

A Communications Renaissance

Upon completing a study for the Rand Corporation on the future of communications in the United States, Ben H. Bagdikian stated that the content of news which affects our way of life so pervasively will be determined by the technology bringing that news to us. He further stated that this technology will result not in less but in more print—printed news and news analyses. The reason: History clearly demonstrates that the better educated a people are, the more they read.

For all news organizations, he concludes, there will be a . . .

vast increase in the scope of their news gathering, in the quantity as well as the speed of their intake of information; and there will be radically new methods of storing and selecting from this expanded reservoir, as well as an increasing versatility in presenting it to the consumer. For the consumer, there will be more control over what information he or she receives and over the timing and form of its arrival in the home.

Thus is the future sure to bring a momentous change in the lives of communicators and a new era in the availability of information to the consumer. Truly does the future promise a Communications Renaissance.

Activities

1. Participate actively in a class project to identify the various printing/publishing shops, the various radio/television stations, and computer companies in your community. (The kinds of establishments to identify are these: small hand-press printing shops, letterpress printing plants, offset printing plants, radio stations specializing in popular (or other kinds of) music, commercial television stations, public television stations, and manufacturers of computers or companies specializing in the storage and retrieval of computerized information.) With your classmates, establish student teams, each of which will visit one of the establishments identified. Planning each team's field trip should be carefully completed well in advance of the date of the trip. Bring back samples of the kinds of materials each establishment uses or produces. (Most companies are happy to provide them.) With your team, prepare and present a class report about your field trip. Develop a classroom (or school) display of the communications facilities in your community.

2. Prepare a television commercial for the year 2000. Help organize the class into small groups. Some students can draw stills, some can plan special effects, some can prepare copy, and some can actually present the commercial—perhaps as a skit. Then, in a class discussion, compare your commercial of the future with present-day television commercials. What major differences do you see between the two?

3. In what ways can the news media—print and nonprint— function as agents of change? In an essay of two or more pages, respond fully to that question.

4. What, in your opinion, is the most exciting development for the journalist of the future? In a short essay, explain your point of view.

5. What potential problems do you see for mass communication in the future? In an essay of two or more pages, respond to that question and explain your point of view.

PART 2

Roles
of the Journalist
in a Democratic
Society

CHAPTER 7

Reporting the News

The urgency in the voice of the police dispatcher catches the attention of the *Northern Star* city editor: "Car 16, proceed to the corner of Howard and Sweetbriar. Three-car collision; several injured. Ambulances and wreckers on the way."

The city editor, his brow furrowed, walks over to the desk of cub reporter Tim Herrmann. "There's been a bad accident at the corner of Howard and Sweetbriar, Tim. Liz Palmer is your photographer. She's getting her car and will meet you in front of the building."

Tim grabs his jacket and notepad. The editor doesn't have to go into detail on what he wants on this story. Tim already knows. His job will be to get the facts—the plain, indisputable facts—about the accident. And he knows, too, that his readers will want answers to questions like these: *Who* was involved? *What* happened? *When* did it happen? *Where* did it happen?, *Why* and *how* did it happen?

Arriving at the scene of the collision, Liz begins taking pictures, and Tim begins his work—finding out the *who, what, when, where, why,* and *how* of the event he's covering.

Approaching a police officer and showing his press card, Tim asks these questions: "How many were involved?" "How many were injured?" "What are their names?" "Where were the injured taken?" "How did the accident happen? And so it goes. From first to last, Tim asks the questions that will give him the answers his readers will be looking for.

While questioning the police officer, Tim notices that one of the drivers involved in the accident is unsteady as he walks toward his car. Had the driver been drinking? However, Tim would never suggest that possibility in his story. He knows that a first-rate reporter *never* expresses an opinion in a *straight news story*—the type he's covering now. An *editorial* writer might express an opinion about the fact that the driver in question was not given a sobriety test. But even in an *editorial*—known as *argumentative writing*—the writer would never accuse anyone of something that could not be proved in a court of law.

Like all conscientious reporters, Tim will write a straight news story that presents the facts—*who, what, where, when, why, how*—in a simple, straightforward manner. Then Tim will turn the story in to his editor.

Roles of the Journalist in a Democratic Society

The News Reporter

News stories vary in news value and in reader/listener/viewer appeal. News stories having the most news value are ordinarily those that appeal to the largest audience.

While it is true that a straight news story presents facts, not opinions, it is also true that news value is determined largely by what interests and holds the largest audience. Yet there are other considerations for reporters and editors to take into account. Because the news influences the thinking and the behavior of people in any community, the reporter cannot be content to cover only those stories that he or she *thinks* will interest readers and listeners and viewers. The alert, conscientious reporter goes much further, seeking out stories about the social awareness of people, stories that focus on the positive, constructive things people do, and stories that emphasize the public good. The alert, conscientious reporter senses an obligation to arouse popular interest in significant news even if there seems to be public indifference or apathy toward that news. At the same time, the alert, conscientious reporter must be a sharp questioner and a thorough researcher of facts.

The News Story Focus

Because reporters and news writers seek news stories that will interest as large an audience as possible, they are alert for any special appeals—known as "makers of news"—a story might have. That is, in reporting the story they seek to *focus* on some element or characteristic in the story that will increase its impact.

Human Interest

Journalists have long known that news stories dealing with the basic human needs—food, clothing, shelter, affection, recognition, and new experience—hold great interest for most of us. News stories focusing on these human needs are "human-interest" stories, and they involve one or more of the following: romance, ambition, humor, sympathy, love, hate, fear, jealousy, vanity, and generosity. A good human-interest story, for example, might chronicle the events leading up to and following the reunion of two seventy-year-old sisters who had been separated in infancy.

The situation pictured here could be the basis of a human-interest story.

Immediacy

News is perishable. Old news lacks the interest of current news. The fresher the news, the more likely it is to capture public interest. That's one reason why metropolitan newspapers publish several editions daily. That's also one reason why radio and television stations air several news "roundups" every day and break into scheduled programs with special bulletins.

Newspapers that are published weekly or monthly often present, as news, information that is not timely. Many newspapers' editors avoid publishing untimely news by becoming informed in advance about events planned to take place when the paper is published. For instance, background articles are often presented about films scheduled to begin when the paper comes out. Important stories that break after a paper's deadline are usually given feature treatment in later editions.

Roles of the Journalist in a Democratic Society

Proximity

A reporter/news writer may cover a story about personalities and issues relevant to the interests of the people living in the immediate community. Many people have more interest in news about themselves, their families, and their friends than about unfamiliar people and unfamiliar situations.

Prominence

News stories about celebrities make good copy, for most of us enjoy news about famous personalities. Human behavior is harder to interpret than fact, and readers/listeners/viewers respond to news about people in a more emotional way than they respond to news about events. In writing straight news stories about people, good news writers remain objective; they guard against expressing personal feelings and prejudices. Editors are constantly on guard against news items that contain innuendo, gossip, libel, or slander about prominent people.

News stories about prominent people make good copy.

Conflict

A news story that focuses on conflict is almost sure to spark interest. If the story involves verbal confrontation, the persons involved should be quoted accurately. For example, if one party to the conflict mangles the English language, good reporters do not correct the mistakes. Instead, they use direct quotations and report the speaker's exact words.

To obtain background material on any conflict, first-rate reporters/news writers thoroughly research several sources for reliability and accuracy of facts. They also try to be as objective as possible by presenting the *what* on all sides of the dispute. Then, with careful handling, they take the *why* approach to both the situation and the various arguments advanced. Objectivity—always necessary in unbiased news reporting—is especially important when reporters cover news events based on conflict.

Emotion

Though good newswriting is neither sentimental nor melodramatic, it can appeal to the emotions. News stories can evoke fear, anger, disgust, grief, joy, surprise, or yearning—or a combination of those emotions. Reporter/news writers who focus their stories on emotional experiences might ask those involved to describe their feelings in detail. For example, an "emotion" story could

Conflict can be the basis of a news story.

A story about a sight-impaired student is certain to evoke emotion.

concern a handicapped student who, having overcome incredible obstacles just to attend school, wins a first prize in chemistry at the State Science Fair. The reporter could ask the student how he or she felt while awaiting the judges' decision, as the winners' names were announced, and, later, when being congratulated by the teacher who had supplied some much-needed encouragement. "Emotion" stories often have the power to inspire others to achieve—or at least to appreciate what they have.

Consequence

It is important for reporters/news writers to become well informed about social problems and issues that make a difference in the lives of their readers/listeners/viewers. Noted columnist Bob Considine has remarked that, second only to the clergy, news reporters have an opportunity to help their communities to develop a sense of values. By squarely facing such problems as how to keep up with inflation or how to elect honest public officials, and by bringing those concerns to the attention of the public, reporters/news writers can help the people in their communities determine the direction they want their lives to take.

Gathering the News

News Sources

News, to be sure, occurs wherever reporters find it. Yet few, if any, reporters can pick up unrelated facts at random and expect them to constitute material for an interesting news story. The job of gathering usable news for any of the mass media calls, instead, for an awareness of news values, an ability to select an appropriate focus, and an ability to organize facts logically.

The reporter who has an assigned beat has a ready-made news source. Sometimes a reporter just happens upon a situation or an event that will make a good news story. But an alert, astute reporter will develop close friendships with people who are themselves interesting enough to make news. Such people are likely to become important sources of information and thus sources of news stories.

Printable and Unprintable News

Printable news consists of accurate information about ideas, events, and people. Stories about them need to be written as invitingly as possible in order to interest a large and varied audience. A news story that has been well thought out, logically organized, and clearly presented is sure to attract many people who, under other circumstances, might consider a news story on the topic dull and boring.

If the definition of news as "timely information of interest to many people," then there is no such thing as *unprintable* news. However, there is such a thing as unprintable rumor, unprintable libel, unprintable falsehood, and unprintable malice. Reporters and editors—students and professionals alike—have a responsibility to refuse to write or publish news stories that are inaccurate, unfair, one-sided, or in poor taste. Responsible journalism has no place for any person who is inaccurate, irresponsible, foulmouthed, or malicious. Chapter 13, "Preserving a Free but Responsible Press," has more to say on the matter. (See page 272.)

Writing the News

Read the following news story, carefully noting the placement of facts in each paragraph:

Free Tennis Lessons

Youngsters from eight to fourteen who want to learn to play tennis can receive free lessons on Saturday mornings from 9 to 11 at the L. J. Brooks Building, West 4th Street, South End. The lessons will begin on June 10, according to Parks and Recreation Director Donald M. Johns, and will be supervised by Coach LeRoy H. Smith, former Olympics tennis coach.

The instruction is intended for city children interested in learning and developing tennis skills. Funds from Project Inner-City have been set aside for equipment and facilities.

Coach Smith advises interested participants to register early. A large turnout is expected.

Had the preceding straight news story appeared in a metropolitan daily, the average reader would have read only the first paragraph, which contains most of the important facts of the story. The opening paragraph tells *who* is concerned in the story —"youngsters from eight to fourteen." It tells *what* the story is about—free tennis lessons." It tells *when*—"from 9 to 11" on Saturday mornings beginning June 10. The *where* is answered by the words "at the L. J. Brooks Building, West 4th Street, South End," and the *why* is explained by the words "who want to learn to play tennis." The reader will understand the *how* from "supervised by Coach LeRoy H. Smith." In short, the *who, what, when, where, why,* and *how* are summarized in the first paragraph. This first section is called the *lead.* For a short news story, the lead generally appears in the first paragraph; in longer news stories it is often contained in the first two or three paragraphs.

After reading the first paragraph of the news story about tennis lessons, the reader may have some unanswered questions concerning the facts given in the lead. The second and third paragraphs extend the *what* by giving details about supporting funds and by giving more information about the tennis lessons themselves. The *where* is obvious and needs no explanation. The news writer wishing to make the story longer might have expanded on the *why* by giving further details concerning the need for tennis lessons and perhaps by supplying more information about Coach Smith and the Parks and Recreation Department.

This example makes it clear that the body of the story is developed logically through the addition of more details about points connected with or mentioned in the lead. The paragraphs are arranged in descending order of importance of details. The following checklist notes the essential characteristics of the straight news story form, whether the story is a routine editorial assignment for the reporter/news writer or a resourceful discovery of his or her own.

CHECKLIST FOR MAJOR ELEMENTS IN A STRAIGHT NEWS STORY

✓ In a straight news story all of the important facts are summarized in the first section, or lead. The lead is often presented in only one sentence or paragraph.

✓ The body of the story consists of facts that amplify or add to the statements in the lead. Usually these facts answer questions that come naturally to the reader's mind after reading the lead.

✓ Within the body of the news story, facts are arranged in descending order of importance, least important facts coming last.

The Inverted Pyramid Style

The typical straight news story, as may be evident from the checklist above, has an inverted pyramid form, with the most important facts appearing first and the least important appearing last. Note the following example:

The Lead—a summary of all important facts.

Leonard Schwartz, noted authority on teenage crime, will be the guest speaker at Thursday's all-student assembly in Hickman Auditorium.

The Body—details of secondary importance in descending order of importance.

In his talk Mr. Schwartz, author of "Teenage Crime in Our Cities," will compare American teenagers with European teenagers.

Recently returned from Europe, Mr. Schwartz has been making a speaking tour of the country's leading schools and colleges.

There will be a brief question-and-answer period following Mr. Schwartz's talk.

Straight news stories that exemplify the inverted pyramid form —the most conventional arrangement for all news stories—do so for the following reasons: They are easier to shorten because material can be deleted from the end. Readers in a hurry can "get the facts" just by reading the lead. The inverted pyramid tells the story in a "natural" way. The inverted pyramid reflects our modern society—a society that is concerned with getting the basic facts as quickly as possible rather than with details.

Writing the Lead

The most important part of the straight news story is a clear, concise statement that presents the basic facts of the story. This statement is called the lead. If the lead is weak or fails to present the basic facts of the story, the story usually fails in encouraging the reader to read the rest of the story.

Types of Leads

The three types of news story leads are (1) the major-idea lead, (2) the summary lead, and (3) a combination of the two. In deciding which lead to use, the writer first weighs each of the facts obtained for the story. Then the writer asks a question like this: "Which of the facts best suggests the focus of the story—the approach that is the best 'maker of news'?" (See pages 143-148.) Each of the "makers of news" is analyzed from the standpoint of reader interest. After deciding on the best approach, the writer then asks a second question: Which of the five *w*'s and the *h* is most important to the reader/listener/viewer?"

The Major-Idea Lead. If, of all the facts obtained for a story, one fact seems far more important than the others, the writer should use this fact in the lead. The others will be used later in the story or discarded.

The Student Council voted Monday to charge a $5 student fee.

The Summary Lead. If several facts are of about equal value, the writer should briefly combine these facts in the lead:

The Student Council proposed Monday a $5 student fee, the establishment of a History Club, and a change in the name of the school newspaper.

The Combination Lead. On occasion, the reporter may start the first sentence with the major idea and then elaborate on the other facts in the rest of the sentence.

Students will pay a $5 student fee as a result of Monday's action by the Student Council, which also proposed formation of a History Club and a change in the school newspaper's name from *The Record* to *The Jacksonian*.

In the following news story, written in the form in which it was turned in to the editor, the lead has been identified, along with every other important element in the story. To become thoroughly familiar with journalistic style and procedures, you'll want to study the news story carefully.

Goldie
Herrmann
Somerset Journal
The object of one of the largest
searches in Cook County's history, Goldie Lox,
was found unharmed in Schiller Woods Monday
evening.
More than 500 volunteers combed the woods for
five hours after Goldie, 11, daughter of Mr.
and Mrs. Jason Lox of 1525 N. Grove St.,
Norridge, failed to return home from school.
Searchers using bloodhounds from
the Cook County Sheriff's Office located Goldie
sleeping in a small cave on the bank of the
Des Plaines River near the center of the forest
preserve.
She was examined and released from
West Suburban Hospital. Doctors said that,
though unharmed, Goldie suffered from ex-
haustion and from a persistent delusion that
she was abducted by bears and hidden in
their den.
Goldie is a 5th grader at Hitch
Elementary School in the West End of Norridge.
She is the youngest of three children.
Her two brothers, Tom, 16, and Jerry, 14,
joined in the search andd were on the scene
when Goldie was found.

-30-

These reporters are working in a busy newsroom.

Newswriting Mechanics

Most news writers follow these general rules when preparing news material:

1. Use 8 1/2 by 11 unlined paper, leaving a one-inch margin on both sides, top, and bottom.

2. Type your name and a slug line (story identification, usually a word or two summarizing the story) at the top left-hand corner of the page.

3. Type the name of the publication under this information.

Jones, Charles
Student Proposal
Wendona Journal

4. Begin the body copy for the first page about one third of the way down from the top of the page. The editor will later use this space for the story headlines and for printer's instructions.

5. Double- or triple-space the body copy so that there will be room to edit between the lines.

6. If the story takes more than one page, type the word *more* at the foot of the first page. At the top left-hand corner of page two, repeat the slug line and add the manuscript page number 2 or "page 2 of two pages" or "add 2." If the story runs longer than two pages, repeat this procedure (changing page numbers) at the foot and the top of each page.

7. Indicate the end of the article by typing the word *end* or by using symbols such as -0-0-0- or ##### or 30 on a separate line.

Elements of Style in Newswriting

The written word is the news writer's medium. Because the basic interest is to communicate, the news writer must be proficient in writing. Most news writers develop a style that is simple, concise, and lucid. Which one of the following sentences gets the message across more effectively? Which elements of style—simplicity, conciseness, lucidity—make better news copy?

1. Each of the teachers shall endeavor to notify all of the student violators that they (the student violators) are to consider themselves suspended until they receive a notice of readmission from the principal's office.

2. Teachers should make this announcement: If students are suspended, they should not return to school until they receive notification from the principal's office.

Sometimes news writers inadvertently write something they do not mean. Results may be humorous and/or disastrous. What errors in structure cause confusion in the following sentences? How would you reword each sentence to clarify its meaning?

1. They worked with a shovel in one hand, and a gun in the other, and a Bible in the other.

2. John Larson said he found France a wonderful country, especially the museums. When he stood in the Louvre, he had really thought he was in paradise until he turned and saw his wife standing by his side.

3. It won't be real Irish stew unless you put your heart into it.

4. No one can take anything from the bookshelves but a librarian.

5. The new reporter wanted to write very badly.

A Style Book

Reporters would seldom finish a story if they had to stop after each word or so to ask their editors (1) how to spell a word, (2) whether it should be capitalized, or (3) whether it could be abbreviated. Proper newsroom practice dictates that reporters do their own work and avoid bothering others. Of course, reporters know that they can consult a dictionary for the spelling of a word, but a dictionary doesn't explain when a word should be capitalized or abbreviated. Thus, questions like these arise: Should the name of a state be abbreviated when used with a city? Should *principal* be capitalized when it is used as a title? If the principal's name is John Smith, Junior, should the word *junior* be abbreviated? capitalized? preceded by a comma?

Ralph Waldo Emerson wrote that "a foolish consistency is the hobgoblin of little minds." Nevertheless, reporters and editors know the importance of being consistent. They know that readers will have less confidence in a newspaper if a principal's name appears as "John Smith, Jr." in one paragraph and as "John Smith Junior" in another. To help staff members conform to a consistent style, most professional newspapers and many school publications have adopted the rules of the Associated Press. The rules are simply conventions that everyone observes in order to facilitate understanding and reduce confusion.

Spelling in General. English spelling is often difficult because some words sound different from what you might expect. The pronunciation of *ough*, for example, has a different sound in each of the following: *tough, though,* and *through*. The vowel sounds for *ouch* and *owl* are the same, but the letter combinations representing the sounds are different. Errors in spelling can change the meaning of a sentence—sometimes disastrously:

> Miss Davenport wore her great-grandmother's bridle outfit and the groom was attired in mourning dress.

Spelling mistakes can confuse meaning, distract the reader, and hamper reading speed. Spelling errors often result from carelessness, reluctance to check a dictionary, and failure to proofread copy thoroughly. Writing is a skill, and good newswriting is the result of a discipline that has no room for carelessness. On page 156 is a list of 100 frequently misspelled words. How many of them are words you're sure you won't misspell?

Spelling of Possessives. To form the singular possessive, add an apostrophe and an *s:*

> She does her homework on her brother's new typewriter.

When a singular or plural noun already ends in s, you can simply add an apostrophe after the *s:*

> It was Lars' typewriter that she used.
> This particular species' popular name is Princess Lila.

100 Frequently Misspelled Words

accessible	disappearance	judgment	repetition
accidentally	discernible	leisure	resistance
accommodate	discipline	likable	sacrilegious
accumulate	dissatisfied	mischievous	salable
adviser	drought	missile	seize
affect	effect	misspell	separate
all right	efficient	ninety	siege
beginning	exaggerate	necessary	sizable
benefited	excellent	noticeable	skiing
business	exhaust	observer	soluble
candidate	friend	occasion	sophomore
ceiling	gaiety	occurred	subtle
changeable	government	offense	supersede
colossal	grammar	parallel	surprise
column	grievance	paraphernalia	temperamental
compatible	harass	permissible	tendency
competent	height	picnicking	tragedy
conquer	hygiene	precede	transmitter
consistency	hypocrisy	preventive	tying
controlled	inadmissible	privilege	usable
criticism	incalculable	procedure	useful
deity	innuendo	proceed	uncontrollable
dependent	inoculate	questionnaire	villain
despair	interrupt	recommend	weird
dining	irreligious	rehearsal	writing

However, the sound of the word ending in *s* and the need for clarity sometimes make it preferable to use the apostrophe and an *s:*

Mrs. Jones's new puppy is a spaniel.

To form the plural possessive of nouns ending in s, simply add an apostrophe:

The officers' names on the artists' petitions were submitted at the engineers' ball.

Many students have trouble with the possessive form of the pronoun *it*. That form is *its—spelled without an apostrophe*.

> The dog wagged its tail.

An apostrophe and an *s* are added to the pronoun it only when you use the contraction *it's*, which stands for *it is* or it *has*.

> It's time to go.
> It's been a long time since dinner.

Hyphenation of Compound Words. Modern news writers hyphenate two or more words when they are used in combination as one word:

> The pilot of the twin-engine plane began to lose radio contact with the tower.
> Mary is quick-witted.

Twin-engine has a hyphen because the two words are used as a single adjective to modify *plane*. *Quick-witted* has a hyphen because the two words are used as one (as predicate adjective) to modify *Mary*.

Over the years many words that were once spelled with hyphens have lost those hyphens and are today spelled as single words. *Teenage, goodbye, today,* and *cooperate* are examples. It is always wise, of course, to consult a dictionary when problems involving the hyphen arise. To avoid inconsistencies, many publications have their own style sheet, listing the publication's usage preference for the spelling of problem words.

Capitalization. Capitalize courtesy titles preceding persons' names; lowercase courtesy titles following persons' names:

> The announcement was made by Principal John Petry.
> John Petry, principal, made the announcement.
> Marie Gomez, Senior Class president, is here.
> Senior Class President Marie Gomez is here.

But—

> It was a miracle that guard Bill Ray wasn't injured.
> The principal presented the scholarship to art major Jane Abbott.

Capitalize academic grade designations only when referring to a specific class as a group; lowercase academic grade designations when referring to individuals:

> The Sophomore Class meets on Thursday.
> Beth Moresby is a junior this year.

Capitalize *high school* only when used as part of the name of a specific school:

> Their children go to Madison Park High School.
> Joe's high school grades are excellent.

Abbreviations. Abbreviate the name of a state when it is used in conjunction with a community in that state:

> The family lived in Wheeling, W. Va.
> The city of Portland, Ore., is south of the Columbia River.

But note these exceptions: *Alaska, Hawaii, Idaho, Iowa, Maine, Ohio, Texas,* and *Utah* (the eight states having fewer than seven letters in their names) should not be abbreviated.

Lowercase the abbreviations for the words *antemeridian* and *postmeridian*.

> The pep rally begins at 7 p.m. on Friday.

Avoid redundancies like the following:

> The pep rally begins at 7 p.m. on Friday evening.
> They'll leave for Mexico at 8 a.m. next Monday morning.

Punctuation of Direct Quotations. Enclose direct quotations within quotation marks. The end-of-sentence punctuation precedes the final quotation marks:

> "Tom is the editor," the adviser said, "and policy decisions are up to him."
> "Where," asked the hall monitor, "are you going?"

To punctuate one quotation within another, use single quotation marks for the internal quotation and double quotation marks for the overall quotation:

> Alice lamented, "The editor shouted, 'You missed the photo!' "

Why is the punctuation in the next sentence different from the punctuation in the first example in this section?

> The adviser said that Tom is the editor and policy decisions are up to him.

Punctuation of Nonrestrictive Clauses. You can substitute *not* for the prefix *non* and the word *essential* for *restrictive* when referring to nonrestrictive and restrictive clauses. Use commas to set off a clause that is not essential to the meaning of a sentence. That is to say, if the sentence makes sense without the clause, then you use commas. If the clause is essential to the meaning of the sentence, do not use commas. Note the following examples:

The reporter, *who is the backbone of the newspaper* staff, has a responsibility to the community.

Because the clause *who is the backbone of the newspaper staff* simply gives additional information and so is not essential to the meaning of the basic sentence, it is a nonrestrictive clause and is set off by commas.

The reporter *who cannot type* is at a disadvantage.

Deleting the restrictive clause *who cannot type* leaves *The reporter is at a disadvantage,* thus changing the meaning of the original sentence. Without the clause, the sentence suggests (erroneously) that every reporter is at a disadvantage. The clause is a restrictive clause; no commas are used.

Agreement of Subject and Verb. The verb in every sentence must agree in number and person with the subject. Singular subject, singular verb; plural subject, plural verb. Confusion about agreement often arises when the subject is compound:

The old news clipping and the photograph that Emily found in the attic *were* musty and faded with age.

A careless writer might be tempted to change *were* to *was.* Why would doing so be a mistake?

The verb in a sentence agrees with its subject, no matter how many words come between them:

Bert Lowry, the basketball coach, as well as three assistant coaches and ten players, is ready to meet Central High School in the playoffs.

Dangling Participles. What difference in meaning do you find between the two sentences following?

I saw the monkey hanging from the chandelier.
Hanging from the chandelier, I saw the monkey.

In the second sentence, who is hanging from the chandelier? Obviously, the speaker—the *I.* But that's not very likely. In short, the speaker does not mean what he or she said. As the sentence is constructed, the participle hanging modifies the subject of the sentence—*I.* But because the meaning conveyed by that construction is ridiculous, we say that the participle "dangles." Here's another example of a dangling participle:

Running down the street, Pop's false teeth fell out.

What this sentence says is ridiculous. The meaning can be clarified as follows:

> Running down the street, Pop lost his false teeth.

or

> As Pop was running down the street, his false teeth fell out.

or

> Pop's false teeth fell out as he was running down the street.

Competent reporters/news writers always make sure that their participles don't dangle!

Misplaced Modifiers. The reporter who wrote the sentence below received a curt reprimand from the editor. Why?

> George Bennett little realized why his ancestors emigrated to America before he tried to trace them.

The editor was justifiably irate because the adverbial clause *before he tried to trace them* modifies the verb *emigrated*, thereby making what the sentence says absurd. The clause, of course, should modify the verb *realized*. The reporter can clarify the meaning simply by shifting the adverbial clause as follows:

> Before he tried to trace his ancestors, George Bennett little realized why they emigrated to America.

Modifiers in sentences need to be placed so that they *clearly* modify the words that logic shows they must modify.

Fragments. Why does the following clause leave you with a sense of incompleteness?

> While at the same time proposing long-range reforms to improve housing, health, civil rights, and to curb the rising crime rate throughout the country.

This fragment can be changed into a main clause or complete sentence by taking out one word, adding one word, and changing one verb ending.

> At the same time Congress proposes long-range reforms to improve housing, health, civil rights, and to curb the rising crime rate throughout the country.

Run-on Sentences. Every sentence deserves to have its own identity. Every sentence deserves to close with the intonation (if the sentence is spoken) or the punctuation (if the sentence is written) that indicates the completion of its thought. Sometimes, out of ignorance or carelessness, writers ignore that principle and confuse their readers/listeners with constructions like these:

Be careful, you never know what's around the next corner.
Mom's not home, she's out shopping.

Each of these two sentences expresses two separate thoughts. They should thus be punctuated accordingly:

Be careful. You never know what's around the next corner.

or

Be careful; you never know what's around the next corner.
Mom's not home. She's out shopping.

or

Mom's not home; she's out shopping.

Conciseness. Avoid using a phrase or a clause if a single word can convey the same idea. For example, instead of writing "tendered his resignation," write "resigned." What phrase in the following sentence could be expressed by one word?

The couple was united in holy matrimony yesterday.

Avoid using flowery, high-flown language:

As my paternal parent was wending his way homeward from the domicile of an old and true friend last evening, he encountered two young gentlemen of a musical persuasion, playing stringed instruments known as guitars. (35 words)

What the writer of the sentence above is saying is this:

As my father was walking home from a friend's house last night, he met two boys playing guitars. (18 words)

Simple, straightforward sentences are much easier to understand than are pretentious, overblown sentences.

Miscellaneous Concerns. In general, use arabic numerals when referring to whole numbers over ten.

There are exactly 1987 students enrolled in this school.
We are taking six courses.

Exceptions:

At 8 p.m. all the lights went out. (Time)
Miranda and Gregory are in the second grade. (Sequence)

Use courtesy titles (*Mr., Mrs., Miss* or *Ms.*) when referring to members of the administration, faculty, or staff.

Guidelines for Rewriting

In the preparation of any article for a newspaper or magazine, or in preparing copy for an advertisement or public-relations brochure, the average writer usually makes at least two revisions before submitting a story to the editor. After conferring with the editor about the article, the writer may wish to revise still further. In rewriting, the writer should correct any mistakes in spelling, grammar, and punctuation. Tim Cohane, professional writer, gives his students the following guidelines for rewriting:

1. Eliminate every word not necessary for clarity or grace. Rewrite to eliminate verbosity.

2. Check all verb forms to make certain that you have used the active voice as often as possible. Use the passive voice when you want to emphasize the result of an action.

3. If the situation calls for the passive, the verb *to be*, or the expression *OK*, use it. But first, examine the entire situation carefully.

4. Check your paragraphs carefully to see if they are in the proper order. Does paragraph 6 belong up between paragraphs 2 and 3? Perhaps paragraph 8 will make a stronger lead than the lead you have. If so, don't hesitate to change it. Whenever paragraph sequence poses a major problem, consider scissoring each paragraph, and then rearrange the separated paragraphs on the table like blocks.

5. Check the sentences within each paragraph to make sure the thoughts are in the proper sequence. Numbering the sentences can prove helpful.

6. Check every sentence closely to see whether it can be invigorated by placing the main thought at the end.

7. Check transitions between sentences and paragraphs. Are they as smooth and as immediate as you can make them? Transition probably contributes more to smoothness than any other single factor.

8. Never hesitate to strive for the offbeat, the unorthodox, the picturesque. No matter how many times you fall on your face reaching, pick yourself up and try again. First, however, get it clearly in mind what you want to accomplish. Get a true picture of the picture, and see whether it is going to work. Your chances of bringing off the picturesque are much better once you have become acquainted with form—and the best way to learn form is first to learn how to put things clearly and simply.

9. Be conscious of the value of parallel forms, but don't overuse them. Don't overuse anything. Writing is nothing without variety. Without variety, the sound of writing becomes a dull thumping.

Roles of the Journalist in a Democratic Society

News Briefs

Since names make news, editors often use a number of news briefs that include names. Such news briefs are usually one or two sentences long and are often used to fill news columns.

Many editors use news briefs to relieve the monotony of long news stories.

A sophomore beat out the upperclassmen in the math competition as Dave LeMaster earned the top score of 58.25. Senior Bill Lipp finished second.

Writing Captions

Captions (sometimes called cutlines) are the identifying lines of print accompanying photographs and illustrations. If an illustration is used without an accompanying article, the story must be briefly told in the caption using the five *w's* and the *h*. The reporter writing captions must be careful with identifications and the spelling of names, always double-checking to make sure the right name has been used and that it is spelled correctly.

Student Council officers for next year were installed at a ceremony May 14 in the auditorium. From left to right, the new officers are Tom L. Jurkowski, treasurer; Marilee Wilson, secretary; Marie Spinaldo, vice-president; and Martin J. McGee, president.

Newswriting for the Broadcast Media

The major difference between writing for the broadcast media and the print media is the length of the story. After covering a major story for a newspaper, a reporter may write 1000 words or more, but the newscaster may use only a dozen sentences to summarize the same event. The news writer for the broadcast media must write with the listener and the viewer in mind and, therefore, must use simple, direct terms. The news writer usually does not place the most important facts at the beginning of the story but places them later to be sure to hold the listener's and the viewer's attention.

Radio

Like the newspaper reporter, the radio news reporter arriving at the scene of an event must first secure the answers to the five *w's* and the *h*. He or she might then tape-record the voices of those involved, attempting to have these people tell the story in their own words. The reporter writes a "lead-in" as an introduction to the story, summarizing the main points. In the conclusion the radio reporter again summarizes the major events—but in more detail—and adds any additional details or developments necessary for a complete presentation of the facts.

Television

Writing for television news programs is similar to writing for radio news programs. There is, however, a difference in coverage. Instead of using a tape recorder, the television reporter uses a camera. Often, of course, the reporter takes a camera operator along to film the entire scene and to film witnesses as they talk with the reporter. The television newscaster writes the news story in the same way that the radio news writer does. The television news reporter may be "on camera" for but a few seconds, usually during the story lead and possibly again at the story's conclusion. As the television news reporter tells the story, the viewer sees the scenes being described. Then the eyewitnesses tell their stories, and finally the reporter reappears for the conclusion or "wrap-up."

Activities

1. There are seven different "makers of news"—seven different focuses that can be given a news story. (See pages 143–148.) From a newspaper or a newsmagazine, find, clip, and bring to class at least five straight news stories, each of which exemplifies a different news story focus. In class, be prepared to exhibit your news stories, to explain the focus of at least one, and to defend your point of view.

2. With a group of three or more classmates, combine and catalog all of the news stories that were brought to class as a part of Activity 1 above. Then develop a classroom news story reference file, wherein examples of each of the seven makers of news are readily accessible.

3. From a newspaper, clip a story of six or more paragraphs written in the inverted pyramid style. Mount the story on a sheet of notebook or typing paper. Underline the lead. Then, below the story, use as few words as possible to summarize the main idea in each of the remaining paragraphs. Next, examine each summary statement. Is the information given in Statement 3 less important than that given in Statement 2? Is Statement 4 less important than that given in Statement 3? And so on. Would you agree that the news story has been written in an inverted pyramid style? Explain.

4. From newspapers and magazines select one news story that best demonstrates the inverted pyramid style. Cut out each paragraph of the story. On the back of each piece, number its order of importance in the story, starting with 1, 2, etc. Scramble the paragraphs and bring them to class for other class members to arrange in the correct order of importance.

5. From a newspaper, clip three short news stories. Mount each one on a separate sheet of paper. Underline the lead in each news story. Below each clipping, write the five *w's* and the *h* in this order: Who? What? When? Where? Why? How?
After each question, supply the answer you find in the information given in the lead. If the answer to any of the five *w's* or the *h* is not supplied in the lead, circle the unanswered question. Bring your three analyzed news stories to class. Compare your analyses with the lead analyses your classmates bring in.

6. Compile a list of subject areas and topics you think your school newspaper should deal with. Then, conduct an informal survey to find out what topics other students want to read about in the school newspaper. From this combined information compile a master list of topics and issues you can submit to your school newspaper editor.

7. Discuss the student relevance of each topic and the possible methods of fact-finding for each topic contained in the master list prepared for Activity 2. Choose the one topic that most interests you and carry out a fact-finding mission, checking for the possibility of any previously published source material. Bring your notes to class and discuss any problems you might have encountered.

CHAPTER 8

Interviewing

Kelley Sturm, young reporter for the *Los Angeles Examiner*, requested and obtained an appointment to talk with visiting Broadway producer Josh Greene. Here's a part of the interview:

Question: How is *Annie* doing at the National Theater in Washington, D.C., Mr. Greene?

Answer: Great! We're sold out—every performance!

Question: How long has the show been running there?

Answer: Five weeks.

Question: Are you still planning to close the show in Washington in a couple of weeks and bring it out here to Los Angeles?

Answer: That's a good question. The show's grossing about $35,000 a performance. And it looks as if it'll keep up that way for the next two months at least.

Question: But the show is scheduled to open here in Los Angeles in four weeks, isn't it?

Answer: That *was* the plan. But because the show is doing so well in Washington, we're thinking of cancelling our engagement here—or perhaps *postponing* is a better word. . . .

And so it goes.

© Punch/Rothco

Every day reporters ask questions of specific individuals whose replies can make news. Of the many ways of gathering and disseminating information for the mass media, the interview is one of the most productive. Straight news stories sometimes leave unanswered the detailed questions people might want to ask about a news event. Readers/listeners/viewers rely on journalists to supply the desired information—frequently as a result of interviews.

Types of Interviews

Whether printed in newspapers and magazines or aired on radio and television, interviews come in several formats: fact interview, roving-reporter interview, question-and-answer interview, biographical interview, historical interview, descriptive interview, the personality interview, specialist interview, and composite interview.

The Fact Interview

The journalist's purpose in conducting a fact interview is to obtain information about a news event—information that might shed new light and so be of general interest to the reading/listening/viewing public. To obtain the facts concerning a news event —an accident, let's say—a reporter would interview victims (when possible), hospital attendants, police officers, witnesses, and any others involved. The more facts the reporter can obtain from interviews, the better the news story—printed or broadcast—will be. Unless such as story is based on clearly defined facts, it will quickly lose its interest and validity.

The Roving-Reporter Interview

People have an interest in the attitudes and reactions of "average" citizens on controversial issues and timely topics. The news media often sample public opinion by conducting "on-the-street" interviews with passers-by chosen at random. Basically, this kind of interview involves asking a number of people the same question(s). Radio/television reporters frequently tape their interviews for later broadcast. Newspaper and magazine reporters write up and publish the accounts of their interviews, sometimes as sidebars to straight news stories.

A newspaper account of a roving-reporter interview might look something like this:

Question: What do you think of the proposed increase in bus fares?

Answer from Harold Wilson, senior citizen: "I don't like it. It'll cost me more to come into town, and so I guess I'll have to spend more time at home."

Answer from Annabelle Quinn, secretary: "Fares were bound to be increased, what with inflation and all. But even with the increase, I'll still take the bus. It's less expensive than driving into town every day and paying to park."

The Question-and-Answer Interview

Although straight news stories seek to present the facts, many readers/listeners/viewers prefer to "judge for themselves" by reading or listening to the remarks made in question-and-answer interviews (also called public interviews). As a rule, a question-and-answer interview involves the questioning of a prominent person by one or more persons. If the interview is intended for airing on radio or television, there may be as many as four asking questions. Examples of televised question-and-answer interviews are *Meet the Press, Face the Nation,* and *Issues and Answers.*

If a question-and-answer interview is intended for newspaper or magazine publication, the reporter/interviewer must make sure that the questions asked are sharp and clear and that the responses are accurately reported. Frequently, an "Editor's Note" giving the necessary background about the interviewee will precede the transcript of the actual interview.

Question-and-answer interviews follow one of two formats. In one, there are no restrictions on the topics introduced for discussion or on the questions put to the interviewee. In the other, questions are limited to previously agreed-on topics. But with either format, the interviewer must have clearly in mind the questions to ask.

Editor's Note: Citizen Advocate Thomas Paine Elliott, for reasons of his own, agreed to the following exclusive interview. The subjects covered are political and personal.

By Angela Norton

Question: Mister Advocate, granted you've recently been ill, isn't it a fact that there's some merit to the charge you've lost interest in your job?

Answer: Yes, I've been ill. Beyond that—well, I have to say Citizen Advocate isn't the most exciting job on Farris Hill. Interest waxes and wanes.

Q: I'll go further. There is talk you're interested in a judgeship. I've heard a story that one of your aides has let it be known you'd resign your present office if you were appointed to the bench.

A: (Silence)

Q: I'm sorry—have I shocked you?

Menachim A. Begin, Israeli Prime Minister, is being questioned on NBC News' "Meet the Press" by reporters Marvin Kalb, Joseph Kraft, and Bill Munroe.

A: I'm thinking how to reply. You're asking me a complicated question there, more than one. First, do I want to be a judge; second, am I trying to barter the job I have for another.

Q: I wouldn't have put it quite that way.

A: The answer is that I've not given any serious thought to the judiciary. I mean beyond the kind of thought any and all lawyers give it. If you've ever practiced law, you've thought about the bench at some time.

Q: Yes? Is that your answer? That's a long silence you—

A: Are you asking another question?

Trading one job for another?

Q: More or less. I'm reporting there is a rumor that one of your aides is—

A: All right. Let me answer you this way. No one—aide, friend, associate—no one has been authorized to discuss my resignation, either as an isolated fact or in terms of some kind of political deal. Anyone doing that is operating without my permission, without, in fact—

Q: Your knowledge?

A: (Silence) I'll just leave it that I've heard the same rumor you have. And I'll rest on my statement. No one is authorized to deal on any basis with my resignation. . . .

If the questions are not direct and pointed, or if the interviewer depends on spur-of-the-moment inspiration to formulate questions, the interview is likely to be meandering and dull.

The Biographical Interview

An interview that focuses on a person's life is a biographical interview. Here, one person interviews another—usually a person who has lived an out-of-the-ordinary life.

"When I was at the University of Iowa, I decided to go into politics. A few years later, as a member of the Jeffersonville City Council, I ran successfully for the state legislature. But never in my wildest dreams did I ever think I would become a United States senator!" Donna Douglas, who yesterday became the youngest person to be elected to the United States Senate, sat at ease in her living room, talking about her life and aspirations. . . .

The Historical Interview

Reporters often consider doing a historical-interview story when they wish to bring the reader/listener/viewer up to date on an event that happened a number of years ago. In conducting the historical interview, the reporter seeks to make an "old" story timely. The following example was prepared by a student reporter who interviewed a chemistry teacher regarding a serious explosion that had taken place in the high school chemistry laboratory fifteen years before.

Fifteen years ago today an explosion in the Weirton High School chemistry lab resulted in serious injury to five students. The tragedy was recalled last week by Mr. J. B. Haskins, who was in the lab at the time. . . .

The Descriptive Interview

In some cases the locale of the interview or the physical appearance of the interviewee or the kind of work one does may be more important than what the interviewee has to say. If so, the journalist may want to conduct a descriptive—a what's-it-all-about—interview. For example, an interview with an engineer at a Cape Canaveral launching pad could emphasize the sights and sounds of the area and the part the engineer plays in creating those sights and sounds. Similarly, a descriptive interview with a 400-pound circus-sideshow performer might stress the performer's appearance.

Following is the introduction to a written descriptive interview that a magazine reporter conducted with a waitress at a youth recreation center. Note how the introduction prepares the reader for the mood and the atmosphere in the interview itself:

> In a quiet, dark booth at the Youth Center, with syncopated musical beats forming the background, you can sit and talk with friends any night of the week. The whole atmosphere is familiar to you: the fake brown leather seats, the green plastic plants on the pink windowsills, the partly emptied bottles of cola—and Esther. . . .

The Personality Interview

Names make news. And interviews with well-known persons are sure to attract attention simply because most of us would like to get to know as much as we can about famous people. The journalist's purpose, then, in interviewing a celebrity is to give the reader/listener/viewer a "close-up" of that public figure. The interview—whether written or broadcast—could focus on the interviewee's mannerisms, personality traits, and achievements. But since celebrities are likely to have a great many facts at their fingertips, the journalist might consider conducting a combination fact-and-personality interview. The following is a good example:

> How does a boy from Libertyville, Ill., get to be president of the biggest pay TV service in the country?
>
> "You go down to the Interstate and put out your thumb," jokes Jim Heyworth, president and chief executive officer of Home Box Office, calling his career history "very simple."
>
> Not quite that simple, however. First you pick up some big-name degrees (BA, Yale, '64; MBA, Chicago '67), with summer internships in international businesses in Japan and Australia. Then you decide on a career in the communications business; land a job at one of the giants; start in print; get called up by the Reserves, and return to the company in cable. From then on it's up the corporate ladder.
>
> If you're Jim Heyworth, you're 38, and, without much fanfare, sitting in a corner office in the Time-Life building on New York's Avenue of the Americas—responsible for more than 700 employes and two pay TV networks; Home Box Office with more than six million subscribers and the year-old Cinemax with more than 400,000.
>
> Heyworth took over the job in January 1980, after moving up the ranks at HBO since 1973 and at parent Time Inc. since 1967. An inside man with a low profile, Heyworth might not be the first name to come to mind when HBO is mentioned. But within HBO, the Heyworth mark is well known.
>
> From *Broadcasting* June 15, 1981

The Specialist Interview

Individuals are often interviewed because they have a fund of knowledge about specific subjects. Many teachers, for example, have done research on a subject in order to add to their own personal knowledge and to human knowledge in general. Their special knowledge is grist for interviews. The following example is an excerpt from a specialist interview conducted by Marlene Cimons of the *Los Angeles Times*.

NEW YORK—When social scientist Patricia Lund Casserly decided to explore the phenomenon of "math anxiety" in young women and girls, she decided to use a different approach.

She did not want to find out why girls were not encouraged to develop skills in math, or why they "clutched" years later as adults when using math, or why their numbers were dramatically fewer than boys in high school math Advanced Placement courses.

"I wanted to know what people were doing right," says Casserly, a senior research associate with the Educational Testing Service. "I knew there were isolated schools where these things were not happening. I wanted to know why. Was it accidental? None of these schools I looked at had specific programs to encourage girls in mathematics. They just expected women to do as well as men."

She laughs, "They hadn't been reading all the literature."

For five years, she has been studying students in nearly two dozen schools across the country under two grants awarded by the National Science Foundation and the National Institute of Education. She picked schools with Advanced Placement math programs which had sent equal numbers of boys and girls to take the Advanced Placement examinations. Advanced Placement programs are college level courses given in high school to exceptional students who, upon passing a special test, can advance to a higher course level upon entering college. . . .

The Composite Interview

Usually, the single-interview news article in a newspaper or magazine and the single-interview broadcast are relatively short. The composite interview, however, is longer because it involves more than one interviewee—sometimes as many as six—and because it is likely to go into greater detail on the topic under consideration. A newspaper/magazine report of a composite interview can run to a thousand words or more. A radio/television composite interview can take up to an hour—sometimes longer. Although one of the basic commandments of journalism is to "keep it short," many of the significant concerns of our time cannot be compressed into a paragraph or two or into a few minutes' air time. As the education of the news-consuming public increases, the demand for news based on composite interviews increases.

Many composite interviews have some of the characteristics of the types of interviews previously discussed. For example, a journalist assigned to report the news on a controversial subject will seek to interview several informed persons. Moreover, the reporter will select persons with opposing viewpoints, thereby ensuring that all sides will have a chance to be heard. Such an interview might combine some of the elements of the biographical interview, the descriptive interview, the personality interview, and the specialist interview.

The finance section of newspapers and magazines often carry composite interviews with a number of economists having different opinions. A well-known television program based on the composite interview is the *MacNeil-Lehrer Report.*

The Interview Story

The newspaper or magazine reporter writing the interview story —that is, the account of the interview—is writing material to be read. On the other hand, the radio/TV reporter writing up the same interview writes so that it will be easy (1) to *read* on the air and (2) to *understand* by the listening audience.

Elements of the Interview Story

The first task of the journalist intending to conduct an interview is to determine which kind of interview best suits the topic to be discussed and the person(s) to be interviewed. Having done so, the journalist must prepare for and conduct the interview and write it up. Like other mass media presentations, the interview story has three parts: the lead, the body, and the conclusion.

Preparing for the Interview

Conducting a successful interview requires thorough preparation. First, the reporter needs to research the subject on which the interview will be conducted. To ask sharp, clear, intelligent questions, the reporter needs to know as much as possible about that subject. Second, the interviewer needs to find out as much as possible about the interviewee—from *Who's Who*, from *Readers' Guide to Periodical Literature*, and from pertinent news stories filed in the newspaper's morgue.

The more complex the interview assignment, the more thorough the research must be. For example, biographer William Manchester, before writing *The Death of a President*, gathered 45 volumes of tapes, notes, and documents about the last few days in the life of President John F. Kennedy. Manchester spent as many as 15 hours a day for 21 months interviewing some 500 persons.

In Dallas he retraced, on foot, the route of the Kennedy motorcade. He watched the film of the actual assassination no fewer than 75 times. Thorough research like this enables a reporter to learn much about a person's achievements, failures, hobbies, likes, and dislikes. The interviewer can then begin to answer a question like this: "What would the average person want to ask this individual?" Because most readers/listeners/viewers would probably want answers to questions of direct concern to themselves, the interviewer lists questions that seem appropriate. Above all, the interviewer prepares questions that will elicit more than mere "yes" or "no" answers.

Conducting the Interview

Once the subject of the interview story and the interviewee have been thoroughly researched, the journalist needs to consider the actual interview situation. Because the interviewee could be a person of importance with many demands on his or her time, the journalist must be sure to make every question count.

Inasmuch as the interview situation is usually a face-to-face, personal confrontation, the journalist should first put the interviewee at ease. Many successful journalists do so by chatting informally for a few minutes before beginning the actual interview. Then, at an appropriate time, the journalist asks the first of the prepared questions. As the interview proceeds, one question leads to another in an informal conversational manner. Of course, the journalist tries to keep the interviewee from wandering from the subject. In doing so, the journalist must be careful not to monopolize the conversation or express personal opinions.

At the end of the interview, the journalist should thank the interviewee for taking the time to be interviewed. The journalist should also ask whether the interviewee might be called upon to double-check facts. Most interviewees are happy to cooperate in order to make sure that they are not misquoted.

Taking Notes. Journalists conducting their first interviews are justifiably concerned about taking notes during the interview. The journalist who has done a thorough job of research won't need to write down everything that's said but instead will be likely to remember much of what was said. Usually, he or she will take notes only about specific dates and statistics. When the journalist feels that certain statements need to be written down, he or she should make the note-taking as inconspicuous as possible. Confronted by a person with a large notebook, many interviewees may think that every word they say will appear in print, and so they become overly cautious. To avoid alarming the interviewee in this way, the interviewer should hold a small notepad low in his or her lap and write as inconspicuously as possible.

The Five Essentials of Interviewing. Conducting a successful interview takes practice. Yet a beginning journalist/interviewer can profit from the experiences of others. Expert interviewers agree on five basic "DO'S" for conducting a successful interview:

The Do's of Interviewing

- Prepare properly.

- Double-check to avoid misinterpretation.

- Phrase questions carefully.

- Attribute statements accurately.

- Use the first-person singular pronoun sparingly.

Prepare Properly. It is essential that the interviewer know the background of the person being interviewed. Ideally, the interviewee will regard the interviewer as a "reporter who knows what I'm talking about." For example, a student reporter assigned to interview a prominent scientist doing government research on infrared rays had not done his research "homework." The student's interview story was written and published and, not realizing how inaccurate it was, a news reporter forwarded it to a news agency. When the article appeared in papers all over the country, the scientist began to receive irate letters—some from government officials. One congressman demanded an investigation to probe the waste of taxpayers' money, leaving the scientist in the position of having to deny the facts contained in the story. Thereafter the scientist refused to grant interviews to students.

Double-check to Avoid Misinterpretation. During an interview, United Press International foreign correspondent Joseph Taylor emphasized certain words, winked while using hyperbole, and laughed after tripping over a word. Near the end of the interview, furthermore, Taylor said that he had recently finished writing a book about Latin America. Then he jokingly added, "It will probably put you to sleep." In writing the interview story, the journalist unthinkingly included this sentence:

> Taylor has recently finished a book on the Caribbean that, in his words, will "put you to sleep."

Although it is true that Taylor made the statement, he did not intend it for publication. What the journalist failed to realize was this: Without elaboration, many quotations became inaccurate. It is sometimes best to avoid direct quotation. The wise interviewer double-checks to be sure his or her interpretation is correct.

Phrase Questions Carefully. Beginning journalists are sometimes not as careful as they should be to phrase questions that interviewees can and will readily understand. Consequently, the reporter takes down and the paper publishes something that was not intended. Questions should be carefully thought out. They should be short, clear, and pointed. When the answer is given, the interviewer—if he or she had any doubt about the intended meaning—should repeat both the question and the answer. For example, an interviewer asked a senator, "Do you favor a ten percent tax increase?" The senator answered, "Yes." To double-check, the reporter asked, "You're saying you favor a tax increase?" "Heavens, no!" exclaimed the senator. "I thought you said *decrease.*"

Attribute Statements Accurately. For each quotation appearing in the interview story, the speaker must be correctly identified so that there will be no doubt in readers' minds about the source of the statement. Although there are a great many synonyms for the verb *to say,* most editors feel that the use of this verb is suitable in the majority of cases. They reason that readers aren't conscious of the verb except when they want to be sure of the source of a statement. Attribution can come at the beginning, in the middle, or at the end of the sentence:

He said, "The President has granted no pardons except on the recommendation of the attorney general."

"The President has granted no pardons," he said, "except on the recommendations of the attorney general."

"The President has granted no pardons except on the recommendation of the attorney general," he said.

Use the First-Person-Singular Pronoun Sparingly. Beginning interviewers often make the mistake of revealing their own feelings by overusing the first person singular in their interview stories. These interviewers fail to realize that the average reader is more interested in what the interviewee thinks. Awkward sentence structure can result from the misuse of the first person singular:

I asked him what he thought of the Letterman's Club. He answered that . . .

Reporting only the answers the interviewee gives will result in a much smoother story. The example line above would be much better if it read as follows:

Concerning the Letterman's Club, he said, . . .

Writing the Interview Story

Organizing the Material. With the completed interview, the journalist often amasses a great deal of unorganized information. If that information is to be properly presented, it must be put into a logical sequence. To do so, the journalist must consult the notes, first identifying the material related to each major point and then separating that material from the rest. The journalist then skeletonizes the interview story and discards all information not pertaining to the major points of that story. Having identified all of the usable information, the journalist then outlines the interview story, listing the major points in the order of their importance. It is this outline that serves as the basis for writing the interview story itself.

Writing the Lead. The type of lead chosen for an interview story is, of course, dependent upon the type of interview conducted and the information obtained. Some common leads are

The Summary Lead. The summary lead summarizes the major points learned from the interview.

Ideal qualifications for foreign correspondents were cited by UPI reporter Joseph Taylor today. Last week he was given the George Polk Award "for courage and enterprise" in reporting an attempted coup in Latin America.

The Salient-Idea Lead. The salient-idea lead contains the main idea emphasized during the interview.

"Be interested in what you are doing." This is the basic qualification of a correspondent, according to award-winning UPI reporter Joseph Taylor.

The Feature Lead. The feature lead, usually presented in narrative style, is used to gain reader interest by supplying a background for the main idea of the interview.

It is from the troubled Caribbean that the storm clouds come with hurricane winds and driving rain. It is from the troubled Caribbean that revolutions spring overnight and governments fall.

And it is from this troubled Caribbean scene that UPI's Joseph Taylor reported and won the George Polk Award for courage and enterprise in journalism.

The Word-Picture Lead. The reporter often uses the word-picture lead when writing about a well-known interviewee or one with a particularly striking personality. This type of lead presents a colorful visual image of the interviewee. To use this lead effectively, the interviewer must watch as well as listen during the interview. The interviewee's mannerisms, dress, and distinctive habits can often make interesting lead material which, when properly presented, will enable the reader to "see" as well as "hear." The following is an example of a word-picture lead:

Bundled up like a ponderous old bear, Leonid Brezhnev labored up the steps of the Lenin Mausoleum early last week....

Newsweek, November 22, 1982

The Figure-of-Speech Lead. To make a striking comparison or an analogy, the writer of the interview story often considers using the figure-of-speech lead. In this type of lead, the writer tries to present a clever, thought-provoking twist.

Interviewing a veteran reporter is like dancing with a politician; it's debatable who's leading whom....

The Thought-provoking Question Lead. To gain reader interest, reporters sometimes begin an interview story with a thought-provoking question.

How radical can you get? Only the most wide-eyed souls in the 1900s thought that a woman who was doing the same job as a man should be paid the same wage.

Writing the Composite Interview Lead. While any of the preceding types of leads may be used for interview stories (as long as they are accurate and lure the reader into the story), composite interview stories use only one of the following types of leads.

The Comprehensive Lead. The most common lead for the composite interview story is the comprehensive paragraph in which the writer reduces the important ideas from the interview into a single, summarizing unit. This type of lead is used when each idea from the interview is of about equal value.

Four area environmentalists yesterday endorsed the movement launched by the County Health Assocation to locate and mark every site in the county where chemical wastes have been indiscriminately dumped.

The Main-Idea Lead. The composite interview story usually uses the comprehensive lead when the interrelationship between those interviewed is the outstanding news factor. However, when one remark is superior to the others, the reporter may want to single it out and play it up in the lead.

> "Protect our people! Stop illegal dumping of chemical wastes!" With those words County Commissioner Ira T. Jacobs drew cheers from the crowd assembled at the high school auditorium last night.

The Combination Lead. The third type of lead for the composite interview story is a combination of the two previous types. One main idea is used; minor points are briefly summarized.

> County Commissioner Ira Jacobs has joined forces with area environmentalists to locate and mark every spot in the county where chemical wastes have been illegally dumped.

Writing the Body of the Interview Story. After determining the type of interview story and deciding on a lead that introduces the topics to be covered, the writer then proceeds to the body of the story. Usually, that part of the interview story concerns only a few major topics, each of which is developed in a paragraph. Paragraphs follow one another in logical order.

The body of the interview story should be presented in a smooth, coherent style. Each topic should be thoroughly discussed before the writer proceeds to the next topic. Doing so will ensure that there are no unanswered questions left in readers'/listeners'/viewers' minds. To achieve variety, the writer can consider alternating direct quotations with indirect quotations. If the interviewee made an especially forceful or a controversial statement or used colorful language, the writer might consider using only direct quotations for those statements, reserving indirect quotations for transitions or for summary remarks.

The strains of an old ragtime tune were drowned out by the scream of an early-model diesel train.

The physics teacher, Dr. Walter Smudski, dismissed the strange mixture of sounds. "The kids are playing," he said with a smile. He said the kids often played in the lab.

The "kids" were two seniors, Harry Pander, "my electronic expert," and Mary Riebling, "my physics whiz."

Actually, they were studying the pitch of each of several sounds. . . .

The use of transitions is even more important in the composite interview story than it is in shorter interview stories. A few transitions that can easily be adapted for use in composite interview stories are "Another development in the story . . . ," "At the same time . . . ," and "Earlier in the day . . ."

Concluding the Interview Story. The final paragraph of the interview story, the conclusion, should give the entire story an air of finality and should summarize the purpose of the story. The writer may wish to use a summarizing statement in a direct quotation preceded by a statement such as "In conclusion, he said. . . ." or "He concluded with. . . ." Another commonly used type of conclusion for interview stories is often referred to as the "picture-frame device." This type of conclusion points the reader back to the lead by repeating the thought contained in the lead, thus indicating that the interview is over.

The conclusion to the interview story should not editorialize, and it should avoid wordy, complicated sentences like the one in the example that follows:

> All of the members of the faculty and the members of the senior class student body wish to thank Mr. Smith for his efforts in their behalf, as well as to extend all of their best wishes to him for success in all of his future endeavors.

How would you rewrite that sentence to make it into a brief, clear, appropriate conclusion?

The conclusion for the composite interview story, also, must have an air of finality. All of the reader's questions should have been answered in the body of the story, and no loose ends should be left hanging.

The Profile

On occasion a reporter may be assigned to do a long, in-depth article—a profile—on a prominent person. Researching for such a profile may take the journalist as long as two weeks. This type of study resembles an English composition more than it does a news story. In other words, the inverted pyramid style of the straight news story gives way to an article with an interesting introduction, a body, and a conclusion. The introduction should be about one eighth of the length of the article; the conclusion should be about that length, too. In the article itself, the journalist strives for freshness of approach. An outline is essential for writing a profile.

Associated Press veteran reporter Saul Pett was assigned to do a profile on New York City Mayor Ed Koch. Here are his first three paragraphs:

He is the freshest thing to blossom in New York since chopped liver, a mixed metaphor of a politician, the antithesis of the packaged leader, irrepressible, candid, impolitic, spontaneous, funny, feisty, independent, uncowed by voter blocs, unsexy, unhandsome, unfashionable, and altogether charismatic, man oddly at peace with himself in an unpeaceful place, a mayor who presides over the country's largest Babel with unseemly joy.

Clearly, an original. Asked once what he thought his weaknesses were, Ed Koch said that for the life of him he couldn't think of any. "I like myself," he said.

The streets are still dirty. The subways are still unsafe. The specter of bankruptcy is never farther away than next year's loan. But Edward Irving Koch, who runs the place like a solicitious Jewish mother with no fear of the rich relatives, appears to be the most popular mayor of the implausible town since Fiorello LaGuardia more than a generation ago. . . .

After the profile was published, several other writers discussed it with Pett. He explained that after he got the idea to do the story, "I started reading like crazy about Koch. Other things that had been done about him—some news stories, some previous profiles—until I got thoroughly familiar with him. Then I went down to City Hall and started to talk to people about him. People who worked for him. Others in politics. City Hall reporters. By the time I got to interview him, which I saved for last, I felt that I knew him."

Before Pett sat down for the formal interview with Koch, he spent a couple of days traveling around the city with him. Pett said he wanted

"to see the man work, especially a colorful guy like this. We got in the car and went over to Brooklyn, where they were dedicating a new shopping mall. Then we went to a new pier, and then we went to one of his 'town hall' meetings. There were any number of little stops where he talked to people on the street. He loves to talk to people, even to be heckled by them. It's part of what he calls 'street theater.' And then I sat down with him in his office and we talked for a couple of hours at least.

"I had a list of questions in mind. I usually do. I find that important. Even though there are spontaneous people involved, you should plan some questions. You're dealing with a busy guy, and you can lose him."

Asked about his interviewing technique, Pett said,

"I kind of plan the opening, either with a little humor or something to relax them or something that will interest them. I think the success of an interview depends

Roles of the Journalist in a Democratic Society

on whether you interest the guy. You get him to where he feels like talking about himself. This sounds like a contradiction: The night before, I'll be sitting in a motel room, nervously trying to think of questions, and it makes for a more spontaneous interview. I want it to be relaxed. Ideally, the interview will come off like a conversation. There's another trick—it's so obvious—but it's a thing I had to learn: Relax, Charlie. Don't be a district attorney. Give the man time. Don't worry about a pause. If you ask him something and he says yes or no, and he pauses, you let him pause. He's thinking about something. You frequently get some awfully good things that way, letting the guy or woman talk. If you get an interview only on the basis of their quick and ready answers, you've got a kind of formal thing."

When Pett had finished his research and his interview, he had a tremendous amount of information that needed organization.

"I've got several notebooks full of stuff," he said. "I've got clips. I've got maybe portions of a book, or magazine pieces, taped interviews which I've transcribed. All that is done. There is my basic material. But it's all kind of in bunches. So then I sit down, and this is just dull donkey work, and I hate it, but I find it necessary, and I kind of outline my material. I try to put in into piles. Here's stuff about Koch's wit. Here's stuff about his independence. Here's stuff about how he can be tough with minorities. Here's stuff about his background. All that exists in my notebooks scattered throughout. So the advantage of the outline is that I've got it on paper in logical segments. It's a lot of dull work. I spend two or three days at that.

"And there's that little thing called a lead. I know that I don't spend as much time on leads as I used to. We make a mistake when we're younger. We feel compelled to hit a home run in the very first sentence. So we spend a lot of time staring at the typewriter. I'll settle for a quiet single or even a long foul—anything that gets me started. When I talk to young writers, that's the most sensible advice I can give them. Perfect anecdotal leads are so rare. Even though Koch was full of good anecdotes, no one anecdote deserved to be the lead."

Finally, Pett defended the fact that his lead on the Koch article had 65 words in it—far more than the 17 or so that readability experts suggest.

"The length of a sentence should not be any kind of barometer unless it ends up unclear. The newspaper writer's first obligation is to be clear. And if he's unclear in a four-word sentence, he's committed the ultimate sin. Whether it's four words or forty words, it has to be clear. I find long sentences now and then a great help, a way of saying a certain thing with a kind of spirit, a momentum, a thrust, a flavor, a rhythm. . . ."

Interviews and the Broadcast Media

Effective interviewers in both the print and the broadcast media know how to listen well, absorb and relate information, and react intelligently. Yet those conducting radio/television interviews face an added challenge. Besides observing the guidelines followed by print media interviewers, broadcasters must "write" the interview while it is in progress. That is, they must constantly keep in mind that the questions they are asking and the answers they are getting are being disseminated at that very moment to thousands of listeners/viewers.

Live News Broadcasts

Paul Elbin of WSYR-TV is at the scene of a mine disaster. With the help of a police captain, he finds a survivor who is willing to talk briefly about the tragedy. Paul knows that he has only 30 seconds or so to be on the air and that he must use that short time to the best advantage. And so before going "live," he asks the survivor a number of questions to determine the best ones for the actual interview. Paul is giving the interviewee a chance to think over his answers and thus avoid stumbling around for words during the interview itself. In addition, Paul knows that the anchorperson in the studio—before switching to Paul for his live report—will have given viewers the facts about the five w's and the h.

Paul's task is to expand on the five w's and the h and to add human interest to the interview. He wants to give the viewers something that isn't available in the studio report. Before they go on the air, Paul gets the survivor's name, age, and job title. Then he probes with questions like these:

- "Where were you when the tunnel collapsed?"
- "What were you doing?"
- "Why were you there?"
- "What did you see happen?"
- "Who are the trapped miners?"
- "How well do you know them?"
- "How is it that you weren't with them?"
- "What did you do after the tunnel collapsed?"

Paul asks the survivor to elaborate on those answers that seem to have a more-than-ordinary interest for viewers. He then decides which of the questions he'll repeat for the actual interview. His questions will bring out the survivor's heroism in carrying an injured friend to safety and the survivor's good luck in starting on his lunch break a few seconds earlier than usual.

On the air, Paul has the survivor quickly establish the facts about the situation (the five *w's* and the *h).* Then he asks the questions that bring out the "quirk of fate" and the "hero" angles. Paul is intense and serious. He keeps his questions sharp and pointed. He uses the present tense whenever possible to add to the sense of immediacy.

Delayed News Broadcasts

After his live report, Paul knows that his station will need a longer report for later news broadcasts. Consequently, for a few minutes he continues the interview, which is filmed. In his questioning, Paul gets the survivor to elaborate even more about the disaster. But Paul is keenly aware that he must exercise discretion, avoiding questions that might elicit overly emotional answers—questions that might bring the survivor to tears and make him appear to be something he is not. In short, Paul puts ethical considerations ahead of his desire to report all the facts of the story.

Having been careful to avoid overdramatizing the disaster or distorting the facts associated with it, Paul returns to the studio to aid in editing the film of the extended interview.

A Window on the World

A frequent theme in student English compositions is ""How I'm Suffocated by My Environment." Regardless of the part of the country in which students live, they often feel that "the grass is greener on the other side of the fence." Many students in New York City and Los Angeles dislike city living and wish they could move to the country, while students living in rural communities often dream of what they think is the glamorous life of the city. Many students living in the North would gladly exchange their climate with students living in the South, and vice versa. These students can be compared to the consumers of the mass media who are discussed at the beginning of this chapter. The average consumer often feels shut off from the "outside" world, or trapped by the four walls of office or living room. The interview story writer can give such a person a "window on the world" —a window that gives readers/listeners/viewers insights into human emotions, human failures, and human accomplishments.

> **INTERVIEW CHECKLIST**
>
> ✓ Did you research your interviewee?
>
> ✓ Did you develop several key questions to guide the interview?
>
> ✓ Did you establish rapport with the interviewee?
>
> ✓ Did your questions flow in a conversational manner?
>
> ✓ Did the interviewee understand your questions?
>
> ✓ Did you use tact in helping your interviewee to stick to the subject?
>
> ✓ Did you conclude the interview tactfully at the appropriate time?

Activities

1. Suppose that you have been assigned to see the vocal music teacher about a concert to be given in the school auditorium in two weeks. In making the assignment, your editor remarked that your story—*with all the facts*—will be featured on the front page of next week's edition of the school paper. Obviously, your first step is to get as much preliminary information as possible. From sources in the journalism classroom you learn the following:

The vocal music teacher is Miss Georgina Kent.
The concert will be given in the school auditorium
at 8 p.m.
The concert will be given in two weeks on Friday evening.

Write out the carefully phrased questions you should be prepared to ask the vocal music teacher as you seek to get the facts for your front-page story.

2. With a classmate, prepare and act in a skit illustrating what to do—or what not to do—during an interview. After the skit, participate in a class discussion of what was done right and what was done wrong. Be prepared to offer suggestions for remedying any mistakes identified during the discussion.

3. To gain experience with the various types of interview leads, write five short opening leads for an imaginary interview, using as the interviewee a celebrity of your choice. Choose the leads that you prefer and discuss your choices with your classmates.

4. As you read the following transcript of an interview, take notes on the important facts revealed. Keep in mind that under the conditions of an actual interview, you would have but little time for taking notes. Thus, for each note you do make you will want to use as few words as possible, and you will want to abbreviate where you can.

Reporter: Good morning, Mr. Dunn. I'm George Lee, reporter for the *Bugle.* I'd like to get some information about last Saturday's Science Fair. Is this a good time to talk with you?

Mr. Dunn: Yes, this is a good time. Sit down, George.

Reporter: Thanks. I'm not sure I understand what the Science Fair was all about. Why was it held? What was its purpose?

Mr. Dunn: Well, the science teachers in the city knew about and were impressed with the experiments and projects some junior and senior high school students were working on. They thought that parents and other citizens would be interested in what the young people of the city were doing in science. And so a committee of science teachers went to the Board of Education, seeking authorization to conduct a science fair. The Board enthusiastically approved. And the fair was held in the Civic Auditorium last Saturday from nine o'clock in the morning until four o'clock in the afternoon.

Reporter: How many students participated?

Mr. Dunn: Twenty-four in all. They came from the six junior high schools and from the three high schools. The participants either exhibited their work or demonstrated some kind of scientific operation.

Reporter: How many students from South High participated?

Mr. Dunn: Four.

Reporter: Who were they, and what did they do?

Mr. Dunn: Well, let's see. Louise Montgomery, a senior, demonstrated several ways in which kinetic energy operates. Josh White, a junior, experimented with a computer, storing and retrieving information supplied by people who stopped by his exhibit. Angela Nuñez, also a junior, exhibited her collection of unusual moths and butterflies of this area. And Jim Higgins, a senior, demonstrated how the sun's energy can be converted into heat to heat water for the home.

Reporter: Let me have those names again. Louise—that's L-o-u-i-s-e —Montgomery, a senior. And then there was Jim Higgins—H-i-g-g-i-n-s, also a senior. The two juniors were Angela—A-n-g-e-l-a—Nuñez— N-u-ñ-e-z with an accent mark on the second *n* and Josh White. Is that right?

Mr. Dunn: Yes, you have their names right.

Reporter: Were there any prizes awarded?

Mr. Dunn: No, no prizes. But there were Certificates of Commendation. Each participant received a Certificate.

Reporter: Do you and the other science teachers consider the Science Fair a success?

Mr. Dunn: Indeed we do! More than 2000 people visited the Fair during the day. That kind of attendance indicates to us that parents and citizens generally are very much interested in what young people are accomplishing these days.

Reporter: Will there be a Science Fair next year?

Mr. Dunn: We certainly hope so. Our committee is planning a larger fair for next year—one that will run for two days.

Reporter: Well, I think I have the information I need. Is there anything else to be said about the Science Fair?

Mr. Dunn: I think that's everything.

Reporter: Thank you, Mr. Dunn, for taking the time to talk with me.

Mr. Dunn: You're very welcome. Come back next year for some information about Science Fair II.

Bring your interview notes to class. With your classmates, decide what facts from the interview are essential for writing an attention-getting interview story for the front page of the school newspaper. Are there any facts the reporter should have asked about but did not? If so, what are they?

5. List the preliminary steps a journalist should take before conducting an interview. List the steps the journalist should take after the interview to prepare for writing the interview story.

6. Make arrangements to spend one or more class periods interviewing one of your teachers on school-related issues. In conducting the interview, keep in mind techniques of interviewing discussed in this chapter.

    a. Be prepared in advance to ask specific questions about the issue or issues being discussed.

    b. Try to have the questions follow one another in an easy, sequential, and informal manner.

c. Keep in mind that the interviewee may have demands on his or her time; try to make every question count.

d. Try to keep note-taking as inconspicuous as possible. Consider using a tape recorder, if available.

e. Try to avoid expressing your own personal opinions about the issue or issues being discussed.

f. If you have any doubt about the meaning of an answer, repeat both the question and the answer.

CHAPTER 9

Covering Speeches, Public Meetings, and Published Reports

Mike Gonzales, reporter for the *Miami Herald,* finds this note on his typewriter:

> James Watt, curator of Asiatic art at Lowe Art Museum, is speaking at the museum at 8 tonight on "Ritual in Ancient China." It's in connection with "The Great Bronze Age of China," the exhibition that opens tomorrow. Get out there and do a couple of takes on Watt's speech.

Convinced that the city editor works him harder than anyone else on the staff, Mike groans. Then he sets to work. A journalism major at the university, Mike has taken several art courses. He has read about the upcoming exhibition and is looking forward to seeing it.

First, Mike goes to the newspaper library and, in an encyclopedia, finds some information about the Bronze Age in China. He then comes upon a museum brochure about the upcoming exhibition. Mike knows that the more information he has about the subject before he goes out to hear Watt's speech, the better his news story about that speech will be. He finds, for example, that in 210 B.C., the Chinese made more than 7000 life-size terracotta warriors and horses to be placed in the grave of the first Emperor of Qin. Some 70,000 laborers constructed those clay figures. Fascinated by the information, Mike is looking forward to the speech.

He arrives at the museum about a half hour early and goes to talk with the public relations representative. From her, he receives an advance text of Dr. Watt's speech. He is glad to have it —especially that portion dealing with the names and dates of Chinese rulers.

Mike prefers to take notes rather than use a tape recorder. Although Mike has never taken shorthand, he uses a number of symbols and abbreviations as he takes notes. For the most part, he summarizes the speaker's words. But when Dr. Watt, in an aside not in the prepared text, uses especially colorful language to describe the facial features and the armor of the clay warriors, Mike takes down the speaker's exact words.

After the speech Mike returns to the office and immediately sets to work writing his story. He considers the several options available for focusing his story and decides that the timeliness and proximity angles are best. Then Mike writes his lead, which focuses on the 7000 replicas of warriors and horses.

In about a half hour Mike is finished. He reads his story, checking for obvious errors, such as typos. Then he reads the story again to double-check dates and the spelling of names.

As he turns his story in to the city editor, Mike feels a sense of accomplishment. He's added some "present-day history" to a story about human life in China centuries ago.

The Speech Story

Since most people aren't able to attend every significant speech, they must rely on the news media to keep them informed about those they miss. Like straight news stories, stories about speeches inform readers/listeners/viewers by answering the questions *who, what, when, where, why,* and *how.* Writing stories about speeches is often more challenging than writing straight news stories. In addition to informing readers/listeners/viewers about an event that has taken place, the reporter must also account for what was *said.* The reporter must, therefore, be an attentive listener as well as a careful observer. He or she must also be able to select the most important ideas in the speech and then organize them into a coherent news story. In addition to reporting the content of the speech accurately, the reporter must be careful to retain the spirit in which the remarks were made. If it is important to the story, the reporter should give background information about the speaker and about the place where the speech was given.

Preparation

The reporter assigned to cover a specific speech should first research all available source materials to obtain as much background information as possible about the speaker. This background information should include the speaker's full name, biographical data, his or her views on various issues, and organizations and activities he or she has been involved in. Second, the reporter should obtain as much information as possible about the speech itself—the correct title, the subject matter, and the time and location of its delivery. Third, because many speeches are followed by question-and-answer periods, the reporter should write out several questions that readers/listeners/viewers would be likely to ask if they had the chance.

The well-prepared reporter arrives at the scene about a half hour before the speech is scheduled to begin. Doing so provides the time to register at the Press Table or Press Room and secure the necessary credentials often required for admission. The reporter may also have time to obtain an advance copy of the speech—mimeographed or printed copies usually are made available to members of the press—and to discuss with the sponsors of the speech any questions he or she has. Finally, an early arrival will permit the reporter to find a seat from which he or she can see and hear the speaker without difficulty.

Writing the Speech Story

The reporter should begin writing the speech story as soon as possible after the speech—while he or she still has a strong impression of the speaker's remarks and of important particulars of the occasion. Before beginning to write, the reporter should read her or his notes to be sure that the speaker's main theme and supporting ideas come through clearly.

Elements of the Speech Story

In reporting a speech, the speech-story writer has three elements to keep in mind: the speaker, the audience, and the speech itself.

The Speaker.   As with the interview story, the writer of a speech story should first inform the reader/listener/viewer of the speaker's full name and credentials. Second, the writer needs to address this question: Why should I (the reader/listener/viewer) pay attention to what this person has to say? Next, the writer might describe the speaker's appearance and manner of speaking. By reporting *how* the speech was delivered as well as *what* was said, the writer can describe the speaker and the audience and thus paint a verbal picture of the event. Did the speaker, for example, point an index finger at the audience in a gesture of admonishment? Did the speaker pound a fist on the lectern or shout when making important points? Details like these will help enliven a speech story.

The Audience.   Estimating the size of the audience, noting what special-interest groups or prominent persons are in attendance, and reporting the audience's reactions to the speaker's remarks make a speech story interesting.

In estimating the size of the audience, the reporter needs to be as specific as possible, avoiding such vague expressions as "full house," "near-capacity crowd," or "standing-room-only crowd." Such expressions mean little to readers/listeners/viewers who are unfamiliar with the size of the auditorium. By adding a phrase like "at the 500-seat auditorium" to these expressions, the reporter can give them more specific meaning.

If it is important to the story, the reporter might want to indicate what groups of people were represented in the audience. Were they taxpayers, union members, teachers, students, bankers? If any prominent persons were in the audience, the reporter should mention them in the story.

The reporter might incorporate into the story the reactions of the audience to the speech. Did the audience applaud or cheer enthusiastically? Did anyone walk out of the hall at a certain point in the speech? In general, was the audience receptive?

The Speech Itself.   The final—and usually the most important—element in a speech story is the content of the speech itself. In reporting the speech, the writer must be sure to answer questions like these: What did the speaker say? What main ideas were advanced in the speech? What supporting arguments did the speaker give to try to persuade others to his or her point of view?

Because he or she will most likely be unable to write down everything the speaker says, the reporter must be able to separate the important statements from those that are less important. Some of what the speaker said will, of course, be summarized. At the same time, the reporter must be alert for statements that merit direct quotation and quote such statements exactly.

The Speech Story Lead

In addition to giving such information as the speaker's name, the subject of the talk, and the occasion of the speaking event, the speech story lead will often contain some important element from the speech itself. The lead will usually be contained in one paragraph. However, the writer choosing to write a lead with a lengthy quotation can place the strictly factual information (*who, what, where, when, how*) in a second paragraph.

The most important element of a speech story is not necessarily the content of the speech. Sometimes beginning with an element such as the speaker's name or the circumstances surrounding the event or an unusual title may be a more appropriate way of leading into a speech story. In most cases, however, the reporter will begin the speech story in one of the following ways:

1. By summarizing the main ideas or general theme of the speech.

   Burton Samson, playwright and actor, last week discussed the modern playwright and the theater. The speech was sponsored by the Drama Club.

2. By directly quoting a significant statement that was made by the speaker and that effectively expresses the theme of the speech.

   "The theater is an arena, an intellectual and emotional sporting event where the actors are sportsmen," philosophized Burton Samson, noted playwright, last week at Wheeling High School.

3. By quoting the speaker indirectly.

   Playwright Burton Samson, speaking at Wheeling High School last week, said attending the theater was like going through customs.

4. By using an interest-arousing quotation from the speech to lure the reader/listener/viewer into the story. (The reporter beginning the story in this way should summarize the entire speech in the second or third paragraph so that the speaker's intent will not be misrepresented.)

"The theater is like going through customs when you're asked what you have to declare," said Burton Samson before a crowd of 400 students at Wheeling High School last week.

"The most mysterious thing I have ever come across is an audience," said Burton Samson as he spoke at Wheeling High School last week.

"In fact," he continued, "the audience makes a sportsman out of an actor."

The Body of the Speech Story

In the body of the speech story the reporter will condense the speech by summarizing and by quoting the speaker directly and indirectly. In doing so the reporter should take care to retain the spirit of the speech, be faithful to the speaker's original meaning, and be concerned with correct and accurate attribution. The length of the story will depend on the news value of the speech —the importance of the occasion or of the statements made, or the prominence of the speaker.

To begin the speech story, the reporter may want to expand on the element chosen for the lead. The sentences that make up the story should be well organized and relate to the main theme of the speech, even if the speaker rambled. As in other news stories, the ideas presented in the speech story should be arranged in order of decreasing importance (inverted pyramid style), even though this order may not be the same one as that in which the speaker made the statements. Thus the body of the speech story, like that of the interview story, will be made up of short paragraphs of direct and indirect quotations and summary statements. Quotations should not be selected at random but should serve to develop and illustrate the main theme of the speech story itself.

In addition to stating the theme of the speech and the supporting arguments, the reporter can also include in the story anecdotes, humor, and specific examples the speaker used to illustrate his or her ideas. Including this material will add life to the story.

Samson described his new three-act play, "The Generation Beat," as "unfashionable because people don't want to drink lemonade twice." This comment was one of many anecdotes that he used to brighten his talk. . . .

The Conclusion of the Speech Story

Like an interview story, a speech story should conclude with an air of finality. Often a speaker will conclude a talk with a summarizing statement. The reporter may wish to use this statement to conclude the story.

> In conclusion, Samson said, "The theater is an instrument with which the playwright can do anything he likes, provided he can hold his audience. The playwrights are among the very few who can say what they think—with no fear."

If the speech is part of a lecture series, the reporter might conclude the story by informing the reader/listener/viewer of the time and place of the next event.

> The next speaker in the Drama Club Series will be Arthur Morton, a scenic designer, who will speak February 23 on the topic, "What High School Students Should Know about Scenic Design."

CHECKLIST FOR WRITING A SPEECH STORY

✓ Did you thoroughly research the speaker and the topic prior to attending the speech?

✓ While covering the speech, did you take accurate and complete notes, including significant direct quotations as well as summarizing statements?

✓ Have you written a concise and effective lead that includes an important element of the story and identifies the speaker, the subject of the speech, and the occasion?

✓ Does the body of your story present the speaker's remarks in an interesting, coherent, and well-organized manner?

✓ Does your story have a conclusion?

✓ Do all direct quotations use the speaker's exact words?

✓ Does your story retain the original tone and intended meaning of the speech?

✓ Does your story show that you thoroughly understood the speaker's main theme and supporting arguments?

Sidebars to the Speech Story

As in a straight news story, a sidebar to a speech story often accompanies the main story about the speech. On occasion, developments prior to, during, or as a result of a speech will make good material for the writing of sidebars. If, for example, a speaker made certain charges against the school system in a speech, the reporter might ask a school authority to answer the accusations. Or if protesters stormed the stage and forced the speaker to delay the talk, the sidebar could be written about this disturbance. Or if certain groups had been barred from attending the speech, the reporter could write a sidebar based on interviews with leaders of such groups. Whereas the speech would be covered in the main story, less important, though related, elements would be included in the sidebar. The following examples, written by a journalism student now with the *Providence Journal,* show the difference between speech stories and sidebars to speech stories.

■ Speech Story

Since we have the most technically advanced society in the world, we have no models. In fact, we are an experimenting station for other countries. "Consequently, we should put more planning into our 'Choice of Communities for Tomorrow,'" Dr. Margaret Mead told 500 students in Hendricks Chapel Wednesday night. . . .

■ Sidebar to a Speech Story

Time—7:30. The lecture was scheduled for 8 p.m. Hendricks Chapel was gradually being filled, until stragglers were forced to use windowsills and balcony steps for seats.

I sat fidgeting, but glad I had arrived early enough to grab a good seat. A crumpled copy of the school paper lay on the floor before me. The boldface headline read as follows: "Margaret Mead on Campus Today." I wanted to pass the time, and so I began to read the article. World famous anthropologist. Author of 11 books. Researcher of cultural patterns in South Sea islands and primitive areas of New Guinea, Bali, and Samoa.

Suddenly, I came to a conclusion. There I sat—a sophomore in college—a sophomore with hopes of being both a newspaper and sociology major—a sophomore who had said so many times, "Education means a lot to me." And

why was I there? Because of a course requirement.

A woman with a master's and a Ph.D. from Columbia University had been asked to share her knowledge and experience with today's students, and I began to wonder how many were awaiting the talk because of their own initiative and desire to learn.

The girl next to me looked at her companion and said, "I'm not taking notes. I'm just here to meet a friend." I gazed about, noting several frosh acquaintances, who were, no doubt, attending because of class obligations.

How many students are sincere? After all, I always envisioned myself as eager to learn, enthusiastic, and grateful for the opportunity to do so. But what had I done about it? Studied conscientiously? Most of the time. But what about *extra* reading, *extra* writing, and taking advantage of *other* guest speakers? Rarely.

The murmuring drifted away. A woman in a green suit came up to the rostrum. She smiled at her audience and began. The audience was appreciative and attentive.

The lecture, "The Choice of Communities for Tomorrow," ended and the bid was made for questions. A seemingly long pause filled the room. *Come on, college students,* I thought. *Are your minds that blank?* Finally, several hands shot up.

Time—9:30. It was over. I wandered toward the exit, purposely listening to comments: "She was great, but I disagree with her point on ..."

"The topic was too generalized ..."

"Her ideas were edging toward Communism ..."

"I'm glad I *had* to come. She really was worth the time ..."

"Gosh," I thought, "those students were *thinking*. Her lecture really stimulated minds."

Maybe this is what education is all about.

The Public-Meeting Report

Speeches—from informal talks to formal addresses—may be given at meetings of any group. For example, at an hour-long PTA meeting, speeches might consist simply of comments from the floor. On the other hand, at a five-day meeting of student editors the schedule may call for a number of formal speeches. The reporter assigned to cover both types of meetings might write a couple of sentences or a short paragraph about each speech listened to. Or he or she might want to summarize all significant speeches given at a meeting. Another choice—as in the following example—is to write about one speech that effectively summarizes the most important developments at the meeting.

As a result of the School Board meeting last week, student social clubs will be allowed if these clubs follow the rules that govern all other school clubs.

Speaking at the meeting, Superintendent Martin said that the name of the club "is of secondary importance."

"Organizations, good and bad, go by the same name," he continued. "What really matters is not the name—but the goal. In setting goals, students have an opportunity for genuine educational experience," he said. . . .

The Grantonian

Panel Discussions

The reporter may find that writing a story about a panel discussion presents more problems than writing a story about a speech. However, many of the suggestions given for reporting speeches will also apply to reporting panel discussions. For example, the reporter should research the topic and the panelists' backgrounds before attending the discussion.

If the panelists are in general agreement about the topic of discussion, the reporter could, as in the examples following, write a lead in a variety of ways. The remainder of the story might then consist of significant comments made by the panelists.

With a prevailing note of pessimism, four high school teachers discussed "The United Nations in a World of Crisis" last week at the Warwood High School Auditorium. Participating in the panel discussion commemorating U.N. Day were Kevin O'Toole, William J. Pearson, Ishwer C. Kobe, and Robert J. Thompson.

Humankind is not yet psychologically ready to achieve international peace and harmony through an organization such as the U.N., concluded four Warwood High School teachers appearing at the U.N. Day panel discussion last week.

At the auditorium last week, an international panel of Warwood High School teachers expressed some grave doubts about the future of the United Nations.

If the participants are in disagreement, the story might well consist of a presentation of the various opposing points of view on the subject of discussion. The fact that they are in disagreement could be used in the lead—as follows:

A panel of experts last week differed sharply on whether the United States should provide military aid to Israel. Participating in a discussion on "The Mideast in Crisis," three authorities often became embroiled in heated and emotional outbursts during the program at the Washington High School auditorium.

The Published-Report Story

Published reports such as government documents, public-relations releases, and magazine articles can be of great aid to the reporter as a source of background information for a news story or as a basis for writing a feature story. To write a news story based on information contained in a published report, follow a procedure similar to that used in writing a speech story: condense the material into a coherent story by quoting some passages directly and indirectly and by summarizing other passages.

NEW YORK—American authors make less than $5000 a year on the average from writing. By the hour, writing books pays no better than being a file clerk or a janitor, according to a Columbia University study.

But most of the authors surveyed can live very much better than the average American, thanks to having other jobs and working mates, the two-year study showed. It also showed that overall, men make more from writing than women.

And, not surprisingly, writers of potboilers do a lot better than poets.

One out of five authors of romance, detective, western, and Gothic books had an income that attained the $50,000 level. Among authors making less than $2500, 55 percent write poetry or academic nonfiction, it said.

A reporter who writes novels at night is a stock character in fiction, but the survey found that only five percent of authors are also journalists. Thirty-eight percent of authors teach at colleges and universities and 20 percent are professionals—lawyers, doctors, and clergy, according to the study.

It found the median family income for all authors was $38,000 a year, which includes what the writer and mate earn from all sources.

The figures, compiled for the Authors Guild Foundation by Columbia's Center for Social Sciences, were based on responses from 2239 authors about their incomes in 1979. An author was defined as a writer who has had at least one book published. None of those surveyed hit million-dollar movie-and-paperback sales bonanzas in 1979, but a few had books that made the best-seller list and accounted for "the few" six-figure incomes of 1979, the survey said.

Associated Press

Government Documents

The U.S. Government Printing Office makes available a great many reports of value to reporters. For example, a reporter writing a story about teenage employment could secure copies of reports published by the Department of Labor. For material on problems of education, the reporter could write to the U.S. Department of Education. The information could be used in a news story as follows:

Two professors have just finished a major study of adolescents in three area high schools and have concluded—broadly speaking—that public high schools tend to inhibit rather than encourage independent thinking.

The recently published report, commissioned three years ago by the U.S. Department of Education, suggests that high schools are failing to stimulate original thought and are, in effect, crippling their students.

Public-Relations Releases

Public-relations offices may supply newspapers, magazines, and the other media with newsworthy articles. If news writers use this material for news stories, they should check the accuracy of the releases and, in most cases, rewrite them. Following is an example of a lead from such a release.

> Baylor University has announced the completion of a major study by leading youth authorities Mario Delio and Rena Wilson. The study, conducted at local high schools, proves. . . .

Magazine Articles

Magazine articles can be used by reporters as sources for background information for many assignments and for factual details needed for writing a story. In using quotations, the reporter should indicate the name and date of the magazine and, in some cases, obtain the magazine's permission to reprint the material.

> Washington High School pitcher Warren Newton is the subject of an article in the April issue of *Sports Consolidated.* Author Tim Rice points out that Newton has signed a $75,000 contract to play professional baseball for the California Angels this spring.
>
> Because of the contract, Newton will be ineligible to pitch in any further Washington High games. Coach Robert Lawson made the following comment concerning the situation: "I'm only sorry that the Angels couldn't have waited until Warren graduated."

Your Opportunity to Think

Learning how to present the content of speeches, meetings, panel discussions, and published reports to readers is a valuable experience for the journalism student. While the reader benefits from reading these reports, the student writer benefits even more. From organizing the material into a coherent, newsworthy story and from writing the story, the student can think about and evaluate the relative importance of ideas contained in the material. Most important, by attending speaking events and reading published reports on important subjects, the student journalist will become more mature and better informed.

Activities

1. The circumstances under which a speech is given—the speaker's appearance or mannerisms, special-interest groups or prominent persons in the audience, audience reaction to the speech, and the place where the speech is given—can help enliven a speech story. During a school assembly or some other school meeting, sharpen your powers of observation by taking notes about the audience's reactions. Compare your observations with those made by your classmates. Discuss which notes (observations) should be included in a story about the meeting.

2. From a daily newspaper, clip a speech story of five or more paragraphs. Read the story carefully. Then briefly write out your answers to the following questions:

    a. What was the speech about?

    b. Of the four kinds of leads available for a speech story, which one does the reporter use?

    c. What kind of person does the reporter make the speaker out to be? Support your answer by quoting from the speech story.

    d. How does the reporter conclude the speech story?

3. Find a speech story in a daily newspaper. Edit by eliminating any material unessential to the meaning of the story. Summarize and paraphrase ideas expressed in long quotations which you think can be stated more concisely in your own words. Do not remove any important facts from the story. Discuss with your classmates your edited paragraphs.

4. If possible, obtain an advance copy of a scheduled speech. Attend the speech. (If an advance copy of the speech is not available, attend the speech anyway.)

    a. If an advance copy was available, compare the speaker's actual remarks with the content of the advance copy. If the speaker omitted or changed any part of the speech, determine why he or she did so.

    b. Write your own brief speech story about the event. Base your lead on any new or important information introduced during the speech.

5. Attend a court hearing, school committee session, town meeting, or similar event, and write a sidebar about a related event or development that took place prior to, during, or following the meeting.

6. Write a news story based on the content of a government document. Your school library may have government documents and pamphlets on various subjects or write to the U.S. Government Printing Office or the appropriate government department.

Covering Speeches, Public Meetings, and Published Reports

CHAPTER 10

Writing Feature Stories

Mary Roberts has a sign on her desk: "Writing isn't hard; thinking is!" Mary has been a feature writer for the *Sioux City Journal* for four years, and she says she has loved every minute of it. Other reporters are secretly a little jealous of her. After all, she's the one who gets to put color in her stories, while the reporters assigned to the City Desk seem limited to facts.

Mary doesn't argue the point; nevertheless, she knows that her job isn't all that easy. Those crisp phrases that make her copy sparkle don't just come off the top of her head; she works hard to come up with them.

Then there's the matter of topics. Those reporters on the city desk have assigned beats that they cover every day. Mary doesn't have a beat. She has to come up with her story ideas herself. Of course, her boss, the Feature Editor, helps, but for the most part, Mary's story topics are her own ideas.

Today's topic is a case in point. Last evening Mary and a friend went out to an ice-cream parlor that has become the "in" place in her community. There were 30 people in line, waiting to buy some unusual flavor such as banana-coffee or chocolate-cinnamon-raisin or strawberry-chip.

When Mary finally got to the counter, she found that the prices were what she considered exorbitant: $2 for a medium-size cone.

This morning she discussed the matter with her editor, who gets just as excited about a story on ice cream fads as Mary does. They agreed on this title for Mary's forthcoming feature story: "The Four C's of Today's Ice Cream: Calories, Content, Cost, Connoisseurs." After spending the next couple of days talking to store managers, food editors, and average ice-cream lovers, and after putting on five pounds sampling the various kinds and flavors of ice cream ("It's my job, boss"), Mary turns in a feature story with those crisp phrases that make her copy sparkle.

The Feature Story

What Is a Feature?

Material written for the mass media—both print and broadcast—that cannot be categorized as straight news or as an editorial or as advertising is called feature material. Almost any topic that would entertain and interest consumers is an appropriate subject for a feature article. (Mary's feature story about ice cream is a good example.) Feature stories, which add color and an extra dimension to news content, lend variety to the newspaper's or the broadcaster's straight news presentations.

Most news features are based in some way on news events: News features present entertaining news, explain and interpret facts, or present the human-interest side of the news. Other types of feature articles, also related to the news, include commentary, detailed speech reports, personality interviews, and fashion news. In addition, news-related features include reviews of books, stage presentations, movies, radio and television programs.

Purpose of the Feature Story

The primary purpose of the straight news story is to inform; the primary purpose of the editorial is to persuade. Although the feature story might inform and persuade to a degree, its primary purpose is to entertain. Above all, the feature story must be *interesting*. While straight news stories and editorials generally appeal to the intellect, features usually appeal to the emotions by arousing joy or sympathy or anger or contentment or some other feeling. For example, Jack Cort, City Editor of the Cocoa (Florida) *Today*, tells about a beginning reporter's first account of a man's

Helping children enjoy and understand museum art

Parents can take an active role in using art museums as educational and fun places for children to explore.

By Jane Anderson
Staff writer of
The Christian Science Monitor

Boston

"Can you see any animals on these mummies?" asked Elizabeth Greene, teacher of a preschool program at the Museum of Fine Arts in Boston.

"Sure," piped up a towheaded four-year-old boy, examining the colorful relics in one of the museum's Egyptian rooms.

"Look very carefully and tell me what you see."

"I see a parrot," offered a pony-tailed girl in pink.

"I also see a snake," another youngster added.

"You have very sharp eyes. Here you can see several birds and all their feathers," said the instructor, pointing to a section of one of the mummies. "These drawings are really telling you a story," she continued as she began to explain about hieroglyphics and the ancient Egyptian way of life.

Later during the short gallery session, the children took pencils and paper to draw birds and other creatures decorating the mummies to use as ideas for a work project in a downstairs studio.

Many art museums around the country offer classes or tours for children, but parents themselves can help their children enjoy and understand art during museum visits.

"The most important thing is to try to enter into a discussion with the child about what they see in front of them," says Lois Raasch, director of the Junior Museum for the Art Institute of Chicago. "Parents may feel hesitant or may not feel they're capable [of discussing] art with children], but they already have a sophisticated eye in many ways."

Questions a parent asks a child should be based on what they both can see in the painting or sculpture rather than on a knowledge of art history or historical fact. The questions, she adds, should not elicit a right or wrong answer.

In a portrait, for example, a parent might ask, "Is there something you would remember about that face?" or "What can you learn about that person from the way he is standing?"

Miss Raasch says her staff at the museum generally covers eight to 10 pieces of art in an hour or an hour and a half. "That gives the child the opportunity to make comparisons."

Parents may want to pick themes for a museum visit such as animals, shapes, or colors, says Lorri Berenberg, coordinator of workshop programs for the Museum of Fine Arts in Boston. Or they may want to focus on a particular culture and discuss what it has in common with their own lives or how it is different.

"The best thing a parent who is not an art historian can do is to bring the painting into the realm of the child's life," agrees Louis Gordon, museum educator for schools at the Fine Arts Museums of San Francisco.

One way to start is to bring the child's attention to clothing, food, or animals in paintings and other pieces of art.

In a room of portraits a parent might ask, "Which person looks the nicest?" "How would it feel like to wear those kinds of clothes?" or "Who would you want to be your brother, your sister, or mother?" Mrs. Gor-

> Questions a parent asks a child should be based on what they both can see in the painting or sculpture rather than on a knowledge of art history or historical fact.

don also points out that portraits often include background objects indicating a person's occupation or interests, which can spur an interesting discussion.

"It's often most beneficial for the parents, because it makes them look at the paintings closely themselves in order to ask the question," she says.

In discussing nonobjective art with their children, parents can focus on colors and shapes or help their children look for brushstrokes or other painting techniques. Another approach is to have children play the part of the artist and ask them questions about the painting from that perspective.

Mrs. Gordon says children show a special interest in decorative arts because they can

Museum of Fine Arts in Boston　　By Barth Falkenberg, staff photographer
Egyptian statue captures the imagination of preschoolers

easily understand their function. She finds children are also attracted to paintings of babies and other children.

After 30 to 45 minutes in the galleries, Mrs. Gordon suggests breaking for lunch or some other activity. "Art museums are fun for young children in small doses," she says.

A new workbook, "Let's Go to the Art Museum," by Virginia K. Levy, provides a good introduction to the art museum experience. Parents can take it along for their children to use while they go through the galleries.

In a bright, easy-to-follow format, the book gives basic explanations about different kinds of paintings such as portraits, still lifes,

seascapes, landscapes, and nonobjective art. It also covers sculpture, prints and graphics, drawings, photography, primitive art, textile art, and other decorative arts.

Each topic includes black-and-white examples of master artworks, questions and suggestions for discussion parents might initiate, and space for children to try similar projects of their own.

Copies of "Let's Go to the Art Museum" may be obtained by sending $6.95, plus $1 postage and handling to, Veejay Publications, PO Box 1629, Pompano Beach, Fla. 33061.

Vacationing with teen-agers offers opportunity to renew family bonds

By Nancy Norton Mattila
Special to The Christian Science Monitor

If your family is like ours, over the years you've enjoyed touring this "absurd, brilliant, angular country" — as Josephine Tey described our beautiful land.

For us it all started when we borrowed that first pup tent and camped our way from Minnesota to the West Coast. Our first child fell easily into this budding family tradition. Eventually both children delighted, during their first dozen years at least, in the annual vacation trip to such far-flung destinations as Big Bend National Park; the Thousand-Mile

Parent & child

Drive around Lake Superior; San Francisco; and Gettysburg, Mount Vernon, and Williamsburg (on a Bicentennial visit).

Time passes, however. The 6- and 10-year-olds amenable to whatever itinerary seems best to their parents are suddenly 14 and 18, with other commitments. Nostalgically they may agree that a family trip is a good idea. But when it comes to all that togetherness in the car, parents might well rethink and discuss travel plans to make this experience more memorable.

With young adults living at home longer, we've found that vacationing together (when feasible) also benefits the home situation, as we relax and enjoy one another under holiday conditions. Here are some ideas that have helped:

● Bring teen-agers in on all aspects of the vacation plan; use some of their imaginative ideas. You can now share responsibility for making this a fun-filled, educational event. Be sure everyone has some influence on (1) how long you'll all be away from home; (2) your major destination and possible sidetrips; (3) the amount of money available and how it will be allocated for gasoline, food, overnight accommodations, entertainment, and souvenirs. Pick a volunteer to keep track of actual expenses.

● Teens will usually offer plenty of good-humored assistance with the mechanics of an automobile trip. If you're properly insured, a licensed teen can provide needed relief behind the wheel. On a budget-wise camping trip (which does require work), we put all that youthful energy to work setting up and taking down tents, scouting out dried wood for the traditional evening campfire, and roasting the hot dogs.

● You may have to submit to a certain number of hours of "their" music. Headsets or a transistor radio in the back can help re-

lieve this problem. If your teens use the car radio for their tapes, compromise by allowing equal time for your own favorite tapes or for blessed silence. As a matter of survival, we were dragged into lukewarm tolerance of rock music somewhere between Syracuse,

> With young adults living at home longer, we've found that vacationing together (when feasible) also benefits the home situation, as we relax and enjoy one another under holiday conditions.

N.Y., and Chatham, Mass., in June 1981. The moment stands out in my mind as the dawn of an inkling of what it's like to be a young adult in the 1980s.

● Teens may miss school friends. Help out by packing plenty of writing materials and stamps. Later there will be post cards, so take along your local telephone directory to supply addresses of friends.

● Imaginative teens always notice what's new to do. They'll spot the motel with HBO and join early risers in the lobby for continental breakfast. They'll while away the hours

contentedly taking a sun bath under the van's sunroof. Not long ago, near the Mexican border, our daughter made a quick stop at a local porch sale and came away with colorful, like-new garments at 50 cents apiece. Souvenir shops were selling such items for $20 and $30.

● Unlike younger children, you don't have to worry about teens amusing themselves. During odd hours, rest stops, and overnights, they may be found swimming, jogging, playing catch with baseball and glove, throwing a frisbee, fishing, working out on a camp basketball court, snapping a camera, painting and sketching, reading and writing. Remind them to bring along materials for their favorite leisure pastimes.

Car travel with teens provides a chance for relaxed conversation and fun together, as well as observation of concerns overlooked in the busyness of daily life. Here parents may empathize with the young man who, if he seems overly concerned with appearance, is having to adjust to his sudden six-foot stature. And they can sympathize with a daughter who seems coolly in control, but still craves encouragement as college studies become increasingly challenging. Living cheek by jowl on these tours reminds us of how very welcome parental understanding can be, even to the most self-assured teen.

A Monday column

operation to restore his sight. The reporter's first story was a simple presentation of facts in straight news-story form. Cort suggested that the reporter rewrite the material as a feature article to show the readers what the blind man had been missing before his sight was restored. Following is the lead from the reporter's article, revised and resubmitted as a feature presentation.

A blind man stood by his window after a summer rain. A cool mist touched his empty eyes.

Across the street, unnoticed, a little girl stirred a puddle with her toe to muss the rainbows and watch them form again.

Sights like the little girl have been missing from the world of Sam Cooper for 16 years. Now he will see again. . . .

The Importance of Style

In the straight news story the news writer follows a definite style in presenting material: the inverted pyramid. In the inverted pyramid style the news writer reveals the most important elements in the lead and enumerates the remaining facts of the story, usually in order of decreasing importance, in an impersonal, straightforward manner. By contrast, feature writing is less rigid in structure and allows the writer the creativity to present a more *human* side of the news. Because the style of feature writing is informal, and because the writer is permitted to express ideas in an imaginative way, feature writing often requires more skill than does straight newswriting.

In feature writing the news writer's personal style (the way he or she puts thoughts into words) is more important than in straight newswriting. Successful feature writers have an original, personal style—an individualism. To develop an individual writing style, students planning to become professional writers should first become familiar with—and study carefully—the elements of style used by skilled feature writers. They should also practice writing feature articles at every opportunity.

Structure of the Feature Story

Although permitted greater freedom in writing a feature story than in writing a straight news story, the reporter should keep in mind the basic elements of structure so that the feature story will have unity. In feature writing, the lead can be thought of as an introduction. Generally, the introduction should comprise about one fifth of the length of the entire story. The body should com-

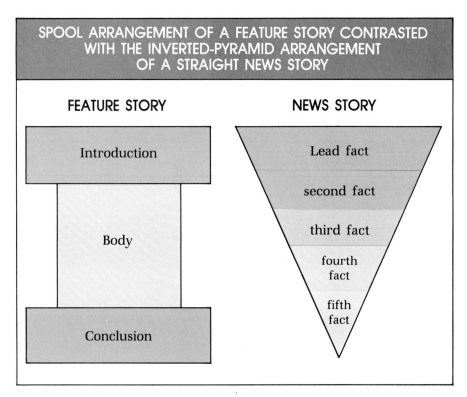

SPOOL ARRANGEMENT OF A FEATURE STORY CONTRASTED WITH THE INVERTED-PYRAMID ARRANGEMENT OF A STRAIGHT NEWS STORY

FEATURE STORY

Introduction

Body

Conclusion

NEWS STORY

Lead fact

second fact

third fact

fourth fact

fifth fact

prise a little over three fifths of the entire length, and the conclusion should comprise slightly less than one fifth of the entire length. In contrast to the inverted pyramid structure of a straight news story, the structure of the feature story can be said to resemble a spool.

Feature-Story Leads

The purpose of the lead (introduction) in a feature article is to arouse interest and acquaint the reader/listener/viewer with the general theme of the article. By using an intriguing idea, a lively vocabulary, and an imaginative approach in the lead, the feature writer can successfully capture attention. The following examples, written by journalism students, indicate a number of ways to begin a feature article.

The Serious and Thoughtful Lead. In a sense, this type of lead says to the reader/listener/viewer: "This material should be important to you—no matter who you are." The tone of this lead is serious and thoughtful. The writer can create a sense of urgency by using short sentences.

Wisdom spoke to Tommie last night. She walked right into his
dream. Tommie told me so.
"Mommie, why is he so quiet?" asked little Susan.

The Problem Lead. This type of lead points to a problem and
says, "Something's amiss here." The problem lead is informative
and often presents conflict—one of the makers of news.

Six out of every ten students entering an institution of higher
learning will never graduate.

The Shock Lead. Another effective way of capturing attention is
to throw readers/listeners/viewers off guard and then shock
them. However, in using this type of lead, the feature writer must
be careful not to resort to sensationalism, not to let readers/lis-
teners/viewers down in the body of the story. The following fea-
feature is based on a report of the American Cancer Society. The
humorous approach and the lightness of tone in the first few sentences succeed in throwing one off guard.

Tobacco is a dirty weed. I like it.
It satisfies no normal need. I like it.
It makes you thin, it makes you lean,
It takes the hair right off your bean,
It's the worst darn thing I've ever seen,
I like it.

Oh cigarette, cigar, and pipe smokers, join the crowd. Chant the
mighty ballad. Enjoy your simple pleasure. Relieve your nervous
and bored natures. Divulge your need to relax with tobacco. Puff
yourself from good health to ill. Curtail your body's usefulness.
Join the fun.
Die, oh die. Die of cancer. Die of heart disease. Die of emphy-
sema. Death comes to all. So what does it matter how we die?
When it comes, it comes. *Que sera, sera.*
Now abide foolish cigarette, cigar, and pipe smokers—these
three; but the most ill-omened is the cigarette smoker, according to
the latest report on smoking and lung cancer released by the
American Cancer Society.

The Mood Lead. Figures of speech are often used to set the
mood in this type of lead. Ideally, the mood lead gives readers/
listeners/viewers a feeling of expectation, a feeling that there will
be more to this story than might first appear.

The winter sunset hinted at snow. The scene was grey, like
the inside of an oyster, and the sun appeared as white and as
precious as a well-kept pearl.

The First-person Lead. The first-person lead indicates that the writer will inject himself or herself into the story and take the reader into confidence.

> Snow fell on Minneapolis the day I flew home to Washington, D.C., for Thanksgiving vacation. I looked out the window when we took off, and as we rose in altitude. . . .

The Alliterative Lead. Alliteration, the repetition of initial consonant sounds in two or more neighboring words or syllables in a phrase, can be used effectively in a lead. Feature writers might use alliteration in a lead to establish a light, easygoing mood. Writers who use alliteration in their leads can be said to be saying to readers/listeners/viewers, "Take it easy. You don't have to be serious all the time."

> Ah, Hollycrest, hilly haven for crazy college kids, overworked snow shovels and perpetual precipitation—snow and hail love you, Hollycrest. They must—they come to us first and leave us last. . . .

The Historical Lead. Since the subject matter of a historical feature article may seem at first like "old news," the writer should try to make the lead as interesting and as lively as possible. In the following example, the words *hugged* and *clawed* create vivid images of conflict early in the story.

> The year was 1973. Intercollegiate wrestling champion "King" Larry Martin had hugged and clawed the challenger for his domain and had reigned supreme for ten years. Now, "King" Martin faces the battle of his life for control of his kingdom. . . .

The Body of the Feature Story

The body of the feature story should incorporate three essentials of all good writing: unity, coherence, and emphasis.

Unity. To ensure unity in their features, many writers summarize the main idea, or topic, of their material in one brief sentence that is similar to a précis or thesis statement. The writer then uses the summary statement as the basis for expanding the topic in the body of the article. All material in the body of the feature article should be related to this summarizing statement. Many feature writers prepare an outline listing all the points that are to be made in the article and that also are related to the summary statement. Each sentence should relate to the summary statement, should expand on the idea contained in the summary

statement by adding specific, pertinent facts, a[...]
interest readers/listeners/viewers.

■ Paragraph Lacking Unity:

The size of a person's hands and their [...]
rest of the body are factors that influence [...]
Very large hands, for example, are those [...]
capable of delicate, intricate work. An op[...]
reveals a person who lacks firm charact[...]
Many people scoff at the mere mention [...]

■ Unified Paragraph:

A long list of important historical figu[...]
have taken an interest in palmistry. Ale[...]
Aristotle were greatly interested in the [...]
times, celebrities who have had palm r[...]
Twain, Helen Keller, Arthur Rubinstein[...]

Coherence. The sentences and paragr[...]
often much shorter than those makin[...]
tion. Coherence—the smooth flow of [...]
more difficult to achieve in feature writi[...]
sition. To guard against misunderstandin[...]
organize their materials and must car[...]
prepared outline. In each sentence of an a[...]
try to use transitional devices (words and p[...]
thoughts contained in preceding sentences. [...]

■ Paragraph Lacking Coherence:

Some people work hard to turn each of us into [...]
Gossamer Albatross flew across the English Channel [...]
mer of 1979. The International Human-Powered-Vehic[...]
tion is an organization dedicated to the invention of [...]
vehicles powered by human muscle only. An asso[...]
was the pilot (and engine) of the Gossamer Alba[...]
bicycle, not the airplane, that is receiving the [...]
attention from association members. . . .

■ Coherent Paragraph:

Some people work hard to turn each [...]
International Human-Powered-Vehicle [...]
tion dedicated to the invention of e[...]
human muscle only. One associa[...]
Gossamer Albatross, the hu[...]
the English Channel in t[...]
member was the pilot[...]
the vehicle receiving [...]
ation's members is th[...]

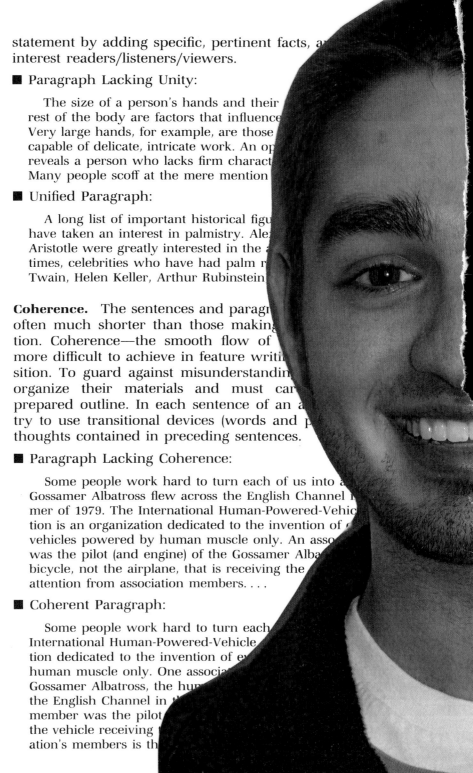

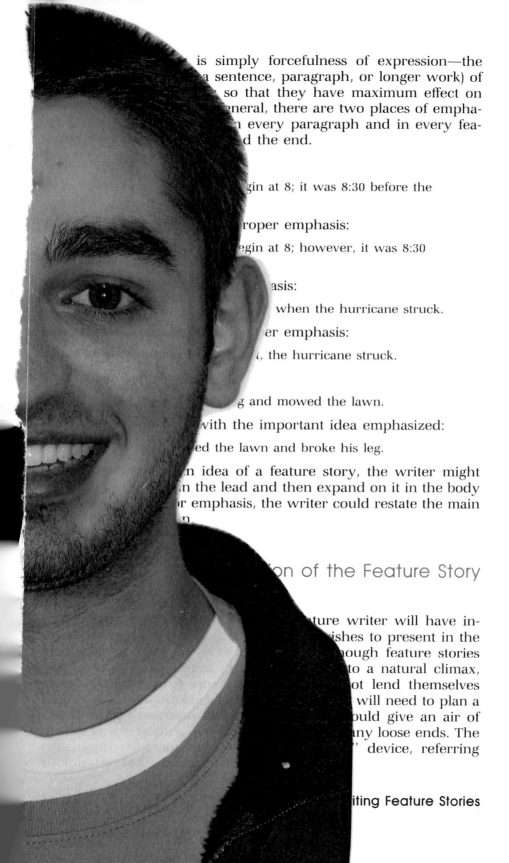

is simply forcefulness of expression—the
a sentence, paragraph, or longer work) of
so that they have maximum effect on
neral, there are two places of empha-
every paragraph and in every fea-
d the end.

gin at 8; it was 8:30 before the

roper emphasis:

egin at 8; however, it was 8:30

asis:

when the hurricane struck.

er emphasis:

, the hurricane struck.

g and mowed the lawn.

with the important idea emphasized:

ed the lawn and broke his leg.

n idea of a feature story, the writer might
in the lead and then expand on it in the body
r emphasis, the writer could restate the main

on of the Feature Story

ature writer will have in-
ishes to present in the
ough feature stories
to a natural climax,
ot lend themselves
will need to plan a
uld give an air of
ny loose ends. The
" device, referring

THE THREE PARTS OF A FEATURE STORY

Headline ——————→ **AGE NOT A HAZARD**

Lead ——————→ There's no salt like an old salt. _____

Body ——————→ The other day Maude Miller stood on her front porch and watched the repaving of the street in front of her home. _____

Conclusion ——————→ As we said at the beginning, there's no salt like an old salt.

Types of Feature Stories

Although the kinds of feature stories are as numerous as the writer's imagination will permit, the most common are identified and discussed in the paragraphs that follow.

The Human-Interest Feature

The human-interest feature, the most-often-used type of feature story, appeals to the reader's/listener's/viewer's feelings by offering a glimpse of the predicaments and successes that ordinary human beings experience. In the following example the writer describes a day in the lives of two college students. Though the feature is based on straight news material, the writer has added a new dimension to the story by using fiction-writing techniques. The tone and the mood are established in the lead. The writer achieves unity by focusing on just one day in the lives of the two students. The reader's senses and emotions are appealed to by describing sights and sounds and human responses.

April Love Blooms in Public Garden

Love is spring sunshine, scented air, and two people who can't seem to stop grinning. If you are a reader who is cynical and jaded, perhaps you should stop now and turn to a grittier story.

At 11:20 yesterday morning, Tom Doherty, 20, sat with his arm around the waist of Jackie Breen, 18, under a tree in the Public Garden. The temperature had just reached 70 degrees, and a squirrel scrambled across the greensward.

It is unclear the extent to which Tom and Jackie, wrapped in a cocoon of euphoria, grasped these facts. Or, in their mutual preoccupation, many other details of the world around them. . . .

And visible on the other side of the park, a Hollywood crew was shooting "Small Circle of Friends," a film fantasy about love—though young love was blind even to this manufactured celluloid valentine.

Someone asked them a question. Are they in love?

"Yes," they said.

Jackie's grin grew so huge it threatened to pinch her ears. Tom smiled too. His legs were stretched out casually across the grass. His foot kept jiggling.

Tom majors in finance at Suffolk University, and Jackie studies accounting there. . . .

The pond reflected the blue sky. A swanboat filled with mothers, children, and older people sent gentle vibrations across the perfect mirror. A bird darted under a branch, chirping.

What's it like to be in love? How a person, he or she, know when it happens?

"It started to happen subcons___ ___y," Tom said. "At first I didn't war___ ___admit it to myself. You don't really r___ a definition. It's just a feeling."

"It feels really good," Jac___ ___ded. "You aren't embarrassed o___ ___amed. If he comes over and I'm in ___ers, I don't feel like a jerk."

Tom introduced him___ ___ Jackie a few months ago in a ___ ___class.

"How did you do___ ___r midterm?" he had asked her.

Jackie astutely a___ ___ined this was a line, but that was ___ with her. Soon, they were sitting ___ ___ther in math class, and then they fe___ ___ love.

Could they fa___ ___ut of love? Could a dark cloud . . . ?

"I hope things get a little more normal," said Jackie, with that dazed grin. "Right now it's kind of confusing. There have been big fights, but we have trouble fighting because we both break out laughing."

Later in the afternoon, Tom was due at his part-time supermarket job. Before then, perhaps they would have a bite to eat. Going to a restaurant, of course, could prove a challenge. They would have to walk there without their feet touching the ground.

From the *Boston Herald-American*
by Robert Garrett

The Autobiographical Feature

Features that deal with the life or personal experiences of the writer can be classified as autobiographical features. Ordinarily, autobiographical features are written by well-known persons. However, anyone may have an interesting story to tell. In the following autobiographical feature, a journalism student explains how she became interested in writing. The form of the example is similar to that of the essay. The sentences flow smoothly because the ideas are well expressed and are presented in chronological order. Use of the "picture-frame" device (in which the conclusion refers back to the introduction) gives the article unity.

Journalism: A Stepping-Stone

When I was ten years old, I fell in love with a library, neither very large nor ornate. It had at the most a few thousand volumes at hand. Just the same, I decided then and there that I would spend the rest of my life in a room whose very walls burst with knowledge and adventure. Perhaps it was the smell so peculiar to libraries, the odor of old pages and new bindings. It might have been the books themselves. Their titles fascinated me; the covers pleaded in various hues to be taken down and read. And of course, being ten years old, and not of a very steadfast nature, I was captured and bound.

Bound did I say? No, the very opposite. They showed me lands and people I had never dreamed of. They loosed the bonds of the here and now and the chains of time and space. . . .

As I grew older, I realized that everyone had dreams, but they had to be kept in their place. I had a responsibility to myself to live in a real world, populated with real people. I was learning to live.

It must have been then that I decided the only vocation possible for me was one in which I could write. To think, in this pen lie a million words. With it, I can draw a picture in your mind of ideas, beauty, moods, emotions, love, glory, eternity, and dreams. What world is not within the ken of my mind, and what can stop me from giving it to you in all its beauty and magnitude?

How will my writing help my fellow human beings? I will create a magic carpet, a spaceship, a gold chariot to help them reach for the stars. I will make people laugh and cry at life and death. I will show people good and evil, right and wrong. I will stimulate rage and despair, sympathy and love, for heaven knows, people do not feel strongly enough about things today. My words may light a fire, whether in a person's mind or in a wastebasket, I cannot know. But this I do know. That someday my books will sit quietly on a crowded shelf, in covers of red and gold and wait for a very little girl, lost in a very big world.

Sandra Altner, Syracuse University

The Personality Feature

Feature stories concerning the life, interests, and accomplishments of well-known or interesting persons can be categorized as personality features. Often a personality feature is based on material obtained from an interview. Whether the interview will result in a straight interview story or in a personality feature depends on how much creativity and imagination the writer chooses to put into the story. Often a personality feature will show how a person gained fame or distinction—as in the following example.

Brother-Sister Rodeo Team Horsing Around

Rodeo. It's all in the family for senior Jodi Courtland and her sophomore brother Jasper. They have been raised around horses, and for as long as they can remember, they have been riding them.

Some people ride horses for pleasure, some race horses, and others—like Jodi and Jasper—ride them in rodeos. Their dad got them started because he is a rodeo competitor himself.

There are many events in a rodeo. Jodi participates in three events, and so does Jasper. For Jodi, it's break-away, team-roping, and barrel racing. Jasper participates in calf-roping, bull-dogging, and team-roping. Both have won money, belt buckles, and jackets. Jodi twice earned her way to the national rodeo finals.

Much hard work goes into trying to make it to the nationals. Jodi and Jasper find their friends and family to be a big help in the support department.

"My dad helps me practice," said Jodi, "and my mom is always there to say I did my best." Jasper added, "Our dad does anything he can to help us, and my friends often ask how I'm doing."

Along with practicing and performing come disappointments. Jodi said that she often gets discouraged when she doesn't do as well as she thought she should have or when she makes mistakes.

Jodi is not sure what level she would like to continue with, but Jasper plans to become a member of the Professional Rodeo Cowboys Association. However, they are still in competition for this year and have set goals for themselves.

"I'd like to compete in the national rodeo finals," said Jasper.

Jodi has been to the nationals and has put her goal a step higher. "I'd really like to win the all-around title," she said; "that would definitely be a great accomplishment for me and my family."

By Penney Jordan

The How-to-Do-Something Feature

Many newspapers and magazines print feature articles which explain to the reader the practical steps to follow in order to do something. Examples of features in this category are "do-it-yourself" articles on crafts and home repairs, articles explaining how to improve your bridge or golf game, articles on diet and exercise, and articles on sewing and cooking. The writer of the following "tongue-in-cheek" feature story seems irritated by persons in public life who avoid giving straight answers to interviewers.

The Historical Feature

Historical features, informative news features about past events, are usually written to observe national holidays, birthdates of historical figures, and anniversaries of important news events. Timely historical feature stories could be written for publication on Independence Day, on Thanksgiving, on the anniversary of a city founder's birth, or to recall such significant events as the ending of World War II. Source material for historical features can be found in your school or community library. The following is an example of an appropriate historical feature written during the Christmas season.

The Color Feature

Color features are sidebar stories concerning the trappings that add glamor to major events. A main story might be written about the outcome of the Homecoming Game; a color feature might concern the crowning of the Homecoming Queen. Other color stories might deal with what happens backstage during a Drama Club presentation or in the football team's locker room during half-time. The following color story describes events occurring during half-time at a football game.

So Who Needs Horses?

The Greeks showed the Romans a trick or two at Syracuse University Saturday.

Romans used horses to pull their chariots. Yesterday the Greeks (SU fraternity brothers) had human pullers for their chariots.

This twang on an old saw came at the second "Greek Games" run off in Archbold Stadium as part of the last act of a campus "Greek Week" sponsored by the Interfraternity Council. The touch of Marx Brothers followed a week of social events, entertainment, speeches, scholastic competition, and alumni programs. The finale occurred during half-time of the Syracuse-Oregon State game.

The chariots—all hammered together in the fraternity houses with wood, bed sheets, flags, and bicycle wheels—carried two riders (flyweight), hauled 100 yards by alternating teams of four students.

"I can't believe my eyes," a football fan said. "Are they really doing that?"

The stadium cinder track was wet, the midfield was wet, and riders and donors of horsepower were freckled with mud. . . .

Richard Case
Syracuse Herald-Journal

The Weather Feature

Weather reporters for metropolitan dailies telephone the U.S. Weather Bureau each day to secure the information for their stories. To gain reader interest, weather reporters try to present interesting facts in their leads. A routine weather story lead might be as follows:

The first major snowstorm of the season is expected to move into the Midwest today with Chicago escaping most of the six inches of snow. . . .

Unusual weather conditions often make good material for imaginative feature stories. During one extended hot spell in the San Francisco area, a reporter wrote this award-winning weather feature. It began like this:

The Quietest Night Ever

"This," said one veteran moon-watcher in the San Francisco police department, "was the quietest night since the blizzard of '88." Inasmuch as San Francisco had no blizzard in '88, that makes it the quietest night ever. . . .

Andrew Curtin

The Humorous—and Perhaps Satirical—Feature

Writing humor requires an understanding of basic human nature. We all make mistakes, and William Safire, well-known columnist, has some fun with the human propensity for error.

Fumblerules of Grammar

By William Safire
New York Times Service

Not long ago, I advertised for perverse rules of grammar, along the lines of "Remember to never split an infinitive" and "The passive voice should never be used."

The notion of making a mistake while laying down rules ("Thimk," "We Never Make Misteaks") is highly unoriginal, and it turns out that English teachers have been circulating lists of fumblerules for years.

As owner of the world's largest collection, and with thanks to scores of readers, let me pass along a bunch of these never-say-neverisms:

—Avoid run-on sentences they are hard to read.

—Don't use no double negatives.

—Use the semicolon properly, always use it where it is appropriate; and never where it isn't.

—Reserve the apostrophe for it's proper use and omit it when its not needed.

—Do not put statements in the negative form.

—Verbs has to agree with their subjects.

—No sentence fragments.

—Proofread carefully to see if you any words out.

—Avoid commas, that are not necessary.

—If you reread your work, you will find on rereading that a great deal of repetition can be avoided by rereading and editing.

—A writer must not shift your point of view.

—Eschew dialect, irregardless.

—And don't start a sentence with a conjunction.

—Don't overuse exclamation marks!!!

—Place pronouns as close as possible, especially in long sentences, as of 10 or more words, to their antecedents.

—Hyphenate only between two syllables, and avoid un-neces-sary hyphens.

—Write all adverbial forms correct.

—Don't use contractions in formal writing.

—Writing carefully, dangling participles must be avoided.

—It is incumbent on us to avoid archaisms.

—If any word is improper at the end of a sentence, a linking verb is.

—Steer clear of incorrect forms of verbs that have snuck in the language.

—Take the bull by the hand and avoid mixed metaphors.

—Avoid trendy locutions that sound flaky.

—Never, ever use repetitive redundancies.

—Everyone should be careful to use a singular pronoun with singular nouns in their writing.

—If I've told you once, I've told you a thousand times, resist hyperbole.

—Also, avoid awkward or affected alliteration.

—Don't string too many prepositional phrases together unless you are walking through the valley of the shadow of death.

—Always pick on the correct idiom.

—"Avoid overuse of 'quotation "marks."' "

—The adverb always follows the verb.

—Last but not least, avoid cliches like the plague; seek viable alternatives. . . .

Featured Brights

Newspaper editors often need short two- or three-sentence stories to fill out a column of type. If these stories are written in straight news-story style, they are known as fillers or boilerplate. If the facts contained in such short stories are presented in feature-story form, they then become featured brights. Featured brights are usually short, humorous features, often ending with a punch line. Some types of featured brights can be thought of as feature sidebars. For example, if, at the scene of a fire, a dog were seen tugging at a fire fighter's coat in order to prevent the fire fighter from entering a burning building, such information could be presented as a feature sidebar to the main fire story. Following is an example of a featured bright:

Two Israeli police officers on a goodwill tour of the United States were not over-awed by New York City traffic after directing cars for 10 minutes in Times Square. Roberta Cohen, 19, conceded only that New York traffic snarls are "worse than Israeli traffic." But Janice Freedman, 20, said, "Traffic is more hectic during the rush hour in Tel Aviv."

Feature Photographs

Human-interest photographs often make good feature material for newspapers. Feature photos can provide the reader with a welcome relief from pages filled with straight news copy. The following classified advertisement provided one photographer with a subject for an interesting feature photograph.

> For Sale: One old hound dog that is lazy and has fleas. Price $500. Call 555-3484.

Intrigued, the photographer telephoned the man who had placed the advertisement. He learned that the dog's owner had given in to his wife's demands that he sell the dog and had placed a classified advertisement in the newspaper. But he hadn't told her how the advertisement would read. The photographer asked if the advertisement had brought results. "Yes," replied the man. "One caller had offered to trade two $250 cats." Faced with the possibility of having two cats rather than one dog, the man's wife consented to keeping the dog. The man was happy to let the photographer take a feature picture of his son showing the dog licking the boy's face.

News Features

News-feature stories often employ any of the devices of form and style that are common to the human-interest story. News features have, as a basis, a timely news happening with a human-interest angle and are generally more timely than straight human-interest or long feature stories. News features are usually about events that have already taken place or that everyone already knows about. Following is the lead from a news-feature story:

Chute Fails to Open on First Jump

Editor's Note: The following story is true. This exciting incident relates a harrowing experience a young sophomore at MHS went through as he made a practice jump from an airplane over Orange, Massachusetts, in his desire to learn skydiving.

"It was my first time jumping from a Cessna 185. I had always wanted to learn how to jump and now my big moment had come. I was to be the first one out. Since I was a beginner, I was to jump at an altitude of 2500 feet. . . ."

Benjy Matta, *Mustang News*

News-Summary Features

News-summary features summarize a series of news events, often by day, week, month, and sometimes years. Many newspapers feature news-summary features in "capsule" form on their front pages, expanding them on the inside pages. School newspapers often use the news-summary feature to summarize such events as all school dances for a particular year, all athletic competitions for a given season, or all of the fund drives. Following is the lead from a news-summary feature story:

Club Roundup—Spring Salute Planned

Boom! Everything but fireworks is aiding Jackson High's salute to spring this year. Style shows, field trips, elections, and special presentations are only a few of the multitude of events scheduled. . . .

Feature Obituaries

Newspapers must, at times, publish obituaries that are presented as features. Such obituaries should be respectful and sympathetic without being overly sentimental. In addition, they should be factual and should be written in good taste. As a rule, feature obituaries are published a few days after the person concerned has died. The following example consists of excerpts from a feature obituary written by noted drama critic Elliot Norton after the death of playwright Paddy Chayefsky.

Paddy Chayefsky, who died last Saturday at 58, one of the few screen writers whose name meant something to the public, was a great professional, a tough-minded, sure-handed craftsman. Though he wasn't entirely happy on Broadway, he learned his trade there and in the last two years had been working on a new play for the stage.

When he came out of the service after World War II, he decided he wanted to be a playwright, but he had had no training and didn't know where to begin. Although he hadn't seen it, he had read and admired Lillian Hellman's first drama, *The Children's Hour,* and undertook to study it as a textbook. It worked for him.

His method of discovering why the Hellman play had succeeded was to examine it line by line. He said afterwards he copied the text on his typewriter and asked himself after each sentence: "Now why does she write that way?"

He didn't know Lillian Hellman at the time. But he knew that her play had been a hit and he had wit enough to recognize that her dialogue, seemingly no more than a flow of "natural" speech, was very carefully and shrewdly contrived. . . .

To conclude his feature, Norton makes a general statement about the treatment of screenwriters and then assesses the degree of greatness Chayefsky achieved.

Hollywood has tended to devour or bypass writers. In the old days of Goldwyn and L. B. Mayer and Harry Cohn they were treated like peons, their stories cut, curtailed and rewritten. More recently, they have been subordinated to dominant directors. But not Chayefsky. Pictures like *Network* and *Hospital* were his. He had the muscle, the courage and the skill in dramaturgy to insist on that.

He had come a long way since he labored over his typewriter copying Lillian Hellman's first play, line by line, and trying to understand just why her words had made a first-rate drama. He had started the right way. He was bright—not brilliant—and he should by right have had many more good years.

Society and Homemaking Features

Most newspapers contain columns and feature articles about homemaking and social events. Such features include news of engagements, weddings, social events, and personalities. Included in this category are columns and feature articles offering information about health, child-rearing, family living, fashion, and "how-to-do-it" features on cooking and homemaking.

Most school newspapers contain feature articles that can be generally categorized as personality, occupation, social event, and appearance features or columns.

Personalities. One of the favorite pastimes of both men and women is "people-watching." Many people interested in news of celebrities enjoy reading about other people. In this category are feature stories about professional women. The following feature is about author and playwright Jean Kerr.

Larchmont, N.Y. (AP)—When Jean Kerr was turning out $300 magazine articles in the back seat of the nine-year-old family Chevy, parked a few blocks from her houseful of boisterous boys, she never considered herself a serious writer. "I consider a writer serious who makes more than $20,000-a-year," was the way she put it.

That was five years ago.

Today, two books, two movie sales, and a hit play later, Jean Kerr has had to revise her standard upward. Her royalties from the five companies of *Mary, Mary* average $20,000 a week. And she approaches her work with the same uncomplicated candor as when she heard MGM had paid $75,000 for the screen rights to her best-seller *Please Don't Eat the Daisies*.

The venerable Chevy still holds down a place of honor in the Kerr garage, alongside a newer, more expensive vehicle, but its back-seat recluse has moved on to larger, more comfortable quarters. Jean Kerr now works in a corner of the bedroom amid a colossal chaos of Coke bottles, cigarette butts, and disorderly mounds of manuscript that, as the children know from past experience, constitute the rubbled construction site of a new play.

The Associated Press

Social Events. Throughout the school year, school newspapers include many feature articles on student social events. Including details (such as a description of the decorations at a school dance) will add life to a feature story and will help re-create the atmosphere of the occasion.

Members of the Junior Class will sponsor a tea as a special Valentine's Day greeting for their parents in the cafeteria this afternoon.

A Valentine motif of hearts and cupids will transform the cafeteria. In charge is a committee of 24 juniors directed by Miss Martha White, junior counselor, who will spend the seventh period decorating.

The tea table centerpiece and the refreshments of . . . .

The Lancer

Appearance. Many people are interested in reading about ways to improve their appearance and the appearance of their homes. Feature articles based on beauty care, fashion, and interior decoration have high reader interest. The following is a fashion feature oriented to the interests of fashion-conscious students.

"Teens today are the best dressed in history," Chuck Mills, co-owner of the University Men's Shop told students in Journalism I and II classes last week.

He speaks often to women's, as well as men's, groups because, he says, "Seventy percent of men's and boys' clothing is bought under the influence of women and girls."

He finds that in schools where there is an ideal or program on proper dress the morale is higher and the influence on grades is enormous.

The Southwest Lancer

Feature Columns

School newspapers contain many types of feature columns. One of the most popular types is the social column, which presents news about students and their activities. Information contained in the social column is usually presented in the form of brief news items. Most social columns are informal in style, often use humor and figures of speech, and are conversational in tone.

Everything in a Mess

You may not sleep tonight after I tell you this, but it's something you have to know.

For 16 years, I have conducted an informal survey among parents that requires a simple answer to a simple question: "Does your son or daughter pick up anything besides a fork?"

Some parents became quite violent. Two had to be sedated. A dozen or so reminded me they had served in the war. And here's the scary part. Of those queried, not one parent had a child who found tidiness a way of life.

Somewhere between boiling the pacifier and buying black towels, we lost 'em. I don't know where we failed, but we have unleashed a generation of kids who think self-cleaning bathrooms have already been invented.

What most parents fear is that they will be considered incompetent for not teaching cleanliness. . . .

I resent people thinking that slovenliness comes from a mother who was too busy to teach organization. When my firstborn was just a toddler, before I would seat her at the table, I'd say, "Did you wash your hands and face?" I never got an answer. Just a 24-inch tongue that came out of the mouth and like a street cleaner made a path, bordered on the north by a nose, east and west by cheeks, and on the south by a chin.

I lost ground every day after that.

I hate to go whining to the government every time there is a problem, but perhaps a Child Neatness Agency could be established to set up some health standards.

Yes, the real problem today is not the threat of UFO's bringing alien people from another planet to earth. It's how are we going to find them in all this mess after they've landed.

Erma Bombeck
The Boston Globe, May 7, 1981

Features for the Broadcast Media

Inasmuch as its primary purpose is to entertain, the feature story fits in ideally with one of the major purposes of radio and television: entertainment. The subjects of broadcast features can be as many and as varied as those published in newspapers and magazines.

Beginning with a clear idea of the general purpose of a feature story, the writer phrases an effective topic sentence and then lists, in logical succession, the important points that support it. Next, the writer works hard on the beginning and the ending of the feature story—the beginning because the deftness with which the story attracts the attention of the audience may well determine whether there will be any listeners/viewers at all. The writer's attention then shifts to the ending because it is important to leave the audience with a feeling of satisfaction—a feeling that may insure memorability. Finally, the writer develops the body of the feature.

Besides their ability to write clearly and interestingly, writers of radio features have at their disposal the human voice, sound effects, and music. Writers of television features use these same elements, but they also must consider the appearance of the studio set and camera angles that will be most effective.

Here is a feature story that was broadcast and telecast recently.

Courtesy seems to be going with the proverbial wind. Not long ago, a colleague shared this story with me. While she was arranging for a rental car, the reservation clerk told her, "My name is Jack." Thinking there could conceivably be another Jack on the car rental's payroll, she asked, "Jack, who?" Not that she was nosy. The extra question was insurance; in event something went awry, she could mention that the arrangements were made with Jack so-and-so, and be credited with some degree of accuracy. Well, it seems this particular auto-leasing firm does not give last names. No reason was offered, save for the comment that first name conversation is friendlier. But we're in a hurry these days, and to address someone as Mr. or Mrs. takes more time than some people wish to use. It's apparently more time than broadcast news services are willing to relinquish to what is deemed superfluous words. This week, for example, one broadcast service announced that it will discontinue using courtesy titles for women in the second reference. And using a story about Jane Doe, let's say, after it's been established who Jane Doe is, she will be referred to as Doe; not Miss Doe, Mrs. Doe, or Ms. Doe, unless of course there is some story when the man and the woman have the same last name. Then, all those salutations of yore would be used all over again. [Some networks] have no set policy on the subject of using last names for women. Each of us can choose the form he or she wishes to follow as preferences or habits dictate. There is something to be said, though, in favor of continuing the practice of courtesy that was a bit of all right for previous generations. Can you imagine if Winston Churchill had a job as a car rental agent. It might be jarring to hear, "This is Winnie, do you want a compact?" Or how would you like to hear a story that refers to the great actress Katherine Cornell, and uses her last name only. There could be confusion with the university of the same name. "Courtesy," as William Butler Yeats once said, "is one of the sensible impressions of the free mind." Familiarities, some might argue, could bring imprisonment. Maybe Ralph Waldo Emerson said it best. "Life is not so short," he wrote, "but that there is always time enough for courtesy."

Use of Feature Stories by Other Media

Newspapers and magazines are not the sole media to use feature articles. Many public-relations and advertising agencies prepare and distribute a variety of public-service feature materials, as well as feature materials concerning clients and advertisers.

Public-Relations Agencies. Since newspaper editors prefer to use the best available feature stories, many public-relations agencies hire writers who specialize in preparing features. Feature articles prepared by public-relations writers usually concern the agency's clients. The following feature article was prepared by a public-relations agency and distributed to thousands of newspapers and magazines.

From: Mapes and Grant, Inc.
510 Madison Avenue
New York, NY 10017

For: The Ross Company

Novice Solves Pressing Problem
A Minnesota woman has a pressing problem.

Literally.

But by solving it she became a successful businesswoman.

This is the success story of Mrs. Maude Lee of Jackson, Minnesota—whose invention now is being sold coast-to-coast by Boyd Bros., a division of The Ross Company.

Like every other woman who sews, Mrs. Lee knew that proper pressing is the secret of custom-made, rather than homemade clothes.

But what does a woman do when her ironing board remains uncooperatively flat when she's trying to iron a curved seam?

Maude Lee invented her own ironing board, suited for tackling those difficult problems.

It has different surfaces—a straight edge, an inside curve, small, medium, and large outside curves, an angle for points and corners, a long curved edge, and a flat working area for small details. All in all, just about any shape that could be needed.

And it's compact enough to fit on any shelf and light enough so that anyone could easily set it up.

Ever since Boyd Bros. bought her invention, Mrs. Lee has been busy with other home sewing ideas.

She isn't talking about them until she has successfully tested each one to her own satisfaction.

Advertising Agencies. The body copy for many advertisements is often presented in feature style. The advertising copywriter may peg a story on something that is in the news. For example, if city drivers were concerned about traffic congestion, a copywriter for a headache remedy might begin his or her copy with a reference to drivers. One major oil company has built an effective advertising campaign based on problems encountered by teenage drivers, and a recent advertisement for a car manufacturer was centered on winter driving problems.

Sources of Material for Feature Stories

Feature-story material is easily found in any community. Any information having interest and entertainment value for readers makes ideal material for feature articles. Schools contain an abundance of feature material, and writers often get feature-story ideas from student activities, student organizations, individual students and teachers, or from offices that are set up to aid students. A student preparing a historical feature that compared the size of the school's first graduating class to the size of the present class might use for research sources the yearbook, the student newspaper published by the school's first class, a teacher who taught the school's first class, and a local citizen who was in the class. These sources could provide the student with basic research materials for a good feature.

The student reading *Canterbury Tales, Romeo and Juliet,* or *Othello* can often see the qualities of the people he or she knows in the characters portrayed. The student may know persons as selfless as the clerk, as innocent as Juliet or Desdemona, or as ugly as Iago. While times may have changed since these masterpieces were written, human emotions haven't. In summary, the feature writer must be concerned with the triumphs and tragedies of the ordinary person and must have the ability to write about them with feeling in warm, human terms.

CHECKLIST FOR PREPARING FEATURE ARTICLES

✓ Has the story topic been thoroughly researched?

✓ Is the story itself interesting and entertaining?

✓ Does the story have one main idea?

✓ Does the story have a lead, a body, and a conclusion?

✓ Is the story written in the familiar-essay style?

✓ Is the lead designed to entice the reader, and is it different from a straight news-story lead?

✓ Does the story have unity? Has it been developed with coherence and emphasis?

✓ Does word choice reflect freshness and originality? Have all clichés and redundancies been deleted?

✓ Is the sentence structure varied?

✓ Does the conclusion wrap the story up neatly?

Activities

1. Select five straight news stories from your daily newspaper. Rewrite each lead paragraph into a feature-article lead, but maintain the basic facts. Use suspense, quotes, and shock leads to change the impact.

2. Each year many department stores select students for part-time employment. Plan an interview with one of these students and find out how he or she got the job, the hours, and the good and bad features of the work. Also find out any other interesting sidelights to the work. Then prepare an outline for a feature article based on the results of the information you obtained. Be sure to start the outline with one brief summary statement.

3. All feature articles are based primarily on news information. Create a human-interest feature story from one of the news items listed under *a* to *f* by making up your own facts. Remember to include the elements of unity, coherence, and emphasis.

   a. Mary Smith's dog was killed by a car.

   b. Petty thieves stole money from the church rectory.

   c. The goalie broke his leg during practice before the big game.

   d. Three false alarms have been rung this month at school.

   e. Cheerleader Mary Jones is very sick with pneumonia. It is believed she came down with it during the rainy football game.

   f. The Tower Ballroom, scene of last week's prom, burned down today.

4. Write a fictional featured bright elaborating on the following sentence:

The car stopped.

5. The Home Economics Department in your school often has available information on fashion news. Members of this department often work directly with local and national organizations that specialize in grooming and teen problems. Obtain any available information you can as the basis for a brief fashion-news feature. Prepare your feature so that it is of interest to a high school audience or an adult audience or both.

6. Personalities make up your student body. Select two students who have different opinions on the same issue (the content of assembly programs might be a start) and prepare a personality feature that stresses the students' attitudes toward this problem. Keep in mind that in writing a personality feature, home conditions, religious beliefs, and even the students' friends all work directly and indirectly to influence opinion. Dig into the students' backgrounds for clues to help you develop a feature angle for your story.

7. Radio and television feature writers sometimes prepare featured brights that are included at the end of straight news broadcasts. Prepare three-line featured brights for a radio or television news broadcast for each of the following subjects:

    a. An apple   **c.** A window

    b. A pencil   **d.** A clock

CHAPTER 11

Reporting Sports Events

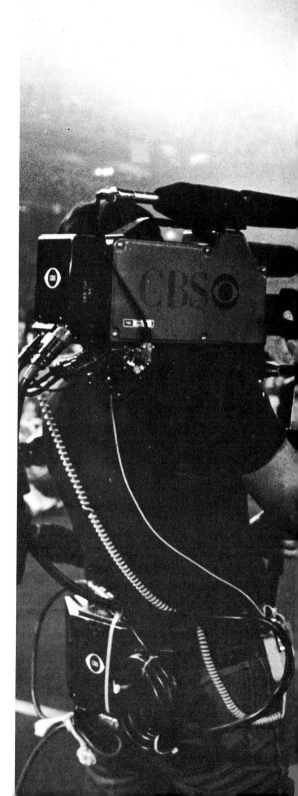

A rnold Lazarus is a walking sports
encyclopedia. Do you want to
know Ted Williams' lifetime batting
average? or Jim Brown's total yardage?
or Larry Bird's free-throw average?
Arnold will tell you. Arnold has been
following the careers of well-known
sports figures since he served as
sports editor on his high school
newspaper. In fact, he traces his
present job as sports reporter for the
Tribune to one Saturday when he
was covering his high school football
team. He was in the press box at the
field and just happened to be sitting
next to the *Tribune* sports editor,
who was covering the game, too.
Arnold struck up a conversation with
him. When the school newspaper
published Arnold's story, Arnold sent
the *Tribune* sports editor a copy. The
editor was impressed and sent him a
note of congratulations. That note
concluded, "If you're interested in
working with us when you graduate
from college, let us know." But Arnold
didn't wait until he graduated from
college. Since he was attending a
college near his home, he worked
weekends and summers on the sports

staff of the *Tribune.* And when he did graduate, he had a full-time job waiting for him.

Like all good reporters, Arnold is after specifics. And he tries to get as many as possible into every sentence. He feels that his accounts should contain all the conflict, drama, color, and emotion found on the athletic field itself.

Arnold knows that the sports world is becoming more complex than ever, that the number of sports events to be covered has greatly increased. He knows, too, that the coming of cable television has created a tremendous demand for sporting events and that viewers are being saturated with athletic contests. He is fully aware that the Entertainment and Sports Programming Network (ESPN) televises sports—80 percent of the events are taped—24 hours a day, seven days a week. That kind of coverage, of course, whets the fans' appetites for more information about sports, and Arnold is happy to have such intense interest in what he writes about.

Trends in Sports Reporting

To meet the demands of millions of sports fans, newspaper/magazine sports pages and radio/television sports broadcasts have changed noticeably during the last decade. Changes have occurred principally as follows:

1. *In the amount of space and time given to sports coverage.* The number of newspaper pages devoted to the reporting of sports events and the amount of radio/television time given to sports reporting have increased dramatically. Today, most daily newspapers publish an entire "Sports" section of from eight to 16 or more pages. Each radio/television news broadcast devotes a portion of time to the reporting of sports events, and radio/television networks block out a sizable amount of time each week for sports events, many of which are covered "live."

2. *In the elimination of trivia.* The amount of space and time given to "general" sports reporting has been considerably reduced. Conversely, much more space and time are given to extended coverage of many different kinds of sports and to coverage in depth. Cases in point: sports columns that analyze the probability of a team's winning a given game; the televising of entire sports events—football, basketball, baseball, hockey, tennis, golf, and swimming.

3. *In the specialization of sports reporters.* Sports editors now give specific assignments to sports reporters who are familiar with the particular sport to be covered. In the past, any writer or reporter was considered competent enough to cover almost any sport. Not so any more. There are sports reporters today who know as much as the players—sometimes more—about almost any given sport.

Nowadays, sports reporters—whether writing for daily newspapers, high school publications, radio, or television—understand the audience for whom they are writing. Many professional sportswriters categorize their audiences as follows:

- *Those who have witnessed the event:* This category is made up of people who have been to the event or who have seen it on television and who want a "behind-the-scenes" story.

- *Those who know the outcome of the event:* This category includes people who did not attend the event but who know the outcome and want to read or hear accounts of the highlights of the action.

- *Those who do not know the outcome of the event:* This category includes people who want to know the outcome of the event and who want to read or hear "highlights" and "behind-the-scenes" stories.

Wrestling At The Fox

Above, in a preliminary-round match of the Suburban West League wrestling tournament at Fox High School Friday Jim Pounds puts the pressure on Dave Bremehr of Lindbergh. At left, unable to make a pin, Pounds looks for advice from his coach.

Above, Keith Saylor of Webster Groves arches his back to forestall a pin by Brady Burgett of Northwest.

Above, Kelly Carr of Parkway South shouts encouragement to her brother, John, in the closing seconds of his match. He won. At left, Cheerleader Kim Schomaker of Fox eyes the clock as one of her team's matches winds down.

Photos By Odell Mitchell Jr.
Of the Post-Dispatch Staff

This is a sports page picture spread of high school wrestling.

Baseball player Reggie Jackson is being interviewed as his fans watch.

Types of Sports Stories

Every major sports event presents possibilities for a great variety of sportswriting including such assignments as sports features, sports "spot news" stories, sports interviews, sports sidebars, sports columns, sports speeches, personality stories, editorials, testimonials, and sports statistical reports. Each of these ten sports assignments can exemplify any one of the three basic types of sports stories: *advance stories*, *game stories*, and *follow-up stories*.

The Advance Story

In the advance story, the reader/listener/viewer is told *who* the participants and stars will be, *when* and *where* the event will take place, *what* the result can mean, and *why* the event is important. (Reporting *how* the event took place is usually reserved for game and follow-up stories.) As in most news stories the more background given, the more interesting the story. The major purpose of the advance story is to inform the audience about the event in the most interesting way possible. The second of the following examples of advance-story leads includes background information and is, therefore, the more interesting of the two.

The Wildcats will meet the Eagles on Friday at the Municipal Auditorium.

Frank Wolf and Ray Denfield, the best the Wildcats and Eagles have to offer, will be out of action Friday night at 8 p.m. when the teams meet for their annual clash at the Municipal Auditorium.

The remaining sentences in the advance story, presented in logical sequence, usually include other facts needed for the complete story. The preceding example would be continued as follows:

. . . Wolf, the leading scorer for Gibson, is hobbled by a badly sprained ankle, and Denfield, Wilson's Center, is suffering from the flu.

In place of Wolf, Coach Rudy Flowers will start Larry Haskins, the number six man on the team. Eagle coach Murray Berman has indicated that he will move sophomore Ray Santamaria into the lineup.

The Wildcats will be defending their 13-6 record for the Blue Division title. The Eagles, who have the same record, won a tryout game played between the two teams earlier this season by a 63-60 score.

Coach Flowers has stressed the importance of the team's winning this game: "We still have a crack at the title, but a loss could hurt the excellent mental attitude our team now has."

The Game Story

From the timeliness point of view, the most important sports story is the one published immediately following the event. To write a game story, the sportswriter must secure as many of the specific facts as possible while attending the event. If such facts are outstanding, they may provide material for the lead. Among

THE WEEKEND TV-RADIO SPORTS

TODAY

TELEVISION
TENNIS—U.S. Pro Indoor Semifinals, (9) .... 9:30 a.m.
GOLF—LPGA Mazda Classic, taped, (26) .... 9:30 a.m.
SKIING—Ski Adventure, (26) .... 11:30 a.m.
FOOTBALL—NFL Week In Review, (4) .... Noon
BASKETBALL—Minnesota vs. Indiana, (3-4-8) .... 12:30 p.m.
SPORTS SATURDAY—Boxing: Baret vs. Starling, (5-10-46) ...... 1 p.m.
BASKETBALL—Washington St. vs. USC, (4) .... 2:30 p.m.
GOLF—Crosby Pro-Am, (5-10-46) .... 3:30 p.m.
BOWLING—PBA Tournament, (7-11-13) .... 3:30 p.m.
SOCCER—International Match, (9) .... 4 p.m.
SOCCER—World Cup Replay; W. Germany vs. Spain, (14-35) .... 4:30 p.m.
ICE SKATING—The Great Skate: Profiles of Skating Champions, (5) .. 5 p.m.
WIDE WORLD OF SPORTS—Figure Skating Championships, (7-11-13) . 5 p.m.
HORSE RACING—Bay Meadows Review, (60) .... 6:30 p.m.
HORSE RACING—Meadows Reports, (36) .... 7:10, 9:10 and 11:10 p.m.
BOXING—Boxeo de Mexico, (14-35) .... 10 p.m.

RADIO
HORSE RACING—Bay Meadows Scratches, KCBS (740) .... 8:40 a.m.
HORSE RACING—Bay Meadows Reports, KCBS (740) .... From 12:40 p.m.
HORSE RACING—Meadows Reports, KNBR (680) .... 2:50, 4:50 & 5:50 p.m.
BASKETBALL—Arizona St. vs. Stanford, KSFO (560) .... 3:30 p.m.
HORSE RACING—Bay Meadows Re-creation, KNBR (1190) .... 5:15 p.m.
BASKETBALL—Santa Clara vs. Loyola, KHIT (1500) .... 7:30 p.m.
BASKETBALL—Hayward St. vs. Sonoma St., KTOB (1490) .... 7:45 p.m.

BASKETBALL—San Antonio Spurs vs. Warriors, KNBR (680) .... 7:45 p.m.
BASKETBALL—Arizona vs. Cal, KGO (810) .... 8 p.m.

TOMORROW

TELEVISION
SOCCER—International Match, (14) .... 9:45 a.m.
TENNIS—U.S. Pro Indoor Final, (9) .... 10 a.m.
BASKETBALL—DePaul vs. Georgetown, (3) .... 10 a.m.
BASKETBALL—Marquette vs. Wake Forest, (5-10-46) .... 10 a.m.
SPORTSWORLD—Boxing: Mancini vs. Feeney, (3-4-8) .... Noon
SPORTS SUNDAY—World Figure Skating Championships, (5-10-46) ..... Noon
GOLF—Crosby Pro-Am, (5-10-46) .... 1 p.m.
FOOTBALL—Pro Bowl: AFC vs. NFC, (7-11-13) .... 1 p.m.
OLYMPICS—Profile: Tracy Caulkins, Carl and Carol Lewis, (4) .... 3:30 p.m.
GENERAL—Superstars, (7-11-13) .... 4 p.m.
GENERAL—Sports Talk, (36) .... 6 p.m.
BASKETBALL—Tenn-Chattanooga vs. Marshall, (54) .... 11 p.m.
GENERAL—Weekend Sports Wrap-Up, (40-44) .... 11 p.m.
GENERAL—Sports Final, (4) .... 11:25 p.m.

RADIO
FOOTBALL—Pro Bowl: AFC vs. NFC, KCBS (740) .... 12:30 p.m.
BASKETBALL—UC-Santa Barbara vs. UOP, KJOY (1280) .... 1:20 p.m.
BASKETBALL—Phoenix Suns vs. Warriors, KNBR (680) .... 2:15 p.m.
BASKETBALL—San Jose St. vs. Fresno St., taped, KCBS (740) ..... 5 p.m.
Sports programs on cable channels are in the regular TV listings.

the specific facts secured at the scene of the event will be answers to the following questions:

What Were the Weather Conditions? The wind, or lack of it, may affect a quarterback's passing. Cold weather may be the cause of fumbles. The sun may blind the outfielder and cause the player to misjudge the fly ball. The All-State runner may lose because of a muddy track.

> Despite a cross-wind that buffeted passes, quarterback Jack Wiseman rifled three touchdown aerials to lead Watkins High to a 21-0 triumph over previously unbeaten Brookside yesterday.

How Large Was the Crowd? If the stands were packed, approximately how many fans were turned away? What was the approximate number of spectators? Did the cheering of the home crowd have any effect on the players? How did the fans behave? Did they celebrate the victory by tearing down the goal posts?

> More than 15,000 fans—the most ever to witness a high school basketball game in Centerville—saw the Lions down Lakeland 71-53 yesterday at the War Memorial.

What Was the Outcome of the Event? Readers/listeners/viewers, of course, want to know who won. How was the event won? Did the victor "come from behind" to win? Any statistics about prior events that might possibly highlight the outcome of the event should be included.

> In the highest-scoring game in Baylor's history, the Generals downed undefeated Auburn 101-83 Thursday night.

What Spectacular Plays Were There? Accounts of spectacular plays may be included in the lead, especially if they affected the final outcome of the game. "The basket from mid-court as the buzzer sounded," "the punt-return for a touchdown," or "the bases-loaded home run" should be included.

> Joan Ashmore speared a line drive deep behind second in the ninth inning to prevent the tying run from scoring and to preserve a 3-2 win for the pennant-bound Orioles at Hanley Field yesterday.

Who Were the Individual Stars? How did the stars perform? And, by the same token, if the star halfback didn't score, there is material for an interesting story.

> Scoring two touchdowns and setting up two others, John Martin led the Hampton Beavers to a 27-14 victory over the Wykoff Tigers Wednesday. Star halfback for the Tigers, Steve Gordon, wasn't up to form when he fumbled. . . .

What Significance Did the Outcome Have? This is another area that should be researched before covering an event. Was one team's undefeated string broken? Did the defeat cost a team the championship? Did the victor move up in the standings?

> Handing Triadelphia the worst beating in the history of the school, Warwood continued its baseball supremacy Monday with an 18-0 shutout.

How Did the Teams Compare? If the winners excelled in certain areas, this fact could well be mentioned early in the story. Did one team outweigh the other? Was the pass-rush effective? Did the full-court press hamper the loser?

> Capitalizing on their height advantage, Moundsville's Trojans trounced the New Martinsville Blue Devils 71-34 last night on the loser's court.

The Follow-up Story

Because many newspapers are published several days after a sports event has taken place, and because radio and television news programs often review sports events, the written accounts of such events are presented as follow-up stories. Since follow-up stories lack timeliness, the writer must give such stories a different treatment than that given to advance or game stories. Follow-up sports stories may be generally categorized as follows:

The Wrap-up Story. If several games have been played prior to publication or broadcast, and if space or time limitations prevent detailed accounts of the individual games, all of the information about the games is combined into one sports presentation called a wrap-up story. The wrap-up story should emphasize the most recent game and should briefly summarize the high spots of earlier individual games.

The Second-day Story. If a team performed spectacularly several weeks prior to publication or broadcast, there will need to be a separate story on that game. However, since such information is "old news," the writer usually gives the story a second-day story treatment by answering any possible questions the average fan might still have. For example, such unanswered questions might be ones like these: Why did the coach alternate the forwards? Why didn't the team use the fast-break more often? Frequently, the writer will interview the coach and the players to find answers to such questions. The most significant of the answers might be used as the lead for the second-day story.

The Evaluation Story. The evaluation story attempts to put the results of an event into understandable perspective. To do so, many writers evaluate an entire sports season and present prospects for the rest of the season by answering questions such as the following: What does the outcome of the last game mean to the team? Can the team still hope to win the championship? Can the team rebound next week from their past mediocre performance? Often, the reactions of players, coaches, and fans help make the evaluation story more interesting. Many sportswriters and editors feel that the best evaluation stories about sports events can be obtained from the losing players' reactions, usually revealed in the locker room. There, the writer finds such elements as human interest, pathos, and drama. The writer can talk with the coach, the stars, and the player whose mistake lost the game. The first of the following examples is an evaluation story by a writer who did not do thorough background research.

> In a driving rainstorm Glenville's Hawks came from behind to edge the Wesleyan Eagles 8-7 two weeks ago, when guard Tom Hinkle tackled Eagle fullback Russ Wilson in the end zone, scoring a safety....

The second example shows better handling of the same story.

> Russ Wilson sat alone in a dark corner of the Eagles' locker room. Other players were silently changing clothes, but Wilson, his head bowed and his eyes fixed on the floor, was trying to figure out what had gone wrong.
> Without shifting his eyes, he muttered, "The rainstorm caused it. The field was just too muddy . . . I just couldn't get up any momentum. Before I knew it, Hinkle came through our line like a Mack truck and was on top of me...."

Writing the Sports Story

Because the sports story conforms in general to the principles that govern the straight news story, the sports-story writer should handle assignments the same way the news reporter handles a straight news story. The sports-story writer must make the necessary advance preparation by researching for background material, must organize the story material, and must write the story (usually using the inverted pyramid style) in as interesting and informative a manner as possible.

Preparation

The sports reporter, if not an expert, should at least be well informed about the event he or she has been assigned to cover. The reporter must be familiar with the rules of the particular game and must also know the backgrounds and past performances of the individual players—especially the outstanding players on both teams. In addition, the reporter should be able to make a reasonable prediction about the outcome of the event.

Organizing the Story

Since good sportswriting is also good newswriting, the sportswriter should organize most stories in the inverted pyramid structure. Ordinarily, the reporter will include the five *w's* and the *h* in the first few paragraphs and will include as many other news elements as possible. Chapter 7, "Reporting the News," pages 149–152, discusses these elements.

Writing the Lead

The lead for most sports stories should include the names of the teams (or players), the score (if it is a game or follow-up story), and the place of the event.

Writing the Body of the Story

In the past, sportswriters were known for their overuse of "sports jargon," language that strained to be colorful and sensational. Such writing, however, soon came to be recognized for what it was—forced and trite. Today, the more experienced professional sportswriters avoid sports jargon in writing their stories. But many amateur writers still resort to overblown, meaningless expressions like "split the ozone," "scorched the cinders," and "booted the pigskin." The best sports stories are written in honest, straightforward language. But that doesn't mean they have to be colorless or dull. Sportswriters are permitted more freedom of style in their writing than are straight news-story writers, and they use that freedom to advantage in expressing themselves in colorful and creative—yet appropriate—ways. To some extent, the specific style of sportswriting depends on the type of story being written and on the type of medium used for presentation.

SPORTS STORY IN INVERTED PYRAMID FORM

By Hal Bodley
USA Today

ST. LOUIS COMPLETES SWEEP 6-2

ATLANTA—St. Louis, determined not to let Atlanta duplicate Milwaukee's heroics, won the National League Championship Series with a 6-2 victory Sunday night.

Right-handed pitcher Joaquin Andujar vaulted the Cardinals to their first World Series since 1968 with relief help from Bruce Sutter.

"We just weren't able to score in the playoffs," said Atlanta manager Joe Torre after the three-game sweep. "I had hoped we would play better than we did....Our guys played their hearts out, but (they) just didn't get the key hits."

The Cards will face Milwaukee in the World Series, beginning Tuesday night at 8:30 EDT in St. Louis. The Cards' Bob Forsch (15-9 during the regular season and 1-0 in the playoffs) is expected to start against Mike Caldwell (17-13 and 0-1).

The Brewers dropped the first two games of their American League series to the California Angels, but then rallied with three triumphs.

The Cards, triggered by Willie McGee's two-run triple, scored four times in the second inning against starter Rick Camp. St. Louis added a run in the fifth, then held off the Braves' late surge.

Sports Features

Because of the high reader interest in sports features, sports editors often request sportswriters to prepare feature stories about the many different aspects of sports. When writing a sports feature, writers follow procedures similar to those suggested in Chapter 10, "Writing Feature Stories," on pages 204–229.

Celebrity Sports Features

The more famous the sports personality, the more articles there are printed about him or her. Sports feature writers preparing a celebrity sports feature usually prepare their material by interviewing a player after having read sufficient background material or after having talked to the player's coach and to the player's friends. The celebrity sports feature often takes the form of a biography, an interview, or a personality sketch.

When it comes to track, Laura Stageberg is a woman possessed—possessed by an obsession to prove that she is the best.

Ever since she was, in her own words, "humiliated" in the 880 in the state meet last year (if you can call a seventh-place finish because of a pulled muscle being humiliated), Laura has trained like a Spartan to prove that this year she is the best.

"I see runners like Crunican (Marge, last year's state champ and state record holder from Roseburg) and I want to be like her," says Laura. "I want to be number one once in a while...."

The Axe

Scene-of-Event Sports Features

Scene-of-event sports features focus on the specific place in which a major event is to be held. For example, a number of scene-of-event feature articles have been written describing Houston's Astrodome. Other stories of this type detail the facilities and dimensions of the ball parks in which a World Series or Super Bowl game will be played. School sportswriters may draw a comparison between the home court and the court on which the championship game is to be played.

The Houston Astros open the season against the Pittsburgh Pirates on Friday in baseball's plushest surroundings.

The SRO crowd of 45,000 will be watching the game in a $31.5 million weatherproof, air-conditioned, mosquito-resistant ballpark that rises some 200 feet above the Texas plain like a misplaced flying saucer.

The Astrodome covers 259 acres, most of it parking space for 30,000 cars. The stadium itself takes up about nine acres. Fans will watch from upholstered luxury in six tiers painted varying shades of red, coral, purple, blue, and gold....

Interpretative Sports Features

Readers are interested in the *why* behind any sports event. An interpretative sports feature supplies the background information concerning sports issues and policies. Such an article might tell why a team won the state championship or how the condition or abilities of the players might affect player performance.

The year of the Panther is here ... again. Thanks to the coaching of Byron Weaver and his hard-working assistants, North Central is out to top last year's fantastic season. Even greater finesse and more speed are the keys to this goal.

With players returning in better condition, the coaches were able to start working toward greater dexterity and speed than ever before.

The Northern Lights

How-to-Do-It Sports Features

As more people become interested in participant sports, the demand for how-to-do-it sports feature articles (sports features of an instructional nature) increases. Sportswriters often prepare features on such subjects as how to play tennis, golf, soccer, or hockey. Many high school newspaper sports editors assign fledgling sportswriters to prepare series of how-to-do-it features for use as fillers or for publication in each issue of their school newspapers. The following example lends a twist to the usual how-to-do-it sports feature. In a light, humorous way, the writer tells how to write a sports story.

Pitching, Sox Achilles Heel

In the good old days, they tell me, writers didn't traipse around baseball locker rooms the way they do now.

Afternoon papers carried pretty much the same game material as the morning, with some sort of fresh angle in the opening paragraph. An afternoon baseball story might go something like this:

Walter Weakarm, veteran curveballer of the Red Sox, will go against Eddie Erratic of the St. Louis Browns as the Hose attempt to square the series this afternoon at 3 at Fenway Park. Yesterday afternoon in the Jersey St. ballyard, the Brownies smashed 12 hits good for seven runs, etc., etc., etc. . . .

Nowadays, that sort of thing doesn't go. An afternoon writer is required to probe the psyche of the athletes, supposed to get down there, amid the

adhesive tape and sweat socks, and ask penetrating questions.

So it was that a writer sat in the stands late Sunday afternoon and watched the Red Sox almost turn another pumpkin into a royal coach.

He saw the Sox score four runs with two out in the ninth and make a game out of a 7-1 runaway. He saw the Twins, who should have had an easy victory, panic over a pop fly that went 12 feet into the infield and about a thousand feet high. . . .

But most of all the writer saw the customers—standing, yelling, screaming for their cardiac kids, who so often battled from behind in the seven games of the present home stand. . . .

by Ray Fitzgerald
The Boston Globe

Sports Features Based on the Writer's Involvement

Sports feature writers often become directly involved as sports participants in order to present readers with interesting feature materials. One such writer talked the coach of an undefeated football powerhouse into letting him participate in a practice session. The writer's lead read: "I felt like an ant among elephants." Author George Plimpton once masqueraded as a football player and went through training sessions with the Detroit Lions. Plimpton's book, *Paper Lion*, was based on these experiences.

Many professional sports figures are becoming sportscasters. They bring with them their first-hand experience and valuable insights into the sport.

Joe Greene (left), a former professional football lineman, has become a sports commentator.

Adding Interest to Sports Features

Now and again, a sports columnist will write a sports feature with an unusual twist by taking advantage of the unexpected. For example, note the following:

Never List-less

It's happened again. Another guy has beaten me to the publishers with a book idea and will probably make the million dollars that should rightfully be mine.

It's not generally known, but I was drawing up an outline for a book about the Brooklyn Dodgers of Jackie, Campy, and Shotgun Shuba when Roger Kahn came out with *The Boys of Summer*.

And I was hard at work on a definitive history of the Red Sox of 1978, tentatively called *The Back Bay Zoo*, when Sparky Lyle hit the market with his *Bronx Zoo*.

The latest blow came a couple of weeks ago in the mail—*The Book of Sports Lists* by Phil Pepe and Zander Hollander.

My idea exactly. Now I'm left with my own useless lists, compiled at night by the light of a 30-watt bulb. Here. You can have them. . . .

■ Ten Vanishing Americans in Sports

1. Punting on third down.
2. Kids choosing up sides with a bat.
3. Black high cut basketball sneakers.
4. Goalies without masks.
5. Two woods.
6. Western Union operators in press boxes.
7. Drop kicks.
8. Scoreless ties.
9. Square wooden backboards.
10. White tennis balls.

■ Eight Most Overworked Sports Clichés

1. I'll have to wait until I see the films.
2. He came to play.

3. He plays with pain.
4. He always gives 100 percent.
5. We'll pick the best athlete available.
6. It's been blown out of proportion.
7. I look on the job as a challenge.
8. I've always wanted to play for this organization.

■ Eight Most Common Alibis for Losing

1. Injuries killed us.
2. We didn't get the breaks.
3. We didn't play our game.
4. They made us play their game.
5. They took it to us.
6. We didn't block out on the boards.
7. We were flat.
8. I lost my rhythm.

■ Ten Most Boring Moments in Sports

1. Kickoffs into the end zone.
2. Icing the puck.
3. Timeouts near the end of one-sided basketball games.
4. One-sided basketball games.
5. Intentional walks.
6. Baseball rain delays.
7. TV commercial timeouts.
8. Carlton Fisk between pitches while batting.
9. Stalling in college basketball.
10. Howard Cosell playing God.

Ray Fitzgerald
The Boston Globe

Pitfalls: "Sports Staffs Beware"

Bill Ward, former sportswriter and columnist, prepared the following list of pitfalls to be avoided by sportswriters preparing material for newspaper sports pages and for radio/television sports news.

1. *Writing in sports jargon.* Outlaw all sports language; write in clearcut language understood by the nonfan. Avoid such tangled constructions as "The hurler unlimbered a blazer which the sticker cracked into the outer pasture for a one-bagger. The left gardener gloved it on the hop and sizzled it to the keystone sacker." One bit of sports slang is one bit too many.

2. *Organizing a game summary in chronological order.* Unless the kickoff is your most newsworthy element, organize the story with the most interesting details at the start. It is easy to tell a story chronologically; it usually is also dull.

3. *Narrating play-by-play.* This is dull, flat, routine, unimaginative, hard for the reader to follow, and stimulates few mental images. "Jones smacked the middle for six yards to the 18. Then Smith fired a pass to Smyth, who took it on the 15 and ran to the 12. After two incompleted passes, Jones snaked to the 9. Funkle was thrown for a two-yard loss." Ad infinitum. Who cares? If you must include a play-by-play sequence, clip it short. Be sure it's important.

4. *Becoming a critic.* Your job is to report a game, not to coach a team. Frustrated athletes who become sportswriters are a bane of coaches. Sportswriters know very little about the techniques of the game; they know even less about the subtle problems that coaches and athletes encounter behind the scenes. I recall a metropolitan sportswriter who criticized a collegiate halfback for loafing and losing. In truth, the halfback was badly crippled, a fact which had been hidden from the press and from the opposition before, during, and after the game.

5. *Failing to get specific, detailed facts.* Lazy, indifferent, unknowing? Whatever the reason, it's inexcusable. A sportswriter must systematically dig, day by day, for any facts he or she may need for a story.

6. *Writing with too many adjectives and adverbs.* I have never visualized a "low flyball," so why a high one? There are also too many "vicious tackles, smoking slides, diving catches, smashing drives, blistering linedrives." Save your modifiers for moments of true impact.

7. *Including too many statistics.* Not many fans can tell what Biff McNasty hit in 1906; most don't care. Statistics are not sports, but merely a side-product. You must write about the action and the human interest. Don't turn a sports event into a bookkeeper's nightmare. "Tonight the Beaneaters (8 wins, 5 losses), averaging 6-2 in height and 195 pounds, meet for the second time the Yellow Sox (10 wins, 3 losses), averaging 6-1 and 184. The Beaneaters with a .321 shooting average came into the game with a 3-game winning streak (the longest in the conference this year thus far) after snapping a 5-game losing streak. . . ."

8. *Posing pictures.* Shoot on-the-spot action. There is little reason for posing athletes before and after games and then relaxing during the action.

Activities

1. From newspaper sports stories, compile what you consider to be examples of both acceptable and unacceptable sports terminology. Use the examples to start your own sports-jargon notebook. Keep in mind that because the average reader finds sports jargon difficult to understand, experienced sportswriters avoid using it. Instead, to keep their language colorful and interesting, they use appropriate synonyms. Make a list of all the synonyms you can think of to replace the word *belted* in the following sentence:

> Jones *belted* off right tackle and scampered 25 yards down Medford's sidelines for the winning touchdown.

2. The standard "5 *w's* and the *h*" news lead is often used in sportswriting. Using the results of the last sports event you attended, write six sports-story leads. Use *who* as the main "w" in the first lead, then the *what* in the second lead, etc., until you have completed six different leads, each based on the same basic facts. To gain practice in writing under pressure, establish a deadline time for completion of these leads.

3. Most schools have an "eager-beaver" athlete, usually a sports enthusiast who comes early and stays late for practice. Often this person cleans the cleats, picks up the dirty towels, and brings water to fellow athletes and is, in many ways, as important as the star player. Seek out such a person and prepare a sports feature that uses the personal approach. Let the class evaluate your article for possible submission to the school newspaper. Such articles lend interest and variety to sports pages.

4. Study the sports pages in at least three recent issues of your daily paper. For each issue, list the advance stories and the reports of games or events. Which type of story appears more often? Which type receives more space?

5. From the sports pages of one or two daily newspapers, clip several columns. Identify each by summarizing the type of topic each sports columnist writes about. Which statements in each column are factual? Which statements are opinions?

6. Cover a sports event of your choice. Then write a brief sports story for possible publication in your school paper. Use colorful words and informal expressions as you think appropriate. Be sure to observe good newswriting practices, too.

CHAPTER 12

Writing Editorials

Roland Steele, editorial writer, sits quietly at the daily news confer- listening to the various editors discuss what they feel are the top news stories of the day. On occasion, the editor-in-chief turns to Steele, seeking his advice or asking for background information.

"Roland, what's the administration's policy on refugee immigration?" asks the editor-in-chief.

With a slight smile Steele replies, "That depends on whether you're talking about immigration because of communist oppression or because of political oppression. But, in general, we've taken a harder line lately on immigration."

The editor relies on Steele to give him honest answers to hard questions. He knows that Steele can see the many sides of a number of issues. And Steele can—because it's his job to know the facts and to take a stand on the side he thinks is right.

Steele is the one person on the newspaper staff who puts his own feelings in print. He's the paper's editorial writer. His background qualifies him to editorialize. After majoring in political science in college, he became a reporter and then, after a couple of years, the city editor of the paper. The publisher admired the evenhanded way in which Steele dealt with people and problems, and one day he called Steele into his office.

"Let me get right to the point, Roland," he said. "We need an editorial writer—a person who can take the heat. Do you think you qualify?"

Steele smiled, knowing that the publisher was referring to the adage, "If you can't take the heat, stay out of the kitchen."

"It'll be quite a change from the type of writing I'm used to," replied Steele, "but, quite frankly, I've always wanted to write editorials. I'll do my best to justify your faith in me."

Now, in his new job, Steele is pretty much his own boss. He decides the topics he'll write on; he also decides where his comments will be placed on the editorial page. Despite the pressures from all sides, Steele likes it in the "kitchen"; he feels certain that he's performing a useful service for his readers and for his community.

Editorials and the Mass Media

Any listing of famous names taken from the history of American journalism would reveal that most of these persons, in addition to being news writers, were also skilled editorial writers—writers who wielded great influence through their editorials. The names of Horace Greeley, Henry Grady, Henry Watterson, E. L. Godkin, Charles Dana, William Lloyd Garrison, William Allen White, Elijah Lovejoy, Walter Lippmann, and editor-poets William Cullen Bryant and Walt Whitman would be included in such a listing. Through effective, convincing editorials these people helped bring to light and resolve many of the major issues of their times.

Just as editorials expressing the opinions of these journalists exposed and helped find solutions for many of the problems of their times, editorials expressing the opinion of today's journalists expose and help find solutions for the problems of our times.

While the role of today's editorialist is, perhaps, not as dramatic as was a similar role during the days when Horace Greeley's writings were eagerly read throughout the country, today's editorialist is still an influential and respected member of our society. The editorial writer in today's society, while being concerned with many of the unsolved problems inherited from previous generations, is also confronted with the challenge of writing about newer problems—problems like nuclear armament, urban crises, overpopulation, race relations, and world peace. Today's editorial writer represents the conscience of the community.

Horace Greeley is shown reading his editorial.

Will *The Express* distinctly inform us whether it includes the *Extension* of Slavery into Territory now Free when it speaks of 'the Slavery question' as one that should not be introduced in a Whig National Convention? Let us fairly understand each other. We agree (or insist, if you prefer that term) that the Federal Government has no power to abolish Slavery in any State of this Union; and we are quite willing that a Whig National Convention should so resolve: is it not equally clear that said Government has no power to *establish* Slavery in a territory subject to its jurisdiction, and wherein Slavery did not previously exist! If it has power to establish Slavery in a Territory, has it not power also to *abolish* it in any Slave region which may be acquired—Cuba for example! We understand the principle to have been settled, that accession to this Union makes no change in the social institutes of the region acquired; but if any change be wrought thereby—if annexation to this country is to work any change at all in the premises—we insist that the benefit shall enure, not to Slavery but to Freedom. Such we understand to be the *Conservative* doctrine—but whatever it is, we think a question of such vital and imminent National consequence should not have been blinked by the Convention.

From *The New York Tribune*, June 27, 1848:

Despite the fact that on any given day more people read their newspaper's comic section than read the editorial section (very few newspaper readers can actually identify one editorial writer by name), the thoughtful, concerned decision-makers of most communities invariably read the editorials. Among the first items the President of the United States reads each morning is a summary of editorials from the country's leading newspapers.

Editorial writing has become increasingly important in the broadcast media. Radio and television stations frequently devote time to airing matters of public concern through editorials "in the public interest" prepared by station writers. Following is an example of a public service editorial for radio and television.

Legal Aid for the Poor

The administration wants to eliminate the Legal Services Corporation. It provides 85 percent of the total funding of civil legal services for the poor. This is a program that has great impact on our area.

During 1980, the Community Legal Services handled 16,518 cases. 31 percent of the casework regarded government benefits; 24 percent were related to housing; 17 percent to family problems. 73 percent of those assisted were white; 16 percent were black and 9 percent were Hispanic. The courts and the judicial system are the proving grounds of democracy. Those grounds are valid only if *everyone* can use them.

The Legal Services Corporation is one of the programs that meet the goals of the administration. The legal assistance it provides has helped eliminate waste, fraud, and abuse in public programs. It has reduced unnecessary bureaucracy and has made government work for the people. It doesn't make sense to eliminate or cripple this program.

There are reports that the Legal Services Corporation may receive partial funding; it deserves to be fully funded. To do anything less would be a slap in the face to poor people and a betrayal of democracy.

WBZ-TV

Purpose of Editorials

The editorials contained on any publication's editorial pages or aired by any radio/television station usually focus on the same general issues found in the news. An editorial, no matter who

Roles of the Journalist in a Democratic Society

writes it, is still a kind of news even though it is written and presented from a viewpoint different from that of straight news stories. Unlike news reports prepared by reporters, which must be impartial presentations of factual information, editorials reflect the writer's or the publication's or the station's own appraisal and interpretation of events. Editorials constitute the "mouthpiece" of a publication or a radio/television station. In no other way is the publication's or the station's character, personality, and policy so clearly shown. For this reason, crusades are often conducted through editorials.

The primary purpose of an editorial is to *convince*. The mark of a truly successful editorial is its ability to arouse readers/listeners/viewers to take action on the issue dealt with in the editorial. The writer of an editorial can be said to be saying, "Here is the evidence. The verdict should be as I have indicated."

What Makes a Good Editorial?

The most important element of an editorial is *effectiveness*. If an editorial is not effective, it will not fulfill its purpose. Because people want news, effective editorials should be *timely* as well as *interesting*. For example, what students were discussing last month may well prove boring to them today. Editorials that preach and editorials containing uninteresting, poorly presented statements and assumptions often lose the reader's interest. "Preachy" editorials are usually ineffective because they fail to arouse a response. With students, "preachy" editorials often arouse resentment; like all human beings, students dislike being reminded constantly that they should or should not do something. But because a major purpose of all editorials is to suggest what people should not do and encourage them to do what they should do, many editorial writers feel obliged to focus their editorial writing on faults and so tend to preach about such faults. To avoid "preachiness," the editorial writer should consider the following:

1. Rather than demand that people do something specific, editorialists can discuss a situation and challenge readers/listeners/viewers to work out their own solutions.
2. Presenting an appropriate example can often eliminate the necessity for further lengthy comments that might sound preachy.
3. Being specific and using definite examples is usually more effective than using general statements and making vague assertions.

The successful editorial writer must be well acquainted with the elements of news discussed in Chapter 7, "Reporting the

News," on pages 143–148—human interest, immediacy, proximity, conflict, emotions, and consequences—and should apply as many of them as possible to editorial writing. Following are important qualities that contribute to making an editorial effective:

Conviction. To be effective, editorials must be convincing. To be convincing, the writer must thoroughly understand the situation or the problem. The editorial must reflect the writer's belief in a particular point of view.

Forcefulness. An editorial must have an obvious purpose, clearly stated, that is the result of careful thinking. It must be

---

Martin Van who?

Perhaps no one has noticed, but upbeat journalism is the new trend. As a trend it is not overwhelming, and it still does not offset the usual violence and crises on which the news media thrive, but it is there and should be noticed.

One item which might be classed as upbeat journalism is that Kinderhook, N.Y., has recently decided to honor Martin Van Buren. As far as upbeat goes, Martin Van Buren is a borderline case, but bringing his name into the news has something cheerful about it . . . .

It is recorded somewhere in the town hall that Van Buren was born in Kinderhook. It is just that up until now nobody particularly cared. Maybe Van Buren himself tried to hush it up.

Some think that [the reason] it took Kinderhook so long to celebrate the fact it is a presidential birthplace is that no one in town knew Martin Van Buren had been president. This isn't peculiar to Kinderhook. A lot of people didn't know it. Evidently, according to some speculation, a few tourists drove through town looking for a monument, and that started the ball rolling.

They found a monument. It was hidden by some weeds, but it was there. From then on, there was a hometown movement to make Martin Van Buren a celebrity.

It turned out, unfortunately, that his birthplace had been torn down in 1920. It was considered an eyesore. Since Kinderhook is not widely known as the Athens of America, it must have been an eyesore indeed. Anyway, it is unlikely it was torn down out of spite. In our modern society, memorials are not as important as parking lots.

The Van Buren mansion, in which he later lived, has been cleaned up. His name is recorded on numerous signs. Parades and grand balls are given in his honor. And, while Martin Van Buren's name still doesn't come up often at parties in Washington, these things can change.

(Taken from a column titled "Lightly Le Pelley")
Christian Science Monitor Tuesday, February 22, 1983.

---

presented forcefully enough to drive the central thought home to the reader/listener/viewer, thereby evoking a responsive note. Forcefully written editorials inspire people to take action; the more people who take action as a result of reading or hearing the editorial, the more successful is the editorial.

Brevity. Well-planned, straight-to-the-point, short editorials are the most effective. When confronted with a solid body of unrelieved type or with a long, emotional tirade, readers/listeners/viewers are inclined to avoid reading or listening. Short editorials of not more than 300 words retain attention and interest more easily than do longer ones. To keep their editorials brief, successful editorial writers zero in on only one aspect of a newsworthy situation or problem.

Consequence. Consequence is one of the most important elements for the editorial writer to consider in choosing a topic. Minor news items are seldom used as the basis for good editorials. In writing editorials for your school newspaper, you should write about what you consider significant in your school and about what concerns the student body.

Relevance. Among the most important factors contributing to a good editorial is relevance. The editorial must be relevant to the concerns, problems, and needs of readers/listeners/viewers.

Editorial Research

One of the most important prerequisites for writing sound editorials is research. The writer must have all of the facts connected with the issue before beginning the editorial. The actual writing usually takes but a fraction of the time spent talking with authorities, taking notes, reading about the subject, and compiling background material. Library reference materials such as the *Readers' Guide to Periodical Literature* are basic research tools for editorial writers. To avoid ridicule and/or condemnation, the editorialist must be sure of and able to substantiate all the related facts.

Types of Editorials

Editorials written for publication in the print media or for presentation on radio or television are either formal or informal in approach. Most of the editorials used by the mass media are of the formal type; school newspapers usually feature informal editorials. The chief difference between the two approaches lies in the writer's point of view. The formal type uses only the third-person approach; the informal type uses the second-person form of pronouns and sometimes the imperative form of verbs. Editorials don't usually use first-person singular pronouns. Most editorials come under any one of the following classifications:

Editorials of Argument and Persuasion.   Also called editorials of refutation or editorials of criticism and reform, editorials of argument and persuasion criticize existing conditions and try to influence public opinion to demand specific changes. Argumentative in nature, such editorials take a definite, convincing stand. Even though the editorial's object of criticism might not accept the writer's point of view, the editorial is effective if the object of criticism ceases the activities being criticized.

The Y Affair

Iowa seems to grow tall corn and reactionaries. Iowa State helps grow tall corn and inflames reactionaries. The continuing and serious YMCA controversy is a good example.

The Y has been changing its image from "that building with the columns" to a campus force for active discussion and inquiry. This change has transformed the Y from an insignificant "religious society" to a dynamic campus organization. Just when the Y was beginning to come into its own as a dialogue-producing catalyst, the Ames community objected. The very roots of their objections pry into the freedoms and rights of expression and discussion. But the worst part of this reaction is its threat to knock the awakening sense of intellectual curiosity and inquiry in the head. If the reactionaries win, the Y will be demoted to the rank of hike leader for 10-year-olds and a meeting place for mental midgets.

Fortunately, members of the University community, who realize what the purpose of a university is, have come to the defense of the Y. Unfortunately, these enlightened persons do not hold the life-or-death purse strings. We were glad to see that the dean of students chose to support the Y with a letter urging it to "continue to stimulate all segments of the University community." They desperately need this type of encouragement and we'd like to add our hope that the Y will continue its programs of rational discussion on controversial topics.

After all, if a university isn't the place for such inquiry, what is? Certainly, the churches won't take up the yoke or the high schools or the Federated Women's Club or the plant or the office. The university is the only social unity that can handle such inquiry into contemporary concerns.

The State Board of Regents realized this fact when it said, "We encourage students and staff to hear and discuss diverse points of view from speakers and programs sponsored by recognized student, faculty, and employee organizations. This policy is entirely consistent with the aims of higher education. It is designed to emphasize that in a democratic society all citizens have not only the right but the obligation to inform themselves on issues of contemporary concern including politics, religion, ethics, and morals."

A democracy must necessarily depend on an informed public —a public that isn't afraid to probe, pry, and ask questions. If a university student can't inform himself or herself now, it is doubtful if the habit will be formed for use in later life. E. N. Griswold of the Harvard Law School has said, "Great ideas can rarely be developed in an atmosphere of constraint and oppression. The university has a unique function, not merely in systematizing the orthodox, but also in providing the soil in which may be nourished the speculative, the unfashionable, and the unorthodox." How can University instructors exhort their students to be open-minded and searching inside the classroom and deny the same right outside the classroom?

The whole controversy boils down to the purpose and autonomy of the university. Maybe the Y should consider breaking away from the stifling Ames community.

Charles S. Bullard, Iowa State University

Editorials of Information. To prevent possible misunderstanding, editorials of information offer informative comments. Their success depends upon the influence of the information presented. These editorials do not attempt to present obvious conclusions, and they limit themselves to a review of the facts.

Lawyer Pool Could Result in Saving for State

Governor Licht has a good idea that might save the taxpayers some money and at the same time increase the efficiency of government. He is considering setting up a lawyers' pool in government instead of assigning lawyers to different departments. In this way he might be able to cut back on the number of lawyers needed. A plus in the proposal is that the lawyers will have a better idea of what's going on, and maybe the gears of government will mesh better when all of the departments find it no longer necessary to have a private corps of lawyers to protect "private" interests.

The Citizen, Providence, R.I.

Editorials of Interpretation. These editorials present the facts or an explanation of the facts about timely situations of interest, including the writer's, publication's, or station's opinion about such situations. Such explanations of facts may be presented as a penetrating discussion and are often of the personal essay type, using "I" and "me" (which are not often used in editorials) in their presentation to make them more forceful.

A Focus on Housing

The proposal by the Senate Ways and Means Committee to create a new state Executive Office of Development, comprised of the current Office of Communities and Development and agencies now within the Office of Manpower Affairs, has raised understandable fears that housing programs at the state level will be downgraded.

Under the reorganization proposal, the business of Communities and Development, now overseen by a Cabinet-level secretary, would be largely handled by an autonomous commissioner, a title of lesser rank, within the proposed new Office of Development. It is by no means certain that a commissioner, without either the trappings of a Cabinet secretary or direct access to the governor and with the deep budget cuts proposed by Ways and Means, could pursue controversial housing policies successfully.

The secretary sitting atop the proposed new Office of Development would have a much broader range of responsibilities than housing-related issues, including oversight of economic development and job-training. He or she might be more inclined to focus on job-creating activities — which, when they work, draw wide plaudits — than on . . . housing and urban development, which often put the state at odds with local officials.

If the Legislature is committed to eliminating the Office of Manpower Affairs, it might consider putting most of its functions within the proposed new Office of Labor and Consumer Affairs and not expand substantially the range of responsibilities within Communities and Development. That would leave that department and its secretary to continue to focus on physical development, most notably the production and rehabilitation of housing, surely among the state's pressing needs.

Boston Globe

Editorials of Commemoration and Special Occasions. Editorials of commemoration and special occasions are usually about special events and occasions, holidays, campaign drives, and fund drives such as the Heart Fund, March of Dimes, and the United Fund campaign. These editorials are often interpretive and narrative.

Our Columbus

Why do we Americans diminish Columbus Day by paying more attention to the rival claims of Spain and Italy on the nationality of the Admiral of the Ocean Sea than to the liberating philosophical contributions the discovery of the New World made to Western civilization? . . .

By sighting the Western Hemisphere, the new Atlantis, Columbus confirmed the belief of the great utopian thinkers in the existence of a more just social order—a belief that would lead millions over the next half-millennium to find refuge in both the northern and southern halves of the New World.

It is puzzling that Latin Americans call Columbus day "Dia de la Raza"—meaning roughly "day of the Hispanic-American people"—and observe it as an affirmation of their Iberian heritage, as though they had fought no wars to throw off the yoke of the Spanish crown. Moreover, don't they occupy, with us, a continent that has experienced the vital convergence of Indian, European, African, and Asian cultures?

For all the talk of pioneer spirit and independence, we remain colonized by a British version of history, just as the Latin Americans remain captive to the textbooks of Spain.

These sectarian, Old World approaches to the commemoration of the date that changed the world illustrate the topsy-turvy perceptions one half of the hemisphere has of the other. How else can we explain the remarkable disregard we have for the basic fact of our shared origins as immigrant communities that fled the political intolerance and rigid social hierarchies of Europe? Have we become so conditioned by parochial European prejudices that we fail to recognize the unique New World quality of our increasingly egalitarian and ethnically mixed societies or that the same frontier spirit that claimed California claimed the Pampas, built Brasilia, Medellin, and Houston and today produces some of the world's most vital literature, music, and art? That freedom and creative impulse is the miracle of the man of the Americas. . . .

To hear some Americans talk today you would think we are living as an island of Puritan virtue in a hemispheric sea of perversity. Meanwhile, Latin American critics thundering away like an Inquisitor assailing the Reformation, accuse us of materialism, godlessness, and imperial pretensions.

Before we can successfully understand the man of the Americas, we must devote more thought to our common history and how it relates to the rest of the world. Perhaps as we approach the 500th anniversary of Columbus' first great transoceanic voyage, we can be inspired to explore the various assumptions that have led to our conflicting interpretations of life in the other half of the New World so that we may be able to celebrate 1992 with the spirit of pride and mutual understanding the event deserves.

Henry Raymont
The Washington Post
October 11, 1982

Editorials of Commendation. Written in praise of something or somebody, as expressions of appreciation, as a tribute to the deceased, or to commend a worthy cause or action, editorials of commendation are nearly always written seriously and are formal in approach.

Editorial

The Sands Point Academy has a self-assured, easy-to-get-along-with leader. His name is Mr. John Heller, our new principal.

Mr. Heller has brought a firm but quiet policy of leadership to our school. Students who have met with him have found him to be definite in his ideas but always open-minded and willing to listen.

This is the kind of leadership that a progressive school like Sands Point should have. Our principal's past experience gives him a unique and qualified basis for taking over at our school. In his years as principal at Jericho High School, he obviously learned the value of treating students, both younger and older, as responsible adults.

Though basically a member of the "old school," our new principal is willing, as administrative leaders too often are not, to give the student the benefit of the doubt. He realizes the value, in terms of mutual respect, that such a policy ensures.

Mr. Heller's honesty is also appreciated. He is a very straightforward man, hardly a typical administrator. The students of our school have such trust and faith in him that they have even found him ready to listen to, discuss, and offer advice about their personal problems, a rare thing in other, less personal schools.

We are very glad to see Mr. John Heller join our school's administrative staff, and we hope that this appointment will help to deepen the relationship of student and administration.

The Sandpaper

Editorial Brights, Fillers, and Liners. These editorials are usually short (often one-sentence) statements on a general or specific subject and can be either serious or humorous, depending on their topic of concern. Purposely brief, they are often placed at the end of editorial columns and are usually related to, or concerned with, the theme of the preceding editorial material.

■ Editorial Bright

Remedy of Nature Perfect Medicine

Mother Nature has managed to save the day again. Just as students and teachers were beginning to fall into a dreary, listless pit, spring entered the scene to shock all of us into awareness.

It's surprising what a little bit of sunshine and blue sky can do to revitalize an entire student body.

Spring's burst of energy may be just the shot in the arm we need to finish the last three months of school.

The Lancer

■ Editorial Filler

Generalities

Attention, students and faculty: Anyone ranging in age from 18-60 and in good health can help now in the treatment of hundreds of hospital patients who need someone else's blood to survive. You can help by donating only one pint of blood on Wednesday from 2:30-7:30 p.m., in the Alameda cafetorium, 2732 N.E. Fremont.

Unmarried persons under 18 years of age who wish to donate must bring a signed parental consent.

Farrell's Ice Cream is giving a free sundae to each donor.

The Grantonian

■ Editorial Liner

For finding out things one never knew about, there's nothing like opening the encyclopedia and reading away.

Editorials of Humor and Entertainment. As their name implies, the purpose of editorials of humor and entertainment is to entertain. Usually written as personal essays, they often use analogy, drawing a parallel between a familiar situation or person and one that is not familiar to show that what is true in one situation is also likely to be true in another. This kind of editorial uses subtle humor to get the writer's point of view across.

Editorially Speaking . . . Turnabout Tale, Spring Cleaning . . .
Girl Shows Date 'How Not to Act'

The car horn blared, interrupting the early evening silence.

"Well, how do you like that?" John said to himself. "It's Turnabout night and she doesn't even come to the door for me."

He finally went out to the car and waited for Mary to get out and open the car door for him. "Hey, this is Turnabout, remember?"

"Yeah, yeah, I know. Just get in," she answered.

"Did you make me a corsage?" John asked after riding in silence for several minutes.

"Oh, I guess I forgot. I was kind of rushed all day. Sorry."

John started to complain. "Why start an argument so early in the evening?" he thought to himself. "Surely she'll be better at the dance."

They continued in silence. . . .

. . . "Well, we came to dance didn't we? You're supposed to ask me tonight, you know."

"All right, all right," Mary said without enthusiasm.

"Dancing sure makes you thirsty, doesn't it," John hinted.

Mary grinned.

John dropped another hint.

Mary grinned wider . . .

. . . They rode home in angry silence.

"This has been a terrible evening," John thought indignantly. "She just treats me like . . . why . . . uh . . . like I treat her."

The Lancer

Roles of the Journalist in a Democratic Society

Editorial Cartoons. Editorial cartoons are used by the print media on editorial pages to emphasize the point of view presented in the editorials. These cartoons catch the reader's eye and generate interest in the related editorial. Editorial cartoons often deal with political or other current topics. Their visual appeal adds variety to the publication's editorial pages. On page 264 is an example of an editorial cartoon.

Editorial Polls. An "Inquiring Reporter" column on editorial topics can lure a great many readers to the editorial page. Many editors base their editorials on the results of such polls.

Sports Apathy Prevails at NE

Amid the talk of student apathy circulating at Northeast, our eyes are opened to another problem—teacher apathy.

In a golden star poll given randomly on April 19 to 32 Northeast teachers, 18 of these teachers said they have attended only five or fewer sporting events this school year. (This includes track, softball, tennis, wrestling, cross-country, football, baseball, and golf.) Of the 32 polled, 27 said they think their presence at school sporting events has a positive effect on the athletes in the games and in their classrooms. Yet, only seven teachers have been to more than ten games. Many teachers have been to no games.

These teachers have reasons for not attending the games. The most popular one is that the game times and dates conflict with family schedules. Also, many teachers hold second jobs.

However, it seems unlikely that, out of the nine months school has been in session and the 77 sporting events that have passed so far this year, some teachers have not been able to sacrifice a few hours of their time to support the athletic department and the student athletes.

On the poll, teachers were asked to rate the overall spirit of the faculty, given the choices of super spirit (the best that it can be), mediocre spirit (pretty good but could be better), poor spirit, or none at all. Two teachers rated the faculty's spirit as super. Twelve teachers said the spirit was mediocre. Ten said that the spirit was at the poor level. And eight teachers rated the faculty as having no spirit at all.

There definitely is a spirit problem at Northeast. The students reflect this problem when they don't attend school-related functions. . . . Yet the problem is not that noticeable in teachers. Their absence at school sporting events reflects their lack of spirit, as do the results of this poll.

Something needs to be done. This is not a problem without a solution. The solution is obviously not easy to arrive at, but something can be done.

Editorial Writer, Northeast High School

Editorials Based on the News. One of the ways of using the power of the press to remedy an injustice is to write an editorial based on a news story. Doing so adds an element of interest— namely, timeliness.

On occasion, a major news story will break and be covered (1) as a news story, (2) as a topic for a column, and (3) as an editorial. Such is the case here:

■ News Story

> Consolidated Textile's president, Ken Wharton, faced with an inquiry by the state Commission Against Discrimination, yesterday rescinded his decision to terminate employment of a 65-year-old worker.

■ Opinion Column

> What is the world coming to when a man like Ken Wharton, Big Boss of America, can't even choose who'll work for him anymore? . . .

■ Editorial

> Consolidated Textile's president Wharton's decision to cancel his proposed termination of employment of a 65-year-old supervisor is a wise and necessary one. The policy of age discrimination, long in effect, is both unwise and unfair.
>
> However, in blaming the press for the avalanche of unfavorable publicity that forced him to take that action, Wharton is aiming at the wrong target. Regressive personnel policies that discriminate against someone because of age do not belong in today's workplace. Forced retirement at age 65, long the practice and policy of Consolidated. . . .

Libel Considerations in Editorial Writing

In the 1830s an editorial in the *Louisville Focus* began, "President General Andrew Jackson is a lying, thieving scoundrel." Today such an editorial would be discredited as libelous. Libelous matter is any material appearing in print that contains false information injurious to a person's reputation or business, whether that person is alive or deceased. Libel laws apply as much to editorial comment as to anything else in a publication or broadcast. In America, in order for printed material to be considered libelous, that material must be proven to be malicious in its intent. The common defense against libel is to prove the truth of the matter published, to prove that the publication or broadcast did no appreciable damage, or to prove that there was no malice aforethought. The school newspaper editorial writer must avoid any material that might recklessly endanger the reputation of anyone and must be careful always to be accurate in the presentation. All school publications support an editorial policy of truth and honesty in their presentation of published materials. There is no place in the school press for loose accusations of any kind.

Improving Editorial-Page Readership

In addition to placing "Letters-to-the-Editor" on the editorial page, the newspaper editor can help improve readership by using attractive layouts that include photos, cartoons, and special features. Editorial pages are visually more appealing when all stories used on the page are short and the editorials are set in a larger type size and at a wider column width than are the regular news stories appearing elsewhere in the publication. Interest-arousing headlines and leads for each editorial also help gain reader attention. Often, when especially significant issues present themselves, editors run them as featured editorials on page one.

Most publications do not run advertising on their editorial pages, thus allowing space for visually attractive groupings of editorial and feature material. Many publications place their masthead (the publication's name, address, names of staff members, and publication's affiliations) on the editorial page.

In order better to judge reader response, editors encourage and evaluate letters from readers. "Letters-to-the-Editor," an essential part of a good editorial page, makes an interesting editorial feature and provides a platform for reader dissent. Such a platform is especially important for school publications; it shows that students are thinking about what they read. A school newspaper editor should make it a rule that all letters to appear in print be signed and should always check that the signatures are authentic.

Because libel laws also govern what can and cannot be published in the "Letters-to-the-Editor" section, the burden of proving the truth of what is stated falls upon the publication's editor—despite the fact that the printed letters are genuine.

Encouraging Constructive Thinking

After Henry David Thoreau had been imprisoned for protesting taxation, he was visited by poet Ralph Waldo Emerson. Shocked by his disciple's plight, Emerson demanded, "Why are you here?" Thoreau, who had merely been following the advice of his friend, responded, "Why aren't you here?" Thoreau had taken a stand and was suffering the consequences.

Despite the advice of an old-time editor who said, "A newspaper's job is to print the news and raise hell," the editorial writer must remember that his or her duty is to attempt to help people think constructively. An editorial writer—any editorial writer—must never tear down merely for the sake of tearing down but should instead emphasize the positive approach. An editorial writer who cannot advance solutions to problems has no business condemning those that do advance constructive, positive, well-intended solutions.

Each year one of the Pulitzer journalism prizes is awarded for the country's most outstanding editorial. The criteria on which editorials are evaluated comprise a basis for preparing a good editorial. The criteria are relevant for judging both mass media and school editorial writing. They are the following:

1. Clarity
2. Moral purpose
3. Soundness of reasoning
4. Power to influence public opinion

In summary, before writing an editorial, an editorial writer must know all sides of an issue, must be qualified to offer opinions on the subject, must be fair and impartial to all sides, and must be positive enough in his or her suggestions to withstand any consequences for what has been written.

Activities

1. Every day for at least one week, watch the same telecast of local news on your favorite television station. In logbook fashion, summarize the topic of each editorial presented. In addition, record the approximate amount of time the newscast gives to editorials. Bring your log to class to compare it with the logs your classmates have kept. In your opinion, are television editorials effective? Why or why not?

2. Examine the editorial page of your daily newspaper. Summarize the main topic of each editorial printed on that page. With your classmates, discuss the relationship, if any, that you find between the editorials and the significant news of the past several days. What, in your opinion, is the purpose of an editorial page?

3. Select an editorial from a recent issue of your daily paper. Bring it to class. After briefly explaining the subject of the editorial and the editor's point of view, evaluate the lead, the writing style, the organization, and the effectiveness of the editorial.

4. Select an editorial cartoon from the editorial page of a recent issue of your daily newspaper. With your classmates, discuss the relationship, if any, between the cartoon and an editorial printed in the same issue.

5. Collect two weeks' editorial pages from the same daily newspaper. Examine the "Letters-to-the-Editor" section from each issue. Analyze how long it took for the newspaper to print responses to editorials and whether or not other sides of the issue and other points of view are represented by the letters. Discuss your analyses with your classmates.

6. The editorial page is read probably more closely than any other in the newspaper except the front page. If that statement is true, why, in your opinion, doesn't newspaper management take advantage of the situation and place advertisements on the editorial page?

7. Examine the editorial comment of one back issue of your school newspaper from 1980 or 1975 or 1970. What were the issues that prompted the editorials? To what extent are the editorials in your school newspaper today concerned with the same issues? To what extent is the presentation of the editorials similar?

8. Call the editor of the editorial page of your local newspaper and/or the editor who comments editorially on local news telecasts. Invite each one to visit your journalism class. Be prepared to ask how he or she decides on, researches, organizes, and writes editorials.

9. List five or so topics you would like to have considered for editorials to appear in your school newspaper. Make a master list, combining your topics and those of your classmates, eliminating duplication. Present the list to the paper's editor for possible use.

10. List five suggestions for increasing your school newspaper's editorial-page readership. Make a master list, combining your suggestions and those of your classmates, eliminating duplication. Present the list to the editor.

CHAPTER 13

Preserving a Free but Responsible Press

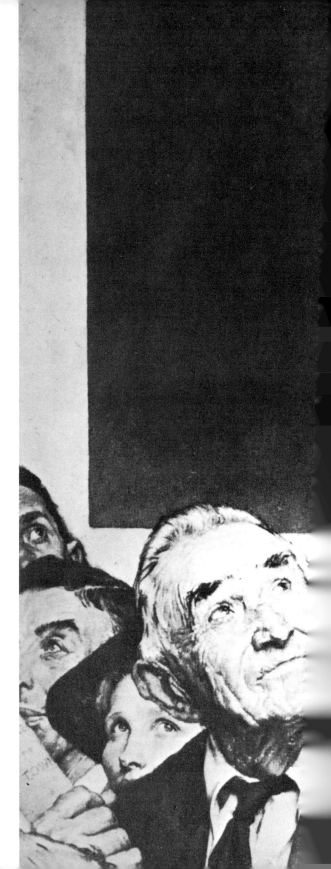

V.I. Lenin, the founder of the Communist Party in Russia, once asked: "Why should freedom of the press be allowed? No government would allow opposition by lethal weapons. Ideas are much more fatal things than guns. Why should any man be allowed to buy a printing press and disseminate pernicious opinion calculated to embarrass the government?"

As Chairman of the Council of People's Commissars and hence dictator of the newly established Soviet state, Lenin made sure that he would not be embarrassed by a free press. Under his direction, the press became the propaganda arm of the government. (The press in all totalitarian countries is the propaganda arm of the government.) The Russian press continues to function in that capacity, telling the people only what the government wants them to know.

What a world of difference there is between a government-controlled press like that of the USSR and a free but responsible press like that in the United States and other Western democracies! That there is that world of difference is no accident. Different

political circumstances, different philosophies of life, different values— all have contributed to the development of the free but responsible press we in this country know and prize.

In the late 18th century Americans found themselves in a life-and-death struggle against tyranny. Once they had won their freedom, they were determined to preserve it; they were determined to prevent the reappearance of any kind of tyranny or capricious despotism. That resolve helped produce the Constitution of the United States and the Bill of Rights.

Of the ten articles making up the Bill of Rights, the first (which is also the First Amendment to the Constitution) guarantees four freedoms: freedom of religion, freedom of speech, freedom of the press, and freedom of assembly. Those four freedoms constitute the very heart of American and Western democracy.

In America, freedom of the press has become an integral part of our way of life. For almost 200 years— since the adoption of the Bill of Rights in 1790—the press in this country has remained free. It is true that during those years there have been numerous attempts to muzzle American journalists. Those attempts continue even in our day. But for the most part, the American press has successfully defended itself against all efforts to limit its operations. Perhaps that's one reason why some Americans tend to take a free press for granted, but to take any freedom for granted is dangerous. Some people, to further their own ends, seek to restrict what newspapers and magazines may publish and what radio and television may broadcast. But so far, their efforts have been thwarted because the press has been willing to guard the freedom it enjoys with eternal vigilance. Sir Winston Churchill, the noted British statesman, put the matter this way: "A free press is the unsleeping guardian of every other right that free men prize; it is the most dangerous foe of tyranny."

But what exactly do we mean when we talk about a "free but responsible press"? The term has at least four important implications: A free but responsible press is (1) an impartial source of information, (2) a guardian of the public's interest, (3) a defender of freedom under law, and (4) an ally of the consumer.

The Journalist—Impartial Source of Information

Newspapers, newsmagazines, and radio/television newscasts are involved in mass communication. Their basic commodity is the news. As was pointed out on page 148, news is "timely information of interest to many people, usually concerning events that have just occurred or are about to occur." Elements in a news story (human interest, immediacy, proximity, prominence, conflict, emotion, and consequence) help to give the story an interest it might not otherwise have. Although *conflict* received considerable emphasis a decade or so ago, editors today feel that the emphasis should be on consequence. Thus, they would define *news* in a slightly different way:

> **News is the unbiased reporting of all sides of a significant event that informed persons want to know about and need to be interested in.**

The Responsibility to Inform

Want and *need* are the key words in the definition just given. Generally speaking, editors—because of their training, concern, and experience— are in a better position than others to decide what should go into a newspaper, newsmagazine, or newscast. One primary function of journalism is to inform the general public about events that affect their well-being. Because editors have access to information about events occurring the world over, they have the perspective necessary to effect an appropriate mix of local, national, and international news affecting the lives of their readers/listeners/viewers.

The Responsibility to Interest

News editors must be concerned with news material other than news stories. Competent editors make sure that along with news stories the newspaper or the newscast offers features that will interest readers/listeners/viewers. News stories frequently report crime, corruption, or disaster; features emphasize the positive, constructive things people do. That's why editors seek to make sure that the news the public receives is not only informative but also interesting. They seek to inform their readers/listeners/viewers, not only about misfortune and tragedy, but also about the positive, encouraging things that happen in their neighborhood, their town, the country, and the world.

The ABCs of Credibility

A is for ACCURACY and ATTRIBUTION, but mostly for ALERT editors who keep problems out of the newspaper.

B is for BALANCE—both sides, remember? And for BOOSTERISM, which (however worthy the cause) may be just one side of the story.

C is for CORRECTIONS—admit them prominently; for CONFLICTS OF INTEREST, for which there should be guidelines; and for CROWD ESTIMATES, which are so often wrong that you should always say who made them and how.

D is for DETACHMENT—reporters should be disinterested observers, not participants or advocates.

E is for ERRORS and ways to ESCAPE them (by providing the necessary time and resources for reporters and copy editors and by cultivating a climate of accuracy in which mistakes are admitted and responsibility taken).

F is for FAIRNESS—even analyses and labeled opinion must meet the standard of fairness.

G is for GRAPHICS AND PICTURES, which can be as misleading and dishonest as a faulty story.

H is for HEADLINES—and the need to be vigilant against the distortion and dumbness that sometimes result from counts that are too short to tell the story.

I is for INTEGRITY—there are some things that just shouldn't be done because they cheapen the news columns, such as running advertising on page 1, taking freebies from PR flaks, using unlabeled advertising.

J is for JOKES AND PRANKS that find their way into the newspaper, or are played on news figures or readers at the expense of the newspaper's reputation.

K is for the courage to KILL tasteless photographs or underdeveloped, unfair stories before they cause trouble.

L is for (gulp) LIBEL, about which editors and reporters should know the basics . . . also for LIBRARY—make sure corrections are made on errors in stories filed in the library, or they'll show up again and again.

M is for MORBID—a particular tastelessness in pictures and stories that screams to everyone, "Death Sells."

N is for NOTE-TAKING, the root of many errors; and for NUMBERS, which always require a second check.

O is for OBJECTIVITY: Whether you believe it is truly possible or not, it should be a goal.

P is for POLLS and their special PITFALLS. (Some of the information that will help establish the credibility of a poll: How many people were sampled? Was it scientifically conducted? What is the margin of error? Who conducted the poll, and when?)

Q is for QUICKLY correcting all errors—moving with the same concern and dispatch to correct an error as you did in getting the story in the newspaper in the first place.

R is for REQUIRING REPORTERS to inform an editor of their confidential sources, and for a whole lot of other things involving REPORTERS' RESPONSIBILITIES to their editors and their newspapers.

S is for SPECIAL SECTIONS—too often, fluff and advertising-promotion features masquerade as news in them. Any advertising that might be confused with news should be labeled, and advertising-promotion copy should not use the same headline and body-type faces as news.

T is for TIE-IN ADVERTISING—it's not all bad. It might offer the reader a more complete shopping service, so long as the tail doesn't wag the dog (make sure the publisher agrees which is the tail and which is the dog!).

U is for UNDERCOVER skulduggery and other reporting tactics that may add up to deceit and deception in the eyes of the reader.

V is for VERIFICATION of facts and statements. Just because somebody said it doesn't make it true, or worthy of print.

W is for WIRE STORIES—editors should hold them up to the same standards as they do local stories, including the standards for sources.

X is for EXPERTISE, which should be developed in reporters assigned to cover technical or complicated subjects.

Y is for YOUR RESPONSIBILITY to ensure the integrity and credibility of your newspaper.

Z is for ZEALOTS—there is no room in the news columns for reporters, editors and publishers with causes and crusades.

The Responsibility to Be Accurate

Besides the responsibilities to inform and to interest their readers/listeners/viewers, journalists have the responsibility to be accurate. Every statement a journalist makes in a news story must be factually verifiable.

Being accurate means being correct not only about specifics but also about the overall impression a news story or a feature makes. Both the reporter and the editor are responsible for seeing that the important—the truly significant—facts are emphasized and that the less important facts are put into proper perspective. Responsible journalism means making sure that neither the news story nor the feature distorts the facts.

The journalist has a responsibility to be accurate—to make sure that what he or she has written is accurate. Carelessness, inattention, or indifference cannot be tolerated. The responsible journalist checks and rechecks the facts—names, dates, places, events. He or she questions sources—at length—to make sure that the information received makes sense, fits together, is consistent.

The Responsibility to Be Believed

In early 1981 the *Washington Post* published a story about an eight-year-old heroin addict by the name of Jimmy. The story received considerable acclaim, even winning a Pulitzer Prize for

Special Reporting. However, a problem soon developed. There was no Jimmy. The story turned out to be a hoax. The reporter responsible for the story was immediately fired, and the *Post* filled three-and-a-half pages with a remarkably frank and thorough investigative explanation of how it all happened. Out of the 18,000 words making up that explanation, one word said it all: "Inexcusable!"

To maintain the time-honored standards of journalism and to be effective, journalists must make sure that their news stories and their feature stories are credible. It is imperative that the news a paper prints and that a radio/television station broadcasts is accurate and believable. To ensure that it is, journalists must exercise constant vigilance, checking and double-checking facts and thoroughly questioning sources of information. The reputation and the reliability of journalism itself is at stake.

The Responsibility to Be Impartial

Besides the obligations already discussed, journalists have the added responsibility to report the news impartially. More than a century ago, Lawrence Gobright, Washington correspondent for the Associated Press, made the point succinctly. He remarked: "My business is to communicate facts. My instructions do not allow me to make any comments upon the facts."

A news story, as you know, is a factual report of an event. It is not a report of the event as a person with a selfish motive might tell it; nor is it a report of the event as the reporter might wish it to be. An acceptable news story is objective, impartial. Although it is sometimes difficult to achieve, complete objectivity is nevertheless essential for truly responsible newswriting. A news story has no place for the reporter's personal opinion, bias, or emotional outburst. Fairness and impartiality are the goals of newswriting.

In today's complex world, however, readers/listeners/viewers often find that their understanding of the facts increases if the news story contains some interpretive and/or evaluative background information. Thus there has emerged a kind of reporting that combines a news-story approach with a feature-story approach. It is called "interpretive reporting." Writing under a byline, the reporter explains the significance of the facts in the story and supplies whatever background information is needed to help people understand what they are reading or hearing. But even though the reporting is interpretive, the responsible journalist scrupulously avoids (1) judging the rightness or the wrongness of the events reported or (2) slanting the story in order to sway public opinion one way or another. If the story involves a controversial subject—and some interpretive reporting does—the responsible journalist presents information that speaks to all sides of the issue. The journalist must be objective, impartial.

The Journalist—Guardian of the Public's Interests

In Sweden when citizens feel that a public agency or executive has not treated them fairly, they go to see the *ombudsman*, an official appointed by the government to receive and investigate complaints made by individuals against abuses or capricious acts of public officials. Swedish citizens know that the ombudsman will thoroughly investigate their grievances and work diligently to achieve equitable settlements. To the ombudsman, everyone—regardless of social position or wealth—is equal, for the ombudsman's job is to serve the public and guard its rights.

A Role as Ombudsman

In many ways mass media journalists in the United States are the ombudsmen for the American public. Though the journalists in each communication medium have developed their own methods for serving the public, most subscribe to the "Statement of Principles" of the American Society of Newspaper Editors, on pages 290 and 291, and to "The Journalist's Creed," on page 302, part of which reads as follows:

> I believe in the profession of journalism.
> I believe that the public journal is a public trust; that all connected with it are, to the full measure of their responsibility, trustees for the public; that acceptance of a lesser service than the public service is betrayal of this trust. . . .

The press, which includes newspapers, newsmagazines, and radio and television news departments, has often been called the "fourth branch of government" because, like the executive, legislative, and judicial branches of democratic government, it too represents the will of the people. By providing the public with news, by reporting and explaining the actions of public officials, and by exposing unjust and illegal activities, the press has played and will continue to play a vital role in the lives of all our citizens. To perform that role responsibly and effectively, the press involves itself in public issues and problems in several ways.

"Ombudsman Columns."   Many newspapers and radio/television news departments receive and investigate citizens' complaints about everything from cracks in sidewalks to the malpractice of public officials. After checking out such complaints for legitimacy, the newspapers publish—radio/television stations broadcast— their responses in "ombudsman columns." Here, for example, is a grievance letter received by one newspaper:

> The sidewalk in front of my house is cracked and uneven. One section is six inches above the one next to it. It's dangerous for passersby, especially children. It has been five years since the city did any work on it. Six months ago, the city repaired the sidewalk across the street but didn't even come near this side. I've called the DPW, but they say I'll have to wait another six months before my sidewalk can be fixed. That doesn't seem fair. I vote; I pay my taxes. Is there anything I can do to get some satisfaction in this matter?
>
> J. Q. Sten

After investigating Mr. Sten's complaint, the editor of the paper's ombudsman column replied as follows:

> DPW Commissioner Michael Walsh admits that you have a valid complaint. He points out, however, that there has been a drastic budget cut since the sidewalk across the street from you was repaired. He said he didn't realize that it has been five years since your sidewalk was checked. He's sending a work crew out this week to take care of the problem.

Investigations by "Spotlight Teams."   Sometimes a newspaper or a radio or television news staff will undertake an extensive investigation of a situation or condition brought to light by a news story. The purpose of such an investigation is to determine the extent of the problem, to expose it to public view, and perhaps to suggest satisfactory ways of solving it. A "spotlight team," for example, might probe alleged wrongdoing on the part of public officials. Or it might try to find out why a public agency requires additional funds to continue its efficient operation. The following article makes clear what a newspaper "spotlight team" does.

The Globe Spotlight Team

The next time someone tells you there is no one around to look after the little guy—no white knights in shining armor—point him in the direction of the *Boston Globe*.

There, in a small first-floor office tucked away in a corner, is the headquarters of the *Boston Globe* Spotlight Team, a four-member investigative reporting unit.

"We're really the only ones to get behind the scenes," said Stephen Kurkjian, head of the group. "A lot of people come to us because they envision the Spotlight Team as independent and crusading—a team which can't be bought."

The current Spotlight Team lineup consists of Kurkjian and veteran staff reporters Nils Bruzelius, Benjamin Bradlee, and John Ellement.

Since the Team's inception 11 years ago, they have received both critical and public acclaim as an effective and forceful new twist in the journalism field.

Included on the list of kudos are two Pulitzer Prizes awarded for outstanding investigative reporting. The first Pulitzer was received in 1972 for the Team's series on corruption in the government of the Boston suburb of Somerville. In 1979, a second Pulitzer was awarded for an eight-part series on the Massachusetts Bay Transit Authority.

"I like doing puzzles," said Kurkjian," and that's what this is all about. So much of our work is piecing together bits of information from various sources and trying to come up with a story. You're never exactly sure of what is going to fit where. . . ."

According to Kurkjian, the researching of facts and the searching of files is often considered the easy part. It's the employees who answer questions with monosyllabic responses who often make the going difficult.

"Some people refuse to talk to us at all for fear of reprisal from an employer," Kurkjian said. "The lower-level people are the ones whose initial reaction is that they're not going to talk until they check with their bosses first."

But he added,"Surprisingly, it's the middle management people who are most responsive to our reporters because they know we're not going to stretch the facts."

Once all necessary information has been collected, checked, and re-checked, the Team will begin to write the story.

"That's the fun part," Kurkjian said. . . .

But what differentiates the Spotlight Team from other types of reporting?

"Other stories just give you the *who, what, where, when,* and *how.* We try to give you the *why,*" Kurkjian said.

"You might say we're the people's watchdog," he says with a smile. . . ."

By James Daly

Editorial Campaigns. Responsible journalists throughout the country know that if newspapers and radio/television news departments are to serve their communities, they cannot become complacent or subservient to special interests. News staffs must fulfill their civic responsibilities through vigorous, independent, courageous journalism.

Journalists who have served the public well have often won the journalism profession's most respected award, the Pulitzer Prize. The newspapers in the Gannett group, for example, won a Pulitzer Citation for excellence in community-service reporting. The president of the Gannett Group first became interested in public-service journalism when he became concerned about ways in which Group newspapers could help improve race relations in American cities. He sent a memorandum to each newspaper editor in the Group:

> Every city has the same problem. If it doesn't now, it soon will have. Every city is trying to find answers. Have any cities found answers that might be useful? If so, what are they?

He then assigned the Group's executive editor to organize and direct a series of editorials titled "The Road to Integration." He spelled out the objectives for the Group's editors as follows:

> We would look for accomplishment and for constructive, workable projects in the fields of jobs, housing, education, rights. We would use all of the techniques of newspapering—straight news reports, feature stories, interpretive pieces, interviews, pictures, and editorials. Our associated radio and television stations agree to cooperate. We would not print just another series, however good, but set up coverage to be continued indefinitely.

To announce the series, each Gannett Group newspaper published a front-page editorial titled "Here's What We Can Do About Integration."

Following the announcement of the "The Road to Integration" series, Gannett reporters wrote and published relevant articles and editorials. Many cities benefited.

The Gannett Group of newspapers was presented the "Brotherhood Award of the Council of Christians and Jews." The Pulitzer Prize Committee called "The Road to Integration" series "a fresh and constructive journalistic approach to a major social problem" and "a distinguished example of the use of a newspaper group's resources to complement the work of its individual newspapers."

Edward R. Murrow, a courageous journalist, is shown broadcasting.

A Voice for the Oppressed

On Thanksgiving Day 1960, the Columbia Broadcasting Company aired a one-hour television documentary about migrant farm workers in America. Titled "The Harvest of Shame," the program is now viewed as a milestone in the history of the development of a free but responsible press. Following in the footsteps of John Peter Zenger (page 21), the documentary continued the tradition of vigilant, courageous journalism in its exposure of flagrant social injustice. The narrator, Edward R. Murrow, concluded the telecast with this remark:

> The people you have seen have the strength to harvest your fruit and vegetables. They do not have the strength to influence legislation. Maybe we do. . . .

In the days following the program, Murrow received both praise and criticism. Some persons praised him for having dramatically and effectively exposed the terrible conditions of the migrant workers; others, however, condemned him for editorializing on a news program. Those who condemned Murrow claimed that by editorializing on a news program he had destroyed its impartiality. When Murrow was questioned about his lack of objectivity, he replied: "Would you give equal time to Judas Iscariot or Simon Legree?"

As illustrated by this incident, journalists in both the print and the nonprint media feel a special responsibility for calling attention to any form of injustice in our society.

In this way, the press provides an indispensable service to the society. Newspapers, magazines, radio and television stations become, in a sense, big brothers and big sisters who are not afraid to question government in order to achieve justice for the average person. And, as a result of their action, many injustices are righted, simply because the press has the power to let the community know what is really happening.

An Advocate of the Positive

Because newspapers, newsmagazines, radio and television stations are basically profit-making business ventures, there is always the threat that enough pressure from the media of persuasion—advertising and public relations—could influence journalistic standards. Journalists are constantly aware that advertising, which pays most of the production costs in the mass media, might be withdrawn if journalistic content does not please advertisers. In general, however, most media editors present the news that they think is factual and that will appeal to the largest number of consumers. Advertisers, also concerned with reaching the largest possible number of consumers, rarely interfere with news content.

Advertising. The medium of advertising, with its power to influence the public to buy certain products, has also become aware of its power to influence the public in other matters. With this increasing awareness, advertising has become more sensitive about its social responsibility. To demonstrate to the public how advertising can play an important role in bettering society in general, the medium banded together with business groups and formed the Advertising Council, an agency solely concerned with public-service advertising. The Council has the following policy:

1. Accept no subsidy from the government and remain independent of it.
2. Conduct campaigns of service to the nation at large, avoiding regional, sectarian, and special-interest drives.

3. Remain nonpartisan and nonpolitical; conduct the Council on a voluntary basis; and accept no project with commercial interest unless the public interest is overriding.

Broadcast, print, transit, and outdoor advertising contribute millions of dollars each year publicizing such organizations as the Peace Corps, the National Safety Council, and the U.S. Department of Justice. The following illustration shows the type of public-service advertisements prepared by the Advertising Council.

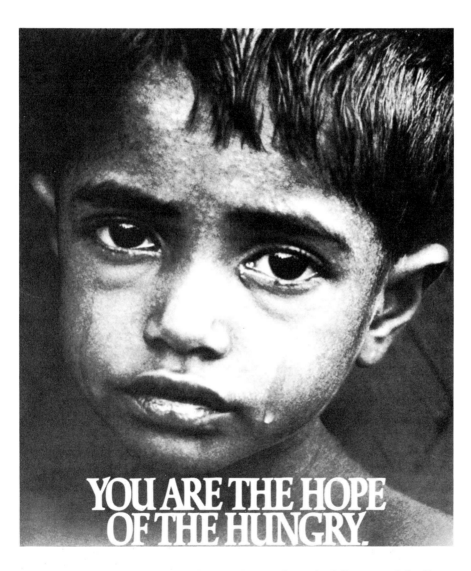

YOU ARE THE HOPE OF THE HUNGRY.

The Broadcast Media. Radio and television stations regularly feature news stories about social problems—for example, the elderly who must get along on fixed incomes, people who are forced to move because of the conversion of their apartments to condominiums, high unemployment among black youth, and the like. In addition, radio and television stations regularly schedule discussion programs that ask listeners/viewers to call in and comment on current issues. They broadcast public-service announcements that supply the public with the names of agencies that can help in problem situations. Another contribution of the broadcast media is the editorial in which the station's news editors take a stand on the problems and issues facing their communities. Such broadcast editorials help stimulate public participation in community affairs.

A Warden for Public Safety

On the morning of April 30, 1980, Boston *Herald-American* City Editor Ken Hartnett arrived at his office, prepared to talk with his staff about a number of ideas he had for features for tomorrow's paper. As the staff gathered in Ken's office, the police radio came alive with a report about a spill of chemicals from a railroad car. The accident had just occurred in the rail yard in one of the nearby suburbs. Hartnett realized immediately that here was news requiring more than routine coverage. He immediately dispatched a photographer and a "spot-news" reporter to the scene.

Within minutes, the reporter was calling on the two-way radio, describing a thick black cloud hovering over the area of the spill. He reported further that Somerville police and fire fighters were hurriedly evacuating residents from the area.

Hartnett realized that this story was too big to be covered by one reporter in the usual 5-*w*'s-and-the-*h* manner. He also realized that he had an obligation to alert the entire community to the potential dangers of spilled chemicals. At the same time, he recognized his responsibility to keep the story in proper perspective, avoiding any possibility of causing the residents in the area to panic.

Hartnett hastily wrote down the topics that he felt should be covered in detail. He then assigned each topic to a reporter who he felt could best handle it. Here are the topics and reporters:

■ *Main story — Earl Marchand:* Magazine-style approach with a focus on the moment of impact and on first reactions.

Journalists are concerned about matters of public safety.

■ *Odyssey of tank car 113009 — Harold Banks:* Detailed account of tank car, its size and specifications, its capacity and safety devices, where it was made. Detailed account of its trip from Monsanto Chemical Midwest to Massachusetts.

Preserving a Free but Responsible Press   287

- *Hazardous materials and Massachusetts — Jean Cole and Howard Carr:* Focus on quantity and variety of hazardous materials moving through the state; the main points of shipment, the precautions and regulations of shipping chemicals, the regulations governing the manufacture and inspection of tank cars and their supervision; adequacy of public protection against disasters; complications, stumbling blocks.

- *The Response — Susan Hand, Shelley Cohen, Jim Morse, Alex McPhail:* What is the emergency system now in use? What is the overall plan? Who calls whom? Who decides what? Should schools be closed, neighborhoods evacuated? What is the chain of command? Are citizens at the mercy of the Somerville police chief? fire chief? anyone else? What's the mayor's role?

- *Profile of a chemical — John Langone:* Exactly what is the spilled chemical? What is its chemical makeup? What's it used for? How widespread is its use? How dangerous is it to human life?

- *The strategy of disposal — John Langone and Tom Donovan:* Just how do we get safely rid of the chemical? What are the hazards? Tell story in *Popular Mechanics* detail, linking options of disposal to what is actually being done in Somerville. Story should also focus on the chemical cloud over Somerville. What dangers, if any, does it pose? How is it safely dispersed?

- *Legal consequences — Jim Connolly:* Who is responsible—or liable—for injuries? The railroad, the chemical manufacturer, the tank-car manufacturer, the state? Why? Are there any legal precedents?

- *Preparedness — all reporters:* Were hospitals in Somerville and nearby towns prepared for a disaster? Did the police and fire fighters have the equipment they needed? Did school officials act coolly and responsibly? How did city officials respond?

- *First-person interview with evicted resident — Bill Duncliffe:* Resident's experiences and reactions.

- *Chronology of day's events as the sense of danger deepened — Dan Zaldiver.*

The newspaper next morning printed a complete coverage of the accident and, at least in part, was responsible for calling the public's attention to the need for the importance of proper precautions for the public safety.

Rather than sit back and let the news come to him by way of the wire services and official news released from city officials and railroad officials, Hartnett went after it. Like all responsible editors, he believed that journalists and the public alike need to know the problems of their communities. And like all responsible journalists, he sought to help the public become informed—not only about the problems but also about potential solutions to those problems. And finally, like all responsible journalists, Hartnett realized that the only way to achieve those ends was to go after the stories that would produce the information needed.

The Journalist—Defender of Freedom Under Law

An often-repeated story tells of an accused man brought before a judge for swinging his arms and hitting another man in the nose. The defendant, pleading innocent, asked, "Haven't I the right to swing my arms in a free country?" The judge, answering the accused, said, "Your right to swing your arm ends where another man's nose begins. Ten dollars!" Though the defendant knew that the First Amendment to the Constitution guaranteed his right to freedom of expression, what he didn't know—and what the past has so often shown—is that freedom of expression has limits. Along with every freedom there is necessarily a parallel responsibility.

Champion of the First Amendment

For journalists the problems of what to print or broadcast and what to omit is constant. In 1947 a commission organized by Time, Inc., sought to define how the press can act both freely and responsibly. In their deliberations the commission divided the freedom of the press into two parts—"freedom from" and "freedom for." The commission defined "freedom from" as follows:

A free press is free from compulsions from whatever source, governmental, or social, external or internal. From compulsions, not from pressures; for no press can be free from pressures except in a moribund society empty of contending forces and beliefs. These pressures, however, if they are persistent and distorting—as financial, clerical, popular, institutional pressures may become—approach compulsion; and then something is lost from effective freedom which the press and the public must unite to restore.

To the commission "freedom for" meant the following:

A free press is free for the expression of opinion in all its phases. It is free for the achievement of those goals of press service on which its own ideals and the requirements of the community combine and which existing techniques make possible. For these ends, it must have a full command of technical resources, financial strength, reasonable access to sources of information both at home and abroad, as well as the necessary facilities for bringing information to the national market.

A Free and Responsible Press
Copyright 1947 by the University of Chicago

Almost 30 years later, the American Society of Newspaper Editors reaffirmed its commitment to a free but responsible press by issuing the following "Statement of Principles:"

1. Preamble

a. The First Amendment, protecting freedom of expression from abridgment by any law, guarantees to the people through their press a constitutional right, and thereby places on newspaper people a particular responsibility.

b. Thus journalism demands of its practitioners not only industry and knowledge but also the pursuit of a standard of integrity proportionate to the journalist's singular obligation.

c. To this end the American Society of Newspaper Editors sets forth this Statement of Principles as a standard encouraging the highest ethical and professional performance.

2. Responsibility

a. The primary purpose of gathering and distributing news and opinion is to serve the general welfare by informing the people and enabling them to make judgments on the issues of the time. Newspaper men and women who abuse the power of their professional role for selfish motives or unworthy purposes are faithless to that public trust.

b. The American press was made free not just to inform or just to serve as a forum for debate but also to bring an independent scrutiny to bear on the forces of power in the society, including the conduct of official power at all levels of government.

3. Freedom of the press

a. Freedom of the press belongs to the people. It must be defended against encroachment or assault from any quarter, public or private.

b. Journalists must be constantly alert to see that the public's business is conducted in public. They must be vigilant against all who would exploit the press for selfish purposes.

4. Independence

Roles of the Journalist in a Democratic Society

a. Journalists must avoid impropriety and the appearance of impropriety as well as any conflict of interest or the appearance of conflict. They should neither accept anything nor pursue any activity that might compromise or seem to compromise their integrity.

5. Truth and accuracy

a. Good faith with the reader is the foundation of good journalism. Every effort must be made to assure that the news content is accurate, free from bias and in context, and that all sides are presented fairly. Editorials, analytical articles, and commentary should be held to the same standards of accuracy with respect to facts as news reports.

b. Significant errors of fact, as well as errors of omission, should be corrected promptly and prominently.

6. Impartiality

To be impartial does not require the press to be unquestioning or to refrain from editorial expression. Sound practice, however, demands a clear distinction for the reader between news reports and opinion. Articles that contain opinion or personal interpretation should be clearly identified.

7. Fair play

a. Journalists should respect the rights of people involved in the news, observe the common standard of decency, and stand accountable to the public for the fairness and accuracy of their news reports.

b. Persons publicly accused should be given the earliest opportunity to respond.

c. Pledges of confidentiality to news sources must be honored at all costs, and therefore should not be given lightly. Unless there is clear and pressing need to maintain confidences, sources of information should be identified.

8. These principles are intended to preserve, protect, and strengthen the bond of trust and respect between American journalists and the American people, a bond that is essential to sustain the grant of freedom entrusted to both by the nation's founders.

But stating principles is not the same thing as implementing them. Maintaining a free but responsible press is actually quite difficult because of the social, political, financial, and legal pressures journalists have to contend with. Among those pressures are accusations from many kinds of pressure groups that the press—both in print and nonprint—is unreliable and that news stories, features, and editorials are superficial. Other accusations are that in general the press panders to sensationalism and violates individual privacy. Still other charges—among the most serious—accuse the press of obstructing justice through pretrial publicity. The press in effect tries criminal cases in print or on the air, thus jeopardizing the basic rights of defendants.

Preserving a Free but Responsible Press   291

Journalists have been accused of obstructing justice when they refused to reveal confidential sources of information. In recent years several widely respected journalists have been found guilty of contempt of court and have gone to jail rather than betray confidential sources of information. From the journalists' point of view, protecting such confidences is a key component of freedom of the press. In fact, they consider the relationship between a journalist and a source of information equivalent to the lawyer-client relationship, which is legally inviolate.

Seeker of Truth

Every journalist understands the adage "The pen is mightier than the sword." It follows, then, that every statement a journalist makes—spoken or printed—must be non-malicious, truthful, fair, and impartial. Although the mass media are looking for courageous men and women to be their reporters and editors, they don't need people with more nerve than discretion.

American journalists have more freedom than do those in any other country. Yet they work in a world of "thou-shalt-not's" in that they are constantly in danger of being held liable if they overstep their bounds.

It is true that the First Amendment guarantees freedom of the press. It is also true that the Fifth Amendment guarantees that "No person shall . . . be deprived of life, liberty, or property, without due process of law. . . ." The implication that the Fifth Amendment has for the journalist is this: Any published or broadcast statement that defames a person operates to deprive that person of a part of his or her liberty. How, then, can any journalist function effectively within these seemingly contradictory amendments? Apparently, the journalist can make *any* statement (because of the First Amendment), but he or she can legally be held to answer for it (because of the Fifth Amendment). Journalists, therefore, know they must be extremely careful about the remarks they make concerning any person. If they are not, they may find that they are defendants in a law suit. The two types of lawsuits of major concern to journalists are those involving libel and slander.

Libel. The majority of legal cases concerning the print media are in the area of libel. A libelous statement is any false or malicious representation, written or printed, which hurts the reputation of a person; exposes that person to hatred, ridicule, or contempt; injures that person in his or her occupation; or financially damages the firm he or she works for.

The two types of libel are criminal libel and civil libel. Criminal covers the publication of obscene, blasphemous, or seditious material. Because this offense is considered a felony in most states, conviction carries a jail sentence. Civil libel consists of publication of material that unjustly defames a person's character or hurts the operation of his or her business. In most cases, civil libel is a misdemeanor; conviction can result in a fine or a jail sentence.

CHECKLIST FOR AVOIDING LIBEL SUITS

✓ Know the libel laws of your state.

✓ Triple-check every story for accuracy.

✓ Remember: There are at least two sides to every question.

✓ Be fair and honorable with your sources and with your readers.

Slander. Libel laws apply to false and malicious written statements; slander laws pertain to spoken defamatory remarks. In the early days of radio and television, a person who felt slandered by a radio or television commentator had little recourse in the courts. If the slandered person sued and won the case, the settlement was often so small that it was hardly worth the time. But because of the large audiences radio and television now attract, suits for slander are now tried under harsher libel laws. Usually, the more persons that hear the slander, the more severe will be the penalty.

Defenses in Suits for Libel or Slander. Despite the fact that journalists are subject to suits for libel and slander, legal defenses have been developed. In general, there are three such defenses for protecting members of the mass media: truth of report, privilege of reporting, and fair comment and criticism.

Truth of Report. Truth is the major defense in any libel suit. The editor or publisher accused of publishing a libelous statement must be able to prove the truth of the statements made. For example, when a national magazine published a report saying that two well-know football coaches had conspired to "fix" a game between their two teams, the magazine publisher was sued by the two coaches. For the libel suit to be dismissed, the law required that the magazine prove the coaches' involvement in a conspiracy. When the magazine's publisher could not substantiate the reported "fix," the coaches were awarded over a million dollars for damage to their reputations.

A person's name need not necessarily be used in a defamatory statement for libel action to take place. If the person about whom the statement was made can be identified, he or she can sue for damages. To avoid libel suits, reporters avoid expressions implying that a person accused of a crime has been adjudged guilty of that crime. The non-suable phrasing used is often something like this: "the person *alleged* to have committed the crime."

Privilege of Reporting. This defense grants the press immunity from libel damages for fair and true reports of government or other official proceedings. For example, if a mayor fires a police commissioner, the mayor's reasons, whether given at a news conference or in writing, can be published without fear of a libel suit being filed by the dismissed police commissioner. Similarly, any comments or accusations made by government officials during public hearings can be published.

Fair Comment and Criticism. Without this defense, many editorials, movie, stage, television, and book reviews, feature stories, and letters-to-the-editor could not be printed. This defense permits editors, feature writers, and columnists the freedom to express their opinions as long as they are not malicious. If fair comment and criticism were not a defense against libel, no reporter would be able to include in a news story any quotations that criticize a person or business.

People in a democracy have the right to know how government officials function. The mass media in a democracy have the duty to inform the public about government operations. Therefore, journalists and government officials are often at odds. Journalists try to uncover facts; government officials sometimes prefer to keep those facts secret. During the war in Vietnam, for example, the government became concerned about unfavorable reports from the battle zone and sought to pressure *The New York Times* into transferring its reporter David Halberstam from South Vietnam to Poland. *The Times* refused to transfer Halberstam, who later received a Pulitzer Prize for his coverage of the war.

Another case in point involves the Watergate scandals of the mid-1970s. Many government officials—including those at the highest levels—sought to deny information to reporters. Then when certain information did appear in print, government officials threatened the offending newspapers with severe legal reprisals. Refusing to yield to such pressure, the national press and national television persevered in bringing to the American public information that the executive branch of the government preferred not to divulge.

No journalist, of course, believes that the press must know everything. Every journalist realizes that some confidentiality is necessary if the government is to pursue its foreign and domestic policies successfully. The conflict between the people's right to know and the government's need for secrecy was summarized by John Hohenberg, a former foreign correspondent for *The New York Times:*

> The responsible news media ... are torn between a desire to respect the processes of government that clearly demand a certain amount of confidentiality and to check the growth of such objectionable official practices as holding unnecessary executive sessions and maintaining unnecessary secrecy over public records.
>
> *The News Media: A Journalist Looks at His Profession.*

The Journalist—Ally of the Consumer

An informed consumer is an intelligent consumer. Information needed to inform consumers is only as good as it is accurate and free from bias. Today, consumers know that they can trust the mass media to provide honest answers to questions about goods and services.

Many consumers feel that they are wasting their time complaining about faulty merchandise to the dealer or the manufacturer. Reporters often can provide two-way communication about a given problem. For example, consumer columnist Margaret Dana gets hundreds of letters weekly complaining about things as "poor workmanship, especially the holes left in fabric to mark darts in dresses; narrow seams, badly stitched; skimped hems and waist-length sections." Ms. Dana relays these complaints to the manufacturers, who, in many cases, correct the flaws.

Until the early sixties the slogan "Let the buyer beware" was the prevailing attitude of manufacturers toward consumers. At that time President Kennedy proposed executive and legislative action designed to guard the health and finances of consumers. In an address to Congress, he asked for major enactments dealing with drugs, foods, cosmetics, and television sets. In a sense this legislation told business people that unless they did a better job of policing their members on matters of consumer protection, Washington agencies would take over this job.

Within a week after she had been appointed the first head of the Consumer Protection Department, Esther Peterson received 3000 letters. One of them contained a shrimp, along with the complaint that the biggest shrimp in the frozen food package was smaller than any pictured on the cover of the package. Most of the letters were angry in tone. A Pennsylvania man sent a cereal box which he said contained "only seven inches of cereal and four-and-one-half inches of air."

Until this time the mass media had had little concern with the dissatisfaction of the consumer. With the advent of national focus on the consumer, the situation changed, and newspapers and magazines began running columns dealing with consumer problems. Television and radio soon followed suit and scheduled talk shows and panels that deal with consumer problems. *Consumer Reports*, a magazine that tests and compares consumer products, had an immediate circulation increase. Consumers became aware of their right to get what was advertised and to get their money's worth, and they increased their watchfulness; manufacturers began to reckon with a more knowledgeable consumer.

Related news events began to mushroom. Shoppers began to boycott supermarkets because of prices or faulty merchandise. States formed their own consumer protection units and brought certain businesses to court. The slogan "Let the buyer beware" had changed to "Let the manufacturer take care." The responsibility would now be shared.

Of course the charge is plagiarism!

Newspapers expanded their homemaking sections and added Sunday supplements dealing with such items as home furnishings, quality of clothing, and consumer services.

Newspapers, radio and television stations began to conduct their own investigations of certain businesses. For example, a reporter on a metropolitan newspaper assigned to investigate the high cost of auto repairs had a mechanic loosen a spark plug in her car's engine. She then took her car to a number of repair centers. Repair bill estimates ranged from "no charge" to $375. The story — citing names — was published. One major advertiser whose estimate was among the highest cancelled its advertising. The editor felt, however, that the story had provided a community service.

Other such investigations dealt with costs of TV repairs, rates of heating oil, and the large amount of sugar in various brands of breakfast cereals.

Guidelines for Journalists

To try to prevent violations of the written and unwritten codes of the journalism profession, the mass media have created some specific guidelines for journalists. The sections that follow discuss these guidelines as they concern covering public disorders, covering the courts, covering the arts, plagiarism, word choice, and impartiality.

Guidelines for Covering Public Disorders

After a number of peace demonstrations and protest marches in which several persons were injured, a group of editors met to set up guidelines to prevent the mass media from contributing to any public disturbance. Among the provisions set forth were these:

> Because inexpert use of cameras, bright lights, or microphones may stir exhibitionism in some people, great care should be exercised by crews at scenes of public disorders. Their presence should be as unobtrusive as possible.
>
> All news media should make every effort to assure that only seasoned reporters are sent to the scene of a disaster.
>
> Every reporter and technician should be governed by the rules of good taste and common sense. The potential for inciting public disorders demands that competition be secondary to the cause of public safety.
>
> From *Rights in Conflict*, by Daniel Walker.

Guidelines for Covering the Courts

To ensure an accused defendant a fair trial, mass media journalists must keep in mind the fact that an accused person is innocent until found guilty by a judge or a jury. The American Bar Association (ABA), an association of lawyers, has frequently charged that the mass media sometimes prevent an accused person from receiving a fair trial as guaranteed by the Sixth Amendment. Though the ABA does not advocate restricting the mass media (to do so would violate the guarantee of the First Amendment), the organization does recommend that police and court officials withhold certain information. An ABA committee on "Free Press, Fair Trial" recommends that the following facts be withheld in criminal cases:

1. The suspect's prior criminal record.

2. Existence or contents of a confession.

3. Lie detector test results or whether the suspect takes the test.

4. Identity of prospective witnesses.

5. The possibility of a guilty plea.

6. General comments about the suspect's guilt or innocence.

Though many journalists have protested that these recommendations constitute censorship of the public's right to know, court officials in most states are following the ABA recommendations. However, mass media organizations, the ABA, and certain universities are conducting studies to determine whether newspaper and television publicity—"trial by newspaper," as it is called—has any effect on the decisions of juries.

The Sixth Amendment

In all criminal prosecutions, the accused shall enjoy the right to a speedy and public trial, by an impartial jury of the State and district wherein the crime shall have been committed, which district shall have been previously ascertained by law, and to be informed of the nature and cause of the accusation; to be confronted with the witnesses against him; to have compulsory process for obtaining witnesses in his favor, and to have the Assistance of Counsel for his defense.

Guidelines for Covering the Arts

Another example of self-imposed restriction concerns the arts. If a reviewer too harshly criticizes every movie, play, art show, or musical event offered in a community, people will either stop attending such events or will soon completely ignore the criticisms. Reviewers, therefore, try to temper their reviews. What they write or say about an event and its participants should, of course be honest. It should seek to criticize constructively. Above all, it should avoid sarcasm, harsh ridicule, and vindictiveness.

Guidelines Concerning Plagiarism

The word *plagiarism* is defined as the presenting as one's own the ideas or words of another. Although news facts cannot be copyrighted, the style of writing them is. A news writer, however, is permitted to rewrite material presented in another story provided that credit is given to the original source. It is not only unethical to use passages of another writer's story; it is also illegal. The original writer may have invested a great deal of time and energy in a sentence and, as the originator, is entitled to compensation if another writer uses his or her work. (It is said that Ernest Hemingway rewrote one particular sentence one hundred times.)

Guidelines Concerning Word Choice

Though journalists are reasonably sure of the distinction between fact and opinion when writing news stories, they are often less confident in their choice of words for their stories. Editors and reporters are people who know that language has power. They realize that certain words in news copy can create positive or negative feelings. For example, does a group "demand" or "request" a change in the zoning codes? If the writer presenting a story on this subject uses "demand," he or she must be sure that the group proposing the change is really "demanding" and not just "requesting" a change, because some readers might react negatively to "protest" but positively to "participation." To avoid taking sides in any dispute and spreading propaganda for any cause through their use of language, journalists take great care in writing a story, deleting any words or sentences that will misrepresent a person or event.

Guidelines Concerning Impartiality

A newspaper's job is to clarify issues and events, not to confuse them. To do so, journalists must decide how to report an event. Newspaper, radio and television coverage of the foreign and domestic policies of the government differ in part from one organization to another because different editors have different viewpoints about government activities. For example, a newspaper in favor of capital punishment might feature a series on "The Death Sentence—A Crime Deterrent," whereas a newspaper favoring abolition of the death sentence might provide front-page space for an article titled "Reforming the Penal System." Individual newspapers usually cannot avoid taking a position on the issues facing the public, though the best newspapers try to prevent prejudice in their news reporting. (During election campaigns newspapers openly support their candidates in their editorials.)

The news media continuously and earnestly attempt to be fair to all sides at all times. But some pictures and stories are so powerful—like the highly publicized picture of a Buddhist monk burning himself in the streets of Saigon—that editors decide to use them even though they may be criticized for sensational and unethical journalism. It is thus a matter of the dual considerations of good judgment and of ethical purpose that often influence an editor to publish or broadcast a story.

Outlook for the Future

Today, the President of the United States and the general secretary of the Communist party of the USSR can communicate with each other immediately on a "hot-line," a telephone link installed to lessen the danger of accidental nuclear war. The general principle behind this "hot-line" is simply this: When two people communicate their thoughts and feelings directly to each other, they are less likely to settle their differences by physical force. Similarly, by keeping the public informed and at the same time observing the guidelines set forth in their own codes of ethics, the mass communications media can contribute to a better, safer, more ethical, more peaceful world. In *A Free and Responsible Press*, the Commission on Freedom of the Press pointed the way for journalism in the future when it said the following:

With the means of self-destruction that are now at their disposal, men must live, if they are to live at all, by self-restraint, moderation, and mutual understanding. They get their picture of one another through the press. The press can be inflammatory, sensational, and irresponsible. If it is, it and its freedom will go down in the universal catastrophe. On the other hand, the press can do its duty by the new world that is struggling to be born. It can help create a world community by giving men everywhere knowledge of the world and of one another, by promoting comprehension and appreciation of the goals of a free society that shall embrace all men.

THE JOURNALIST'S CREED

I believe in the professionalism of Journalism.

I believe that the public journal is a public trust; that all connected with it are, to the full measure of their responsibility, trustees for the public; that acceptance of a lesser service than the public service is betrayal of this trust.

I believe that clear thinking and clear statement, accuracy, and fairness are fundamental to good journalism.

I believe that a journalist should write only what he holds in his heart to be true.

I believe that suppression of the news, for any consideration other than the welfare of society, is indefensible.

I believe that no one should write as a journalist what he would not say as a gentleman; that bribery by one's own pocketbook is as much to be avoided as bribery by the pocketbook of another; that individual responsibility may not be escaped by pleading another's instructions or another's dividends.

I believe that advertising, news and editorial columns should alike serve the best interests of readers; that a single standard of helpful truth and cleanness should prevail for all; that the supreme test of good journalism is the measure of its public service.

I believe that the journalism which succeeds best—and best deserves success—fears God and honors man; is stoutly independent, unmoved by pride of opinion or greed of power, constructive, tolerant but never careless, self-controlled, patient, always respectful of its readers but always unafraid, is quickly indignant at injustice; is unswayed by the appeal of privilege or the clamor of the mob; seeks to give every man a chance, and, as far as law and honest wage and recognition of human brotherhood can make it so, an equal chance; is profoundly patriotic while sincerely promoting international good-will and cementing world-comradeship; is a journalism of humanity, of and for today's world.

Walter Williams
School of Journalism
University of Missouri

Activities

1. What problem in your community most angers and upsets you? Is anything being done about it? What stand have your local newspaper and radio station taken? To what extent is the community aroused or apathetic about the problem? What can the local mass media do to change the situation? If you were a professional journalist, how would you attack the problem? List some ways in which community action might be stimulated.

2. Bring to class two different newspaper or newsmagazine stories covering the same news event. Compare the headlines, pictures, amount of coverage, depth of coverage, placement of the story, and style of reporting in the two different publications. Which publication seems to provide the more accurate, detailed, and impartial information? Which one seems more responsible? What reporting changes would you make in the less responsible publication?

3. Do you think that a newspaper can "hang" a suspected murderer before he or she goes on trial? Why are reporters and photographers sometimes banned from courtrooms in major criminal cases while artists are not? What problems do newspaper reporters face in covering the murder or the kidnaping of a prominent person? Do you think that the legal restrictions on trial coverage violate the public's right to know, or that they guarantee an accused criminal a fair trial? Explain.

4. Select an evening when all members of your class can watch the same two or three nationally televised news programs. In class the next day, discuss the following questions:

    a. Did any program give a distorted picture of events, people, and facts? If so, how?

    b. Did you find any program (or part of it) annoying or offensive? If so, what and why?

    c. Would you censor any of the programs? Why? How?

    d. Which program(s) showed the greatest social responsibility? In what way(s)?

5. Select a controversial public figure to write a short news story about. In your story make up an incident involving that person. Read your story aloud to see whether the class can identify what your feelings are about the individual. If your feelings did come through, what sentences, words, or phrases gave you away? Did those who agree with you about the individual like your story? Can opinion ever be completely concealed? Rewrite your story, trying to be strictly impartial.

6. How can book, play, and movie reviews be considered unfair? Can a critic be sued for writing a review that insults an artist? To what extent should student critics have the same freedoms of expression as their professional counterparts?

7. Attend a movie and write a review of it. Assume that you are the reviewer for an influential publication and that your review can make or break the film. Read your review aloud to see if your classmates think your review is accurate and fair.

8. Prepare a report explaining the conflict that has developed between the government and the press in any one of the following areas:

    a. Censorship   **d.** Antinuclear demonstrations

    b. The "credibility gap"   **e.** National security

    c. News "leaks"

Part 3

The High School Journalist and the School Media

CHAPTER 14

The School Newspaper: Staff Organization

The time: Spring, two weeks before the end of the school year.

The place: The journalism classroom at Jordan High School.

The event: A review of the newspaper publishing year just ended.

The cast: The 25 journalism students who, during the school year, put out 35 issues of *The Jordan Times* and who have just published the 36th and final issue.

The director: Mr. Bob Oberfelder, journalism teacher and faculty adviser for *The Jordan Times*.

For over 35 minutes, the class members have been examining the past issue of the paper and commenting on what was good about the various issues and what improvements they think they might make if they had the chance to relive the year.

"All in all," remarks Mr. Oberfelder, "it has been a really good year. In December, you recall, the paper

received the Kiwanis-Rotary Community Service Award for the four-part series we did about the Hospital Development Award fund. Then in March the paper received the State Journalism Award for Editorial Excellence. That was because of the editorials Dave and Marcie wrote about school-building use. And then just a week ago, *The Jordan Times* received an Honorable Mention from Quill and Scroll. Besides that, our bank statement shows a balance of $1500. OK!"

A buzz of agreement.

"All of you," continues Mr. Oberfelder, "and I mean *all* of you—rate a special commendation. But right now, those who've been in charge of things around here should be singled out. Dave, Marcie, Beth, Mac, Mei Ling, Miriam, Lil, John, Anne, Scott— stand up and take a bow."

The ten staff members rise to enthusiastic applause.

"Dave, as editor-in-chief, you must have something to say."

"I sure have," grins Dave Jackson. "As Mr. Oberfelder said, we've had a really good year. We've made *The Jordan Times* one of the best high school newspapers in the state—and probably in the United States, too. And all of us want it to go on being a top-notch paper. That's why we have to think now about next year. Let's see. How many of you are juniors?"

Twelve hands go up.

"OK. How many of you will be taking journalism next year?"

Again, twelve hands.

"Great! Well, you're the ones who'll be running *The Times* next year because you're the ones who'll fill the key jobs I've listed on the board." Dave points to the list of eleven key posts:

- Editor-in-chief
- Managing Editor
- News Editor
- Sports Editor
- Feature Editor
- Layout Editor
- Chief Copy Editor
- Business Manager
- Advertising Manager
- Circulation Manager
- Chief Photographer

"If you are interested in any one of these jobs, give me a piece of paper with your name on it, the name of the job you'd like, and a sentence or two explaining why you think you'd be good at that job. OK?"

"How soon do you want that paper?" asks Joe Sanders, who served as a sports reporter during the year.

"By Friday afternoon at the latest. Bring your papers here to the journalism room."

"Can we recommend various persons for specific jobs?" Carmenita Alvarez has been a copy editor.

"Sure can. We're glad to have all the recommendations we can get. But if you do recommend someone, it'd be good if you'd give one or two reasons for your recommendation. Any other questions?"

"When will we know who's going to be doing what on *The Times* next year?" The questioner is Scott Washington, this year's chief photographer.

"At the Awards Assembly next week. So get your applications and your recommendations in pronto."

The entire class—in groups of twos, threes, and fours—begin to speculate on who'd be good in what job. Their buzzing fills the room as the bell rings.

When students begin working on school publications, they may not realize that they have become a part of a distinctive group with a long tradition in school publishing. But they have. The first student newspaper in America, *The Students Gazette*, was published at Friends Latin School—now the William Penn Charter School—in Philadelphia on June 11, 1777. The bicentennial of secondary school publishing in America was marked in 1977.

The Students Gazette was patterned after the prevailing style of the professional newspapers of the day. Interestingly enough, the professional press is today still the role model for student publications. A comparison of school newspapers with professional papers over the years clearly demonstrates the close similarity.

Although many readers are unaware of the *historical* relationship between student publications and professional publications, they seem to sense that there *is* such a relationship—especially when they criticize school publications. But what those critics seem not to understand is that student publications constitute a training ground and are not professional publications.

This student prepares copy for the school newspaper at the VDT in much the same way as her professional counterpart.

Students and teachers often question the fairness of any criticism aimed at student publications, but their arguments are frequently ignored. One reason is that the student press, like its professional model, insists (1) on all the rights guaranteed by the First Amendment and (2) on all the prerogatives enjoyed by the professional press. In a way, then, the criticism directed at student publications may be a sign of the importance granted to student newspapers, especially by the reading public.

Today's secondary school students are increasingly aware of and concerned about the world they live in; they are well aware of the important role mass communication plays in their lives. After all, they have grown up with radio and television; they have grown up in an age of space exploration, satellites, laser beams, and computers. In short, they have grown up in the midst of a revolution in communications technology.

Today's journalism students are playing an important part in this communications revolution as they work with the last of linotype-set school newspapers, as they try their hands at VDT (Video Display Terminal) composition, and as they prepare copy to be set by computer. Technological advances like these offer a welcome challenge to today's high school journalism students.

The Need for Staff Organization

In the United States and Canada the production of school publications has mushroomed into a big business. Each year hundreds of school newspapers, yearbooks, and magazines are written, edited, and published by thousands of secondary school journalism students. What's more, the influence of professional newspapers on student newspapers extends to the organization of the school newspaper staff. While it is true that many school newspaper jobs resemble those performed by professional newspeople, there are significant differences between the two in purpose and in organization. One important difference is this: On professional papers, persons are hired to fulfill specific job assignments for which they have the necessary academic training and professional experience. The school newspaper staff, on the other hand, is often made up of inexperienced first-year journalism students who have had no previous training in producing school publications. Such students, therefore, must learn *on the job.*

Because of the differences from school to school in the numbers, the interests, and the capabilities of students enrolling in journalism classes and because of differences in the amounts of time provided in the school schedule for journalism classes, the organization of the newspaper staff may vary widely from school to school—even from year to year in the same school. The chart (page 311) showing the organization of a "typical" school newspaper staff is, therefore, but one possibility. Furthermore, the job descriptions that follow—descriptions of the duties of key members of the school newspaper staff—are subject to modification as may be warranted by individual school conditions. As presented in this chapter, the job description seeks to fit the schedules and the abilities of journalism students rather than to fit students to specific jobs. The chart on page 311 represents newspaper staff organization in a school where there are at least twenty journalism students to place. Where such is not the case, the school journalism staff will need to modify its organization to ensure the satisfactory performance of key functions and the meeting of key responsibilities.

Like a professional staff, the school newspaper staff has three major areas of responsibility: (1) editorial, (2) managerial, and (3) financial. A successful newspaper—whether school or professional—must attain a balance among those areas. Although a school newspaper staff may at first be primarily concerned with

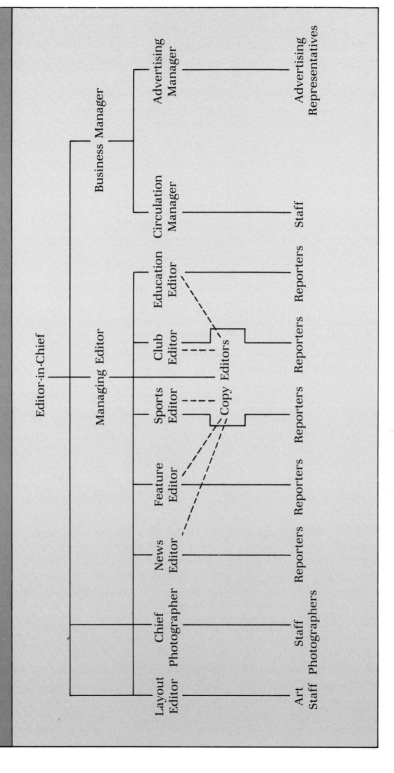

TYPICAL STAFF ORGANIZATION FOR A SCHOOL NEWSPAPER

Editor-in-Chief

Managing Editor

Business Manager

News Editor

Feature Editor

Sports Editor

Club Editor

Education Editor

Circulation Manager

Advertising Manager

Copy Editors

Reporters

Reporters

Reporters

Reporters

Reporters

Staff

Advertising Representatives

Layout Editor

Chief Photographer

Art Staff

Staff Photographers

the editorial function, staff members are certain to find that the editorial function cannot long continue successfully without adequate funds or efficient management.

In this chapter we are concerned with the effective organization of an efficient staff. In subsequent chapters, we shall focus respectively (1) on what the paper should print, (2) on how the content should be presented to readers, and (3) on how the paper can be made an editorial and financial success.

Purposes of Staff Organization

An organizational plan of the staff of a school newspaper has these purposes:

1. To divide the staff into functional groups that can work independently much of the time and yet contribute significantly to the work of the entire staff. A parallel can be made to the offensive and defensive squads of a football team: Each has its specific job to do, yet each contributes to the success of the whole team.
2. To provide the greatest amount of learning opportunity for students and, at the same time, to complete the tasks that must be done.
3. To define the responsibilities of each person on the staff so that individual performance can be evaluated fairly.
4. To provide for easy movement from one task to another, thereby permitting maximum opportunity for students to explore and experiment in a number of staff positions.
5. To provide opportunity for continuous in-service training for all members of the staff.
6. To meet the needs and interests of school newspaper readers.

Staff Members and their Responsibilities

Responsibilities of newspaper staff members may differ from school to school and from year to year. The following discussion, however, will help individual staff members get started in their work as school journalists.

The Editor-in-Chief

The school newspaper editor-in-chief should have the ability to write—and rewrite—news stories, to write effective editorials, to suggest effective headlines, and to design attractive page layouts. This person should have the ability to suggest ideas for stimulating articles, headlines, and layouts.

1. The editor-in-chief understands the duties of all staff members—the editors, the reporters, the copy editors, the photographers, the business personnel, the sales personnel, the circulation personnel—and is sensitive to their problems.
2. The editor-in-chief is well acquainted with the writing abilities of each member of the staff and often authorizes the use of bylines as a reward for outstanding work.
3. With the help of the managing editor (see page 318), the editor-in-chief plans specific staff assignments, usually assigning articles to reporters according to the reporter's special interests and ever-increasing abilities. Many new reporters not yet capable of handling more complex assignments will be assigned to minor stories. The more a reporter writes, the more competent and skilled he or she can become. New reporters can often be encouraged by being given assignments that are well within their capabilities.
4. The editor-in-chief can expect some staff members to lose their enthusiasm for working on the paper. To keep up the morale of other staff members, the editor-in-chief should make no concessions to unmotivated staffers. Staff members who are deadwood often cause trouble with other more productive workers. It is usually a good policy not to retain such people.

Attending Staff Meetings. Planning and conducting staff meetings, with the consent of the faculty adviser, is an important function of the editor-in-chief. In fact, he or she chairs all such meetings.

The editor-in-chief* serves as the "contact" person to whom the papers' readers address complaints. With the help of the faculty adviser, the editor-in-chief has the responsibility to respond diplomatically to such complaints.

The editor-in-chief performs many key functions and must be a responsible person. Among the more important of these responsibilities are the following:

---

*This discussion of the responsibilities of the editor-in-chief stresses the point that a student editor-in-chief is learning how to be an editor, just as a student reporter is learning how to be a reporter.

RESPONSIBILITIES OF A SCHOOL NEWSPAPER'S EDITOR-IN CHIEF

✓ Cooperates with the faculty adviser in organizing the staff for the year's work.

✓ With the adviser's help, assigns news beats.

✓ With the adviser's approval, delegates duties to other staff members and is available to help them overcome problems.

✓ With the assistance of the staff, oversees beat coverage.

✓ Sees that all news in the school is covered and that all news stories are properly written.

✓ Helps in the editing of copy for all pages of the newspaper.

✓ Working with the business manager and the faculty adviser, determines the paper's publishing schedule.

✓ Sees to it that all staff members meet deadlines.

✓ Helps with the layout for all pages.

✓ Coordinates the work of the entire staff.

✓ Works with the printer to coordinate on-time publishing and distribution of each issue of the newspaper.

✓ Plans and chairs all staff meetings.

✓ Keeps a calendar of school events, important dates, and other newsworthy information.

✓ Writes some editorials.

✓ With the other staff members and the faculty adviser, helps identify readers' interests.

✓ Responds to all letters addressed to the editor.

✓ Participates actively in journalism organizations.

Working with the Staff* The student editor-in-chief—with the guidance of the faculty adviser—oversees the work of the entire newspaper staff.

---

*While it is generally true that most of those working on the school paper are journalism students, the editor-in-chief sometimes seeks the services of non-journalism students who represent other school groups.

The student editor-in chief confers with the faculty adviser and the managing editor.

1. The editor-in-chief regularly schedules and conducts meetings with the staff. To keep informed, he or she often schedules informal get-togethers with individual staff members.
2. Prior to each issue of the paper, the editor-in-chief holds planning sessions and editorial meetings with staff members to discuss suggestions, assignments, content possibilities, problem areas, and various ways for improving each issue.

Keeping Informed. The editor-in-chief devotes many hours to publishing the school paper and does not have much opportunity to participate in other school organizations and activities. He or she should, however, keep informed of possibilities for newsworthy material involving all school organizations and activities.

1. To ensure that school-related organizations and activities are properly covered, the editor-in-chief should prepare a beat sheet—a listing of all of the school's organizations and activities to be covered for news possibilities. The editor-in-chief usually prepares the beat sheet by obtaining from the school administrative office a listing of all of the organizations and activities connected with the school, plus the name of the president and the faculty adviser of each organization. From this information the editor-in-chief can have typed an alphabetical list of the various groups. Several copies of this list can be posted in the newsroom. At one of the first general staff meetings, the editor-in-chief and the managing editor can use the beat sheet to make

reporters' assignments. At this meeting student reporters should be impressed with the need for thoroughness in their coverage of assigned beats.

2. Recognizing news that has importance and interest to readers takes experience and perception. The editor-in-chief must determine the importance and potential interest of each story and, based on that experience, decide where to locate each story to be published. He or she must also decide how much space is to be allotted to each story.

BEAT	REPORTER
Principal's office	Rogers
Deans' offices	Littell
Faculty	Smith
Student Council	Martin
Music	Shen
Drama	Franke
Clubs	Robaton
Features	Cooke

This is a beat sheet for a high school newspaper.

Writing Editorials. One of the most important functions of the editor-in-chief is to stimulate student thinking through thought-provoking editorials. Often, the editor-in-chief writes all the editorials or else asks other staff members—and sometimes other students—to write editorials for specific issues of the paper.

A detailed discussion about the writing of editorials appears on pages 252–269.

Establishing and Meeting Deadlines. Because of the time needed by printers to set stories and headlines into type, have engravings or negatives made, make up pages, and print the school paper, the editor-in-chief must plan carefully and schedule editorial preparation time well in advance of the paper's proposed publication date.

1. Ideally, the editor-in-chief should meet with the printer *before* the beginning of the school year. At that meeting they work out the scheduling details necessary for establishing realistic deadlines for submitting all copy from the editorial staff to the printer. If such a meeting is impossible before the school year begins, the editor-in-chief and the faculty adviser need to meet with the printer as early in the school year as possible.
2. Although printers usually want all photographs and most of the news copy as early as possible, it is often necessary to submit last-minute stories, heads, and layouts at a later date so that the news can be kept timely.
3. Established deadlines should be prominently posted in the journalism classroom and in the newsroom.
4. Preparatory work on the school paper should never be put off until the last minute. Editorial work should be scheduled far enough ahead to avoid any chance that the paper might come out late.
5. The editor-in-chief maintains files of general feature stories and pictures. Such files are helpful in the event that a story or a picture for which space has been saved is received too late to be included in a particular issue.
6. The editor-in-chief is responsible for seeing that staff members are constantly made aware of the importance of meeting deadlines.

Working with the Printer. Printers of school publications are usually conscientious persons who cooperate with the editor-in-chief to help make each issue of the school newspaper the best it can be.

1. The editor-in-chief should cooperate with the printer; the printer's advice can be invaluable.
2. The editor-in-chief should see to it that all stories are typed neatly. When copy has been heavily edited, the editor-in-chief should make arrangements to have it retyped.
3. Many editors-in-chief help the printer by writing fillers (one- and two-sentence stories). The printer sets the fillers into type and uses them to fill extra space at the foot of any column, thus making unnecessary any last-minute rearrangement of stories to fill a column.
4. If there will be a late-breaking story, the editor-in-chief should call the printer and explain the situation. For example, if the school's basketball team was scheduled to play in the state finals on the day established as the deadline date for submitting copy to the printer, the printer should be requested to leave space on the front page layout to insert the last-minute copy for the game story.
5. The editor-in-chief is responsible for seeing that all copy and photographs to be submitted to the printer are checked to ensure that they meet the printer's specifications.

Working with the Faculty Adviser. The editor-in-chief must maintain close communication with the faculty adviser on such matters as publishing policy, staff, budget, deadlines, printing, and editorial campaigns.

1. Because some stories may involve poor taste, inaccuracy, or potential libel, close communication with the adviser is essential.
2. School newspaper advisers are usually chosen on the basis of past experience. The professional advice obtainable from an interested, experienced adviser is invaluable.
3. Staff members who are not working to the best of their abilities should be discussed with the adviser. Often, the adviser can suggest discreet solutions to personnel problems.

The Managing Editor

Although the editor-in-chief is responsible for the overall administration of every operation connected with the school paper, it is the managing editor (sometimes called the news editor) who is re-

RESPONSIBILITIES OF A SCHOOL NEWSPAPER'S MANAGING EDITOR

✓ With the help of the editor-in-chief and the faculty adviser, assigns feature stories and interview stories.

✓ Cooperates with the editor-in-chief and the faculty adviser in coordinating the work of the entire editorial and reportorial staff.

✓ Makes out a daily schedule to be observed by the staff; posts that schedule on the newsroom bulletin board.

✓ Assists in the production of news copy.

✓ Assists in editing all copy.

✓ Sees to it that deadlines are met.

✓ Does page layout and writes headlines.

✓ Helps revise copy.

✓ Edits all feature copy.

✓ Keeps a notebook of ideas for feature articles.

✓ Attends all staff meetings.

✓ Takes an active part in journalism organizations.

sponsible for day-to-day editorial operations. The managing editor makes sure that each department editor is doing a thorough job in covering and reporting on assigned news beats. The managing editor helps prepare the beat sheet, often supervising its preparation. On many school papers, the managing editor is also responsible for editorial production (editing and layout). Directly responsible to the editor-in-chief and the faculty adviser, the managing editor carries out their instructions—whether or not he or she agrees with them. The managing editor keeps a copy file of all stories published in the school paper. If the editor-in-chief is absent, the managing editor fills in.

Department Editors

Department editors, together with the staff members assigned to them, cover and report the news obtained from their appointed beats. For example, the education editor assigns staff reporters to cover stories affecting the education of all students in the school. In addition, the education editor assigns reporters to cover faculty members and school facilities. A member of the education editor's staff should periodically consult with the principal on matters concerning the overall educational environment. Department editors need periodically to discuss with the editor-in-chief and the managing editor the major coverage of all beat areas. Each department editor should know approximately how many stories the managing editor expects his or her department to submit for each issue of the newspaper. Department editors are often in charge of makeup for the pages on which their material is to appear. Finally, department editors are directly responsible to the managing editor and the editor-in-chief and are indirectly responsible to the faculty adviser.

RESPONSIBILITIES OF A SCHOOL NEWSPAPER'S DEPARTMENT EDITOR

✓ With the help of the faculty adviser, plans, produces, and edits all materials scheduled for release.

✓ With the aid of the editor-in-chief, the managing editor, and the faculty adviser, makes assignments and edits copy.

✓ Sees to it that deadlines are met.

✓ Maintains a morgue of news stories and news photos.

- ✓ Keeps a scrapbook of printed releases.

- ✓ Keeps a schedule of future school events.

- ✓ Cooperates with the sponsors of school activities and organizations to publicize their work.

- ✓ With the help of the faculty adviser, cooperates with the school office of public information.

- ✓ Prepares exhibits of the work of the journalism department.

- ✓ Attends all staff meetings.

- ✓ Produces copy of news releases, television news shows, and radio news scripts.

- ✓ Provides a minimum output per week as follows:
  - **a.** Delegates assignments to news staff members.
  - **b.** Posts assignments and meets deadlines.
  - **c.** Secures the faculty adviser's approval on all news releases before sending them out.
  - **d.** Keeps a check sheet in duplicate of all news releases sent out.
  - **e.** Orders supplies.
  - **f.** Writes at least three news releases.
  - **g.** Keeps news-release scrapbook up to date.
  - **h.** Approves one or more photos to accompany news stories.
  - **i.** Writes and occasionally broadcasts the school TV news.
  - **j.** Occasionally gives flash news on the school radio.
  - **k.** Maintains a posted schedule of school TV shows and radio tapes, listing the names of the students involved. (Completes such a list a month in advance, if possible.)

RESPONSIBILITIES OF A SCHOOL NEWSPAPER'S SPORTS EDITOR

- ✓ Cooperates with the editor-in-chief and the faculty adviser in coordinating the work of the newspaper staff.

- ✓ With the help of the editor-in-chief and the adviser, makes sports-story assignments.

- ✓ Oversees the work of sportswriters and sports reporters.

✓ Edits all sports copy.

✓ Keeps a notebook of sports-story ideas.

✓ Maintains a sports morgue.

✓ Writes sports copy.

✓ Does sports-page layouts and writes sports headlines.

✓ Keeps a schedule of all school sports events.

✓ Attends all staff meetings.

✓ Participates actively in journalism organizations.

✓ Sees to it that all sports-story deadlines are met.

The Business Manager

The primary function of the school newspaper's business manager is to keep the paper financially sound. To do so, the business manager must maintain thorough records. In working closely with the advertising and the circulation managers, the business manager keeps a close check on the two main sources of revenue—advertising and circulation.

The business manager is responsible for preparing the school paper's budgets—the budget for the entire school year and the budget for each issue of the paper. In doing so, he or she takes into account the anticipated income from advertising and from subscriptions, as well as anticipated expenses for printing, supplies, and general operations.

The business manager is responsible for recording all of the newspaper's financial transactions, receiving all the money collected from advertising and subscriptions, and depositing that money in the newspaper's bank account. With the approval of the editor-in-chief and the faculty adviser, the business manager allocates money to be expended for newspaper supplies and equipment.

The responsibilities of the business manager are discussed at greater length in Chapter 17, "The School Newspaper: Production, Finance, Public Relations," pages 411–417.

The Advertising Manager

The advertising manager, together with the advertising sales representatives, is responsible for the sale of all advertising space in the school newspaper. The advertising manager works closely with the editor-in-chief, the managing editor, the business manager, and the faculty adviser.

The advertising manager's role is essential to the financial security of the paper. He or she prepares a list of business establishments in the community and assigns advertising sales representatives to canvass each such establishment to arrange for an advertisement to appear in the school paper. To be profitable, each issue of the paper should have about 60 percent of its space devoted to advertising.

The responsibilities of the advertising manager and sales personnel are discussed in Chapter 17, pages 417–421.

The Circulation Manager

The major responsibility of the circulation manager is to supervise the distribution of the paper (delivering, mailing, and the like) to all subscribers. He or she must keep careful records of all money collected and must submit such records to the business manager. Ideally, the circulation manager should have access to a car, in order to oversee the distribution of each issue of the paper.

To help plan and carry out circulation campaigns, the circulation manager needs an assistant—even several assistants. The circulation manager, in continual touch with the public, must be constantly aware of his or her responsibility for promoting good will toward the school paper.

The responsibilities of the circulation manager are discussed at greater length in Chapter 17, pages 421–423.

Copy Editors

Copy editors work with the managing editor in proofreading, editing, writing captions (cutlines), and supplying headlines for all of the stories printed in the paper. Usually, copy editors are students who have been reporters and so are aware of the problems reporters can face.

The extent of the editing copy editors do depends on the proficiency of the writer of each story. In some cases, a story might need complete rewriting; in others, only minor copy editing may be necessary.

Copy editors are directly responsible to the managing editor and indirectly responsible to the editor-in-chief.

The responsibilities of copy editors are discussed at greater length in Chapter 16, "The School Newspaper: Copy Editing, Layout and Design, pages 360–380.

Reporters

The reporter—the backbone of the newspaper—is one of the most exciting and rewarding positions on the school newspaper. The contributions of reporters can make the difference between a paper that is uninteresting and a paper that is fresh and alive.

The reporter is "where the action is," often having a front-row seat for news events, and many reporters—both school and professional—have passed up promotions in order to continue to cover news events.

The reporter is directly responsible to his or her department editor and to the managing editor.

For an extended discussion of the reporter's functions and responsiblities, see Chapter 15, "The School Newspaper: Content," pages 326–357.

Chief Photographer

As a representative of the school paper and of the school itself, the chief photographer must be a conscientious person, who is neat, courteous, and professional.

From the managing editor and departmental editors—and sometimes from the editor-in-chief—the chief photographer receives assignments to photograph newsworthy events of interest to school newspaper readers. He or she is directly responsible to the managing editor and indirectly responsible to the editor-in-chief. The chief photographer is in charge of developing and

RESPONSIBILITIES OF A SCHOOL NEWSPAPER'S STAFF REPORTER

✓ Discusses story assignment in depth with department editor or managing editor.

✓ Researches the assigned story, using such sources as the encyclopedia, back issues of the school paper, back issues of the local and/or metropolitan papers.

✓ Writes the story as soon as all research and interviewing are completed.

✓ Double-checks facts for accuracy.

✓ Double-checks for correct spelling.

✓ To prevent misunderstanding or misinterpretation, double-checks the story for clarity and sharpness of expression.

✓ Meets all deadlines (but turns in copy ahead of the deadline if possible).

✓ Makes two copies of the story—one for the copy files and one for the editor's files.

✓ Attends all staff meetings as requested by the department editor, managing editor, editor-in-chief, or faculty adviser.

✓ Conducts oneself professionally at all times while on assignment.

printing all of the photographs taken for the school paper. He or she is also responsible for seeing to it that photographs selected for printing in the paper have been appropriately cropped and are ready for the printer.

The responsibilities of the chief photographer are discussed at greater length in Chapter 23, "Photography and School Publications," page 529.

Activities

1. Draw up a staff organization for a school newspaper, filling all of the positions on your chart with the names of classmates who, in your opinion, would most suitably fill those positions. To what extent do your job assignments coincide with those made by other students? Why is it sometimes difficult to assign people to specific jobs? How can friction between staff members on a school newspaper best be avoided? What procedures would you suggest to ensure harmonious relationships among school newspaper staff members?

2. Using an agreed-on organizational chart of staff assignments resulting from class consideration of Activity 1 above, plan a class newspaper and set a deadline for its completion. Structure its content, size, and format according to the time and the facilities you have available. Prepare a list of business establishments that might want to advertise in your class paper. Do you think your class newspaper could succeed? Why? Why not?

3. Prepare a beat sheet for your school paper, and assign yourself to cover one of the beats. List all of the school activities that you would cover as the reporter for your beat. Prepare your beat sheet with that posted by the paper's editors. How does your coverage differ from theirs? How is it similar?

Chief Sarah Winnemucca
Paiute peacemaker, author, leader of her people

1844-1891

Chief Sarah Winnemucca
Paiute Peacemaker

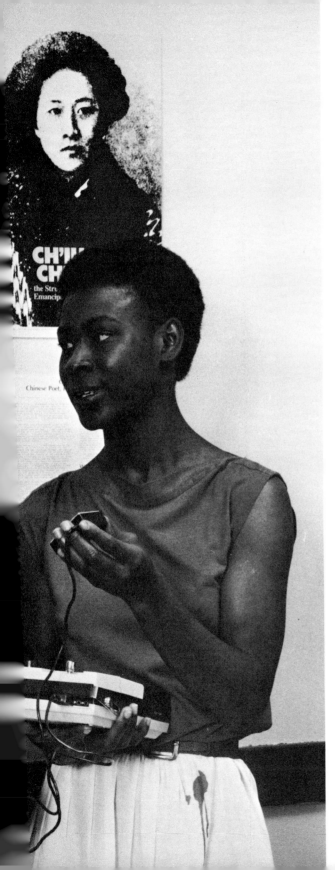

CHAPTER 15

The School Newspaper: Content

Pat Loiko, reporter on the Mannington High School *Monitor*, sits at the VDT in the journalism classroom, writing a story for the next issue. Managing Editor Andrew Stentovich walks over, peers at the screen, and after a few seconds says, "Looks like you've got a good story in the works there, Pat."

Pat smiles and kids him, "Sure, Andy. It's OK for today, but what about tomorrow?"

Andrew goes along with her kidding and replies in a mock-stern manner, "I've been meaning to speak with you about that, Pat."

They both laugh.

"Seriously, though," Andrew goes on, "I've got what I think will be another good assignment for you."

Pat turns from the VDT, picks up her notebook and pencil, and says, "Fire away!"

"Well," Andrew begins, "you know how the kids are complaining about the food in the cafeteria."

"So what else is new?"

"But this time it's different," persists Andrew. "The Student Council has voted to lodge a protest with the School Board."

"They're making a mountain out of a molehill, Andy. The food may not be as good as it was last year, but it's still OK as far as I'm concerned."

"Maybe so. But we need some facts. How about going over to Fairmont High tomorrow? That school's cafeteria is about the same size as ours. Find out how much their cafeteria spends on food. Find out how many cooks and servers they have. How long do they spend preparing the food they serve? Have they had the same number of employee cutbacks as we have had this year?"

"Sounds good, Andy. And then you think I should ask the same questions here about our cafeteria. Right?"

"Right. And I wouldn't be surprised that once you find out the facts and present them in a straight news story, the kids here will sing a different tune about the cafeteria food."

"OK," agrees Pat. "As soon as I finish getting this story on the VDT, I'll get to work on some good questions to ask at Fairmont tomorrow."

And with that, both Pat and Andrew turn their attention to the immediate job of getting out the next issue of the *Monitor*.

The abilities of the members of the school newspaper staff are best revealed by the quality of the paper's written content. News stories, editorials, speech stories, interview stories, sports stories, and feature articles must be honest, objective, and accurate presentations that reflect the school to the best of the student writer's ability.

Writing for the School Newspaper: Copy Preparation

Stories should be typed on standard 8 1/2-by-11-inch copy paper. When more than one of the school's publications use the same editorial room—or the same printer—it is advisable to color-code the copy paper. For example, the newspaper might use white copy paper; the yearbook, yellow; and the school magazine, pink. All news copy should be double-spaced, leaving generous margins at the top, bottom, and sides of all pages. More space should appear at the top of the first page of copy—for possible use by the copy editor. In addition, as an aid to the printer, it is preferable to end a page with the end of a paragraph. In general, copy preparation should follow the procedures outlined in Chapter 7, "Reporting the News," on pages 149–163.

The more "makers of news" (pages 143–148) included in school news stories, the better. News stories, of course, can range from brief stories of about 40 words to very long stories. A beginning news writer will most likely be assigned to write a short, straight news story. That same news writer, after gaining experience, will no doubt be asked to write inverted pyramid stories, stories about meetings and speeches, sports stories, feature stories, sidebars, and even editorials.

But probably most important in his or her training as a journalist, the beginning reporter/news writer will be assigned to write a story structured in the conventional news-story form—the inverted pyramid. (The structure of the inverted pyramid story was discussed in some detail in Chapter 7, "Reporting the News," page 150.) In the inverted pyramid story the important facts relating to *who, what, when, where, why,* and *how* constitute the key to the structure of the story—a structure, incidentally, that works well for most news stories. The inverted pyramid story, you will recall, serves two practical functions:

1. It enables the reader to scan a newspaper quickly to learn the important news of the day.
2. It allows the editor to delete paragraphs toward the end of the story —paragraphs that deal with nonessential information. When a news story can be shortened in this way to fit the available space, it is said to meet the "cut-off test."

But just how does the beginning journalist turn out an inverted pyramid news story that will capture and hold reader attention? Following is an example of the development of such a story, starting with the reporter's notes and ending with the final copy submitted to the news (department) editor.

Reporter's notes

■ Junior Achievement mtg at Central, Friday, Oct. 30, 2 p.m. Central gym.

■ More than 300 Central students to attend. All have applied for JA projects.

■ About 25 local business firms to be represented.

■ Representatives to serve as advisers or consultants to kids doing JA projects.

- This is 1st mtg this yr.
- Purpose of mtg: to organize projects.
- One kid (don't know name) said: "I don't know much about the JA program, but it has to be better than sitting in study hall."
- In project, kids form a company by selling stock, mfg a product, or creating a service.
- Associate Prin. says that projects will fit students' interests. Also says: "If a student wants to start a business for which there is no immediate adviser, JA will find an adviser."
- Associate Prin. is Sam Smith.
- JA is a nonprofit, economic education program.
- Central has worked with JA 6 yrs.
- In spring, advisers and kids to evaluate success or failure of projects.

Identification of the important facts. A veteran journalist would mentally analyze those notes and spot the important facts to use in the lead. The beginning journalist, however, may find it helpful to identify and write down the facts that make up the five *w's* and the *h*—as follows:

- **WHO:** 300 Central students
  Advisers from 25 local business firms
  Sam Smith, Associate Principal
  Student who commented re JA
- **WHAT:** JA Program at Central
  Organizational mtg of business advisers and students
  1st mtg of yr
- **WHEN:** Friday, Oct. 30, 2 p.m..
  In spring, advisers and students to evaluate success or failure of projects
- **WHERE:** Central gym
- **WHY:** To organize projects
  For students and advisers to meet
- **HOW:** Other relevant information:
  Statements from Sam Smith, Associate Prin.
  Quote from student (didn't get name) about JA
  6th yr Central has participated in JA
  JA—a nonprofit, economic education program

The lead. After organizing all the relevant information, the student journalist goes on to compose an acceptable, usable lead. Here is what might be the student's first try:

(1) "I don't know much about Junior Achievement yet,"said one JA applicant today, "but it has to be better than sitting in study hall."

Discarding this lead because it fails to focus on the most important facts of the story, the student reporter would try again:

(2) For the sixth year, Central High will participate in the Junior Achievement program.

Again, this lead fails to zero in on the important facts. And so the reporter might try another one:

(3) More than 300 Central High student applicants for the Junior Achievement program, together with their advisers from 25 local business firms, will meet to organize projects at 2 p.m. on Friday, October 30, in the Central gymnasium.

This third trial lead focuses on the major idea of the story. But the lead is obviously wordy and overburdened with ideas. So the reporter rewrites and sharpens it:

(4) More than 300 Central High applicants for Junior Achievement projects will meet with their local business advisers at 2:00 p.m., Friday, October 30, in the school gymnasium.

The reporter reviews this lead and decides (a) that it does indeed reflect the major idea to be reported, and (b) that the message it conveys is sharp and clear. The reporter then puts the remaining information contained in trial lead (c) into a second paragraph:

The advisers are representatives of 25 local business firms who have agreed to guide the students in establishing their own small business companies this year. In the Junior Achievement program, the students form a company by selling stock, manufacturing a product, or creating a service.

Here is the reporter's final version of the story as it was submitted to the news editor:

More than 300 Central High applicants for Junior Achievement projects will meet with their local business advisers at 2:00 p.m., Friday, October 30, in the school gymnasium.

The advisers are representatives of 25 local business firms who have agreed to guide the students in establishing their own small companies this year. In the Junior Achievement program, the students form a company by selling stock, manufacturing a product, or creating a service.

Associate Principal Sam Smith states that the projects will fit the interests of the students. He added, "If a student wants to start a business for which there is no immediate adviser, Junior Achievement will find an adviser to help him or her."

The business advisers and the students will evaluate the success or failure of the projects next spring.

Junior Achievement is a nonprofit, economic education program. Central High has participated in the program for six years.

One student applicant said, "I don't know much about the Junior Achievement program, but it has to be better than sitting in study hall."

That the student journalist followed good inverted pyramid structure in developing this news story is evident from the diagramed resetting of the story below.

THE JUNIOR ACHIEVEMENT STORY IN INVERTED-PYRAMID FORM

Lead
More than 300 Central High applicants for Junior Achievement projects will meet with their local business advisers at 2:00 p.m., Friday, October 30, in the school gymnasium.

Fact

Fact
The advisers are representatives of 25 local business firms who have agreed to guide the students in establishing their own small companies this year. In the Junior Achievement program, the students form a company by selling stock, manufacturing a product, or creating a service.

Fact

Quote
Associate Principal Sam Smith states that the projects will fit the interests of the students. He added, "If a student wants to start a business for which there is no immediate adviser, Junior Achievement will find an adviser to help him or her."

Fact
The business advisers and the students will evaluate the success or failure of the projects next spring.

Fact

Fact
Junior Achievement is a nonprofit, economic education program. Central High has participated in the program for six years.

Quote
One student applicant said, "I don't know much about the Junior Achievement program, but it has to be better than sitting in study hall."

From our discussion so far, it is clear that the most important part of a straight news story is the *lead*. The reader should be able to get the basic facts of any news story from the headline *and the lead*. Yet for the beginning journalist, composing an acceptable, usable lead is often the most difficult part of writing the story.

Leads—as you will recall from the discussion on pages 151–152—come in three forms: (1) the major-idea lead, (2) the summary lead, and (3) the combination lead.

Since most news stories are concerned with events, the lead that tells WHAT and WHEN is the one used most often. To try to include all of the five *w's* and the *h* in one lead usually makes that lead cumbersome and difficult to read.

As a part of learning to write leads, a beginning journalist needs to experiment, using one or more of the five *w's* to fit the immediate situation. In doing so, the writer will quickly realize that the lead directs and controls the organization of the resulting news story.

There is no one correct way to compose a lead. The writer must use his or her best judgment to decide which facts are of greatest importance, which are of secondary importance, and which are of least importance. Following are some guidelines for writing acceptable, usable leads.

Guidelines for Writing Leads

1. When in doubt, make the lead simple and direct.
2. Make the first few words of the lead focus on the most important fact in the story.
3. Try to limit the lead to one sentence—with the subject and verb as close as possible to the beginning of the sentence.
4. Limit the lead to between 20 and 30 words.
5. News story leads usually focus on WHAT and WHEN —BUT—
   a. If a prominent person constitutes the major newsmaker of a story, the lead may well begin with WHO.
   b. If a story focuses on a problematic situation, the lead may begin with a question.
   c. A lead may begin with a quotation if that quotation focuses on the major idea of the story.

The following examples illustrate lead variations—depending on the FOCUS of the news story:

1. WHO lead:

   The President was the picture of confidence as he began his third televised news conference yesterday.

2. Question lead:

Who will be the next mayor of Springfield—Andrew Rice or George Mason?

3. Quotation lead:

"The period for debating the gun-control issue is over. It is time now for citizens to stand up and be counted." So declared Moderator Ben Collins at the town meeting on Tuesday evening.

4. Verse lead:

"I never saw a purple cow."
But I saw many other strange animals at the San Diego Zoo.

5. Allusion lead:

"When I consider life and its few years"—it becomes a wisp of time between pajamas with feet and one's first date.

6. Suspense lead:

Last Monday the pilot of a small, single-engine plane turned to his nonpilot passenger, said, "Take the controls!" and then lost consciousness.

So far as sentence structure is concerned, the lead usually follows the regular pattern—subject, verb, complement. Occasionally, however, journalists seek to vary that order by using other structures. Here are some examples:

1. Inverted order with introductory prepositional phrase:

Onto the floor of Central's gymnasium last Friday night streamed 700 shouting, deliriously happy basketball fans.

2. Gerund phrase:

Passing the 80-cent school levy has to be the most important single action to be taken by this community this year.

3. Infinitive phrase:

To help conserve school funds, Jordan High's Senior Class has pledged 100 hours of free custodial and office work.

4. Participial phrase:

Maintaining a five-yard lead over his closest competitor, Nat Daly yesterday won his fifth 100-yard dash in as many outings.

5. Clause of concession:

Although the Bulldogs lost the state basketball championship by one point, Coach Brown declared that just being in the finals was an honor.

6. Clause of condition:

> If yearbook sales continue at the rate set this week, East High will set an all-time record.

7. Time clause:

> When the lunch bell rings at 11:45 each day, 1400 Centralites hit the halls like a giant tidal wave.

8. Noun clause:

> That Jim Clark won the giant slalom by two seconds is crystal clear from a rerun of the film taken at Lake Placid last week.

After having composed the best lead possible, the writer goes on to tell the facts of the story in descending order of importance—as was done in the news story on pages 329–332. The reporter may, of course, add color and credibility to the story by including human-interest information. Other than that, the reporter must keep strictly to the facts, omitting all personal comment. If, however, the reporter does find it necessary or desirable to express personal feelings about the facts, the story must carry a byline. The byline is a signal that the story is slanted in that it contains expressions of personal opinion. It is in this way that both the reporter and the newspaper maintain credibility with their readers.

How to Write Spot News Stories

Similar—yet significant—news stories appear year after year in school newspapers. Aware that such stories may bore their readers, staff writers often capture interest by using "secondary" or "feature" leads. The following is an example of a spot news story with a feature lead:

Student Power Finds New Leader

R-r-r-ring—The sound of the first bell on the opening day of school marked the beginning of a new era of Belmont High School life as Mr. Robert J. O'Donnell assumed the duties of principal. With his leadership have come his views that students should be involved fully in the business of their school. Under the fresh administration the once dormant Student Council shall have more power and make decisions concerning their "own" issues. . . .

The Highlander

Unexpected newsworthy events of general interest to the student body are also written and presented as spot news stories. The following example of a school newspaper spot news story bases each paragraph on a specific fact.

JUNIOR HURT IN CAVE ACCIDENT

Junior Chad Hall is currently in serious condition in Community hospital.

Saturday, December 28, Chad was with his Explorer Scout troop on a weekend outing of spelunking in Bloomington, Indiana.

As he was descending by rope further into a cave, his hands slipped, and Chad fell from 40 to 65 feet into the cave. Chad remained helpless until the Sputniks—

Professional Rescuer team arrived some four hours later.

Chad is now suffering multiple bone fractures, including a broken back.

Chad's sister, senior Patty Hall, commented that although visitors are not encouraged, any cards would be appreciated. His room number at the hospital is 2517-A.

The Lancer

Writing Interview Stories

In the interview story, the writer presents the opinion of the student, teacher, or administrator being interviewed. Many school papers carry an interview story in each issue. Such stories gain reader interest by dealing with significant topics. The following is an example of such a story—printed under a standard news headline.

OPINIONS VARY HERE ABOUT BOOK BANNING

To Kill a Mockingbird, The Merchant of Venice, The Catcher in the Rye, The Grapes of Wrath, Of Mice and Men, and *Black Boy.* Many of the books we read in English classes are being banned at other schools throughout the nation.

Most of the parents, faculty members, and students interviewed by the *Midway* oppose book banning. They feel that parents or a council of administrators and faculty members should not have the authority to decide what high school students should or should not read. . . .

"High school students are smart enough to know what a book represents, compared with what really happens in life," said Senior Emile Levisetti. "It's too bad people are being deprived of what are often very good books."

Allowing high school students to develop their own ideas is an important reason not to ban books, most people interviewed by the *Midway* felt. "Libraries should provide an open market place for people to formulate their own ideas," said Librarian Mary Biblo. "If we feed students only one type of information, it's like brainwashing them. They have to be exposed to many philosophies."

Parents, in general, were pleased with the books included in our English curriculum. "I'm glad the school uses interesting books to teach," said Mrs. Ruth Ditzian, mother of Michelle, a junior. "It allows students to expand intellectually as well as emotionally."

Some parents, however, felt that . . . some books should be banned. . . . Questioning the ability of high school students to differentiate between right and wrong, Mr. Chung-Yuan Lin, father of John, a sophomore, said, "Books which contain anti-American material are unsuitable."

The Midway

In some high school newspapers the editorial page often carries an inquiring-reporter column, combined with an interpretive interview article. These columns generally interest readers. The following is an example:

THE GENERAL's COMMENT . . .

Marriage: the union of a man and a woman in holy wedlock. Do teenagers really realize the meaning of the word marriage, and the responsibilities, advantages, and sacrifices that lay between the lines of its definitions? Do teenagers jump into marriage with their eyes closed, or are they actually awake to the joys and problems marriage may present?

"I'm against teenage marriage," commented senior Pat Neupert, when asked about the situation. "I don't think most teenagers are grown up enough to realize that in marriage you must give as well as take, and many times you must give a little more than you take.

"Also, a lot of kids don't realize they will continue to change and mature after

getting married early," continued Pat. "These further mental developments could cause problems in a marriage," Pat asserted.

"No," stated Matt Hewitson, a junior, firmly. "I don't think a teenager can support a family. I think one reason many marriages break up is that the couple can't afford to live comfortably and is struggling with money problems.

"A lot of marriages also break up because the couple thought they were in love before they were married, but after they were married they realized they didn't know the real meaning of love," concluded Matt. . . .

The Grantonian

The preceding article served as a sidebar for the following in-depth story on teenage marriages—always a subject of interest to high school students. The story includes source material obtained from the Census Bureau, Family Service Association, and from an interview with a school administrator.

SUCCESSFUL MARRIAGES FOR TEENAGERS?
CENSUS BUREAU STATISTICS OFFER ANSWERS

Can teenage marriage really be a success? According to the Census Bureau it depends upon four things: age, education, income, and where you are living after you get married.

Statistics prove that 21 percent of the men who marry before the age of 18 are divorced or separated within three to five years. Women that marry before the age of 18 are twice as likely to be divorced or separated as women who marry after the age of 22.

Sixty-four percent of the women that get married after the age of 22 are usually married to the same man when they are 60. By 1985 this percent is expected to rise to 72 percent.

It has been proven that couples that marry as teenagers and do not finish high school are most likely to end up in a divorce court or in separation. Those who wait until they have finished their educational training and marry when they are older usually have a much longer, more stable marriage.

"It is all wonderful the first year or so," commented Mrs. Melva Andersen, girls' vice-principal. "When the bills start to pile up, and the pressure gets so bad that the husband can stand no more, he can just take off, leaving the wife to support herself. . . ."

Teenage marriages are considered just another fun experience that teenagers want to try. When the fun stops, marriages end, either in divorce or separation.

If a man and a woman want to get married they should take into consideration three things: Can they support a family now? Are they ready to face the future? Are they really in love? If they feel they can answer these questions honestly and meaningfully then they actually are ready to be married.

The Grantonian

Writing Speech and Meeting Stories

Speeches and meetings of interest to school newspaper readers should be considered by reporters as possible material for news stories. The managing editor or a department editor often asks reporters to attend and write articles based on speeches and meetings of concern to students. Such articles can vary from reports on the status of a student council committee to reports on meetings at which several speakers present material of interest. Here is an example of a story based on a meeting:

On Thursday at City Hall, in a joint meeting aimed at counteracting violence in the schools, the City Council and the School Board designated April as School Safety Month and signed the School Safety Covenant.

Councilor Maura A. Kenton, Chairperson of both the Public Safety Committee and the Committee on School Matters announced the month's aim: "To involve parents, teachers, students, law enforcement officials, the judiciary, public officials, church groups, and the media in a cooperative effort to curb violence in the schools."

Those who attended the signing included Mayor George R. White; Police Commissioner Norman Ayres; John Stacey, President of the Citywide Parents Advisory Council; members of the clergy; and concerned parents, teachers, and students.

Pleased at the large turnout, Ms. Kenton said, "The support visible today is an indication of the strong commitment that the people of this city have toward eliminating unrest in our schools. If our children are to lead productive, happy lives, it is essential that they get an education that will enable them to make responsible decisions."

She stressed that the signing of the covenant is only the beginning; other re-lated events and activities will follow.

In his brief remarks Reverend Walter Taylor supported Ms. Kenton: "We need a thousand beginnings," he said, "if we are to work for peace in our schools. Let there be a new beginning each year."

After the signing ceremony Ms. Kenton explained how the covenant aims to promote school safety. Individual junior and senior high school students will be invited to design and sign their own covenants for display in their schools. Elementary school students will be involved in poster contests and essay-writing contests about school safety.

Kenton also hopes to involve members of the city and county judiciary. She will invite the judges to commit themselves to visiting schools and talking with students about rights and responsibilities under the law.

Powatan Ledger

Writing Feature Stories

Writing feature stories for school newspaper publications affords talented writers the opportunity to be creative. Feature stories can appeal to the reader's emotions as well as supply information. Gifted feature writers have the ability to make the approach to almost any newsworthy situation interesting. For example, the basis for the following story was a program established by a school's drama coach.

COACH STIRS DEBATERS TO PEAK OF SUCCESS

It may be as old as Socrates, but debating is as "in" and "now" at Northwest as the Bugaloo. This isn't just another happening. It is the labor of love of a dedicated coach, Mrs. Charline Burton, who in two short years has more than doubled enrollment in debate classes, filled several cases with trophies, and made a lasting name for herself in the state annals of forensics.

Why are pupils enrolling in a course they once bypassed? Students are attracted to debate for the same reasons they participate in sports; it is an outlet for their natural competitive drive.

Not all students are physically endowed for participating in athletics or performing in musical organizations, but all can and do talk. With proper direction in research and logistics, they can channel this natural inclination into debate.

"Life itself is competition," Mrs. Burton explained. "I feel we need more competition, and more tournaments are the only answers."

There are no "bench warmers" in Mrs. Burton's classes. Everyone, not just the varsity, is permitted to engage in tournament competition. Winning is not the prime consideration, even though they do a lot of that, too.

Matching wits with a serious opponent is "game experience" that all enrolled in debate get. This is the part of the excitement that is padding the enrollment at Northwest.

"We go to tournaments for the same reason the football team plays games. Of course, this takes time outside of class,

but no speech teacher refuses to work after hours," she laughed.

As a result of their active participation, her teams have chalked up an impressive record. They have in two years attended 28 different tournaments, compiling the enviable record of 49 debate trophies: 25 firsts, 17 seconds, and 7 thirds. Her teams have been ranked third in the national forensics, and school trophies include first, second, and third, in regionals. . . .

This year's question: Resolved: That Congress should establish uniform regulations to control Criminal Investigation Procedures, has sent scholars even into court rooms and judges' colleges. Legal libraries and newspaper morgues are gleaned for information to add to their bulging briefcases. They learn to interview public figures. Classwork also includes instruction and practice in extemp speaking, radio speaking and oratory.

Revitalizing the high school debate program really is worthwhile, and it can be done!

The Shield

Writing Sports Stories

Many kinds of sports events are covered in school newspapers. Every major athletic contest in which school teams participate should be the subject for advance and follow-up stories. Because of space limitations, however, many sports activities must be presented as wrap-up stories. Sportswriters can also write sports features, columns, and interview stories based on interviews with players or coaches. Following is an example of a follow-up sports story.

SWIMMERS DISPLAY ABILITY IN FINAL MEETS OF WINTER SEASON

After three weeks with no meets, Loyola's swim team roared back to upset a heavily favored St. John Bosco team by

five points and in the process set three school records. Three days before, the Cubs smashed an outclassed Hawthorne

High by sweeping all divisions. Also the team did fine in the Inglewood Invitational and won the Statewide Divisional Diving Championships.

For the St. John Bosco meet the varsity squad of Pete Worden, George Kerker, Jerry Hankins, Tim Ryan, Jim Henneberry, Roger Burshe, Dan Terheggen, and Rick Hayes was beefed up by the addition of Dave Oyster, Alex Vdacin, and Chris Richard. Greg Spinner led the Bees and Kevin and Phil Doi led the Cees.

It was a cold, windswept, rainy day when Loyola challenged St. John Bosco in their own outdoor pool. After a slow start and a new 200 Medley record by Jim Henneberry, the Cubs came back with a 1-2 in Diving and Butterfly. George Kerker placed first in the 100 freestyle setting a school record. The team of Jerry Hankins, Pete Worden, Tim Ryan, and George Kerker won the 400 free relay setting a record and winning the meet. An elated Coach Gubser received an untraditional, fully clothed swim in the pool after the meet.

On a windy afternoon three days before, the Cubs smashed Hawthorne High by sweeping all of the firsts and most of the seconds and setting a record in the 200 Medley. The Bees also won by a good margin, and there were no Cees.

At the Inglewood Invitational the team performed excellently against L.A.'s best swimmers. Pete Worden placed third in the 100 Butterfly and set a school record. He also placed first in diving and his younger brother Kevin placed sixth.

The Loyalist

The following article is an example of a featurized wrap-up sports story:

WITH A RUMBLE AND A SHAKE

Opposing teams cringe, the ground shakes, and Middlebury citizens quake. What is this phenomenon that casts fear into the hearts of all those associated with it? Could it be superman? No, it is only the extraordinary athletic ability of the girls at Westover.

Hockey at Westover has become the most popular fall sport, and is of an unusually high caliber. (How could we fail to be good with all that energy supplied by recess-lunch sparking through the student body?) The Varsity captain is Whitney Neville, while Claudia Orr heads the J.V. This year's squad has led an undefeated season so far with victories over Forman with a varsity score of 6-0 and J.V. score of 5-0, and St. Margaret's (played the first day of snow) with the Varsity winning 6-2 and the J.V. 7-0. The game with Kent was unfortunately called off because of bad weather, as was the Farmington game, which has been rescheduled for later in the season. Ethel Walker and, of course, The Marvelous Mothers of Middlebury will be the only other opponents Westover will face this season. Can we keep our record?

For those not on the squad, however, a playday may be scheduled when Westover can once again prove its phenomenal athletic prowess. And just so Trinity will not be the only boys school to challenge and confront Westover skill on the hockey field, a game with Hotchkiss may be arranged.

Hockey this year looks promising, and who knows what heights this fall's team will attain?

Fall tennis this year has been given a new lift by the new tennis teacher Mrs. Shealy. She and her son Eric are new faces at Westover this year, and we would like to extend to them a warm welcome. Our new pro handles two periods of tennis daily; one made up of underclassmen, and one composed of seniors. Though her pupils range from beginners to advanced, Mrs. Shealy has done a terrific job in coaching Westover's Wimbledon aspirants.

Toni Walker captains this year's expanded soccer squad. From a total of sixteen a year ago, the squad this fall has jumped to twenty-six girls. Although most of the girls are inexperienced, everybody seems to be full of spirit. The fact that

everyone eventually ends up on the ground has not dampened their enthusiasm for a possible game with Ethel Walker. Whatever the soccer-squad does this year, we'll all be behind our team of potential Pélés.

Obviously, then, athletics at Westover are something with which to be reckoned. So, the next time you hear of something fantastic happening in the Middlebury area, you can be fairly sure it is Westover marching on to another of their countless victories.

The Wick

Like the editorial writer, sports columnists often have the opportunity to express their own opinions in their writing. Many sports columnists base their writing on short interviews with athletes and coaches. Many sports columnists resort to the colorful use of language and sports jargon in their written presentations, sometimes to an extreme. Other than to keep in mind that the material should always have reader interest, the sports columnist needs to follow few rigid writing "rules." School newspaper sports columnists may comment on a variety of sports happenings taking place at their school, or they may choose to feature only one sports topic as was done in the sports column shown in the following example.

MEET THE MAN BEHIND THE MIRACLE . . .

Once upon a time long ago, after a football game between Boone County High and Beechwood, the coaches were rapping about the action. Beechwood's coach admitted that, during play, he had scolded his defensive end for failing to hold down his Boone counterpart. He said his player threw up his hands in dismay and cried, "Coach, I just can't stop that big horse!"

That "big horse" was Mason County's basketball coach, Allen Feldhaus. The nickname "Horse" stuck with him, even through his U.K. basketball career. And, to this day, there is no stopping him. He

just proved it again in the recent Sweet Sixteen basketball tournament. There he led an unheralded underdog team to the runner-up position in a state where basketball is almost a religion and the state tournament its mecca.

The "Horse's" interest in sports was sparked during his youth as an only child who lived 24 miles from the nearest town, Burlington, KY. His closest neighbor lived a mile away, so to entertain himself, Feldhaus rigged up his own basketball goal, hanging the ring of a discarded stove on a smokehouse wall. "Everytime I sank one, the thing flopped up and down," he chuckled. But there he spent hours and hours playing alone.

By the eighth grade, Feldhaus had the opportunity to play organized sports on a real team. "I wasn't actually good," he said. "I was just BIG."

A multitalented athlete, Feldhaus received college scholarship offers in basketball, football and baseball. He claimed he was best at baseball, but added, "When you live in Kentucky and have a chance to play U.K. basketball, people will convince you that's what you should do." Another motive behind his decision to play basketball was the problem of conflicting schedules between baseball and spring football training. He wanted to play baseball, and the basketball schedule left him free to participate in both sports. . . .

The whole Feldhaus family is dedicated and hard-working, and it showed at the Kentucky High School Basketball Tournament. This was Feldhaus' first appearance at the Sweet Sixteen as a coach, and he had his two older sons playing for him.

About the tournament, Feldhaus said, "I didn't think we could possibly go as far as we did. You read about all those other teams in the papers, and we're not even in the top 40. But we prepared for the Shelby County game just like any other.

We analyzed three films, broke them down, and ended up feeling that we could play with them—if our players would dedicate themselves to winning and not just be satisfied with the regional title."

His strategy worked, and his calm planning carried them on through to the final. Feldhaus said they actually made more shots, good shots, during that critical third quarter than any other, but the shots just wouldn't fall. Still, he said, "There was no loser in that game; these were the two CLASS teams of the tournament." That showed in the 22,000 people who turned out to see them play. . . .

Dreams are fine with Feldhaus, but they don't count for too much. He believes strongly in hard work. He said, "The great experience these players have had will give incentive to younger players. But we have to be careful of the Dream World. We've lost six big seniors. We'll have to go back and rebuild—start another group and go from there."

"Dreams don't just come true," according to Feldhaus. "We have to work hard at our goals, and if this year's experience gives new players motivation to work, then that's good. Maybe their dreams will come true."

Royal Decree

Writing Effective Editorials

Nature and Purpose of School Newspaper Editorials

Editorials can and should be an important part of every school newspaper. Depending on the subject discussed, the fairness and the logic of the reasoning, and the quality of the writing, every editorial should seek (1) to stimulate student thinking and (2) to further the development of a truly cohesive student body.

RESPONSIBILITIES OF THE SCHOOL NEWSPAPER EDITORIAL WRITER

The writer of editorials for a school newspaper must—

✓ Keep constantly in mind that to be effective an editorial should be timely, interesting, forceful, and relevant.

✓ Base the editorial on matters related to the well-being of the school and the student body.

✓ Keep in mind that the editorial writer speaks for the paper and should plan editorials with the guidance of faculty adviser.

✓ Keep in mind that an effective editorial can have far-reaching results. Thus it must be planned and written with care.

Through editorials, student journalists have the opportunity to speak directly to their readers about news, actions, ideas, decisions, and changes that influence the lives of those readers. The very fact that a school newspaper carries one or more editorials in each issue says to student readers, "Look. This matter is important to you." By implication, an editorial poses a question like this: "Have you considered how this (news, action, idea, decision, change) affects you?"

Although every editorial appears on the editorial or "opinion" page of the school paper, it is not exclusively an opinion piece. It is, instead, a commentary on the news or on an idea or an issue or a decision. Like a news report, it is based on facts, research, and analysis. Usually the editorial represents the point of view of the newspaper rather than that of the individual editorial writer. Because of this fact, the editorial writer does not write from the viewpoint of *I*. Instead, he or she uses *we* and *you* and sometimes the name of the paper. For example, suppose that a new ruling about smoking on the school grounds has just been announced by the school administration. The staff members of the paper, *The Weekly Scribe*, consider the ruling unfair. In an editorial on the subject, the writer would state the point of view of *The Weekly Scribe*, namely that *we* (the news staff) urge a reconsideration and a modification of the ruling. The writer might even specify the changes the paper recommends. The editorial would not be signed because it represents the position of the paper, not just of one student.

By contrast, "Letters to the Editor," which usually appear on the editorial page, reflect the opinions of individual writers. Each is written from the *I* viewpoint and is signed.

Thus, in a well-balanced school newspaper, the reader finds news, entertainment, analysis, and opinion.

The Editorial Writer

While professional newspapers regularly employ several full-time editorial writers—the larger daily newspapers often have eight to ten—the average high school newspaper usually has but one—the editor-in-chief. Because of the many responsibilities inherent in the job, the editor-in-chief usually does not have the time to write an effective, hard-hitting editorial, issue after issue. To help resolve this problem, the editor-in-chief can ask other staff members to write editorials for specific issues of the paper. Other student leaders—the student body president, officers of the student council, leaders of other student organizations—can be asked to write guest editorials on matters of concern. Research indicates clearly that those students have much to contribute.

In writing an editorial, the editor-in-chief—or whomever he or she has designated—engages in a distinct kind of creative writing experience. The editorial writer functions as a spokesperson for the paper and, at the same time, expresses personal attitudes and beliefs. In short, the student editorial writer not only experiences the satisfaction of creative expression but also enjoys a sense of pride in having contributed to the school and perhaps to the larger community, too.

Most successful editorial writers—whether professional journalists or school journalists—demonstrate the following characteristics: the ability to think clearly, a keen interest in and an extensive knowledge of society at large, and the ability to express a point of view clearly and convincingly. To become skilled, an editorial writer needs a knowledge of many fields and an aptitude for doing careful, thorough research. He or she may find it necessary to write on matters that are unpopular with certain segments of the community and must be able to withstand pressure and criticism.

Then there is the matter of an appropriate writing style. Like any other writer, the editorial writer has the task of conveying a message to a reader. To do so effectively, the editorial writer must (1) organize material in such a way as to facilitate reading, (2) say simply and clearly what there is to say, and (3) be honest and sincere throughout.

In preparing to write an editorial the student journalist has certain advantages: He or she knows (1) what the subject of the editorial is to be, (2) what the components of an editorial are, and

(3) what kind of audience the writing is for. But every editorial writer must decide what style to use and at what language level to write.

In terms of style, the editorial writer should be write as if talking with a friend. Avoid adopting or copying another person's style, and scrupulously avoid any kind of affectation.

For language level, standard English usage is the only kind appropriate for an editorial. The writer should avoid anything that sounds pretentious. Formal, scholarly expression (the use of five-dollar words and long, involved sentences) should give way to a comfortable, straightforward, conversational tone. Finally, the writer should try to say what is meant and mean what is said, giving the reader no occasion for misunderstanding the message.

Types of Editorials

Although editorials can be written about virtually any topic and although writing styles can differ markedly from writer to writer, there are ten distinct types of editorials. Each was discussed in some detail in Chapter 12, "Writing Editorials," on pages 250–270. In high school newspapers the most common types of editorials are these: editorials of argument and persuasion, editorials of information, editorials of commendation, and editorial cartoons.

Today's school newspaper editorials vary widely in subject and in treatment. While many school papers publish editorials on what are considered "safe" subjects—supporting the United Fund, for example, or giving thanks at Thanksgiving or returning library books promptly—other school papers publish effective editorials on controversial subjects.

PLANNING THE SCHOOL NEWSPAPER EDITORIAL

The editorial writer—

✓ Thoroughly understands the problem or situation about which he or she is to write (has researched the topic).

✓ Decides what is the basic purpose of the editorial.

✓ Analyzes the causes of the problem or situation and determines a proposed course of action.

✓ Plans an effective way for getting the point across to the reader.

✓ Organizes material into a working outline.

The determinants of editorial subjects and of the style of presentation can be found in community values, in the philosophy of administrators and teachers, in the experience of the journalism instructor, in the maturity of the newspaper staff, and in an understanding of the purpose of the school editorial. Given a knowledge of the purposes of editorials, given competent guidance in selecting topics, given an understanding of how to write clear, forceful prose, many high school students can compose effective editorials. And many do.

Sometimes disagreements about suitable and unsuitable topics may arise between the news staff and the school administration or other readers. Most disagreements can be satisfactorily resolved through frank and honest discussion. But before seeking such discussion, school journalists should examine the editorials written during the previous school year and make a list of the topics discussed. Were those editorials critical more often than not? Would a more balanced selection of subjects and types of editorials help dispel disagreement? Do disagreements arise because of misinformation, inadequate research, faulty, illogical reasoning, inflammatory remarks, or appeals for the wrong reasons?

In general, these conditions must be met: the topic is timely and important to students, the research has been thorough, the position taken is supported by fair and well-reasoned argument. When these conditions are met, and if the writing is clear and forceful, and if the conclusion is logical, any proposed editorial stands a better-than-average chance of wide approval, no matter what the subject of the editorial is.

Any member of the newspaper staff may suggest subjects for editorials. The final selection of the topic for any given editorial, however, should result from open discussion and general agreement at a staff meeting. This procedure can be particularly helpful because the editor-in-chief or other editorial writer, having heard the various viewpoints presented, will be more likely to offer reasonable arguments to support the position agreed on at the staff meeting.

Matters of concern to the school community are always appropriate subjects for school newspapers. Problems, common to all schools, that make grist for the editorial writer's mill also include overcrowded conditions in the school, traffic problems in and about the school, and the quality of food and services in the school cafeteria, as well as more controversial subjects, such as the grading system, attendance policies, and the athletic program.

Structure of School Editorials

Although creativity and originality are encouraged, most writers of school editorials follow a standard form that embraces the following three divisions:

1. The lead
2. The body
3. The conclusion

The *lead* should invite reading and should acquaint the reader with the main idea of the editorial. The lead should include a brief presentation of facts in support of the main idea and should state the viewpoint or position of the school paper on the matter being discussed.

Effective editorials can begin in any of the following ways:

1. Presenting an interest-arousing statement that quickly gains the reader's attention.

   Dan Mahoney is a student's student. . . .

Newspaper sets editorial restrictions; describes purpose

The opinion pages are to be a forum of expression. Editorials will comment on relevant issues and attempt to influence the student body and the surrounding community. Their function is to condense problems, issues, and events, evaluate them, and recommend a course of action. Guest editorials are subject to approval by adviser and editor-in-chief, but will occasionally be printed. Letters to the editor are welcome. They must however, not include invasions of privacy, personal attacks, or libel of any sort. Names will be withheld upon request. These pages are open to free expression of ideas from students, staff members, faculty, parents, and community members.

The purpose of the Tower is to inform the public of issues, events, and policies which are relevant to it and about which it has the right to know. It will also influence readers on issues of student concern. The newspaper will do its utmost to remain an educational and entertaining publication. The Tower will:

- enjoy all rights guaranteed in the First Amendment.
- have the freedom and responsibility to uphold unpopular beliefs and challenge the administration, the government, and any other public or private institution when appropriate and necessary.
- not be governed or "used" by any person or organization inside or outside the school.
- do its best to seek the truth and uphold justice.
- report objectively and accurately.
- keep its articles (excluding editorials) free of bias or opinion.
- encourage written reader response to editorials or stories published by the paper.
- not mock any person or organization, regardless of the paper's views.
- keep all criticism constructive and tasteful.
- not publish personal attacks, invasions of privacy, or obscenity.
- never print gossip or hearsay.

The Tower, Thomas Carr Howe High School, Indianapolis, Indiana

2. Exhorting the reader to take a definite course of action, thus presenting an effective challenge.

> For the betterment of Northcentral, students should elect Dan Mahoney present of the student council. . . .

3. Giving, in a simple statement, an interpretation of the situation or problem which the editorial is to present.

> The best-qualified presidential candidate in the Student Council election is Dan Mahoney. . . .

4. Leading with a narrative statement. (Caution: While narrative leads can gain reader interest, they can often run so long as to be out of proportion with the body and conclusion of the editorial.)

> Last fall, when our Student Council was hampered by internal strife, a young delegate took the floor and made an eloquent plea for unity. . . .

5. Using a thought-provoking question that will gain the reader's attention and interest.

> Do you want the best possible leader for the student body next year? . . .

6. Using an interest-arousing quotation which is a vital part of the editorial's subject matter.

> "I will give the students a stronger voice in the operation of their school," Dan Mahoney has promised.

The *body* (middle) should develop a logical case for the viewpoint expressed in the lead. The logic of the arguments presented should make a convincing case for the point of view expressed, and every point should lead naturally to a reasonable conclusion.

The *conclusion* may summarize the points made in the body of the editorial. But the editorial might just simply stop, allowing readers to make up their own minds. Most editorials, however, conclude by suggesting a solution, by challenging the reader in some way, or by driving home the central argument of the piece.

The following example shows the structure of an actual school editorial of acceptable length.

Head	**ELECT STUDENT OFFICIALS FOR STUDENT OFFICES**
Lead	It is unfortunate that the Executive Committee of the Student Council chose the election process that it did for this year's officer elections. This method—having all the candidates run together and choosing the ones with the five largest numbers of votes as officers—turns these elections into popularity contests that might place some people in jobs for which they have no desire or qualifications.
Body	This type of election process was chosen so that no qualified person's talents would be lost if he or she should lose one office. In other words, the candidate who came in second for president would be vice president rather than defeated.

Body   However, it seems that this plan does not live up to its ideals; but rather, it may place people in office who do not feel they are fit for the job.

Since the purpose of an election is to choose the best person for each job, this method does not fulfill its objective.

If this is the case, then a better process should be found. This "better process" is the one used in all other campus elections—from classroom to student body.

Each candidate is required to file for a particular office, and then the voters choose whom they want to serve them in each capacity. In this way the aspect of a popularity contest will be lessened by the fact that the students will be choosing between only a few qualified persons for each office. Also, only a person who really wants a certain job can be elected to that position.

Conclusion   It would seem advisable, then, that this method be adopted for all Loyola elections.

Development of School Editorials

Procedure. In preparing to write an editorial, the student journalist proceeds as follows:

1. With the assistance of the newspaper staff, the writer chooses the general subject of the editorial.
2. The editorial writer must thoroughly understand the problem or situation that has given rise to the need for an editorial, must seek and analyze information, conduct interviews, and research other pertinent sources of information.
3. The writer analyzes all of the information gathered and decides on the major purpose and theme of the editorial.
4. The writer then thinks about and decides on the angle—the focus—to be stressed and roughs out a first trial lead.
5. The editorial writer limits what is to be said in the editorial by listing the points to be made and may write out a tentative ending.
6. Having listed the important points to be made, the writer organizes those points into a rational, logical outline.
7. Using the first trial lead, the journalist writes the editorial, following the outline.

8. Having written this first draft, the editorial writer rewrites, revises, and polishes the editorial to make it as effective as possible.

Length. How long should the editorial be? Most school newspaper editorials contain from 300 to 350 words. There are several reasons for this length. Space on the editorial page is often limited. Sustaining a long, complex argument brings quickly diminishing returns in terms of the effect upon readers. Research indicates that average readers rarely read editorials that run longer than 350 words.

Libel Considerations in Editorial Writing

In the 1830s an editorial in the *Louisville Focus* began, "President General Andrew Jackson is a lying, thieving scoundrel." Today, such an editorial would be discredited as libelous. Libelous matter is any material appearing in print that contains false information injurious to a person's reputation or business, whether that person is alive or dead.

Libel laws apply as much to editorial comment as to anything else in a publication. In America, for printed matter to be considered libelous, the law usually requires that the material be proven to be malicious in its intent. The common defense against libel is to prove the truth of the matter published, to prove that the publication did no appreciable damage, or to prove that there was no malice aforethought. The school newspaper editorial writer must be accurate and must avoid any material that might recklessly endanger the reputation of anyone.

All school publications support an editorial policy of truth and honesty in everything they publish. There is no place in the school press for loose accusations of any kind or for statements that are unsupported.

Improving Editorial Page Readership

"Letters to the Editor." To judge reader response better, editors encourage the writing of letters from readers. "Letters to the Editor," an essential part of a good editorial page, makes an interesting editorial feature and provides a platform for reader opinion. Such a platform is especially important for school publications, for it shows that students are thinking about what they read.

A school newspaper editor should make it a rule that all letters that will appear in print must be signed. It is the job of the editor also to make sure that every signature is authentic.

In a specially designed box in the "Letters-to-the-Editor" section, the editor-in-chief should print a notice specifying the rules that govern the publication of letters to the editor. The first rule is that every letter must be signed. A second rule might specify a limit on the length of letters to the editor. And a third rule should state whether letters from nonstudents will be published. (Many school papers publish letters from enrolled students only. Certain exceptions can, of course, be made. However, exceptions should be made only after discussion with the editor-in-chief and the faculty adviser.)

A LETTER TO THE EDITOR

letter . . .
Parent commends band, pommers for pep

Dear Editor:

At the Turkey Day game, I witnessed the epitome in school spirit. The KHS Marching Band was lined up to go on the field to present its well-rehearsed halftime routine, to honor the senior band members, and to provide the excellent background for the ever exciting pom pon girls to give another precision routine— and then the rains came.

Over the PA system the announcement came "All band members report to the band room." The band didn't move. Even after several announcements, the band held fast (the drummers never stopped their cadence). They wanted to go on with their show.

Only after the rain reached monsoon status, did the band members disperse reluctantly, only to regroup at the foot of the main bleachers where the pom pon girls immediately joined them, and a halftime show I'll never forget went into action.

To see the tears of disappointment on the girls' faces washed away by the realization that the band was there and ready to go "on with the show"—and then to witness the performance our girls gave—was an event I'll long remember (It even made me forget how wet I was.)

I just want our halftime performers to know that this beautiful display of school spirit did not go unnoticed, and was deeply appreciated by the many parents who stayed and felt the same pride in our young people as I did.

Sincerely,
Elaine Boyd

Libel laws also govern what can and cannot be published in the "Letters-to-the-Editor" section. The burden of proving that what is stated in any letter is the truth falls upon the paper's editor—despite the fact that the printed letter is genuine.

Editorial Page Appearance. In addition to placing "Letters to the Editor" on the editorial page, the school newspaper editor can help improve readership by using attractive layouts that include good photos, cartoons, and special features. Editorial pages are visually more appealing when all the materials used are short and when the editorials are set in a larger type size and at a wider column width than are the regular news stories appearing elsewhere in the paper. Interest-arousing headlines and leads for each editorial also help gain reader attention. When especially significant issues present themselves, editors run them as featured editorials on page one.

Most school publications print no advertising on their editorial pages, thus allowing space for visually attractive groupings of editorial and feature material. Page two is usually set aside as the editorial page. It's the page on which many school newspapers place the masthead (the paper's name, address, names of staff members, the paper's affiliations, and advertising rates).

The Editorial—A Positive Force in Your School

The editor of a Chicago newspaper once said, "A newspaper's job is to print the news and raise hell." That may well be. But the editorial writer for a school newspaper must ever keep in mind that his or her responsibility is to help the student body think *constructively.* An editorial writer—*any* editorial writer—must never tear down merely for the sake of tearing down but must, instead, emphasize the positive. If an editorial writer cannot advance solutions to problems facing the school and the student body, he or she must not condemn those persons who do propose constructive, positive, well-intended solutions.

If the editorial leadership of a school newspaper fails to live up to its opportunities and responsibilities, the paper can become weak or troublesome—even useless. On the other hand, if the editorial leadership is effective, that newspaper can be a strong, positive force for the well-being of the school. The potential exists for constructive leadership in school affairs.

Passage of bond referendum urged

The current Construction Fund has $4,105,000 available which will be put towards the costs

An important School Bond Referendum which will be included on the ballot of the November 3 general election should be passed because of the need for new and improved school facilities.

All county bond sales are handled by the Fairfax County Board of Supervisors who are allowed to bond only an average of $60 million per year This year they are asking for $57,230,000 in the referendum to construct and renew a total of 22 educational facilties.

Out of 3000 counties in the U.S., Fairfax County has one of the top nine credit ratings. Bonds for Fairfax County, therefore, sell at exceedingly low interest rates. The last bonds floated by the county had a 7 percent interest rate. The bond should be passed now to take advantage of this low interest rate.

If the bond is not passed, whether or not any construction would occur would be a "Decision made by the Board of Supervisors," says Mr. Edmund Castillo, Director of Public Affairs for the Fairfax County Government. The County could not provide anything even slightly approaching that money made available by the bond issue The projects would be deferred and go to voters in another year How much taxes would then be raised depends on what happens, but they would definitely have to be raised

Other options to the referendum were carefully studied by the School Board and subsequently rejected for their impracticality They include a busing plan which was rejected because students would have to be bused beyond an acceptable distance, or appropriating monies from the regular budget at the cost of instructional programs.

New construction costs will be higher than updating older schools for the understandable reason that although more schools are included in the renewal program, costs of material for constructing new buildings are higher than the costs for upgrading an existing facility.

Most new elementary schools will consist of 21 rooms with support facilities for 32 rooms in the event of an increase of students in that area. If there was a surge in population, more rooms or relocatable buildings could then be added to those schools

All residents of Fairfax County who will be 18 years old or older by election day and are registered to vote by October, will be able to vote on the referendum

For information on registration, voting, and absentee voting, call 385-8100 For information on the School Bond Referendum, call the Office of Community Relations, 691-2291

To benefit the students of Fairfax County with modern school facilities, and to prolong the lives of older schools, the School Bond Referendum must be passed.

Sub-minimum wage:

deemed absurd
promotes discrimination

One proposal to help with unemployment is a special sub-minimum wage for teenagers and young adults. The proponents argue that by some magic youthful unemployment would disappear if only employers were allowed to pay them at a rate less than they pay adults. The youth are frozen out of the job market because employers are unwilling or unable to pay them the minimum wage, $3.35 per hour.

This is utter nonsense. Older skilled and semi-skilled workers are not paid the minimum wage, they are paid at a much higher rate. The minimum wage is paid to the unskilled, the teenagers, the unreliable and the lazy. To propose that honest, reliable, hard working teenagers be paid less is ridiculous.

Sub-minimum wages would not create new jobs and it would certainly not create any new jobs for that group of teenagers where the youth unemployment rates are high, namely the minority groups. What it would actually do is reduce the rates now being paid to hard working teenagers who work principally in the retail industry or or just a few cents above the minimum wage.

There are substantial numbers of teens working, and working hard earning what little they are paid. Almost all of them are paid the minimum wage. People do not see teens working in places that pay good wages. Teens get just as much experience working for the minimum wage, as they would making half or three quarters of the minimum.

An individual should be paid according to his worth to the business for whom that individual works not by his or her age. The days of cheap labor did not end with the demise of slavery, but continued until a decent minimum wage was established. Now some employers want to make second class employees out of its teenage workers by paying them less because of their date of birth. These are the same employers who hire their employees at the

minimum wage and they want to save money at the expense of youth.

There is already a special sub-minimum wage applicable for employees who are working in an approved apprenticeship program preparing them for a better paying job. This should be the limit of special sub-minimum wages.

These young employees deserve the same wage protection from their government as do other workers. The same wages for the same work. Do not discriminate against youth in the pay check.

Activities

1. If the last issue of your school newspaper had to be made smaller, what articles, features, and editorials would you leave out? Why? Which stories would you cut in length? Why? Select one story and rewrite it so that it occupies only half of the space it now fills.

If the paper were to have four more pages, what stories, features, editorials, cartoons, photographs would you add? Why? What stories now in the paper could be meaningfully expanded? How?

2. Prepare a list of questions that you might ask if you were assigned to interview a student who had won some special recognition. From the imagined responses to your questions, write an interview story of three or four paragraphs. Be prepared to read your story to the class to have their suggestions for improving it.

3. What student, faculty, and community activities that will occur within the next month do you think should be covered by your school newspaper? Plan to attend one of those activities and then write a news story about it. Perhaps you can get a classmate to act as photographer for the event. Present your meeting story to the class, inviting them to compare it with the story appearing in the school newspaper. How does its coverage differ from yours? Why?

4. Examine the editorials printed in one back issue of your school newspaper from the years 1982, 1980, and 1976. What were the issues that give rise to those editorials? To what extent are the editorials in your school paper today concerned with similar issues? To what extent are those issues presented in a similar way?

5. Invite the editorial-page editor of your local newspaper to a meeting of your school's newspaper staff. Ask your guest how he or she researches, organizes, and writes editorials.

6. List five topics you would like to have considered for editorials in your school newspaper. Then choose one and write an editorial that succinctly states your point of view. Submit your editorial to your editor-in-chief for possible publication in the next issue of your school paper. At the same time, submit your list of editorial topics.

7. How can the readership of the school paper's editorial page be increased? List five suggestions; then present them to the paper's editor-in-chief.

CHAPTER 16

The School Newspaper: Copy Editing, Layout, and Design

"Are there any special secrets to copy editing, Dad?" Margo Kelly looks quizzically at her father across the breakfast table. Unlike most high school journalism students, Margo has grown up with journalism. Her father is copy editor for the local newspaper.

"Secrets? I don't keep *any* secrets," jokes Mr. Kelly.

"I mean special things to look for. My journalism assignment for the next two weeks is to copy edit the West Roxbury *Rocket*."

"Going to start a family tradition and be a copy editor, eh?" chuckles Mr. Kelly. "Well, let's see. I guess the steps are the same no matter whether you're working on a professional paper or a high school newspaper. I'd say that, first of all, you need to see yourself as the 'court of last resort' for every story you handle. If you overlook something that's wrong or, even worse, change something that's right and make it wrong, it'll get into print that way. And people

NOPQRSTUVWXYZ
nopqrstuvwxyz
567890

NOPQRSTUVWXY

DEFGHIJKL
RSTUVWXYZ

stymie medium

18 point

ABCDEFGHIJKLMNOPQRSTUVWXYZ
abcdefghijklmnopqrstuvwxyz
1234567890

point

ABCDEFGHIJKLMNOPQRSTUVWXYZ
abcdefghijklmnopqrstuvwxyz
1234567890

ABCDEFGHIJKL
NOPQRSTUVWXYZ

Trump o

Makari

abcdefghijklmnopqrstuv
ABCDEFGHIJKLMNOPQRS
1234567890 & .,?-S

MOORE CO

ABCDEFGHIJKLMNOP
(P .:;""!?--[] '$¢%

xtra

TRA
MI CONDENSED

RA
RA CON

6–8	abcdefghijklmnopqrstuvwxyz
7–11	abcdefghijklmnopqrstuvwxyz
8–15	abcdefghijklmnopqrstuvwxyz
9–19	abcdefghijklmnopqrstuvwxyz
10–21	abcdefghijklmnopqrstuvwxyz
11–24	abcdefghijklmnopqrstuvwxyz
12–27	abcdefghijklmnopqrstuvwxyz
13–29	abcdefghijklmnopqrstuvwxyz
14–31	abcdefghijklmnopqrstuvwxyz
15–32	abcdefghijklmnopqrstuvwxyz
16–33	abcdefghijklmnopqrstuvwxyz
17–34	abcdefghijklmnopqrstuvwxyz
18–35	abcdefghijklmnopqrstuvwxyz
19–35	abcdefghijklmnopqrstuvwxyz
20–36	abcdefghijklmnopqrstu

Jefferson

aabccddeeffghhiijjkkll
AABCCDEFGGHHIIJ
TTUUVWXYZ 112345

g controlled completely elec
board and an integrated co
ideal text setting mach
equirements.

old

nœpqrrsstuvwxyz
EF FGGH HI JJKKL
EP PQR RSSTT TUV
1234567890

Mistral

abcdefghijkllmmnoopqrs
ABCDEFGHIJKLMNOP
123456789 (A.:;''"

nir Bold Italic

ijklmmnnœpqrrsstuvwxyz
CD-DE EEF FGGH HI JJKKL
BCD-NNœEP PQR RSSTT TUV
XY YZ 1234567890

Style Script

abcdefghijklmnopqrstuvw
ABCDEFGHIJKLMNOPQRSTUVWXY
YZ 1234567890 &

ENCIL

EFGHIJKLMNOPQRST

who know what's right will get a bad impression of your paper."

"That makes sense," muses Margo. "But are there any special things to do—any special steps to follow?"

"Steps? Yes, indeed. First, find a quiet spot—if there is one in your classroom or the newsroom—where you can concentrate. Second, keep your dictionary at your elbow, and use it—even when you think you know the proper spelling of a little-used word."

"But where do you find out how to spell names correctly?" asks Margo.

"Good question. That is important. I guess the best place for your purposes would be in the principal's office. Make a list of names you come across in the stories you're editing.

Then, when you can, stop in at the office to check on all of them at the same time rather than making several trips. Another good source is the city telephone directory."

"OK. but what about copy editing itself?" persists Margo.

"Oh . . . well. Hmmm . . . OK. Here are three pointers that you can't go wrong on. First, put in paragraph marks where they belong. They tell the typesetter where to indent, and they help you keep track of your place in case you get distracted."

"So I don't have to go back to the beginning and start over. Right?"

"Right. That's the first thing you want to do when you're copy editing. Second, since your editors have already gone over each story for content, your primary concern is with grammar, spelling, punctuation, and accuracy. And third, you're looking for the ideal combination of words to use in your headlines. Active verbs and short words make the best headlines. Odds are that you'll skip the adjectives and five-dollar words. Do those three steps make sense?"

"Yes, they do," agrees Margo. "But they probably aren't as simple as they sound."

"No, they're not. But with a little experience. . . . I'll tell you what. On your next vacation, come on in to the newspaper office and spend part of the day with me, watching what I do."

"You mean it?"

"And since you seem to like steps," continues Mr. Kelly, "I'll point out some of the steps involved in laying out a newspaper page. And maybe you could even help design a page for the paper."

"Great, Dad. I'd like that. Thanks. West Roxbury *Rocket*, here I come!"

Those Indispensable Copy Editors

From our discussion of staff organization (Chapter 14, pages 306–325), you know that one of the critical jobs on a school newspaper is that performed by copy editors. Working closely with the managing editor, copy editors scrutinize and edit the stories the reporters turn in. That is, with reference to grammar, spelling, punctuation, capitalization, word choice, phrasing, and sentence structure in the stories assigned to them, copy editors function as a court of last resort. And equally important, copy editors are the persons who write the headlines for most stories printed in the school paper. A large part of the credit for excellence a school newspaper receives is due to the competence and dedication of their copy editors.

Below is a checklist summarizing the major responsibilities of copy editors. Such a checklist is, of course, useful for a general understanding of what copy editors do. To serve as copy editors is excellent training for high school journalists. If they are to perform effectively, however, they must know how to carry out the day-to-day responsibilities of the job. The first part of this chapter focuses on those responsibilities.

CHECKLIST OF RESPONSIBILITIES OF A SCHOOL NEWSPAPER'S COPY EDITOR

✓ With the editor-in-chief and the faculty adviser:
   a. Develops guidelines to help reporters become careful news writers.
   b. Develops standards for maintaining accuracy and reliability.
   c. Develops guidelines for determining what is good taste in a news story and what is not.
   d. Establishes a procedure to facilitate an efficient copy flow from reporter to printer.

✓ When copy is submitted, reads each story several times:
   a. To ensure that all statements are accurate.
   b. To ensure that all pertinent facts have been presented.
   c. To check for logical, understandable organization.
   d. To make sure that what is said is in good taste, that what is said avoids any possibility of libel.
   e. To eliminate wordiness.
   f. To check for standard grammar, usage, spelling, and punctuation.
   g. To uncover buried leads.
   h. To identify content that would make effective headlines.

✓ Double-checks the spelling of all names.

✓ Submits proposed headlines for the editor-in-chief's approval.

✓ Attends all staff meetings.

Copy Editing

Like professional papers, school newspapers have an obligation to be accurate and reliable in their presentation of the news. Student editors must constantly be aware of this obligation and must, at all times, protect their readers from carelessness, inaccuracy, and deliberate bias. That responsibility applies not only to the editor-in-chief and the other editors but also to the copy editors. They, too, must accept responsibility for accuracy, reliability, and good taste.

The content of all stories submitted for publication must be approved by the editor-in-chief and the faculty adviser. The stories are then scrutinized by the copy editor, who is usually a more experienced news writer than is the reporter. Following an editorial style sheet like that shown on pages 364–365, the copy editor checks for correct grammar, spelling, punctuation, logical organization, and accuracy. As a rule, the copy editor first marks all errors found in the stories being edited. Next, all proposed corrections are checked with the faculty adviser, and with the latter's approval, the copy editor then makes those corrections. Only when a story is very poorly written does the copy editor rewrite it completely.

The copy editor's specific concerns are the following:

- **Accuracy.** Every fact should be double-checked. In doing so, the copy editor uses such reference works as encyclopedias, dictionaries, almanacs, and previous issues of the school paper and other newspapers. In addition, the copy editor checks facts with the reporter who submitted the story and, if necessary, with the faculty adviser.

- **Spelling.** Every competent copy editor keeps a standard dictionary handy for ready reference. For the spelling of names, he or she consults the student directory (usually kept in the principal's office) and the community telephone directory.

- **Grammar and Punctuation.** The competent copy editor also has a comprehensive handbook on grammar and punctuation available for ready reference. After all, a major reason for publishing a school newspaper is to provide students with a laboratory where they can develop their abilities to communicate correctly, clearly, and succinctly.

- **Succinctness.** In editing news stories, the copy editor seeks to make each story succinct—that is, make each story convey its message clearly in as few words as possible. For example, consider the following sentences. The first statement is wordy and repetitive. The second shows how a copy editor might make that statement succinct.

Wordy: Prices that consumers pay in the city of Houston and the surrounding area went down to the degree of 1.5 percent during the month of March. This is only the second time that the price index has fallen in this area since 1980. This announcement was made by federal officials yesterday morning at 10 a.m.

Succinct: Consumer prices in the Houston area fell 1.5 percent in March, according to federal officials— the second time since 1980 that the price index in this area has fallen.

■ **Sentence Structure.** The competent copy editor shortens long, convoluted sentences to clarify meaning and rewrites a series of short, choppy sentences to relieve monotony and provide variety. In short, the copy editor strives to ensure that each sentence means what it says and says what it means. (A detailed discussion of sentence structure was presented on pages 159–162.)

■ **Libel.** The competent copy editor keeps constantly in mind that truth is the only defense against charges of libel. The burden of proof is not on the person who claims he or she was libeled but on the publication. The copy editor, therefore, deletes any material that might, however remotely, damage a person's reputation.

■ **Good Taste.** If, on religious or moral grounds, readers might object to a word, a phrase, or a picture used in a news story, the competent copy editor deletes it. Each story for which he or she is responsible—no matter how controversial the topic— must be in good taste. Highly emotional words are changed or deleted. Such words tend to draw attention to themselves, distracting the reader from the ideas being presented.

■ **Buried Leads.** The competent copy editor seeks out statements within a story that might possibly serve as the lead. For example, suppose that at a school assembly the principal spoke about "Good Citizenship" and, following the talk, mentioned that construction on a new science wing was about to begin. A school reporter assigned to write up the talk might simply end the story with a sentence about the new science wing. An observant copy editor, however, might decide that the information about the science wing would make an interesting lead. Or the copy editor might suggest that the reporter seek further details about the science wing and then write another story about it.

EDITORIAL STYLE SHEET

Numbers
In most cases, write numbers *one* through *ten* as words.

Write numbers from *11* on as numerals.
> *Examples:* 11, 23, 45, 162

When several numbers are used in sequence and include those both larger and smaller than *ten,* use numerals.
> *Example:* Exercises, 3, 5, 8, 12, and 22

Place a comma after the first digit in a four-digit number.
> *Example:* 3,194

Spell a number if it begins a sentence.
> *Example:* Sixty-three faculty members make up our staff.

Dates/Times
Spell the names of the months **except** when they are followed by specific dates.
> *Examples:* August, October
> **But:** Jan. 19, Sept. 30

Do not abbreviate the names of these months: March, April, May, June, July.

Place a comma after the name of a month when a specific year is given as a part of the date.
> *Examples:* May, 1984
> November, 1990
> April 3, 1985

Use lower case to designate the abbreviations for morning and afternoon.
> *Examples:* a.m., p.m.

When inclusive dates employ only two figures, write the end date without apostrophe.
> *Examples:* 1976–79 1983–84

Forms of Address
On first reference to a specific person, give that person's full name.
> *Examples:* Mrs. Marilyn Perkins,
> Mr. John Gray,
> Ms Jane Brown

After the first reference to a specific person, use *Mr., Mrs., Ms,* or *Miss* and the person's last name.
> *Examples:* Mrs. Perkins, Mr. Gray,
> Ms Brown, Miss Smith

Omit the designations *Mr.* and *Ms/Miss* with names of students.

Capitalization
Capitalize grade and class designations only when they refer to specific groups.
> *Examples:* The Seventh Grade at
> Carver Jr. High School
> The Senior Class
> The Class of 1984
> They are in the seventh grade.
> They are seniors at
> East High.

Capitalize a title appearing before a person's name. Do not capitalize a person's title when it appears after the name.
> *Examples:* President Joe Morgan
> Joe Morgan, president
> **Exception:** If the name of a specific organization appears after a title that follows a person's name, capitalize the title.
> *Example:* Joe Morgan, President of Speed, Inc.

Capitalize *Student Council.*

Capitalize references to the school colors when they are used as a substitute for the name of the school.
> *Example:* The Orange-and-Black triumphed over North High.
> **But:** Our school colors are orange and black.

Capitalize *congress* whenever it refers to the legislative branch of the United States Government.

Example: He has been a member of Congress for ten years.

Do not capitalize *congress* when the word is used as a synonym for *convention.*

Example: The organization is a congress of youth groups.

Do not capitalize adjectives derived from the term *congress.*

Example: The congressional delegation has arrived.

Special Spellings

Spell the designations of specific grades or classes.

Examples: She is in the eighth grade.
He is a sophomore.

Spell *percent* as one word. Avoid using the symbol %.

Note the spelling of these informal terms: *emcee, DJ, OK.*

Use the accepted two-letter post-office abbreviations for states when the name of a city precedes the state designation.

Examples: Miami, FL San Diego, CA
But: He lives in Florida.
She has gone to California.

Hyphenation

Use a hyphen to join two or more words when they are used as one.

Examples: part-time job
an I-dare-you attitude
a never-to-be-forgotten experience

Abbreviations

When first referring to names that can be abbreviated, write out the names.

Examples: They joined the National Honor Society.
They work in the Office of Management and Budget.

On second reference, abbreviate the names in the conventional way, omitting periods.

Examples: As members of NHS, they...
In their work at OMB, they...

If a word is ordinarily abbreviated in everyday writing, use the abbreviation.

Examples: They go to Grant Jr. High School.
Manning Sr. High School

A Copy-Edited News Story

The results of one copy editor's work appear on the next two pages. The news story involved is one that a reporter submitted to the managing editor for publication in a school paper. The first example shows how the copy editor marked the story for correction. The second example shows the same story copy edited, retyped, and ready for the printer. (See Appendix V for the standard symbols used in preparing copy for the printer.)

Example 1:

¶ Tridel's Senior class has topped the (jr.) class in the school spirit contest sponsored by the student council, edging the ~~Upperclassmen~~ *juniors* by 3%. ¶ Having just (twelve) per cent, the sophomores are behind the Eleventh Grades 16 percent and the Senior *class* average of 19 per cent. This contest will be continued ~~thruout~~ *throughout* the home basket ball season. ¶ Two council members take the tallie during the ~~hardwood contest,~~ *basketball games,* and ~~a sign is~~ posted *a sign* on the second-floor bulletin board announcing the weakly class standings. ¶ Supervised by Vice-President Judy Jefferson, the contest, which began on Jan. (twenty-fifth) is designed to increase ~~the~~ schools spirit. At the end of the year, the President of the winning class will be presented with a pewter cup.

Example 2:

Tridel's Senior Class has topped the Junior Class in the School Spirit Contest sponsored by the Student Council, edging the juniors by 3 percent.

Having just 12 percent, the Sophomores are behind the Eleventh Grade's 16 percent and the Senior Class average of 19 percent. This contest will be continued throughout the home basketball season.

Two council members take the tally during the basketball games and post a sign on the second floor bulletin board announcing the weekly class meetings.

Supervised by Vice-president Judy Jefferson, the contest, which began on Jan. 25, is designed to increase school spirit. At the end of the year, the President of the winning class will be presented with a pewter cup.

Writing Headlines

After a news story has been copy edited, the copy editor has the responsibility of supplying an appropriate headline. To meet that responsibility, the copy editor must first determine, in terms of action or unusualness, the one essential element of the story to be used as the basis for the headline.

One good way to identify headline material is to read through the story in question and then write down a thesis sentence—a sentence that states the central idea of the story. The copy editor then rephrases that thesis sentence in telegraphic style. That is, he or she eliminates all nonessential words so that the resultant statement will fit into the space allowed for the headline.

Thesis sentence: The East High Panthers defeated the North High Rangers by a score of 56 to 50.

Telegraphic style: Panthers defeat Rangers, 56-50.

Determining Headline Size

The newsworthiness of a story determines how much space (on a newspaper page) a headline and its accompanying story will be allotted. By the time the copy editor is ready to compose the headline for a story, the managing editor—or the editor responsible for page makeup—has already determined the amount of space the headline and the story can have. That editor has also determined (a) the *size* (height) of the letters making up the words of the headline and (b) the *width* into which all of the letters and spaces making up the headline must fit.

After condensing a story's thesis sentence into a telegraphic statement which will be made into the headline for that story, the copy editor must fit it into the space allotted for it. (If the headline doesn't fit, the copy editor must revise it to fit or compose another one that will fit.)

Height. Headline height is measured in points. There are 72 points in one inch. If you measure a 72-point headline from the top of an ascender (the part of a letter that rises above the body of that letter—for example, the tall line of *h*) to the bottom of a descender (the part of a letter that extends below the body of the letter—for example, the long line of *y*), you'll find it to be about one inch. The illustration below identifies the ascender and the descender of a word set in 72-point lowercase type (type without capital letters).

72-POINT LOWERCASE LETTERS SHOWING AN ASCENDER AND A DESCENDER

Since 72 points make up one inch, 36-point type measures one-half inch and 18-point type measures one-fourth inch. The type size most often used for the body of a news story is 9-point type (which measures one-eighth of an inch from ascender to descender). Some examples of 9-point type follow.

9-POINT LOWERCASE TYPE, WITH CAPITAL LETTER

This line is printed in 9-pt Zapf Book Light (roman).

This line is printed in 9-pt Avant Garde (roman).

Classified ads, stock market listings, and sports box scores are usually set in 5- or 6-point type known as *agate*. The top of page 369 illustrates 6-point type.

6-POINT LOWERCASE TYPE, WITH CAPITAL LETTER

This line is printed in 6-pt Mallard (roman).

This line is printed in 6-pt Oracle (roman).

Width. Editors indicate the width of a headline in one of two ways—in columns or in picas. If the total print space of your school paper is 59 picas wide, it can be made up of three columns of type, each 18 picas wide, or four columns of type, each 14 picas wide, or five columns of type, each 11 picas wide. The newspapers below illustrate three- and five-column page makeup.

A pica is a width measure; there are six picas in one inch. If your school newspaper uses a variety of column widths, the only way the editor can indicate headline width is in picas. If, however, the newspaper uses a set format of three 18-pica columns or four 14-pica columns of five 11-pica columns, the editor can indicate the headline width in columns.

Story Significance. When determining headline sizes, editors assign the largest sizes to major stories, which ordinarily are placed at the top of the news page. Less important stories, placed in the middle of the page, usually have smaller headline sizes. The least important stories, placed in the lowest third of the page, have smaller still headline sizes. For example, the top story may have a 48-point or even a 60-point headline; the second story, a 42-point headline; the third story, a 36-point headline; the fourth story, a 30-point headline; and so on. Least important stories are given 24- or 18-point headlines. An exception occurs when a story is used as an "anchor"—that is, it is positioned horizontally across the bottom of the news page. The headline for such a story is usually assigned a larger type size than that given to stories above it. The following shows an anchor story with a 36-point headline.

Story Length. A final consideration for determining headline size is story length. Esthetically, a news page would look very peculiar if a one-inch-long story began with a 72-point headline. As a rule, the more important the story, the more detailed it will be and the more space it will merit. Longer stories, therefore, are assigned larger headlines.

Indicating the "Head Order"

As a rule, editors indicate a "head order" for each headline. They do so by writing the head order across the top of the story to be copy edited.* Each head order indicates, first, the type size to be used for the headline; second, the specific type face to be used; third, the number of lines the headline is to have; and finally, the width of the headline. And all of this information is set down in a very much abbreviated form. It might well look like this:

$$48 \text{ TB}^2 \text{ 29 pi}$$

Or like this:

$$48\text{TB}/2/29 \text{ pi}$$

Or like this:

$$48\text{TB} = 29 \text{ pi}$$

All of these figures and letters mean that the headline is to be set in 48-point type, that the type face is to be tempo bold, that the headline is to consist of two lines, and that it is to be set in a width of 29 picas (4⅞ inches).

Obviously, the number of letters and spaces that make up a headline depends on the size of the type used and the width of the line. An editor, therefore, must allocate enough space to permit the copy editor to summarize each story properly. Naturally, the copy editor must use fewer letters in a 72-point headline set across 14 picas than in an 18-point headline set across 14 picas. The reason, of course, is that 72-point type is four times larger than 18-point type. Editors know, therefore, that when assigning large type sizes to headlines, they must at the same time assign wider measures.

What's more, they know that bold and expanded type faces take more space than do condensed and light type faces. To determine the number of letter "units" available in a specific type

---

*The copy editor also indicates the head order on the makeup dummy and draws a line indicating headline width.

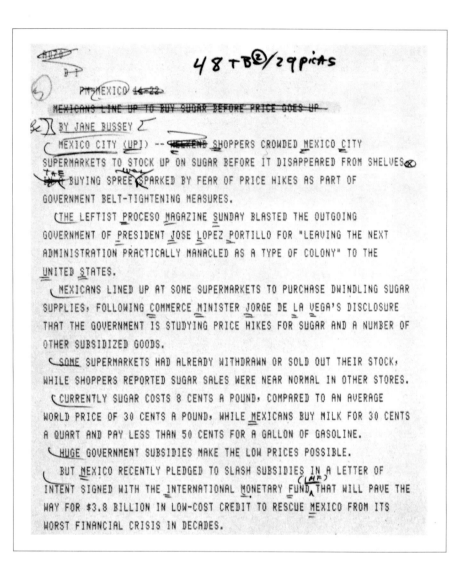

PM-MEXICO 14-22

~~MEXICANS LINE UP TO BUY SUGAR BEFORE PRICE GOES UP~~

BY JANE BUSSEY

MEXICO CITY (UPI) -- SHOPPERS CROWDED MEXICO CITY SUPERMARKETS TO STOCK UP ON SUGAR BEFORE IT DISAPPEARED FROM SHELVES THE BUYING SPREE SPARKED BY FEAR OF PRICE HIKES AS PART OF GOVERNMENT BELT-TIGHTENING MEASURES.

(THE LEFTIST PROCESO MAGAZINE SUNDAY BLASTED THE OUTGOING GOVERNMENT OF PRESIDENT JOSE LOPEZ PORTILLO FOR "LEAVING THE NEXT ADMINISTRATION PRACTICALLY MANACLED AS A TYPE OF COLONY" TO THE UNITED STATES.

MEXICANS LINED UP AT SOME SUPERMARKETS TO PURCHASE DWINDLING SUGAR SUPPLIES, FOLLOWING COMMERCE MINISTER JORGE DE LA VEGA'S DISCLOSURE THAT THE GOVERNMENT IS STUDYING PRICE HIKES FOR SUGAR AND A NUMBER OF OTHER SUBSIDIZED GOODS.

SOME SUPERMARKETS HAD ALREADY WITHDRAWN OR SOLD OUT THEIR STOCK, WHILE SHOPPERS REPORTED SUGAR SALES WERE NEAR NORMAL IN OTHER STORES.

CURRENTLY SUGAR COSTS 8 CENTS A POUND, COMPARED TO AN AVERAGE WORLD PRICE OF 30 CENTS A POUND, WHILE MEXICANS BUY MILK FOR 30 CENTS A QUART AND PAY LESS THAN 50 CENTS FOR A GALLON OF GASOLINE.

HUGE GOVERNMENT SUBSIDIES MAKE THE LOW PRICES POSSIBLE.

BUT MEXICO RECENTLY PLEDGED TO SLASH SUBSIDIES IN A LETTER OF INTENT SIGNED WITH THE INTERNATIONAL MONETARY FUND (IMF) THAT WILL PAVE THE WAY FOR $3.8 BILLION IN LOW-COST CREDIT TO RESCUE MEXICO FROM ITS WORST FINANCIAL CRISIS IN DECADES.

face, editors and copy editors use a "headline schedule" (available from most printers). A "headline schedule" shows the alphabet set in each type face and each type size the printer has in stock. A sample "headline schedule" is shown on page 373..

School copy editors can determine letter "units" by placing a pica ruler over each type face shown and by drawing a vertical line at each of the following widths: 11 picas, 14 picas, 18 picas, 22 picas, 29 picas, 33 picas, 44 picas, 55 picas, and 59 picas. News staffs will find it helpful to post a "headline schedule" in a prominent place in the newsroom.

Headline Schedule

This headline schedule lists the unit count (maximum count) per line of headlines of the indicated column width and type size. It does not list each headline by number of lines since, for example, the count per line for a 1-24-2 would be the same as that for a 1-24-3.

Bodoni Bold and Bodoni Bold Italic

Headline	Maximum	Headine	Maximum	Headine	Maximum
1-14	21	4-36	39	4-60	23 1/2
1-18	18	2-48	14	5-60	30
1-24	13	3-48	21	6-60	36
2-24	26 1/2	4-48	29	2-72	7
1-30	10 1/2	5-48	37	3-72	14 1/2
2-30	23	6-48	44	4-72	20
1-36	9	2-60	11 1/2	5-72	24 1/2
2-36	19	3-60	17 1/2	6-72	30
3-36	29				

Avoid using headlines not listed above. For example, 14BB would not be used across two columns.

Bodoni Light and Bodoni Light Italic

Headine	Maximum	Headine	Maximum	Headline	Maximum
1-14	22	4-36	42	4-60	25 1/2
1-18	19	1-48	7	5-60	32
1-24	14	2-48	15	6-60	38 1/2
2-24	29	3-48	23 1/2	2-72	7 1/2
1-30	11	4-48	31 1/2	3-72	15 1/2
2-30	24	5-48	40	4-72	21 1/2
1-36	9 1/2	6-48	48	5-72	26 1/2
2-36	20 1/2	2-60	12 1/2	6-72	32
3-36	31	3-60	19		

Poster Bodoni

Headline	Maximum	Headine	Maximum	Headline	Maximum
1-14	16	1-30	8	1-60	4
1-18	13	1-36	6 1/2	1-72	3
1-24	10 1/2	1-48	5		

Note: To figure the maximum count for Poster Bodoni headlines of more than one column, multiply the maximum for one column by the number of columns.

Italic and Roman versions of the same headline type size should count the same.

In all cases, count spaces between words as one-half. Count numerals (except 1), the dollar sign ($), the percentage symbol (%) and devices of similar width as one and one-half (1 1/2).

Counting Units in a Headline

There are several methods for counting the units of space in a headline. Many school newspaper copy editors find it easiest to count each letter and each space as one unit. A slightly more complicated—yet more precise—way is to count the narrow lowercase letters (f,i,j,l,t) as one-half unit each and the wide lowercase letters (m,w) as one and one-half units each. All other lowercase letters are counted as one unit each. Capital letters are counted as one and one-half units each, except for *M* and *W,* which are counted as two units each, and *I,* which is counted as one-half unit. The safest count for figures over *1* is one and one-half units each. Punctuation marks are counted as one-half unit each, except for the question mark, which is counted as one and one-half units. Because a good bit of space between words makes reading easier, most editors count spaces as one unit each, regardless of the type size.

For example, in a 72-point headline set in a face called Times Roman, the headline writer has a total of 22 units in 59 picas. The count in 59 picas cannot exceed 22 units, but it can fall short by as much as three units and still allow the headline to look good. Count the following headline to see whether it fits in 59 picas:

72tr/1/59 pi (head order)

Wheeling Wildcats win!

An accurate headline count reveals that the headline will indeed fit because there are a total of 21½ units. Here's how those 21½ units are counted:

2	1	1	1	½	½	1	1	1	2	½	½	1	1	1	½	1	1	1½	½	1	½
W	h	e	e	l	i	n	g		W	i	l	d	c	a	t	s		w	i	n	!

Consider another case. A copy editor is to fit a 36-point, three-line headline—set in a type case called helios bold—into one column (11 picas). The copy editor has eight units of space per line. Count the following headline to see whether it will fit:

36hb/3/11 pi (head order)   or   36hb/3/1 (head order)

Photogs

focus on

top prize

A careful unit count reveals that the headline will indeed fit. The top line has seven units; the middle line, seven and one-half; the third line, eight units. Here's how to count the headline:

1½	1	1	½	1	1	1	
P	h	o	t	o	g	s	

½	1	1	1	1	1	1	1
f	o	c	u	s		o	n

½	1	1	1	1	1	½	1	1
t	o	p		p	r	i	z	e

Headline Content

Counting the units in a headline is relatively easy. Making the headline say something to attract reader attention is more difficult. Persons with extensive vocabularies probably make the best headline writers because they can use precisely the right words and—at the same time—use words that fit the headline count.

The student copy editor, you will recall, first composes a thesis statement summarizing the central idea of the story being copy edited. He or she then strips that thesis statement of all nonessential words, producing a statement phrased in telegraphic style. The examples given on page 367 were as follows:

Thesis sentence: The East High Panthers defeated the North High Rangers by a score of 56 to 50.

Telegraphic style: Panthers defeat Rangers, 56 to 50.

Closer examination shows that there is still more work to do. The copy editor must seek the most effective combination of letters and spaces to make the headline as forceful as possible. The headline writer must choose each individual word with care—especially the verb in the headline. In the telegraphic statement above, the verb *defeat* seemed to the copy editor to be too formal, who felt that a more vivid verb would be more forceful. Here is the new headline:

Panthers trip Rangers   (Unit count 20½)

To write forceful headlines, copy editors give particular attention to verbs—short, active, vivid verbs. Verbs derived from Anglo-Saxon usually have more force than do those derived from Latin or Greek. Verbs in the active voice are more forceful than verbs in the passive voice.

The tense of the verb in a headline is usually the historical present (for example, *speak, speaks*). (The historical present is used because even though the action being reported is a past action, the news story about it is presumably the first time that the average reader has become aware of that action.) The verb in a headline can also be used in the future tense (*will speak*, for example). Future tense can also be suggested by the use of the infinitive (for example, *to speak*). The past tense of a verb is used in a headline only when the story concerns something that occurred in the distant past. For example, in a story dealing with an explosion that 50 years ago leveled the high school, the copy editor would use a past-tense verb:

50 years ago, blast destroyed high school

All forms of the linking verb *to be* are usually omitted from a headline. For example:

Andrews elected to Council

Headline writers try to find a happy medium between being boring and being too clever. TV star Dick Cavett was once scheduled to be the master of ceremonies at a dinner given by a regional newscasters' association. At the last minute, however, he cancelled because of a conflict in scheduling. A newspaper columnist wrote about the cancellation and chided Cavett for his action. Because the story was written by a bylined columnist, the copy editor fully expected the personal opinion expressed in the column. Feeling that the headline for the story should reflect the columnist's attitude, the copy editor wrote the following headline:

Dick Cavett cancels local appearance

But this headline seemed too matter-of-fact; it didn't convey the columnist's attitude very well. And so the copy editor rewrote the headline like this:

Is Dick Cavett a "stand-up" comedian?

But the pun in the headline seemed too cute. And so the copy editor tried a third headline:

Newscasters learn about Cave(a)tt emptor

This one pleased the copy editor but left one serious misgiving: Would readers be likely to know that *caveat emptor* is Latin for "Let the buyer beware"? Talking the matter over, several other editors agreed with his concern about *caveat emptor*, but they also felt that the headline told the story in a unique way and urged the copy editor to use it. It ran—and later the copy editor received an award for an unusual, attention-getting headline.

Types of Headlines

News: This headline tells as many of the five *W*'s and *H* as possible in a simple, straightforward way.

Track team vies in finals
on Saturday

Editorial: This headline takes a stand and reflects the editorial it summarizes.

Administration wisely supports
King memorial

Feature: Classifications for feature headlines vary. Examples:
  Emotion: This headline summarizes the story, telling of the problems faced by a handicapped student.

Handicapped student
sings toward stardom

  Directive: This headline summarizes a story on the importance of friends to high school students.

Here's how to find
key to happiness

  Hornblowing: This headline tells of a teacher who uses humor to make points in class.

Teacher's humor becomes
a class act

  Humorous: This headline is a take-off on the advice given actors: "Break a leg!". The story is about a high school drama club.

It was only a couple of
broken legs

  Offbeat: This headline cleverly sums up a story about Rubik's Cube.

A colorful twist of insanity

Headline "Rules"

To make headlines effective, competent copy editors observe a number of guidelines or "rules":

1. Except for abbreviations, headlines contain no periods.
2. Only abbreviations that are readily understood appear in headlines.
3. As a rule, headlines are set "flush left." That is, the first letter in each line is set at the left margin of the column.

Cougars win;
survive rally
by Bengals

Setting headlines flush left is easiest and least expensive. However, if a headline is to appear in a box—as the headlines for feature stories often do—it might look better if each line were centered in the column. For example

Cougars win;
survive rally
by Bengals

4. Each line of a headline must stand alone.
   a. A line may not end with a modifier—an adjective or adverb.

   Faulty: Former MHS   **Better:** Veteran teacher
                teacher here   joins CHS staff

   b. A verb form may not be divided between lines.

   Faulty: Principal to   **Better:** Principal eyes
                climb peak   Matterhorn

   c. A word at the end of a line may not be hyphenated.

   Faulty: Band con-   **Better:** Band to give
                cert Friday   Friday concert

   d. A line should not end with a conjunction.

   Faulty: Terriers and   **Better:** Terriers, Colts
                Colts tangle   tangle for lead
                for top spot

5. A comma may replace the conjunction *and.*

Johnson, Burdick star

6. A semicolon may be used to indicate separate ideas.

Honor Society awards
trophy; praises Romney

7. A colon may be used to replace the verb *says.*

Governor Mosely:
'No new taxes!'

8. A headline containing a quotation uses single quotation marks.

Coach Myers: 'Tournament
postponed because of flu'

9. Vague, confusing expressions make poor headlines.

Faulty: Council sets   **Better:**   Five juniors
             deadline—so   beat deadline
             avoid the rush   for class race

10. Personal feelings have no place in a headline. However, with a review of a play, a book, or a musical event, the headline writer may summarize personal feelings, provided that the assessment is fair.

Juniors' 'Our Town' inspirational

Three C's of Headline Writing

When breaking in new copy editors, Steve Lynch, veteran copy-desk chief of the Boston *Herald-American*, emphasizes three *C*'s that are of critical importance in the writing headlines.

■ **Comprehension:** Never try to write a headline until you completely understand the story.

■ **Clarity:** Never turn in a headline whose meaning isn't crystal clear to the reader.

■ **Count:** Never turn in a headline that doesn't fit. The best headline ever written is worthless if it won't fit into the allotted space.

Writing Cutlines (Captions)

Because newspaper engravings are called "cuts," the words set in type under a photograph or drawing to identify and describe it are called *cutlines.* (At one time the image of the picture to be printed was cut into a block of wood. Thus, lines of type that identify a cut are cutlines.) Illustrations add impact to the news stories they accompany; therefore, newspaper editors seek to publish a photograph or a drawing (artwork) with each major story. To help readers understand what the photo or drawing depicts, editors supply an explanation—a cutline (or caption)—with each piece of artwork published. Indeed, many publications have two rules regarding illustrations:

■ Use at least one piece of artwork per page.

■ Print a cutline to identify every piece of art published.

Content

Every editor wants what his or her newspaper prints to be completely understandable to its readers. Thus an editor—often the copy editor—is given the responsibility for writing an intelligible cutline for every piece of artwork for pointing out anything (in the artwork) that readers might miss.

With an illustration that accompanies a news story, the editor responsible for writing cutlines must be careful not to duplicate the story. He or she should simply describe—as briefly as possible—what the illustration shows.

If, however, an illustration is printed without an accompanying news story, the cutline writer must compose a mini-story based on the five *w's* and the *h*. For example, suppose that a sports picture shows a football play. The cutline writer must then point out *who* (the fullback), *what* (carried the ball), *when* (during the final minute of play), *where* (on the one-yard line), *why* (he eluded being tackled by three defenders), and *how* (by aggressive running tactics). Finally, the cutline should call attention to the ball—as it is shown in the photograph.

Ranger fullback Nicky Nunez wins the game for Weston last Sunday at Memorial Field. Nunez carried the ball on the one-yard line during the final minute of play, eluding South's three defenders, Mike Lucas, Dave Wolf, and Richie Rollins, to win the game, getting the Regional Cup for Weston.

Style

In writing cutlines, the copy editor (or designated editor) must keep the basic style of the publication in mind. For example, the editor may have called for (1) a 24-point headline above the photograph, (2) a cutline set in 10-point type below the photograph, and (3) a photo credit line set in agate type immediately below the lower right corner of the picture. Or the editor may have indicated that a 14-point headline is to be set flush left below the photograph, followed by a 10-point cutline set in italic type.

The photo credit, which is as important to the photographer as a byline is to a reporter, might be printed in agate type directly under the lower right corner of the photo. Or it could be run vertically along the lower right side of the photo. Or it could be run immediately after the cutline and enclosed in parentheses.

Finally editors and copy editors often encourage photographers to use a rubber stamp to imprint their names of the backs of their pictures. In this way, not only will the credit go to the proper photographer, but it will also be easier for the cutline writer to ensure that the photographer's name is spelled correctly.

Page Makeup and Layout

The Tabloid-Size Paper

Although a few high schools still publish standard-sized newspapers (about 22 inches by 14 inches, with six or eight columns per page), the most common size for high school newspapers is the tabloid size—approximately 17 inches by 11 inches. The width of the print space on the tabloid-size page is approximately 59 picas —almost ten inches. Editorial policy determines the number of columns to be printed in that width. Most high school newspapers use one of three formats. Two of these formats are shown on page 369.

1. The 11-pica page: The print space (about 59 picas wide) is divided into five columns of type, each column set 11 picas wide. A pica of white space (or a column rule) separates one column from another.

2. The 14-pica page: The print page (about 59 picas wide) is divided into four columns of type, each 14 picas wide. A pica of white space (or a column rule) separates one column from another.

3. The 18-pica page: The print space (about 59 picas wide) is divided into three columns of type, each 18 picas wide. One-and-a-half or two picas of white space separate one column from another. The depth of the columns in a tabloid-size paper is about 17 inches, but that depth will vary, depending on page layout, press capacity, and overall paper dimensions.

Basic Types of Tabloid Page Makeup

The basic types of tabloid-size page makeup are the following: balanced (or formal), horizontal, vertical, focus-and-brace, combination horizontal with focus-and-brace, circus, modular, big picture, and picture. Each of these types of layout is discussed and illustrated beginning on this page through page 388.

Balanced, or Formal, Page Makeup. Balanced, or formal page makeup balances each headline or picture with another element of equal weight. That is, every element on one side of the page is balanced by an element of equal size and weight on the other side of the page. For example, on an 11-pica page, a two-column headline or picture in columns one and two would be balanced by a two-column headline or picture in columns four and five. An example of a balanced layout appears in Figure 1. Figure 2 shows a school newspaper page made up from balanced layout.

Fig. 1 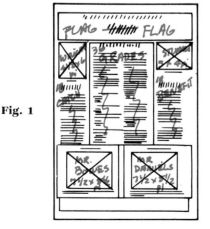  Fig. 2

Horizontal Page Makeup. In horizontal page makeup, headlines and stories and photographs are located so that they appear to form large horizontal blocks. Stories with multicolumn headlines form horizontal bars from left to right. Wide, shallow photographs are ideal for horizontal page makeup. An example of horizontal page makeup appears in Figure 3. Figure 4 shows a school newspaper page based on horizontal layout.

Fig. 3 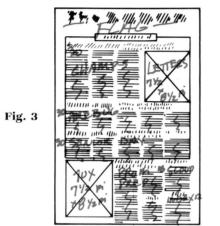  Fig. 4

Vertical Page Makeup. With vertical page makeup, headlines, stories, and photographs are set in single columns. The length of each story in its column is determined by the number of stories the editors decide to place on the page. An example of vertical page makeup appears in Figure 5. Figure 6 shows a newspaper page made up from vertical page layout.

Fig. 5 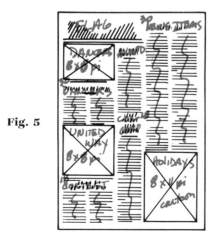  Fig. 6

Focus-and-Brace Page Makeup. With focus-and-brace page makeup, the main story is placed in the top right-hand corner of the page. Other stories are located on the page—in order of decreasing importance—in such a way that one can draw an imaginary line from top right to bottom left and from top left to bottom right.

Many school newspaper editors feel that the focus-and-brace layout is the best for a tabloid-size paper because it creates an impression of action. Focus-and-brace layout is used by many professional newspapers and by some magazines. An example of focus-and-brace page makeup appears in Figure 7. A school newspaper page made up from a focus-and-brace layout appears in Figure 8.

Fig. 7 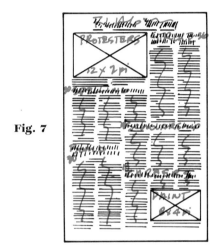  Fig. 8

Combination Horizontal with Focus-and-Brace Page Makeup. Sometimes horizontal layout is combined with focus-and-brace layout. This type of page makeup often uses a page-width photograph across the top of the page, with a four- (and sometimes five-) column headline serving as an anchor for the page. Masses of type in the center of the page are broken up with one-column headshots or boldface headlines referring to important stories and articles on inside pages. Boldfaced, capitalized lead-ins sometimes break up any stories placed in the center of the page. Adding extra space (leading, lĕd′ing) between paragraphs gives desirable white space and attractiveness to the page. An example of combination horizontal with focus-and-brace page makeup appears on page 386 in Figure 9. An example of a school newspaper page made up from this kind of layout appears in Figure 10.

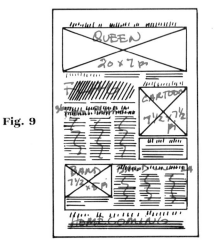

Fig. 9

Fig. 10

Circus Page Makeup. The so-called "circus" layout employs what seems to be a random placement of headlines and stories and photographs. Big headlines and at least one large photograph are important characteristics of the circus layout. The page may look busy, but it also looks interesting. An example of the circus layout appears in Figure 11. Figure 12 shows a school newspaper page based on circus page makeup.

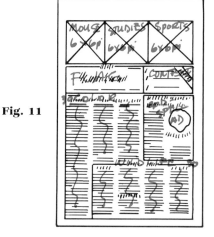

Fig. 11

Fig. 12

Modular Page Makeup. With modular page makeup, every print element and every photograph squares off, making the page look neat and attractive. Some editors feel that the modular layout is the ideal layout. An example of modular page makeup appears in Figure 13. Figure 14 shows a school newspaper page based on modular layout.

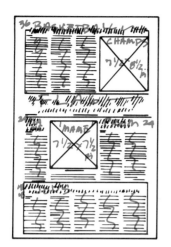

Fig. 13

Fig. 14

Big Picture Page Makeup. Big picture page makeup consists of one dominating photograph of excellent quality, plus two or three news stories of importance. Figure 15 illustrates big picture page makeup, and Figure 16 shows a school newspaper page laid out according to big picture page makeup.

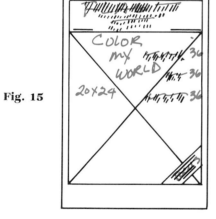

Fig. 15

Fig. 16

Picture Page Makeup. Picture page makeup consists of one attention-getting photograph of excellent quality taking up most of the page. There may be a headline or two serving to anchor the page. Figure 17 on page 388 illustrates picture page layout. Figure 18 shows a school newspaper page laid out with this kind of page makeup.

The School Newspaper: Copy Editing, Layout, and Design

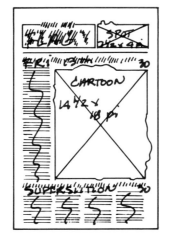

Fig. 17

Fig. 18

Planning of Page Layouts

One of the prerequisites for success as a layout editor is the ability to recognize what constitutes news, plus the ability to judge what is *important* news. Using the "makers of news" as criteria (see Chapter 7, pages 140–165), the layout editor, together with the editor-in-chief, the managing editor, and the news editors, decides the importance of each news story. With that order of importance clearly in mind, the layout editor lists all newsworthy stories and then decides on the location of each story.

The layout editor can begin planning preliminary page layouts as soon as editorial and news assignments are made, realizing that some changes will be necessary before final layouts can be prepared. In many schools the pages of the school paper follow the same general layout (or format) in every issue. Because page one is considered the most important page, layout editors usually work on it first. Most page-one stories will be hard news; however, layout editors sometimes place well-written feature stories at the foot of page one. Once the photographs have been selected for that page, there is usually only enough room left for five or six short news stories. In the typical eight-page school paper, page two is usually the editorial page. The first two columns are usually given over to editorials; the right columns are devoted to cartoons, letters to the editor, or feature material. Usually most of the advertisements appear on pages three and five. Page six often begins the sports section. In general, the top of each inside page (pages three through eight) carries an important story with an accompanying picture and a large (three-to-five-column) headline.

Before starting their layouts, layout editors usually sketch out a tentative layout plan for each page, often attempting to make slight variations from the layouts used in previous issues. The news value of the stories to be used can often contribute variety to the layout. For example, with a lead story concerning a student council election that affects the entire student body, a five-column headline might be appropriate; with a lead story concerning the drama club's spring production, a two-column headline with a three-column picture across the top of the page might be suitable.

Having decided on which pictures and stories to use, the layout editor next writes the name of the newspaper (called the nameplate or flag) in the designated location on the *dummy* (a diagram or template of the page). If dummy sheets are not available, a sufficient supply can be duplicated from a ruled-off master. On the layout dummy, the layout editor indicates, in inches, the space allotted for each story and each photograph. (See the layouts in Figures 1, 3, 5, 7, 9, 11, 13, 15, 17.) After writing the name of the newspaper in location on the dummy, the layout editor next indicates the main story, each photograph, and every other story to appear on the page. He or she makes sure that every corner of the page is anchored with a short two- or three-paragraph story.

Layout editors often consider using two- or three-column headlines in the middle of a page to prevent the page from looking too gray, a condition that can result from too solid a mass of type. Omitting column rules (lines between columns) adds white space. To help give the page an open look, the layout editor can use kickers (small headlines) above the main headlines. The white space that results makes the page more inviting to the reader.

Drastic Cuts Predicted
COUNCIL VOTES MAJOR CUTBACKS

Variety in Page Layouts

Layout editors can achieve visual variety on each page by breaking up solid masses of type with headlines, white space, and photographs. They avoid placing photographs or headlines side by side (an arrangement known as *tombstoning*). But when such placement of headlines cannot be avoided, layout editors achieve the appearance of variety by setting one of the headlines in an italic type face.

Knowledgeable layout editors try to avoid continuing a story from page one to an inside page. It is preferable to print the entire story on page one. Because news stories are written in the inverted pyramid style it is possible to shorten a story by deleting the last few paragraphs, retaining an accurate news presentation with the remaining facts (the five *w's* and the *h*) contained in the beginning (usually the lead) of the story.

In school newspapers that have advertisements, the advertising manager should dummy in the ads for the inside pages. (Usually no advertising appears on page one.) The layout editor must then fit the remaining pictures and stories around the advertisements, attempting to locate at least one picture on each page and using any of the remaining, less-important news stories to fill the pages. Advertisements are usually pyramided, the larger advertisements being located at the bottom of the page and the smaller ones placed above them.

Length of Copy

The easiest way to determine how long a story will run when set in print is to count the numbers of typed lines in the article. When typed on an 8½ by 11 sheet of paper with one-inch margins on each side, four lines of copy will equal approximately one inch of standard newspaper print. For example, if the story consists of 24 typed lines, it will be approximately six inches long when set in type. The headline depth can be approximated by adding one more inch to allow for the average one-column, two-line headline.

A more complex system for keeping track of how much copy is needed is as follows: If a page runs 15 inches deep and is four columns of 14 picas in width, 60 inches of heads, stories, advertisements, and pictures will be needed to fill the page. Following is a suggested form for keeping track of the amount of copy needed to fill pages. For each page in their papers, layout editors usually maintain similar charts that list each story and picture scheduled to appear on a particular page. When the total number of inches reaches 60, they have enough material to complete a page.

One way layout editors prepare copy (preferred by many printers) is to use the paste-up method. With that method, a dummy page is laid out as previously described and is retained by the editor while the printer sets all stories and headlines into type. The printer then has proofs made of all copy and pictures, and returns the proofs to the layout editor. The layout editor next pastes these elements onto actual-size master dummies (or templates), which are then returned to the printer. Using the pasted-up master dummy as a guide, the printer places the type, headlines, and the cuts for the pictures in the exact positions indicated on the master dummy.

SCHEDULE FOR COPY NEEDED TO FILL A TABLOID-SIZE NEWSPAPER PAGE

Head Size	Length of Story and Head	Total No. of Inches	Slug
1. 2/48/2	12	12	Council
2. 3/36/1	10	22	Musical
3. 1/24/3	7	29	Library
4. Picture (2x5)	10	39	with Library

Effective Photographs

To ensure that they have selected dynamic pictures, school newspaper editors should be able to answer the following questions with a "yes."

1. Is the picture of good quality?
2. Does it tell a story?
3. Does it create a favorable impression of the student body?
4. Will using it help create an attractive layout?

Is the picture of good quality? Although noncolor photographs are referred to as "black-and-whites," such prints actually consist of many shades of gray, plus some black and some white. A photograph will reproduce well only if it has many gradations of gray, together with some solid black and some pure white. If a photograph has too much contrast (mostly black and white with few grays), or if it is too flat (overall gray), it should be reprinted.

Does it tell a story? If the picture shows nothing more than a group of students in a row, the editor might suggest that the photograph be retaken. Head-and-shoulders photographs are usually more effective if the person portrayed is doing something. Instead of using full-face headshots, many editors prefer to print action shots—a football player about to catch a pass, for example, or a stagehand moving scenery or a uniformed band member marching in a parade.

Students at work on the school newspaper create a favorable impression of the school.

Does the picture create a favorable impression of the student body? Photographs can often create undesirable impressions. In choosing photographs for use in school papers, editors should make sure that the pictures they select create a favorable impression of the school.

Will using the picture help create an attractive layout? At least one photograph should appear on each page. Strong vertical and horizontal pictures add variety and lend a feeling of action to the pages of any newspaper.

Photographs in Layouts

Sometimes editors responsibile for page makeup make a serious mistake by designing a page *before* seeing the illustration(s) to be printed on that page. The results can be downright embarrassing. Suppose, for example, that the staff photographer has taken a picture of the band director with baton raised, ready to lead the band in the playing of a march. And suppose further that the makeup editor had earlier allocated a space 14 picas wide by two inches deep for that picture. Upon publication of the school paper, however, the photo shows the band director from his chest up to the top of his head. But his arms have been lopped off so that neither his hands nor the baton appear at all!

To repeat: Laying out a page prior to seeing the actual illustration(s) to appear on that page can be disastrous.

To avoid this kind of error, makeup editors should observe these four steps:

1. Carefully select the photograph(s) to be used.
2. Carefully crop the picture, eliminating all dead space. Seek to crop the photo so that it makes a strong vertical or strong horizontal composition.
3. Transfer this same composition format to the layout. Keep in mind, however, that the size of the photograph being used has little, if any, bearing on the size in which it will appear in the paper. The photograph can be enlarged or reduced to almost any size the editor feels the photo is worth.
4. Make sure that the printed photo will be large enough so that everyone shown can be clearly identified.

Placement of Photographs

After choosing photographs that meet the preceding requirements, the editor must decide where to locate them. If a photograph accompanies a story, both should appear on the same page. In fact, it's a good idea to select a picture of the same width as the headline of the accompanying story. For example, when using a 29-pica picture in the top left-hand corner of page one, the layout editor usually places the picture above the story's 29-pica headline.

For layout purposes, the layout editor needs to know the approximate size of the photograph. The final size can be estimated by looking at the cropped photograph. If it is a vertical composition that is planned for a two-column width, chances are that it will run approximately five inches deep (length). A horizontal two-column photograph will usually run approximately three inches deep. Headshots usually run about one column wide by three inches deep. Since most high school editors have proofs submitted to them by the printer, the depths of photographs can be accurately measured from the printer's proof. The cutline, or caption, will, of course, add depth to the photograph. Captions, incidentally, should be planned for all photographs. A rule of thumb to follow when preparing captions is to keep them as short as possible. When a photograph is used without a story, the caption should tell the story as briefly as possible.

Cropping of Photographs

Unless the photographer has had experience in cropping photographs, the layout editor will need to crop pictures in order to eliminate dead space. Pictures that are not properly cropped often show more background or foreground than subject. By placing two L-shaped cardboard strips over the picture (see the illustration), the layout editor can zero in on that portion which will be most effective. Next, to ensure that only the best part of the picture will appear in print, the layout editor draws heavy lines on that part of the photograph to be eliminated. By careful cropping, the layout editor can convert vertically shaped pictures into horizontally shaped pictures, and vice versa.

If a layout editor feels that a story might not fit into the space allotted under a photo, sometimes the picture will be made deeper than necessary. Then, if the story runs longer than expected, the photo can be trimmed to allow the story to fit.

In Conclusion

The layout editor is often called the story's surgeon, the writer's conscience, and the reporter's best critic. Like the members of the stage crew for a dramatic production, the successful layout editor has a skill that gives the production a quality that brings lasting applause. Competent newspaper staffs without layout editors sometimes produce fair newspapers; mediocre staffs without competent layout editors often produce acceptable newspapers; but excellent staffs, backed by competent, experienced layout editors, almost always produce newspapers of outstanding quality.

Activities

1. **a.** Selecting a newsworthy event that occurred recently in your school or community, write a short (two- or three-paragraph) news story about it. Make sure your lead includes the 5 *w's* and the *h*.

   b. Write an appropriate headline and a kicker for your news story.

   c. Select a classmate to be your copy editor and exchange news stories.

d. Using the copy-editing symbols that are given in Appendix V, copy edit your classmate's news story for unity, organization, grammar, punctuation, capitalization, and spelling.

e. With your classmate, discuss the reasons for the copy-editing corrections made in each story.

f. Rewrite your news story to conform to your copy editor's specifications.

2. From a recent issue of your school newspaper, select five headlines that you think could be improved. Rewrite each headline, retaining its original unit count. Then rewrite each again, using five to ten fewer units per line.

3. Using a printer's rule, measure the point sizes of the type used in ten of the headlines in the latest issue of your school paper. What is the one-column unit count for each measured headline? Prepare a "headline schedule" for your school paper, listing the one-column count for each size of headline type.

4. Using each of five of the page makeup examples discussed on pages 383–388, make up a page-one dummy layout for the first fall issue of your school newspaper. In each case, keep the paper's present size and number of columns. Specify the amount of space to be allotted for whatever stories and photographs you intend to use.

5. a. Analyze the page-one layout of a recent issue of your school newspaper for the following:

    (1) Readability

    (2) Variety and placement of headlines

    (3) Size and placement of photographs

    (4) Space between columns and between stories

b. Select another page from that newspaper and analyze it for the following:

    (1) Readability

    (2) Variety and placement of headlines

    (3) Placement of advertising

    (4) Eye-catching devices like cartoons, photographs, and unusual type faces.

c. Select a third page from that newspaper and explain how you would rearrange it, using the stories and photographs that now make up the page.

The School Newspaper: Copy Editing, Layout, and Design   **395**

CHAPTER 17

The School Newspaper: Production, Finance, Public Relations

It's three o'clock on a Wednesday afternoon at South High. The staff of *The Clarion* is in the newsroom for an important meeting about the "graduation" issue. Dennis Paolo, the paper's business manager, has the floor:

"... And last winter, if you'd asked me, I was skeptical about *The Clarion's* finishing the year in the black. But thanks to the cost-cutting measures we all agreed on at the beginning of this semester, we're now in great shape."

The tension eases. Applause.

"In fact," Dennis goes on, "we'll have enough money to add four pages of photos to the graduation issue. That ought to make everyone happy—especially Linda and Bud and Mr. Taylor."

"Hey, Dennis," exclaims Linda Jeffries, the editor-in-chief, "that's super! Our decision to limit each issue of *The Clarion* to four pages and to skip the March 15th issue has really paid off!"

"And now four extra pages for the graduation issue!" Bud Patrinos, the staff's chief photographer is ecstatic. "Wow! That'll mean some changes in the picture schedule for sure."

"You bet it will," chimes in Mr. Taylor. "In fact, it'll mean changing the entire production schedule."

"That's right," agrees Linda. "And, Tom, that'll mean that all copy will have to be ready for composition earlier than we'd counted on. And, Beth, the same holds for all advertising copy. And, Josh, maybe there'll need to be some adjustments in the circulation and distribution schedules."

Everyone agrees that putting out the graduation issue will require some schedule changes.

"Tell you what," says Linda, "tomorrow in journalism class, let's spend the period working out a 'graduation-issue' production and advertising schedule. Any objections?"

There are none. As the meeting breaks up, there's a new tension—a tension of anticipation—felt by everyone on *The Clarion* staff.

Producing the School Newspaper

The successful production of school newspapers, like the production of professional newspapers, is the result of careful thinking and planning. An efficient system for (a) obtaining news, (b) converting that news into attention-getting stories and articles, and (c) readying those stories and articles for publication doesn't "just happen."

Successful, efficient newspaper production results from the careful planning and scheduling of all operations involved in getting the paper into the hands of its readers. To institute an effective production system, the school news staff and the faculty adviser must first determine how often the school paper is to be published—daily, weekly, biweekly, triweekly, monthly, or bimonthly. To make that critical decision, they need to consider at least three questions:

1. How great a demand is there for the paper?
2. How large a staff will be required to publish the paper?
3. How much editorial time can staff members devote to planning and publishing the paper?

The answer to the first question, of course, will vary from school to school. Student interest, school spirit, the availability of printing facilities, and the status of school finances—these are among the major considerations involved in deciding how often to publish. Answers to the second and third questions make up the detailed discussion of Chapters 14, 15, and 16, pages 306–395.

In this chapter we are concerned with these three questions:

1. How can the newspaper staff make sure that each issue of the school paper is published on schedule?
2. How is the paper to be printed?
3. How is the paper to be financed?

Scheduling

To ensure a regulated and a consistent flow of editorial materials, the news staff—especially the editor-in-chief, the managing editor, the business manager, the circulation manager, the advertising manager, and the faculty adviser—must carefully map out an editorial production schedule. Such a schedule specifies exact deadlines and designates clearly the time to be allotted for each step in the production process. Most school newspaper staffs program their editorial schedules by days—rather than by hours, as is the case with professional papers. Production schedules should be posted prominently on bulletin boards in both the journalism classroom and the newsroom. The chart below shows a suggested production schedule for a school paper published monthly.

October 10th Edition

August 20	September 1	September 5	September 8
Prepublication planning session with adviser and all staff members.	(first day of school) General news assignments made from beat sheet. Feature assignments made. Editorial page assignments made. Sports page assignmments made. Pictorial assignments made.	Editorial page assignments due. First advertising copy due.	Advertising layouts made. Editorial and news page layouts planned. First third of picture assignments due. First third of sports copy due. First third of feature copy due.
September 10	**September 12**	**September 17**	**September 19**
News assignments made for scheduled events. First third of general news copy due.	Second third of picture assignments due. Second third of sports assignments due. Second third of feature copy due. Second third of general news copy due.	Copy starts to printer. Advertising and page layouts completed.	Second third of copy (pictures, sports, features, and news) starts to printer. Last third of picture assignments due. Last third of sports copy due. Last third of feature copy due. Last third of news copy due.
September 23	**September 29**	**September 30**	**October 3**
All remaining copy to printer.	Galley proof checked and proofread.	Final layouts made for all pages.	All proof and layouts released to printer.
October 6	**October 8**	**October 9**	**October 10**
Page proof checked and proofread.	Newspapers are printed.	Newspapers collated and folded.	Newspapers are distributed.

*Note: 52 days—30 school days—have elapsed between initial planning and distribution.

The School Newspaper: Production, Finance, Public Relations

In addition to having an *editorial* production schedule to follow, the news staff will find it useful to have an advertising production schedule as well. Such a schedule will help increase operational efficiency. Similar in form to an editorial production schedule, an advertising production schedule can be readily drawn up by the editor-in-chief, the business manager, the advertising manager, and the faculty adviser.

After deciding how often to publish and after setting up realistic production schedules, the news staff—with the input of the faculty adviser and perhaps the school administration—must decide how best to get the newspaper printed. Besides settling on the printing method that will best serve their objectives—the news staff needs to consider (a) appropriate methods of getting copy set into type and (b) efficient routines for proofreading.

Typesetting/Composition

Linotype Composition. Sitting at a keyboard resembling a typewriter keyboard, an operator types from the copy to be set. Overhead is a supply of thin pieces of metal—called a magazine—each of which contains a letter mold, which is called a mat. As the operator strikes a key, the correct letter mold falls into place. (A space band of metal falls into place to form the variable widths between words.) After one line of type has been set in this way, the operator casts the entire line—or slug—in front of a mold where molten lead is forced into the letter molds, thus forming a solid line of raised type. A linotype operator can set an entire tabloid-size page in three to four hours.

Another type of linecasting machine, the Ludlow Typograph, is used to cast headlines into type.

Today, because of the increased use of electronic typesetting method, few linotype machines remain in operation.

Computer Typesetting. Research during the second half of the 20th century has produced radically new methods of setting type; indeed, that research has brought about radically new ways of printing entire newspapers.

Two inventions have made computer typesetting possible—the video display terminal (VDT) and the optical character reader (OCR).

The **VDT** allows a reporter to compose a news story by typing it out on a keyboard (resembling a typewriter keyboard) and having the words appear on a video display screen similar to a small television screen. The reporter can make corrections, delete

Newspaper pages used to be set in type by skilled operators using lino-type machines.

words and sentences, insert words and sentences, and rephrase entire paragraphs without touching a piece of paper. Satisfied with the story, the reporter activates the phototypesetter, which prints out the entire story in a matter of seconds. When the print-out has been copy edited, the story is "called up"—again on the video screen—and any needed changes are made. Then the pho-totypesetter is programmed to reprint the story in a specified type face, type size, and column width. The resulting printout is trimmed and pasted into place on a page makeup sheet. The completed page makeup sheet is photographed; the negative goes to the printer, who prepares the printing plate.

Using the **OCR** method, the reporter types the story on a spe-cial electric typewriter, edits the story on the same machine, and then feeds the story into the OCR. As the machine "reads" the story, the phototypesetter prints out the story in a prearranged type face, type size, and column width. When the story has been copy edited and, if necessary, reprinted, the completed story is ready to be pasted into place on the page makeup sheet.

Phototypesetting. Phototypesetting consists of (a) placing a disc-shaped film negative of the alphabet in front of a light source and then (b) shining the light sequentially through the appropriate letters so that entire words appear on a light-sensitive photo-graphic paper. The result is a picture of words and sentences in

Today, most newspapers are set using VDT's.

readable lines of type. Photographing at the speed of light, the phototypesetter can produce a photographic positive or negative that can be pasted onto a page makeup sheet, which is then converted into a printing plate.

Direct Impression.   In some schools, machines resembling typewriters are used for typesetting purposes.

As a typist types on a Friden Justowriter, each key perforates a paper tape. The finished tape is then run through the machine a second time. During this operation the machine automatically spaces words evenly and even produces lines that are justified at the right. The typed copy is then trimmed to the appropriate size and pasted into place on a page makeup sheet.

A second method of direct impression involves the use of a VariTyper. The typist first types out a story. When the story has been copy edited, the typist reinserts the story into the machine and "tells" the machine how the finished story is to look. For example, the typist would instruct the machine to print the story in 10-point type in a column 14 picas wide. The machine then retypes the story, spacing words correctly and justifying lines at the right. The finished copy is then trimmed to size and pasted into place on a page makeup sheet.

A third method of composition by direct impression involves the use of stencils. Using any standard typewriter and following the copy submitted, the typist types directly on the stencils. This method of composition involves the publishing of a duplicated (mimeographed) newspaper. Further discussion of this kind of publication appears on pages 408–409.

Proofreading

Before any material goes to the compositor/typesetter, it is copy edited. (See Chapter 16, page 362.) With the completion of that process, it is assumed that the copy is error free.

Once copy has been set into type, it must be *proofread.* That is, the printed material must be read to make sure that it is exactly the same as the copy that went to the compositor/typesetter.

The compositor/typesetter returns proof in the form of galleys, long strips of paper containing single columns of print. Usually the compositor supplies three copies of each galley. One copy is proofread and then returned to the compositor, who will make all of the corrections marked. The second copy is used for page makeup. The third copy—containing the same corrections marked on the first copy—is kept by the appropriate editor for reference.

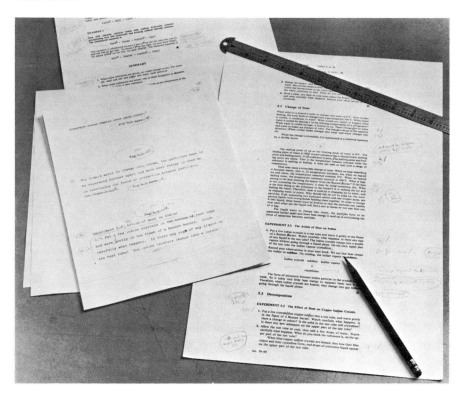

Each galley must be carefully checked with the original copy. The usual procedure calls for two proofreaders, who work together as a team. Reading aloud from the original copy, one member of the team—the copyholder—reads words, capital letters, and punctuation marks and also indicates the beginning of each paragraph. The copyholder even spells out certain words. For example, suppose that a news story about rebuilding a playground contains the word *re-creation,* meaning "a renewal, a rebuilding." To be sure that the typesetter has not confused that word with *recreation* (meaning "play, diversion, relaxation"), the copyholder spells the word aloud: "r-e-hyphen-c-r-e-a-t-i-o-n."

As the copyholder reads aloud, the other member of the team —the proofreader—follows along and, *in the margins of the galley or the VDT printout,* notes and corrects each error the team finds. The corrections are made in the margins (not directly over the errors) to make sure that the compositor/typesetter notices and corrects each one. The photo on page 403 shows a proofreader's corrections on a galley and on a VDT printout. In marking and correcting errors, the proofreader uses standard proofreader's marks, which are shown in Appendix V.

As each galley is proofread, the proofreader initials it—usually in the lower right corner—to show that it has been processed. Corrected galleys are then returned to the compositor/typesetter. When all errors have been corrected on revised galleys or on page proof, a staff member checks to make sure that all errors have been corrected and that no new errors have been made.

It is important to point out that the proofreading team's responsibility is to correct all errors—those that may have slipped by the copy editor and those that were made by the typesetter. There should be few, if any, errors in the original copy. However, if any such errors are found, they should, of course, be corrected. But correcting those particular errors is expensive. The school newspaper pays extra for the correction of errors made by the news staff. Errors made by the compositor/typesetter are corrected at that company's expense.

Proofreaders need to be aware that a change in only one letter in a line of type requires the resetting of the entire line—and sometimes more. Furthermore, if one or more words are to be inserted or deleted, several lines of type—and sometimes the entire paragraph—are affected. Making corrections costs money. Proofreaders should, of course, make all the corrections necessary to ensure that a story is clear and accurate but should make only those corrections that are essential. Above all, they must avoid rewriting the material they are proofreading because doing so would severely strain the newspaper budget.

Printing the School Newspaper

Nowadays most high school newspapers are printed by either the letterpress method or the offset method. Of the two methods, offset printing is the more common. If a high school has its own printshop, the school newspaper is very likely to be printed there. In the majority of cases, however, the school newspaper is printed in a commercial printshop.

School newspapers printed by the letterpress method or the offset method have these advantages:

■ They are easy to read.

■ They look like professional newspapers.

■ They afford more opportunity for effective layouts and advertising displays than do newspapers printed by other methods.

■ The news staff—not having to be concerned with the details of the printing process itself—can spend their time to advantage by striving for editorial and reportorial excellence and for financial stability.

The chief disadvantage of printing the school paper by the letterpress or the offset method is its cost. The approximate cost for printing 1000 copies of a four-page tabloid-size newspaper (including composition and photoengraving) ranges from $1000 to $1500. This cost, multiplied by the number of issues per year, constitutes the basis on which most school newspapers establish their budgets.

There are other methods—low-cost methods—of printing school newspapers. Accordingly, our discussion will focus on several printing methods.

Letterpress Printing. In the 15th century when Gutenberg invented movable type, individual letters were cast in reverse on a raised surface. To print whatever was to be published, an apprentice set each letter by hand—one at a time—in a chase, a quadrangular iron frame which prevented the type from moving during the printing process. The chase was placed on a horizontal flat surface; with a roller, a worker then applied ink to the type; another worker placed a sheet of paper over the chase; then pressure was applied to force the ink onto the paper. Hence the term *letterpress*.

Entirely a hand operation, this process could produce about 20 impressions an hour.

Over the centuries a number of inventions and improvements —including the linotype machine—permitted an increasingly faster operation. Today, in a matter of minutes, an entire page of

Using an antique press that prints one page at a time, this country editor uses a mallet and wooden plane to level the type he set by linotype.

type and engravings can be cast on a curved plate and fitted onto a large rotary printing press. As the press operates at high speed, a roller automatically inks the plate. The raised type on the plate then comes into direct contact with the newsprint, which is fed automatically from huge rolls into the press. Letterpress presses are capable of printing more than 40,000 papers an hour.

Although printing by the letterpress method has pretty much given way to the offset method, some metropolitan dailies are still printed by the letterpress method.

Offset Printing. Offset printing traces its origin back to the invention of lithography by Aloys Senefelder in Munich, Germany, in 1796. Senefelder had discovered a kind of stone that would absorb both oil and water. With a wax crayon he made a design on the stone, spread ink over the entire stone, and then bathed it in water. Surprisingly, he found that only the wax design prevented the ink from being absorbed. He found, too, that only the wax design would transfer ink to paper.

Offset printing makes use of the same principle—the principle that oil and water do not mix. The offset printing process involves the use of a smooth plate surface (as contrasted with the raised

A FLAT-BED CYLINDER LETTER PRESS

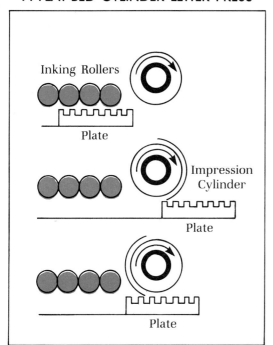

AN OFFSET PRINTING PRESS

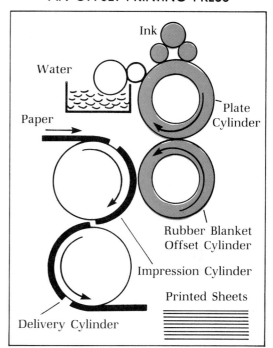

surface used in letterpress printing) on which letters and other images are "burned"—that is, transmittted photochemically. The process involves the formation of light and dark areas on light-sensitive negative plates. The transferred letters and images constitute the light areas; the dark areas are the non-image areas. Only the light areas—the image areas—are receptive to ink (oil). With the application of ink to the image areas, the letters and images are then transferred to a rubber blanket, or roller, which in turn faithfully impresses those images onto paper that comes into contact with it, as shown above. The process is called *offset* because the printing plates never come into direct contact with the paper.

Offset printing is ideal for the relatively small press runs characteristic of the typical high school newspaper.

Gravure Printing. Gravure printing, or intaglio, is a third method in common use. Letterpress printing involves plates with type on a raised surface; offset printing involves type on a treated flat plate; gravure printing uses an *etched,* or sunken, surface.

Lines called *wells* are etched into a copper plate or cylinder. The deeper the etching, the greater the amount of ink that can be transferred to paper. When an etched copper cylinder has undergone an ink bath, a device called a doctor blade wipes the excess ink from the surface, leaving ink only in the etched lines. Pressure is applied to paper brought into contact with the copper cylinder, ink is drawn onto the paper, and a printed page results.

The gravure method produces a print of high quality, especially in the reproduction of photographs. But the high cost of platemaking makes printing by the gravure method expensive.

Mimeographing. School newspapers can be printed inexpensively by means of the mimeographing process.

When news stories, features, and even advertisements have been copy edited, they are typed on *stencils,* 8½-by-14-inch

GRAVURE METHOD OF PRINTING

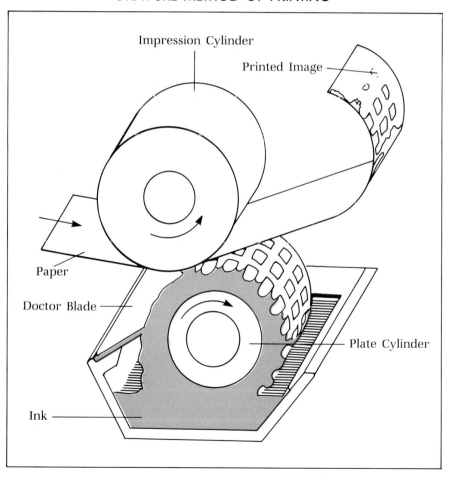

Impression Cylinder

Printed Image

Paper

Doctor Blade

Ink

Plate Cylinder

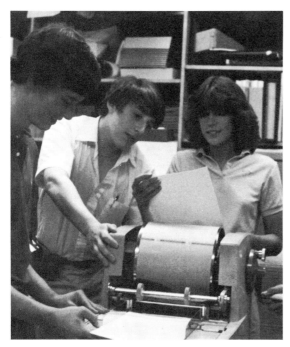

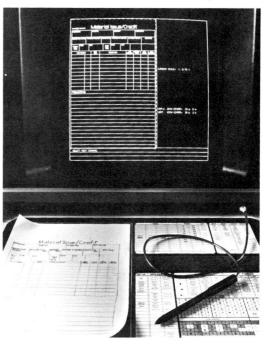

School newspapers can be printed at low cost with a mimeograph machine.

An electronic stylus can be used to reproduce photos on mimeographed material.

sheets made of a tough, fibrous, coated tissue that is impervious to ink. As the copy is typed, each typewriter key perforates the stencil. The typed stencil is then placed around the cylinder of a rotary duplicator, which may or may not be electrically operated. As the cylinder rotates, paper is automatically fed into the machine. When the paper comes into contact with the impression roller, the pressure forces ink from the ink pad on the cylinder through the perforations in the stencil to reproduce what was typed on that stencil.

Headlines and line drawings can be cut on stencils by means of a stylus, a metal penlike instrument with a rounded tip. Black-and-white photographs can be reproduced by means of electronic stencils.

Previously, mimeographing permitted the use of only one color. Today, however, it is possible to use two colors of ink on the same ink pad. In fact, through the use of a two-cylinder machine, multicolor printing of mimeographed newspapers is possible.

The mimeographing process permits printing more than 500 copies of a four-page newspaper at a cost of from $3.75 to $7.00.

The School Newspaper: Production, Finance, Public Relations

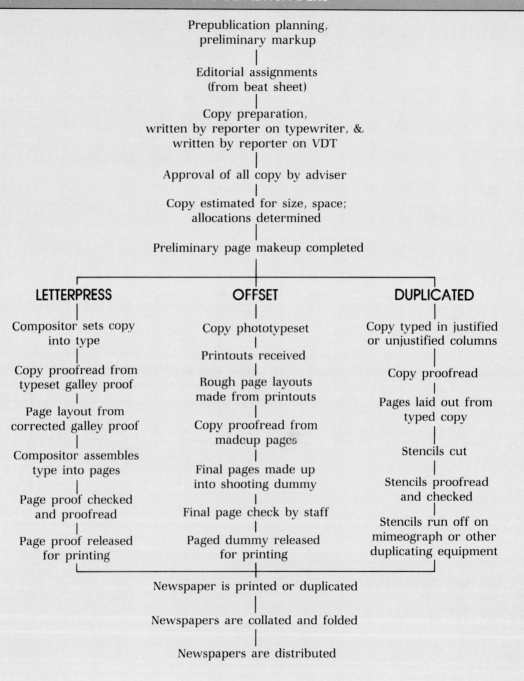

MAJOR STEPS FOR PRODUCING LETTERPRESS, OFFSET, AND DUPLICATED SCHOOL NEWSPAPERS

Prepublication planning,
preliminary markup

|

Editorial assignments
(from beat sheet)

|

Copy preparation,
written by reporter on typewriter, &
written by reporter on VDT

|

Approval of all copy by adviser

|

Copy estimated for size, space;
allocations determined

|

Preliminary page makeup completed

LETTERPRESS

Compositor sets copy
into type

|

Copy proofread from
typeset galley proof

|

Page layout from
corrected galley proof

|

Compositor assembles
type into pages

|

Page proof checked
and proofread

|

Page proof released
for printing

OFFSET

Copy phototypeset

|

Printouts received

|

Rough page layouts
made from printouts

|

Copy proofread from
madeup pages

|

Final pages made up
into shooting dummy

|

Final page check by staff

|

Paged dummy released
for printing

DUPLICATED

Copy typed in justified
or unjustified columns

|

Copy proofread

|

Pages laid out from
typed copy

|

Stencils cut

|

Stencils proofread
and checked

|

Stencils run off on
mimeograph or other
duplicating equipment

Newspaper is printed or duplicated

|

Newspapers are collated and folded

|

Newspapers are distributed

Distributing the School Newspaper

Once the pages of the school paper have been printed on an off-set (or letterpress) press, they are automatically trimmed, collated, and folded. Complete copies of the paper then emerge from the press. These newspapers are collected and bundled and delivered to the school. (In cases where the school paper is duplicated, the news staff is responsible for collating the printed pages and for folding and bundling the individual copies.)

Under the supervision of the circulation manager, staff members distribute copies of the newspaper to students. In some cases, staff members deliver papers directly to designated classrooms. In other cases, staff members deliver the paper to areas in the school designated as distribution centers, where students can obtain their copies.

Financing the School Newspaper

Every school newspaper receives money from subscribers and from advertisers—and perhaps from special funds allocated to it in the overall operating budget for the school. Every school newspaper spends money for printing, for supplies, and for equipment. Sound business procedure, as well as the maintenance of the paper's financial health, demands that accurate records be kept of all money received and of all money spent. Thus, the need exists for a business manager.

The Business Manager

As was pointed out in our discussion of the newspaper staff (Chapter 14, page 320), the primary function of a school newspaper's business manager is to keep the paper financially sound. To do so, the business manager has the critical responsibility of preparing and adhering to a budget.

Preparing the Budget. Working closely with the editor-in-chief and the faculty adviser, the business manager examines the paper's budget from the previous school year. (Our assumption is that the newspaper budget covers income and expenses for the

In 1975 the Columbia Scholastic Press Association conducted a nationwide survey of high school newspaper funding. Significant findings are as follows:

Funding by the sale of single copies or by student subscriptions:

No funds received
from student purchases
or subscriptions: 45.8%
1–25% of total revenue 28.1%
26–50% of total revenue . . .12.7%
51–75% of total revenue . . . 4.9%
76–99% of total revenue . . . 3.8%
100% of total revenue 5%
No response 5.0%

Funding from the sale of advertising space:

No funding received 23.0%
1–25% of revenue 21.0%
26–50% of revenue 19.0%
51–75% of revenue 21.0%
76–99% of revenue 10.0%
100% of revenue 1.0%
No response 5.0%

Funding supplied by student councils:

1–25% of budget 3.2%
of responding schools
26–50% of budget 2.1%
of responding schools
51–75% of budget 5%
of responding schools
76–99% of budget 5%
of responding schools
100% of budget 1.0%
of responding schools

Funding supplied by Boards of Education:

1–25% of budget 8.%
of responding schools
26–50% of budget 10.0%
of responding schools
51–75% of budget 8.0%
of responding schools
76–99% of budget 10.0%
of responding schools
100% of budget 7.0%
of responding schools

entire school year.) With the information available there, the business manager carefully and realistically estimates and itemizes the year's total income from all sources—subscriptions, advertising, and administrative funds. Next, the business manager estimates and itemizes all expected expenses for the current school year, taking into account that inflation may have increased printing costs. The business manager should consult the printer for the best estimate. Furthermore, editorial and production plans may entail added expense. When all estimated expenses have been itemized, the business manager totals those costs and then *adds 10 percent* to create a contingency fund for the unexpected costs that are bound to occur.

The next step in budgeting involves comparing the total estimated income with the total estimated expenses. If they are the same, the budget is in balance. If expenses exceed income, the

CHECKLIST OF RESPONSIBILITIES OF A SCHOOL NEWSPAPER'S BUSINESS MANAGER

✓ Cooperates with the editor-in-chief and the faculty adviser in setting up the year's budget.

✓ Prepares a monthly financial report.

✓ With the aid of the editor-in-chief and the faculty advisor, assigns/delegates the newspaper's business/financial tasks and supervises their execution.

✓ Signs all checks drawn on the newspaper's bank account.

✓ Supervises and assists the circulation manager and the advertising manager.

✓ Inventories all supplies and equipment used in the business operations of the newspaper.

✓ Attends all staff meetings.

✓ Takes an active part in journalism organizations.

business manager and the editor-in-chief must find ways to increase income or ways to reduce expenses. If income exceeds expenses, the excess is put into what is called a reserve fund, from which cash can be withdrawn (at the beginning of the school year) to pay bills that come in before any income is generated.

Once a satisfactory budget has been worked out, the business manager submits it to the editor-in-chief and to the faculty adviser for their approval. (In some schools the newspaper budget must be approved by a school administrator—usually the principal.) If any of the newspaper's income comes from a student activity fund, the organization in control of that fund must also approve the budget.

Two sample budgets for school newspapers appear on page 414.

Drawing Up Contracts.   With the budget approved, the business manager can proceed to draw up contracts with compositors, engravers, printers, and any others who supply materials or perform services for the school paper. In signing a contract, the business manager assures a supplier that the school paper will not take its business elsewhere and that the news staff will meet agreed-on deadlines. The supplier agrees that prices will not increase during the contract period and that supplies will be delivered or services performed according to an agreed-on schedule.

Sample Budget for a Semimonthly Printed Newspaper

Income		Expenses	
Student subscriptions	$2,200.00	Printing	$4,920.00
Subscriptions to alumni and townspeople	900.00	Photography and engraving	660.00
Sales of advertising space	3,500.00	Postage	240.00
		Office supplies, telephone	180.00
		Reserve	600.00
	$6,600.00		$6,600.00

Sample Budget for a Semimonthly Mimeographed Newspaper

Income		Expenses	
Subscriptions	$200.00	Paper	$240.00
Mail subscriptions	20.00	Stencils, ink, mimeograph service and supplies	150.00
Sales of advertising space	300.00	Office supplies, postage	80.00
		Reserve	50.00
	$520.00		$520.00

Keeping Records. Publishing a school newspaper is a business operation and, as a rule, is conducted on a cash basis. Consequently, the business manager and staff need to follow sound business procedures. Doing so requires that each financial transaction be recorded in at least two places.

First, the business manager or a designated staff member must maintain a cash record book or register. (An ordinary checkbook can serve satisfactorily.) When income is received or when money is spent, each transaction must be recorded in that record book, along with the resulting bank balance.

Second, the business manager or a designated staff member must maintain a budget account ledger. Each item in the budget has its own separate page in the ledger. For example, one page might be headed COMPOSITION, another headed PRINTING, another

A TYPICAL CONTRACT

Purchase Order No. _____

South High *Record*

Date _____

To _____

_____

_____

Deliver the following to the South High *Record*, South High School, Newington, or to the bearer. Please refer to the number of this Purchase Order when submitting your invoice.

Quantity	Item	Price	

Approved:

_____

Authorized Signature

headed OFFICE SUPPLIES, and so on. At the top of each page appears the total amount budgeted for that item. Each time money is spent, the amount (a) is recorded on the appropriate page and (b) is deducted from the total. This method clearly shows how much money has been spent and how much remains in the account for each budgeted item.

The budget account ledger contains pages, the headings of which identify sources of income. Examples include SUB-SCRIPTION, ADVERTISING, and so on. Examples of pages from a school newspaper's budget account ledger follow.

A CASH RECORD BOOK   A BUDGET ACCOUNT LEDGER

Expense Account

Printing

Date	To	Amount	Balance
	Total budgeted............................		$4,920.00
Sept. 24	Acme Printing Co.	$332.12	4,587.88
Oct. 8	Acme Printing Co.	344.50	4,243.38
Oct. 22	Acme Printing Co.	326.20	3,917.18

Income Account

Sales of Advertising Space
(Budget: $3,500)

Date	From	Amount	Total to date
Sept. 24	Cash collections*	$112.00	$112.00
25	Cash collections	48.00	160.00
Oct. 8	Cash collections	140.00	300.00
9	Cash collections	24.00	324.00
12	Cash collections	30.00	354.00
12	General Hardware Co.	16.00	370.00
13	Cash collections	28.00	398.00
15	North Way Clothing Co.	24.00	422.00

Handling Money. The business manager is responsible for depositing in the newspaper's bank account all money received from advertising, from subscriptions, and from any other source. To provide adequate safeguards for handling the money deposited, all expenditures are made by check.

For each deposit made, the business manager receives a bank deposit slip stating the date of the deposit and the amount deposited. The transaction is, of course, recorded in the cash record book and in the budget account ledger.

When paying a bill or otherwise spending money, the business manager has a check drawn for the exact amount and then signs it. (In many schools such a check must be countersigned by the faculty adviser.) Again, the transaction is recorded in the cash record book and in the budget account ledger.

To take care of incidental daily expenses, the business manager might set up a petty cash fund, withdrawals from which are made only with the knowledge and consent of the business manager and the faculty adviser. The person who withdraws cash from the petty cash fund signs a receipt for the exact amount. At regular intervals the accumulated receipts are recorded in the cash record book, and a check is then drawn to replenish the petty cash fund.

Supervising Other Business Operations. The business manager works closely with the advertising manager and the circulation manager in order to be aware of any changes in the newspaper's two main sources of revenue—advertising and circulation.

The business manager is also responsible for billing advertisers and others who owe the newspaper money. An example of the kind of statement the business manager might send out is shown on page 418.

Another of the business manager's responsibilities is the issuing of purchase orders for supplies and equipment. An example of a purchase order is shown on page 419.

Finally, the business manager has the responsibility of issuing a monthly financial report detailing all financial transactions during the month and indicating the newspaper's financial status. Copies of the monthly financial report go to the editor-in-chief, the faculty adviser, and the principal. An example of a school newspaper's monthly financial report appears on page 420.

The Advertising Manager

The financial success of a school newspaper depends largely on the effectiveness of the advertising manager and the advertising staff. In addition to contributing to the financial stability of the school paper, advertising contributes a genuine service to the school's business community by fostering good will and making the entire community aware of the total school program.

Estimating Advertising Revenue. During the preparation of the newspaper budget, the advertising manager works closely with the business manager, submitting careful estimates of expected

South High *Record*

Statement

Date _____

To _____

_____

_____

For advertising in the South High *Record*: Date _____ $ _____

Please pay amount due to the sales representative who presents this statement or mail to the *Record*, South High School, Newtown.

revenue from advertising. To arrive at such estimates, the advertising manager, along with the business manager, the editor-in-chief, and the faculty adviser, establishes a schedule of advertising rates.

Assigning Advertising Beats. With the help of the advertising staff, the advertising manager draws up a list of community businesses that are potential advertisers. Then staff members are assigned to call on each of those businesses to sell advertising space in the school paper.

Keeping Records. The advertising manager has the responsibility of keeping accurate records of the businesses called on and of those that purchase advertising space. For each client, the advertising manager records the size (the number of column inches) of the advertisement to be run, the number of issues in which the advertisement will appear, and the advertising rate to be charged.

Drawing up Contracts. Another of the advertising manager's responsibilities is drawing up contracts with advertisers. As an official representative of the school paper, the advertising manager

A PURCHASE ORDER

Purchase Order No. _____

South High *Record*

Date _____

To _____

_____

_____

Deliver the following to the *Record,* South High School, Newtown, or to the bearer. Please refer to the number of this Purchase Order when submitting your invoice.

Quantity	Item	Price	

Approved:

_____

Authorized Signature

signs each contract. (In some cases, the business manager and the faculty adviser also sign each contract.) When a contract becomes effective, the advertising manager—under the supervision of the business manager—is responsible for submitting bills to advertisers, collecting money from them, and depositing all such income in the newspaper's bank account.

Submitting Reports. The advertising manager is responsible for submitting to the business manager a monthly report detailing the amount of advertising space contracted for, all money spent, all money collected from advertisers, and all money due from accounts payable.

A FINANCIAL REPORT AS DRAWN UP BY A SCHOOL NEWSPAPER BUSINESS MANAGER

South High *Record*
Financial Report, November 1, 19 _____

Expenses	Budget	Expenses to date	Amount remaining	Estimated expenses to date
Printing.........................	$4,920.00	$1,002.82	$3,917.18	$ 990.00
Photography, engraving	660.00	102.12	557.88	132.00
Postage	240.00	82.50	157.50	48.00
Office supplies, telephone...........	180.00	24.19	155.81	36.00
Reserve	600.00	0.00	600.00	
Totals	$6,600.00	$1,211.63	$5,388.37	$1,206.00

Income	Budget	Income to date	Amount still due	Estimated income to date
Student subscriptions	$2,200.00	$1,912.50	$ 287.50	$2,200.00
Subscriptions to alumni and townspeople	900.00	721.30	178.70	900.00
Sales of advertising space	3,500.00	544.00	2,956.00	642.00
Totals	$6,600.00	$3,177.80	$3,422.20	$3,742.00

Cash on hand, September 1	$ 216.90
Income to date	3,177.80
Total received	$3,394.70
Expenses to date	1,211.63
Cash on hand, November 1	$2,183.07

CHECKLIST OF RESPONSIBILITIES OF A SCHOOL NEWSPAPER'S ADVERTISING MANAGER

✓ With the editor-in-chief and the faculty adviser:
  a. Establishes the percentage of newspaper space to be devoted to news and to advertising, respectively.
  b. Establishes the fee to be charged for each column-inch of advertising.
  c. Establishes guidelines for accepting and rejecting advertisements.
  d. Determines the number of persons needed for the advertising staff.

✓ With the advertising staff:
  a. Determines the number of prospective advertisers to be approached by each staff member.
  b. Sets up guidelines and deadlines for submitting advertising copy.
  c. Establishes an effective system for billing advertisers and for collecting money.

✓ Turns over to the business manager all money collected from advertisers; receives a properly signed receipt.

✓ Attends all staff meetings.

The Circulation Manager

The school newspaper circulation manager and staff are responsible for newspaper sales, subscriptions, deliveries, and mailings and for promotional campaigns aimed at increasing the paper's circulation.

The sale of advertising, a major source of income for any newspaper, depends on the circulation. Advertisers have the right to expect the newspaper to reach all of the students. The circulation manager's responsibility is to ensure that the school paper is distributed to as many students as possible. Representatives are designated to sell the paper and to make sure that all students have access to the paper through a distribution system involving homerooms or strategically located distribution points within the school.

Selling the School Newspaper. The sale of the school paper to from 75 to 80 percent of the student body is considered satisfactory, but every circulation manager seeks to increase that sale to as close to 100 percent as possible. In many schools, subscriptions are sold either for one semester or for one year. Subscription rates, of course, may vary from year to year, depending on the financial condition of the newspaper, the number of issues printed, and the cost of production.

Mail subscriptions are usually sold at the student rate plus postage. Subscriptions are often sold to residents of the community, who often become buyers of advertising space.

Developing Sales Campaigns. The circulation manager is responsible for planning and executing sales campaigns designed to increase circulation. Usually developed around a theme, sales campaigns can involve contests and other activities to spark student interest in subscribing to the school paper.

Keeping Records. The circulation manager is responsible for maintaining accurate records of the numbers of newspapers sold, delivered, and mailed. The efficient use of receipt books and ledgers will expedite the task. All such records must, of course, be made available at any time to the business manager, the editor-in-chief, and the faculty adviser.

Exchanging Newspapers. Many schools maintain a newspaper exchange agreement with other schools. Usually the circulation manager designates a staff member to supervise the exchange operation and to keep accurate records. An exchange arrangement permits the circulation manager and the entire staff to study newspapers received from other schools and then to try new ideas for page makeup, copy flow, production procedures, and promotion campaigns.

CHECKLIST OF RESPONSIBILITIES OF A SCHOOL NEWSPAPER'S CIRCULATION MANAGER

When the newspaper is distributed free of charge:

✓ Meets with the editor-in-chief and the faculty adviser (and perhaps the school principal) to determine
   a. The most efficient way of distributing each issue of the paper.
   b. Suitable drop-off locations—places for effective schoolwide distribution.

c. The most appropriate time for delivering the paper to the agreed-on drop-off locations.

d. The optimum size of the circulation staff.

✓ With the circulation staff, develops a building map on which each drop-off location in the school is clearly identified.

✓ Assigns a circulation staff member to each drop-off location to check on the adequacy of the number of papers delivered and to supply any additional copies needed.

✓ Assigns a circulation staff member to each drop-off location to collect any unclaimed papers.

✓ Attends all staff meetings.

When copies of the paper are sold to individual subscribers:

✓ With the editor-in-chief and the faculty adviser, plans and implements effective sales procedures.

✓ With the editor-in-chief and the faculty adviser, determines the optimum size of the circulation staff.

✓ With the circulation staff, plans and implements a sales campaign that emphasizes the purchase of yearly subscriptions to the school paper.

✓ Makes sure that each homeroom (or room designated for the daily taking of attendance) is canvassed by a circulation staff member to sell individual subscriptions to the school newspaper.

✓ Gives each circulation staff member the responsibility to see to it that the required number of copies of the paper are delivered on time to designated drop-off locations and that the papers are properly distributed to student subscribers.

✓ Assigns a responsible staff member to collect the subscription fees paid by student subscribers; makes sure that all money collected is properly accounted for.

✓ Turns over to the business manager all money collected.

✓ With the circulation staff, plans and carries out an effective public-relations program. (See the third item of this section.)

✓ Attends all staff meetings.

Maintaining Good Public Relations

With efficient production procedures in place and with a sound financial operating plan established, one important matter remains for the news staff to consider—the maintenance of good relations with the newspaper's readers.

Identifying and Holding the Paper's Readers

In Chapter 2, "Newspapers" (pages 18–45), we pointed out that professional newspapers sometimes experience difficulty in reaching and holding a reading audience. High school newspapers may also face the same problem. Editors—both professional and school—need to find a way to narrow whatever gap may exist between their newspapers and their readers. No one has yet found the perfect way to close that gap, but many have tried. Some practical steps a high school newspaper can take to identify and hold its readers are as follows:

1. Increase the dialogue between readers and news staff. To do so, the staff might conduct audience studies—room-to-room studies, spot studies, random interviews, invitations to readers to react to the newspaper, and the regular printing of a column of "Letters to the Editor."

2. Identify the students (freshmen in a four-year high school, sophomores in a three-year high school) who took journalism in junior high, and make them "stringers" for the school paper. In addition to helping the staff, such an arrangement can give these students a sense of serving the school. The "stringer" idea can also be extended to include club and organization officers.

3. Thoroughly understand the "makers of news." Being able to recognize these traditional elements of news, along with the information gained about the changing newspaper audience and the school itself, will help the beginning reporter keep readers' interests in mind.

4. Set up an *ad hoc* advisory committee of students representing all classes in the school. The committee should include students from all academic, social, and ethnic groups and should mirror a wide spectrum of interests—from members of the student council to students taking auto mechanics.

5. Conduct a staff study that will give some ideas of the readership at the school and of the activities that hold the greatest interest for students and teachers. (This suggestion is one that can be adapted to any school situation.) The purpose is to find out as much about the school and the student body as possible. Then when tough editorial decisions need to be made, the editor has access to the information needed for making valid judgments. To conduct such a study, the staff can develop a questionnaire. A good example of a questionnaire, shown below, was drawn up by the news staff of *The Purple Sage*, Greendale Senior High School, Greendale, Oklahoma.

KNOW YOUR READER
WHO IS THE READER OF THE PURPLE SAGE?

1. *The Purple Sage* is the official school newspaper of Greendale Senior High School.
2. The enrollment at Greendale is _____ .
   Freshmen _____
   Sophomores _____
   Juniors _____
   Seniors _____
   Teachers _____
3. The school curriculum offers _____ solid classes and _____ electives.
4. There are _____ organizations that have a total of _____ students enrolled.
5. There are _____ activities that have a total of _____ students enrolled.
6. There are _____ students enrolled in work-study programs.
7. The school has these major sports, each with enrollment shown. (Include all teams.)
   Football _____
   Basketball _____
   Others _____
8. Student Expenses:
   Books and instructional materials:
       $ _____
   Yearbook: _____
   Newspaper: _____
   Athletics (participant): _____
   Athletics (audience): _____
9. Regularly elected student officers:
10. Classes with largest enrollment: _____
11. School levy: _____
12. Total amount of school budget: _____
13. Favorite leisure-time activities: _____
14. Student officers _____
    Student Body Officers: _____
       _____
       _____
       _____
    Room representatives (attach list)
    Class officers: President _____ Vice-President _____ Secretary _____ Treasurer _____
    Freshman _____
    Sophomore _____
    Junior _____
    Senior _____
15. Major annual projects of each class:
    Freshman _____
    Sophomore _____
    Junior _____
    Senior _____
16. What is the major goal for the school this year? (See Principal.)

NOTE: Each department of the news staff will add questions and seek answers that are valuable to it. A mathematics class with access to computers might work with the staff in setting up and analyzing answers given on this readership study.

Informing the Community about the School and School Events

On occasion the school news staff may encounter protests—even condemnation from the school administration, and from the community itself. The clash of cultural differences, differing values, differing religious beliefs, the generation gap, and general misunderstanding can produce such conflict. For example, students and adults alike are aware of problems that may arise concerning teenagers. Although the high school news staff may write about these subjects fairly and honestly, such subjects may—by their very nature—elicit strong emotional reactions. It is at this point that high school news staffs find themselves facing possible censorship. They ask, "Will we be allowed to print this material?"

If high school journalists understand the traditional "makers of news" and if they understand further that newspaper audiences change, they will be better prepared for possible disagreements with parents, teachers, and fellow students. Instead of asking, "Will we be allowed to print this material?" student journalists might avoid possible censorship by asking questions like these: "What kinds of information about these subjects do our readers need?" "How can we write in a mature, intelligent way about these sensitive subjects without inviting emotional school/community protest?"

One positive approach is to make sure that all avenues of communication are kept open. Those involved in doing so include (a) the school news staff, (b) the faculty adviser, (c) the school administration, and (d) community advisory groups like the PTA. Keeping avenues of communication open means seeking to handle potentially controversial subjects in ways that everyone concerned can live with.

Many stories about school events are often newsworthy enough to be of value to the editors of local newspapers. School newspaper editors-in-chief often appoint students—preferably students who plan to make a career in public relations and/or newspaper journalism—to serve as the newspaper's press representatives. Such representatives, in effect, constitute a kind of school news bureau. The press representatives are responsible for preparing and sending school news to the local newspaper editor. When there might be some question about the editor's interest in a particular story, the press representatives can check by telephone. Most school news bureaus prepare and maintain listings of all major school events worthy of news coverage.

Following is a checklist, prepared by the National School Public Relations Association, that may be used as a guide to determine coverage of specific school events. The guide may also be used by school press representatives to determine the types of school news usually of interest to local newspaper editors.

CHECKLIST FOR COVERAGE OF SCHOOL EVENTS

Elementary School
✓ Special unit features

✓ Field trips

✓ Special day projects (Valentine's Day, Thanksgiving, etc.)

✓ Students entertain parents

✓ School plays, pageants, etc.

✓ Kindergarten events

✓ Intraschool sports, contests

✓ Music programs, operettas, etc.

✓ Special education

Junior High School
✓ Shop and homemaking features

✓ The junior high guidance program

✓ Clubs

✓ Music, dramatics, and dance activities

✓ Students study foreign languages (use of displays, foreign books)

✓ Student publications

✓ Honor societies, student council

✓ Honor rolls

✓ Students help in office, library

✓ Special trips, projects

Senior High School
✓ Business education feature

✓ Clubs, publication, etc.

✓ School productions-drama, music

✓ Special projects (shop, physics, home, etc.)

✔ Students prepare for jobs after graduation

✔ Scholarships, guidance talks

✔ Honor rolls

✔ Contests, sports events

✔ Print shop, auto shop

✔ Student government

General School

✔ School board

✔ School elections, referendums

✔ Teaching staff

✔ School finances

✔ Parent-teacher associations

✔ Citizens' committees

✔ Professional conferences

✔ Maintenance and janitorial activities

Activities

1. With a classmate, work out a realistic production schedule and a realistic advertising schedule for a future issue of your school newspaper. Submit your completed schedules to the editor-in-chief for consideration and possible adoption.

2. What method does your school newspaper use for setting copy into type? What is the cost of setting type by this method? What typesetting methods might reduce the paper's typesetting costs? If the paper changed to another method of composition, what changes might be required in content and format?

3. By what printing process is your school newspaper produced? What is the cost of printing the paper by this method? How does this cost compare with other printing methods? If the newspaper changed its printing method, what changes would be required in content and format?

4. How does the process by which a school newspaper is printed influence what that newspaper prints?

5. With two or three classmates, work up a comprehensive plan to ensure the financial stability of your school newspaper. To do so, you will need to consider questions like these:

- **a.** How will you create a demand for the paper?
- **b.** How will you ensure—perhaps increase—readership and interest?
- **c.** How will you persuade local business people to advertise in the paper?
- **d.** How will you increase the amount and the effectiveness of the advertising?
- **e.** How will you control production costs?
- **f.** What kind of record-keeping system will you adopt?

6. Assume that you are the advertising manager for your school paper. As such, you will need to have a schedule of advertising rates to show prospective advertisers. Work up what you consider to be a realistic and attractive schedule of advertising rates. Submit your schedule to the business manager and the advertising manager of the paper for consideration and possible adoption.

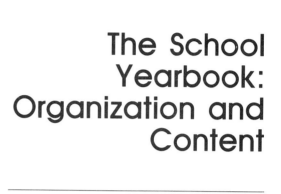

CHAPTER 18

The School Yearbook: Organization and Content

"I've called us together this afternoon"—it's Violet Evanson speaking—"to see if we can agree on a theme for this year's *Banner.*" Vi is the editor-in-chief of the East High School yearbook. "Dan and I were talking yesterday, and we thought that maybe a theme would help make all of our jobs easier."

"That's right, Vi," nods Dan Vickery, the business manager of the *Banner.* "Having a theme seems like a good idea. It'll. . . ."

"Well, last year's *Banner* didn't have a theme," interrupts Christy McDougall, the advertising manager. "And all the kids thought it was a great yearbook."

"Maybe so," continues Dan. "But Mike Swenson—you know, last year's business manager—told me that they barely squeaked through financially."

"That's true." Mrs. Montoya, the faculty adviser, confirms Dan's remark. "This year's reserve fund isn't very healthy."

"But I don't see," persists Christy, "how a theme will help us get ahead."

"Well, you sure need one," Joel Hayes, the subscription manager is impatient. "What's wrong with considering a theme? It seems to me that having a theme and letting everybody know what it is might help boost sales right from the start. We're starting our subscription campaign on the first of October; and if we can focus the campaign around a theme for this year's *Banner*—the theme has to be a good one, of course—boy, what a business we might do!"

"How about 'East High—the Salt of the Earth'?" suggests Boyd Feldman, the managing editor.

"Not enough pepper," laughs Nell Bostick, the art editor. "We'd have a tough time illustrating nothing but salt!"

"Well, I mean . . .," Boyd starts to explain.

"I've got it! I've got it!" exclaims Ted Bashefsky, the photo editor. "How about 'Up, Up and Away'? Great picture possibilities!"

"Hey, m-a-y-b-e." Vi seems to like the suggestion.

"Yeah, maybe," agrees Dan. "But I think we need to let the idea bubble a while. Let's not rush it."

There is general agreement.

"OK," says Vi. "Nell, will you and Ted and Boyd—and Christy— act as a 'theme committee'? See whether 'Up, Up, and Away' can be related to each section of this year's *Banner*. Do you think you can have a recommendation for us by next Monday?"

"Yes, I think so," says Nell.

"It'll soar!" Ted is enthusiastic.

"Next Monday then," says Vi. "At two we'll meet again—here."

Planning the Yearbook

Few books in the average home are read and referred to as often as the school annual, or yearbook. Because the information, the pictures, and the layouts in the yearbook will be seen by the children—and perhaps the grandchildren—of the members of the graduating class pictured in it, it is essential that the writers and the editors chosen to work on the school yearbook be intelligent, responsible individuals. They must be capable of giving future readers an accurate view of what took place that year at that school.

Planning the yearbook should begin as early in the school year as possible. Many yearbook staffs begin their planning the summer before the school year; however, a full year is usually sufficient time in which to complete the average yearbook, provided that the staff is well organized and competent. The techniques used to produce successful yearbooks do not differ greatly from the techniques used to produce successful school newspapers. Like work on the school newspaper, all work on the school year book must be carefully scheduled. Organizing, copy editing, proofreading, writing selections, and cropping photographs—all techniques similar to those used to produce school newspapers—are the techniques that members of the yearbook staff will need to utilize. Because you have studied many of these techniques in previous chapters in this book, this chapter will deal only with those necessary to organize and write for the school yearbook.

Organizing the Staff

Schools select their yearbook staffs in various ways. Sometimes the yearbook adviser selects the students who will fill the major staff positions. Sometimes members of the staff of the year just past select their successors. And sometimes a board of publications does the selecting. The chart on page 434 shows the staff organization for a typical school yearbook. The following paragraphs describe the functions of key members of the *editorial staff*. Although other staff members are noted here, too, their functions are described at greater length in the appropriate sections of Chapter 19, "The School Yearbook: Copy Editing, Layout and Design," on pages 458–473 or Chapter 20, "The School Yearbook: Production and Finance," on pages 474–487.

The Editor-in-Chief. The yearbook editor-in-chief must be a competent organizer, capable of supervising the yearbook staff and scheduling the flow of materials to and from the printer. Directly responsible to the faculty adviser, the editor-in-chief has the overall responsibility of meeting established deadlines. To accomplish this task, he or she must select a competent staff, who will help produce the kind of yearbook that everyone can be proud of. Final decisions concerning the yearbook cover, theme, sections, budget, and overall policy rest with the editor-in-chief. This person must be capable of commanding respect from printers and suppliers and must be tactful but firm in dealing with staff members.

The Business Manager. The yearbook business manager has a function equal in importance to that of the editor-in-chief. A detailed discussion of the business manager's responsibilities begins on page 482.

The Managing Editor. The managing editor is responsible for all of the yearbook editorial functions: writeups, captions, photos, copy editing, layouts, and proofreading. The managing editor must check all this material before it is sent to the printer and

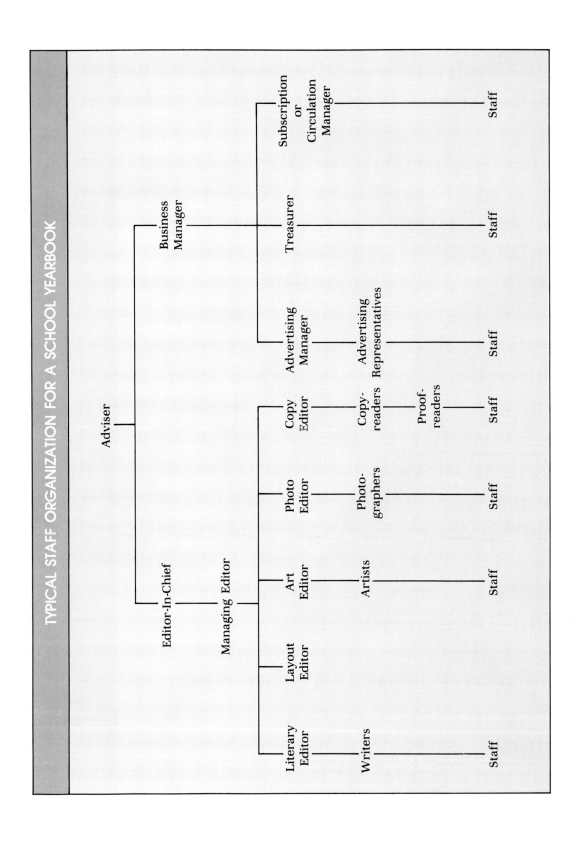

TYPICAL STAFF ORGANIZATION FOR A SCHOOL YEARBOOK

Adviser

Editor-In-Chief

Business Manager

Managing Editor

Literary Editor

Layout Editor

Art Editor

Photo Editor

Copy Editor

Advertising Manager

Treasurer

Subscription or Circulation Manager

Writers

Artists

Photographers

Copy-readers

Advertising Representatives

Proof-readers

Staff

Staff

Staff

Staff

Staff

Staff

Staff

therefore should know what comprises a good writeup, photo, and layout. This position requires a person who can work smoothly with the editor-in-chief and with the entire yearbook staff. In many schools the managing editor will submit a list of candidates for the major editorial posts: literary editor, layout editor, photo editor, and copy editor. These recommendations must then be approved by the editor-in-chief.

The Literary Editor. The yearbook literary editor must know what constitutes effective prose. When choosing staff members, the literary editor should seek students who share an interest in and a love for the English language. It is essential that the literary editor and the literary staff be well grounded in the basics of English: grammar, syntax, spelling, and punctuation. Because most of the stories, captions, and headlines in the yearbook will be written by the literary editor and the literary staff, they must strive constantly for accuracy.

The Layout Editor. The layout editor of the school yearbook is the person responsible for all the layouts on all pages of the yearbook. To do layouts requires looking at blank dummy pages and visualizing the placement of headlines, print, illustration, and white space. The most effective layouts are the ones that are the most pleasing and readable. The layout editor establishes guidelines about the size of pictures. For example, the decision might be made that all pictures showing fewer than three persons would be no larger than four inches wide. Other major responsibilities of the layout editor are helping to choose the theme of the yearbook and helping to plan the opening section.

The Art Editor. The art editor chooses the art, illustrations, and cartoons and sees to it that themes and major ideas are carried through on every page. Good planning of the art will contribute in a major way to the unity of the yearbook.

The Photo Editor. The yearbook's photo editor should have many of the qualities of the art editor. Knowing what constitutes an excellent picture for the yearbook will enable the photo editor to encourage staff photographers to take pictures that tell a story, that have action, that emphasize closeups, and that possess good technical quality. The photo editor should never accept prints that do not have solid blacks and whites, plus a complete range of grays. The photo editor works closely with the managing editor to make certain that all requests for photo coverage are fulfilled. If the layout editor wants a photograph of unusual dimensions, the photo editor is responsible for relaying the specifications to the photographer. The photo editor is responsible for the safe-keeping and distribution of school-owned photographic equipment and supplies.

The Copy Editor.   Among the hardest workers on the school yearbook staff are the copy editor and the members of the copy-editing staff. A detailed discussion of the responsibilities of the copy editor and staff begins on page 460.

The Advertising Manager.   As with the school newspaper, year-book revenue comes principally from two sources—circulation and advertising. The advertising manager's main goal is to help publish the best yearbook possible without incurring any debts. Further details about the responsibilities of the advertising manager make up the discussion on page 484.

The Treasurer.   In many schools, bills sent to yearbook sub-scribers and payments made to yearbook suppliers are the re-sponsibility, not of the business manager, but of the yearbook treasurer. The yearbook treasurer is responsible for supervising all financial matters and for dealing with the bank. Much of the bookkeeping for the yearbook comes under the treasurer's su-pervision. In many ways the yearbook treasurer's duties are simi-lar to those performed by the business manager of the school newspaper, as discussed in Chapter 17, ''The School Newspaper: Production, Finance, Public Relations'' on pages 396–429.

The Subscription Manager.   An important staff member on the yearbook team is the subscription manager. Without sales, the best written, edited, and produced yearbook would be a failure. The subscription manager's chief responsibility is to sell the year-book. Further discussion of the subscription manager's duties appears on page 486.

Determining the Format

Two major concerns in the planning of any school yearbook are unity and emphasis. To give the yearbook unity, the staff should select a theme—a central idea. To give the yearbook balance, the staff should give equal emphasis to all elements in the life of the school during the year. The yearbook should reflect an honest appraisal of the entire year so that years later a reader will be able to look at the yearbook and say, ''That's the way it was.''

Yearbooks reflect the personality of the school.

The Theme. The central idea underlying a yearbook is its theme. The format for the entire year is planned around that theme. If it is to be effective, the theme for any yearbook must be pertinent to each of the following:

1. A specific school
2. A specific senior class
3. A specific school year

It is better to have no theme at all than to have one that fails to emphasize any one of these criteria. The advantages of having a theme are many: A theme gives unity to all sections of the yearbook; it helps make the yearbook different from any other yearbook; it makes the yearbook timely; it helps make the yearbook creative; it can give the yearbook real meaning to the graduate in the years to come.

An example of the successful use of a theme is one high school's decision to make *time* the focus of its yearbook. The cover and the opening section made good use of the following quotation from *Ecclesiastes* III, 1-8:

> To everything there is a season, and a time to every purpose under heaven; a time to be born, and a time to die, a time to keep silence and a time to speak, a time to weep, and a time to laugh, a time to embrace and a time be be far from embraces. A time to get, and a time to lose, a time of war, and a time of peace.

The School Yearbook: Organization and Content

"Time, you old gypsy man, will you not stay, Put up your caravan just one day?"
Ralph Hodgson

"to everything there is a season, and a time to every purpose under heaven. . . ."

Photos throughout the opening section illustrated phrases from this quotation. Division pages throughout the yearbook used other quotations concerning *time.*

When searching for an appropriate theme, yearbook staff members need to consider pertinent questions like the following:

1. Is this theme right for your school? Does it show the school at its best? Does it typify the school? Does the administration approve? Does it represent the entire student body?
2. Can the theme be translated effectively into visual and written expression? Can it be effectively illustrated with the time and the talent available? Can it encompass all sections of the yearbook?
3. Is the theme trite or contrived? Is it childish, crude, or otherwise incapable of reflecting the talents and abilities of the yearbook staff?
4. Would the yearbook be better off without a theme? Will carrying out the theme cause so much difficulty that not enough time can be given to other features of the yearbook? Does the theme constitute an honest effort to say something worthwhile, or is it simply a way of filling up empty division pages?

Layout and art editors design division pages to carry the theme of the yearbook.

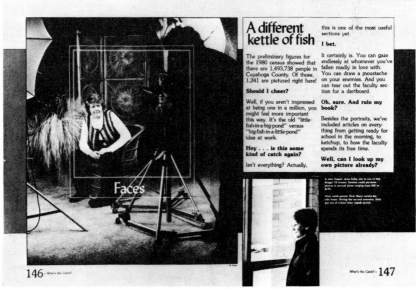

When searching for a theme, the editor-in-chief and the layout editor should try to select one that gives satisfactory answers to all of these questions above. After screening several possibilities, they should submit their results to the entire editorial staff and to the faculty adviser, listening to constructive comments before making a final decision. In considering a theme possibility, the editor-in-chief should consult with the photo editor and the staff photographers to discuss picture possibilities.

Ideally, the theme should be carried through on the cover, the end pages, the table of contents, page one, the opening section, and the division pages. The yearbook staff should, of course, be prepared to abandon any chosen theme they find too difficult or too time-consuming to carry out effectively. Choose a theme carefully, for what may seem clever or witty or humorous today may seem trite or in poor taste a few years from now.

End pages of the yearbook sum up and carry out the theme.

Yearbook Sections. Before the yearbook staff can begin their work, they need to know what sections will be included, approximately how many pages will make up each section, and what the page size will be. In making these decisions, the editor-in-chief and other key members of the staff should look at the yearbooks from preceding years. Those yearbooks can give general ideas about the number of pages to allocate to each section. Then once the business manager presents the yearbook budget, the number of pages in the book can be established. The overall number of pages will, of course, depend both on the budget and on the amount of material to be included. The overall number of pages desired can be determined by first estimating the number of pages that the pictures will occupy, and then estimating the amount of space to be devoted to all other sections based on their relative importance.

When choosing a page size, yearbook staff members should avoid nonstandard sizes. Standard page sizes for most yearbooks are 9″ by 12″, 8½″ by 11″, and 7¾″ by 10½″. Irregular sizes should be avoided to prevent printing problems and paper wastage. Margins are determined with the help of the printer, based on the amounts of space necessary to achieve the most attractive-looking pages.

If it has been decided to use a theme, an opening section devoted to words and pictures depicting this theme might be suggested. Although the arrangements and names of sections can vary considerably from school to school, most yearbooks include the following sections: opening, faculty, graduates, classes, features, organizations, athletics, and advertisements. Larger schools having larger yearbooks often have several other feature sections. A discussion of yearbook covers appears in Chapter 20, "The School Yearbook: Production and Finance," page 481.

The Opening Section. First impressions mean a great deal: the opening section should have major impact on the reader. This section usually presents the greatest opportunity for creativity. (Often, the other sections of many yearbooks retain about the same general format from year to year.) As with every section in the yearbook, the opening section should be broken down into workable units. Considerable thought must be given to the opening section's end pages, the title page, table-of-contents page, and to illustrations. Usually, each part of the opening section is assigned to a different person.

1. *End pages*—Since most printers prefer (for binding purposes) to use heavier paper as stock for the end pages, it is best not to place photographs on end pages. However, many school yearbooks do place line

The opening-section end pages announce the theme.

drawings on the end pages. The end paper should match or complement the color of the cover, and it is usually best not to use solid black ink on them or on any other pages in the book. When a line drawing is used on the end pages in the front, the same illustration is usually repeated on the end pages in the back.

2. *Title Page*—The yearbook's title page represents an opportunity for a great deal of creativity in the use of type, art, and overall design. The title page should always include the name of the yearbook, the year, and the name and address of the school. Whether or not it precedes or follows the pictorial portion, the title page should be an odd-numbered (right-hand) page.

3. *The Table of Contents*—Included on this page will be the various section titles and their page numbers. In listing the contents the material contained within each major section may be broken down into comprehensive descriptions. Many yearbooks place a full-page picture on the page facing the table of contents, balancing such elements on the table-of-contents page (another odd-numbered page) as the school seal or large type faces. As on all other special pages, it is best not to crowd too many elements onto one page. Combined masses of typographical elements with white space usually produce an artistic effect. Some schools reproduce small pictures of the division page illustrations on the contents page.

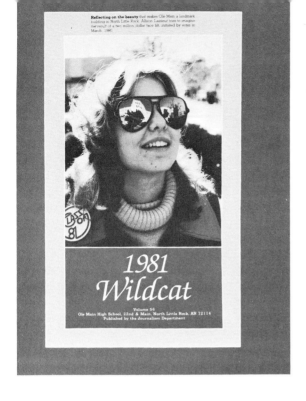

Reflecting on the beauty that makes Ole Main a landmark
building in North Little Rock, Allison Lassieur tries to imagine
the result of a two million dollar face lift, initiated by voters in
March 1980.

1981
Wildcat
Volume 56
Ole Main High School, 22nd & Main, North Little Rock, AR 72114
Published by the Journalism Department

This interesting title page invites readers to open the yearbook.

4. *Illustrations*—Ideally, the photos used in the opening section should set the theme for the yearbook. They should be top-quality pictures, and should be given enough space to make an impact. Their sequence should have unity and coherence. If a poem is used as the theme, an attempt might be made to have each photograph illustrate a few lines of the poem. Editors should consider having a professional photographer take the pictures for the opening section and division-page pictures. Division-page photographs should continue the yearbook theme and should also depict the subject of the section. Some yearbooks use one full page as the division page; others use two full pages. Before taking any pictures, it can be helpful for photographers to know how their pictures are to be used. For example, if a picture is to appear on page one, the photographer should take a vertical picture; if the picture is to appear over two pages, the photographer should take a horizontal picture.

The Faculty Section. A formal arrangement of photos and layouts is often used for the faculty section. Some schools use candid photos of faculty members, taken while teaching or in their offices. A photographic montage division page (many photos cut apart and mounted as a composite) can be used to introduce the faculty section. It should show as many faculty members as possible.

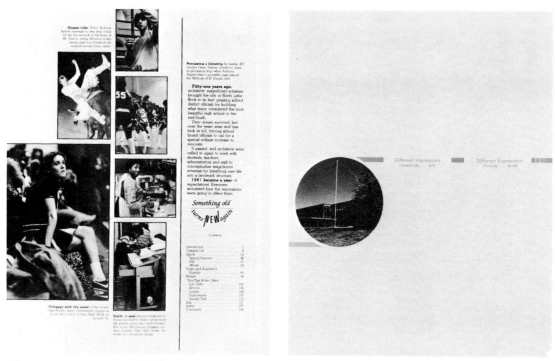

These pages are two different and interesting ways to show the table of contents.

Sometimes civic or school officials write congratulatory messages to the members of the graduating class. These messages should be placed on the same page as the picture of the official who wrote the message. A handwritten message must be reproduced large enough to be easily read. Because yearbook editors can usually complete this section early in the school year, such messages and their accompanying pictures should be secured as soon after school starts as possible.

Some yearbooks use formal faculty portraits. Sometimes faculty members do not have portraits available, and yearbook staff members assigned to the faculty section will need to request that faculty members obtain satisfactory portraits. Some schools have descriptive material of faculty members set in type for emergency use when photos are unobtainable.

Many schools place faculty pictures in alphabetical order; others lay out pictures of teachers by the departments they teach in. Still others place teachers in the faculty section according to their length of service at the school. Yearbooks sometimes print each teacher's degrees, along with colleges attended, with the teacher's photograph.

Human-interest photos add appeal and give impact to the yearbook.

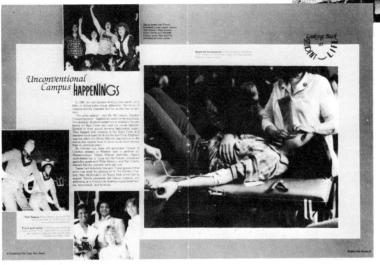

This faculty page shows imagination and creativity.

The Class Section. The class section can often be scheduled for early completion. The class section is usually one of the most important and popular sections of the yearbook, provided that each student is pictured in it. The portrait photographer, often chosen the previous year or during the summer, can usually schedule sittings immediately after the opening of school. A number of schools have found it convenient to have the portrait photographer take the group pictures as well.

The yearbook editors often place candid photos throughout the class section that show the activities of the various classes. Other editors frown on this practice because experience has shown that candid shots detract from the formal pictures.

To help achieve uniformity, editors should work with the photographer to see that students know what type of clothing to wear for their portraits. The photographer should be experienced in doing yearbook photos and should know what color background to use for every picture. Poses and headsizes must be uniform, and the photographer must submit identical picture sizes to the yearbook staff. A popular size for class section portraits is two inches wide by three inches deep. Glossy prints are generally preferred.

The class section is the most looked-at part of the year-book.

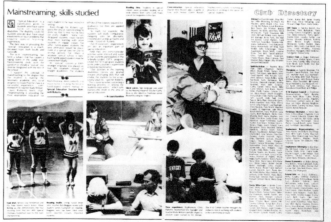

446

After all of the yearbook pictures have been obtained, they should be filed in alphabetical order. Some yearbooks use only the student's name and picture; however, most yearbooks use other descriptive information such as course of study, student organizations, and offices held. Be certain to spell the student names correctly. Spelling—in this and in all other sections—should be triple-checked. No degree of artistic perfection in the other sections will be compensation to a student whose picture and writeup are not perfect.

The Feature Section. The feature section usually singles out students who have made outstanding contributions to the school and contains material about activities students will want to remember. Some schools place a dedication in this section; others locate the dedication in the opening section. Regardless of placement, the dedication must be well written. The student assigned to write the dedication must research the subject thoroughly. The dedication should not be overly sentimental, nor should it sound like a sermon. It is usually more effective when kept light and informative. A large, excellent-quality photograph usually accompanies the dedication.

This is an interesting example of an opening spread of a feature section.

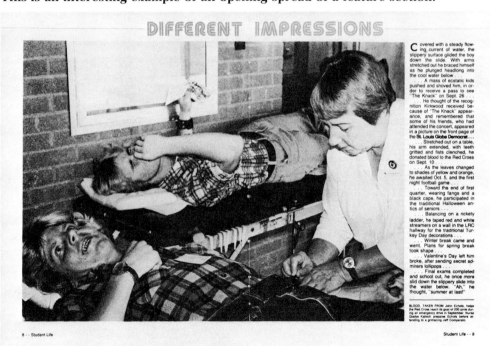

This feature section shows education in the school.

Although the feature section is an ideal place to recognize the class valedictorian and other honored students, close deadlines sometimes make it impossible for the yearbook to identify and applaud the students who might win those honors. An alternative suggests that yearbook editors devote the space to students named to the National Honor Society, thus helping to present the school as an educational institution. Often yearbooks tend to overemphasize extracurricular activities.

The feature section can also include such other items as homecoming activities, holiday programs, dramatic productions, student council elections, and special assemblies.

The Organizations Section.   Yearbook editors often devote considerable time and effort to the organizations section. In addition to scheduling pictures and getting accurate identifications, yearbook staff members must produce interesting, well-researched writeups about each of the organizations in the school.

First, staff members for the organizations section usually plan to have the yearbook photographer come to the school to spend an entire day or two taking group pictures. Schedules for such pictures are approved through the school's administrative offices and usually allow for at least a half-hour to photograph each organization. Organizations should be informed a few weeks in advance of the scheduled dates. In addition to notifying the officers of each organization, yearbook staff members can put up posters and insert notices in the school newspaper to remind students. Students should be told how they are expected to dress; for example, cheerleaders should be in uniform. A yearbook staff member should be available at all times during the shooting schedule. A membership list should be obtained from each club or organization president or adviser to be checked a few minutes prior to the time scheduled for the organization's photograph. A mimeographed form that facilitates the accurate recording of identifications could be made available. Staff members should be sure that proper photograph identifications are taken before allowing a group to disband. Identifications can be checked with the organization after the photographer submits prints.

After all organizations have been photographed, the photographer should provide glossy prints in the proper size. When prints are delivered to the yearbook staff, great care must be taken with them to prevent the emulsion cracking and the print being ruined. Prints should be filed and the organizations' names written lightly on the backs. Writeups for each organization should be completed by the time the photographer delivers the prints. Writeups, captions, headlines, and photos should be shown to the club president and faculty adviser.

This organizations–section opener attracts readers interest.

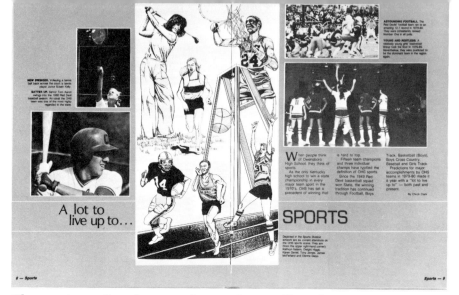

The sports section shows variety and versatility of sports activities.

The Sports Section. The amount of space given to the sports section is usually determined by the intensity of student interest. Although football, basketball, baseball, and track are the major sports at most schools, other sports such as hockey, soccer, swimming, golf, and tennis also deserve coverage.

Once priorities and amounts of space have been assigned for each sport, coverage should get under way. Group pictures of each team (in uniform) will, of course, be needed. The sports department of the local newspaper can often provide glossy photos. Extensive photo coverage should be planned early in the school year. Football action pictures should be assigned early in the school year because weather conditions may be bad later in the season. The photographer should watch for "color" shots: the coach on the sidelines, cheerleaders in action, spectators cheering, the band playing during halftime, and the team coming onto the field.

Yearbook basketball coverage is similar to yearbook football coverage. However, since the yearbook sports deadline is close to the basketball season, basketball action shots should be taken during the first few games of the season. Spring sports present still another problem. Because they take place after the yearbook deadline is past, some yearbooks use pictures taken during the previous season; other yearbooks limit their coverage to posed shots of the various teams. Talk to the coaches in the fall. Coaches have a pretty good idea of the makeup of their teams, and the staff photographer can take posed "candid" shots of team members.

The Advertising Section. Although work on the yearbook's advertising section is actually done by members of the advertising staff, the yearbook editorial staff can help the next year's sales representatives by making the advertising section as attractive as possible. If the advertising section doesn't look good, advertisers will often be reluctant to renew their advertisements. The introductory division page for the yearbook's advertising section might be a general view of the community's commercial area.

The advertising section is usually a good place for candids that don't fit into other portions of the book. Advertisers are pleased to have photographs included in this section, as it ensures that students will then see every advertisement.

For practical reasons, the advertising section is usually one of the last sections of the yearbook to be completed. It is always advisable to plan to have a number of photographs available for fillers in this section. When advertising space is sold, the photos can be replaced with advertisements. If space remains, the photographs can, of course, be retained. Sometimes school yearbooks carry the label "Autographs" at the top of each blank page of the advertising section. But they remove the label if and when last-minute advertisements are obtained.

Imaginative handling of the advertising section is essential because the revenue derived from it is of utmost importance to the financial success of the yearbook.

The advertising section can be handled in a wide variety of attractive and appealing ways.

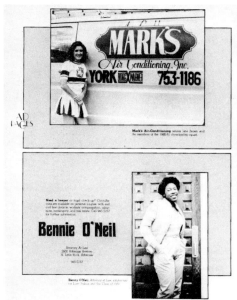

Writing for the Yearbook

Sections

Since the words published in the school yearbook will live for many years, they should be chosen with the utmost care. Skilled student writers who have done well in their composition classes are usually assigned to a yearbook section according to their special interest areas and abilities (such as feature writing or sportswriting.) Ordinarily the yearbook editor-in-chief will write the dedication, the foreword, and the epilogue. Reporters should interview the presidents of the various school organizations to get the facts for the stories that accompany the pictures of each school activity. The reporter should find out the group's major accomplishments and "the story behind the story."

There is an art to the ability to summarize the year's activities of an organization in a few sentences, and yearbook writers should concentrate on learning how to say a great deal in a few, well-chosen words. Yearbook writers must also concentrate on what the organization has done during the year, supplying facts rather than vague generalities. All writeups and photographs should complement each other. Writeups should be kept concise.

Because most yearbook articles are written early in the school year, writers must include activities that have not yet taken place. When interviewing an officer of an organization, the writer must be sure to ask what future events the group is planning. Then the writeup itself should mention only those activities that are definitely scheduled. Yearbook writers must be sure that what they write is correct insofar as grammar, usage, spelling, and punctuation are concerned. Above all, yearbook writers must be sure that what they write is accurate. Following is an example of a writeup for a yearbook's organization section:

> One of the outstanding honors a student of Gloucester High School may receive is election to the Sherman B. Ruth Chapter of the National Honor Society. To be considered for membership, a student must exhibit not only scholarship but also leadership and character.
>
> Each year a scholarship is awarded by the Honor Society to one of its members who plans to further his or her education. The organization sponsors many fund-raising activities, such as selling stamps and candy. Members also act as guides for all official ceremonies of the school. Miss Claudia Perry is the Chapter's sponsor.
>
> *Flicker*

Features like the foreword, the epilogue, and the dedication offer opportunities for creative writing. However, the writer must be brief and make every word count. Using the title "Blithe Spirit," one yearbook published the following dedication:

> A bubbly personality . . . an exuberant spirit . . . a zest for life and her work— the essence of the teacher whose warm heart and understanding nature have helped us bear the "slings and arrows" of our year at HHS. She was not only a teacher but a friend. Her classes and her homerooms were always exciting. We have been guided by her friendly cooperation, her enthusiasm— and we shall remember it always. In grateful appreciation we dedicate this yearbook to Mrs. Olga Garick.
>
> *Hanoverian*

In the foreword, the yearbook editor-in-chief may want to establish the yearbook's theme. This aim is often achieved either by choosing an appropriate poem or by presenting the editor's own words. Choice of an appropriate poem for the foreword is usually made by the literary editor in consultation with the editor-in-chief. The following foreword is on the theme of "friendship."

> The students with whom we share our days and experiences are truly our friends. The strong ties among them are obviously held as the Alma Mater is sung at the assemblies and games, and there is a friendly atmosphere throughout the halls.
>
> A friend is, as exactly defined, more than one whom you know; a friend is one who answer all your needs and brings special happiness into your life.
>
> As we gaze at the individual pictures of all the students, we remember the joy and fun each one brought Stonewall. The great bond of friendship is truly a General Quality.
>
> *Jacksonian*

Class writeups should summarize, in a concise way, the *unique* aspects of the year. How did this year differ from all the others? The following is an example:

> BWH's Senior Class spent their last year of high school actively participating in the many school activities of the year. Seniors served in their school faithfully through the many service clubs and organizations at West High. The members of the class discov-

ered many rewards in being upperclassmen during an exciting year of games, pep assemblies, and dances. There were disappointments such as a wet, snowy Homecoming, and triumphs such as the third consecutive victory over East High on the gridiron, and then finally the Senior Banquet, Senior Week, Baccalaureate, and Commencement. The Senior Class ended the last year of high school with a profitable year behind them and the future they had been preparing for throughout their years at West waiting ahead of them.

Westward

Some yearbooks publish a Class Ode written by one of the senior staff members. Ordinarily, this poem summarizes the writer's philosophy of life. Here is an example:

Quickly we must climb aboard,
The ship will wait no more.
We must leave now this snug harbour
And embark for a strange, new shore.

We must leave that which is familiar
And sail toward what is new.
So powerlessly we watch and wait
As our harbor fades slowly from view.

Straining, we try to recapture
The moments that slip away.
But the progress of the ship is steady.
Only memories are left us today.

We should not linger at the stern,
For we must hurry to the bow.
Only there, we may hope to catch a glimpse
Of the new life which beckons us now.

What will this new life mean for us?
What events does it secretly hold?
Only God knows the answers
Which He will in time unfold.

For God is the weathered pilot
Guiding always our ship of time.
And in His hands lies the destiny
Of the crew—all of humankind.

Westerdays

In the Epilogue, the writer—most often the editor-in-chief—has an opportunity to give advice to the senior class and to express a philosophy about life. Here is an example:

How difficult it is to relinquish the carefree ways of youth and assume the responsibilities of adulthood. As a child's first steps are often unsure, so are our first ventures into the adult world. We are eager for new experiences, challenges, and achievements. Yet, are we ready to tuck away our youthful irresponsibility?

The era in which we live has an atmosphere of constant change. As the growing child discards toys and games, so does youth reject the ideals of adults. Time proceeds, and no segment of the population can impede progress. What we reject today as absurd and ridiculous will probably be an accepted part of our life in later years.

So we are no longer children; we must try to assume the responsibilities of society. As we seek success in diverse fields we shall discover it also will come in varied guises. For some individuals, wealth will measure success; others will attain power or prestige. Perhaps our success will be the personal satisfaction derived from knowing that we have found our identity and place in a complicated society. We all hope that success will be the attainment of happiness. This quest is the challenge of youth. As part of a perceptive generation, the Senior Class must now accept life's challenges. Youth contains hope for the future; awareness is the hope for youth.

The Witch

Captions

A glance at any yearbook will show that the majority of material set in type consists of the names that are included in the captions. Every picture (even the candid photos) used in the book should have some sort of identification. Such identification often consists merely of labels such as "Gary and the Gang." Often, picture identifications need not be complete sentences. Usually, the more names used, the better. Captions for pictures accompanying writeups should be short; in addition, they should always contain the names of all persons shown. If no writeup is used with a picture, the story should be told in a caption. Organization pictures must always have complete name identifications. If two pictures of different organizations are placed on the same page, yearbook editors should accompany the name of the organization with any list of names. An example of such a caption follows at the top of page 456.

Index

Yearbooks containing more than 100 pages usually have an index that includes the names of all organizations, activities, and persons appearing in the book. A number—or numbers—after every entry indicated the page—or pages—on which information about the index entry can be found. One general index, presented as an easy-to-read reference section in which everyone is listed, is preferable to several smaller, complicated indexes. The index should be prepared from the final dummy as each section is completed, usually with each entry typed on a separate 3 by 5-inch file card. The cards are then organized alphabetically and a master list, from which the printer sets the copy, is typed from them.

An index can use art and photography to make it lively and interesting.

1. List five ideas for suggested themes for your school's next yearbook.

    a. In class, discuss all ideas submitted, comparing your theme possibilities with those offered by your classmates.

    b. With your classmates, select the one theme possibility that has the most appeal.

    c. As a class project, plan ways to utilize the chosen theme in the school's next yearbook.

    d. Present the theme and its possible use to the yearbook committee for consideration.

2. What yearbook position do you feel that you are best qualified to fill? Briefly explain why you think you could fill this position satisfactorily.

3. Study a copy of last year's yearbook and make a list of suggested improvements for this year's yearbook.

4. With your classmates, identify any faults you have found in last year's yearbook, and suggest how similar mistakes might be avoided in this year's book. Add these suggestions to the suggested list of improvements you made in your consideration of item 3 above. Submit your list of suggestions to the yearbook committee for consideration.

5. Write a short article about a school organization of interest to you. Make the article suitable for publication in the school yearbook. Submit your article to the editor-in-chief.

6. List five ideas for picture stories suitable for the opening section of this year's yearbook. Expand your listing by including ways of handling photo assignments for the picture stories.

7. In outline form, suggest a unique way to handle material for the feature section of this year's yearbook. Be specific about ways of achieving a balanced representation of both academic and extracurricular activities.

8. Write a 200-word yearbook dedication about a faculty member of your choice. Interview the subject to obtain pertinent information to include in your dedication. Be sure to solicit reactions from your classmates about your subject. Consider their reactions for inclusion in the final draft of your dedication.

CHAPTER 19

The School Yearbook: Copy Editing, Layout, and Design

"Hey, Maureen, when will the writeup for the Sophomore Class be ready?" Joe Unland, copy editor for the West High *Pioneer,* calls over to Maureen Roberts, the literary editor.

"Two minutes. OK?" replies Maureen. "I'm just finishing the rewrite of the first paragraph."

"OK, Betty," Joe turns to copy assistant Betty Mayo, "have the sophomore photos come in yet?"

"Yes, Josh developed them yesterday and then brought them to me. I've shown them to Susie. She thinks they'll need to be cropped to fit the two-page spread she has laid out."

"Cropped? How?"

"Well, Susie thinks—and I agree with her—that the school building in the background of both photos should be cropped so that the photos will fit the horizontal space allotted."

"Does Phyllis think so, too?" (Phyllis Brustein is the layout editor.)

"She hasn't seen them yet. But she told me she'll be over as soon as she and George finish their examination of the Senior Class layouts."

"Here's the Sophomore Class Section writeup." Maureen hands the paper to Joe. "Mac Ansaldo did a good job. The only thing is that maybe the writeup is too long."

"Thanks, Maureen." Joe looks at the writeup. "It may be too long, but we'll see."

"I'll have the yearbook dedication writeup ready for you on Thursday," says Maureen. "In the meantime, let me know whether Mac's writeup has to be cut, will you?"

"Sure will, Maureen. Ben Sanchez will copy edit the writeup. If he has to cut it, I'll let you know."

"Hey, Ben, here's the Sophomore Class Section writeup. Get out your style guide for copy editing."

Ben comes over to Joe's desk. "Hmm," he muses as he looks at the writeup, "it looks longer than the writeups for the other class sections. I may have to cut it to fit the layout."

"OK. But if you do cut, let me see the final version. I've told Maureen I'd let her know."

"Sure thing," says Ben. And off he goes to copy edit the writeup.

"Betty," says Joe as he turns toward her, "will you hold the fort for a while? I've got to go over those Senior Class layouts with Phyllis and George. George has scheduled them to go to the printer tomorrow."

Once the yearbook budget has been approved and the theme determined, and once the writeups and the photographs for the various yearbook sections start coming in, the copy editor, the layout editor, and the art editor take charge. Their competence and dedication in carrying out their respective responsibilities can result in an attractive, successful yearbook. The copy editor and the copy-editing staff are responsible for the polishing of all raw copy submitted; the layout and the art editors and their staffs are concerned with the effective and artistic placing of materials on the yearbook pages. The contributions of these three editors are critical to the overall success of the yearbook.

The first part of this chapter suggests useful procedures for the copy editor and staff to follow. The second part of the chapter focuses on procedures for the layout editor and the art editor and their staffs to follow.

Copy Editing the Yearbook

As suggested on page 361, the copy editor and staff must be reliable, dedicated workers. In handling writeups, headlines, captions, and photographs, they are often the last staff members to see yearbook material before it is released to the printer. Careless copy editing, trite headlines or captions, improperly cropped photographs, sloppy layouts, or negligent proofreading—any of these shortcomings can ruin the yearbook.

Developing a Style Guide

When the literary editor finishes a writeup or article, the copy editor must double-check each word. To expedite the task and to ensure uniformity throughout the yearbook, the copy editor and the staff should prepare a style guide consisting of at least four sections: spelling, punctuation, capitalization, and abbreviations. See the example style guide on page 364 in Chapter 16, "The School Newspaper: Copy Editing, Layout, and Design."

Spelling. Although dictionaries frequently list more than one acceptable spelling for a given word, the copy editor and staff should choose one spelling of such a word and use it consistently. For example, this word has three "correct" spellings: *goodbye, good-by,* and *goodby.* In developing a style guide, the copy editor and staff should decide on the one spelling they prefer and then stick with that spelling throughout the yearbook.

Punctuation. All written material in the yearbook should conform to established conventions of punctuation. The "when-in-doubt,-leave-it-out" rule used by some school newspapers is seldom permitted in the use of yearbook materials. It's a good idea, for instance, to insert a comma before *and* in a series. (Example: "Boyd, Chambers, Swenson, and Moore won the relay.") A hyphen should connect two or more words used as one. (Example: "Helen is a three-time winner of the slalom.") A colon should follow the words *as follows* or *the following* when those expressions introduce a list. (Example: "Left to right, the officers are as follows: J. Hornby, R. Schneider, S. Thibault, B. Waters.") Use *no colon* after any form of the verb *to be.* (Example: "Left to right, the officers are J. Hornby, R. Schneider, S. Thibault, B. Waters.")

Capitalization. Most school yearbooks follow an "up" style; that is, they capitalize the first letter in each important word of a title and in each word of a proper name. (Examples: Wykoff High School; Roger Qualman.) Although some school newspapers use a "down" style (Wykoff high school) the "up" style has preference.

Abbreviations. Most yearbook copy editors avoid abbreviations when they can. However, when abbreviations must be used, they should be consistent—used the same way each time. For example, editors in states like California and Pennsylvania must decide whether to use *Cal.* or *Calif.*, and *Penn.* or *Pa.*, and then stick with whichever abbreviation they choose.

Following Style

Once a style guide has been developed, the copy editor or a designated staff member uses it to copy edit every writeup, every feature article, every headline, and every caption to appear in the yearbook. In addition, the copy editor makes sure that all written material is grammatically correct and that all sentences are easily read and understood. The copy editor should also seek to eliminate clichés and cute or precious expressions. Examples of clichés include "busy as a bee," "worked like a beaver," "a gentleman and a scholar," and "that's for sure." Examples of cute or precious expressions include "li'l darlin'," "cutey pie," "my one and only," "like Mother used to make," "sweetums."

Meeting Other Responsibilities

After a writeup has been copy edited, the copy editor has it retyped, making at least one copy for the files. That copy can serve as a ready reference when the original has been released to the printer. In case the original is lost or misplaced (something that does happen), the file copy can serve as a replacement. When the copy-edited material has been retyped, the copy editor checks it once again to make sure that it contains no typographic errors.

It is the copy editor's responsibility to know how much copy is needed to fill each page of the yearbook. Because writeups about the various school organizations are best kept to about the same length, the copy editor must often shorten an article that runs too long. On the other hand, if an article is too short, the copy editor must become a writer-reporter and add sufficient copy to lengthen the article appropriately.

Competent copy editors—decided assets on any yearbook staff —follow the copy-editing procedures discussed on pages 361–362 in Chapter 16, "The School Newspaper: Copy Editing, Layout, and Design." They also follow the standard copy-editing symbols shown in Appendix VI.

Proofreading

Yearbook copy editors are usually the last staff members to see the final yearbook materials before the materials are released for printing and binding. They have the additional responsibility of proofreading all final copy. Because changes made on final galley proof are costly and can often introduce further errors, proofreaders and copy editors should not rewrite merely for the sake of rewriting. If a sentence is acceptable as it stands, it should be left as is. Unnecessary rewriting takes time and often demoralizes staff writers. The standard proofreading symbols used by most yearbook proofreaders appear in Appendix V.

Writing Headlines

Before making decisions on the type of headlines to be written for each group portrayed in the yearbook, copy editors must know the total number of pages planned for the book. When more than one organization is placed on each page because of space limitations, copy editors often use, with the pictures for each organization, a headline consisting of only the organization's name. When each group is allocated an entire page, more creative, lengthier, headlines and kicker lines can be considered.

Creative headlines add impact.

Once the headline type sizes have been selected, the maximum count for each headline should be determined. (The count refers to the total number of letters and spaces contained in a line of print. See pages 367–382.) A simplified count of one unit for each letter and space is usually acceptable. For example, if a 36-point type face is selected for many of the yearbook's headlines, the editor might decide that each headline should be between 20 to 25 units in length.

When writing headlines, copy editors should try to prepare phrases that are interesting but that aren't juvenile or trite. Headline writers often try to be unusual in their presentations by using portions of well-known sayings, popular songs, or alliterations. Headline writers find that sometimes they don't have enough room for necessary verbs. They then try to "peg" the headline to the accomplishments of the group being written about. For example, following an undefeated basketball season, one school headlined its yearbook basketball squad's picture page with "Quite a Quintet!" Another school used "Miami's Math Marvels" above a picture of its math club, and "The Reel McCoys" was used with the picture of an audiovisual club. Other examples of unique yearbook headlines are these: "A Goalie's Nightmare," "The Groups Behind the Teams," "Thespians of the Future," "Latin Linguists," and "Neophyte Nurses."

Cropping Photos

Since the largest portion of space in yearbooks is devoted to photographs, establishing the correct proportions for photographs is of major importance in yearbook production. In doing the layout for a given page, the layout editor should instruct the photographer to print photographs in dimensions that will add eye appeal to the page layout. If the layout editor has only a vertical photograph when a horizontal shape will better suit the format, the layout may suffer. A good practice is to encourage photographers to take several photographs, each one from a different angle, in order to present a choice of sizes for use with differing formats.

Once the photograph to be used has been selected, the layout editor must indicate any of the unnecessary portions not to be printed. Grease-pencil crop marks (delete marks) are usually used to indicate the portions to be deleted. The pencilled crop marks show how the print is to be reduced or enlarged to the specified size, giving emphasis to the most important area of the photograph. When too much of the photograph has been marked for cropping, it is often necessary to have the photographer reprint,

Cropping a photo changes its shape to fit a specific shape. At left photo is cropped vertically, right, same photo cropped horizontally.

reproducing only the area specified. Sometimes a cropped photograph that has been enlarged too much may suffer from a loss of quality of the remainder of the photograph. After cropping, the layout editor must determine the amount of space the photograph will occupy on the page. When a photograph is reduced in height, it reduces proportionately in width. The diagram on page 466 shows how the width and height of a photograph are affected when the original is proportionately reduced. In the diagram *A, B, C,* and *D* represent the four corners of the photograph. The measurements for a reduction can be determined by drawing a ruled line diagonally across the back of the photograph (dotted line *E-F*) and marking off the desired height *(G-B),* and drawing from the bottom of that point *(G)* a horizontal line *(G-H)* that intersects the ruled dotted line *(E-F),* then drawing a vertical line *(H-I)* to the top of the print. The measurements of the rectangle *(I-B-G-H)* will be the measurements for the reduced print.

Next, the exact size of the reduced photograph is drawn in location on the page layout. The final size is marked lightly on the back of the print (or pasted so that the front of the print is not harmed). The picture should be checked against its caption to make sure that both are accurate. For identification purposes, the picture, its caption, and the layout should each be coded with the same coding symbol, letter, or number.

DETERMINING THE REDUCTION OF A PRINT

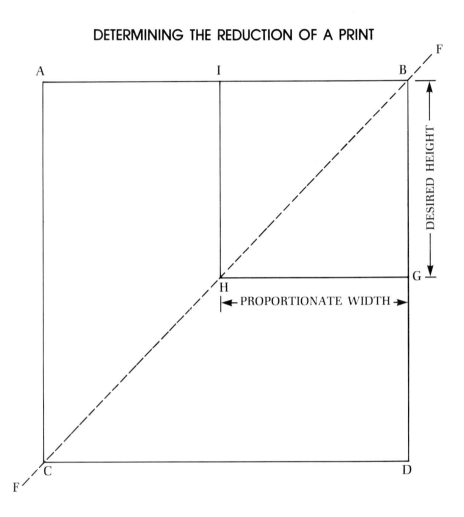

Laying Out the Yearbook

Just as an architect works with wood, stone, and space to plan a building, a layout editor works with pictures, type, illustrations/ artwork, and space to plan the yearbook layout. Both the architect and the layout editor are artists. There is an art to handling yearbook layout elements, and yearbook layout editors, using artistic skills, have the opportunity to create an artistic achievement. Every school has students who are creative and artistic. These students can effectively place layout elements on a page with an inherent sense of order and simplicity. They know that the three critical elements characteristic of all good writing—unity, coherence, emphasis—are equally important in laying out the yearbook.

CHECKLIST FOR YEARBOOK LAYOUT EDITORS

✓ As soon as the yearbook editor-in-chief and adviser establish a stylesheet and the ground rules for layouts, begin working on rough, thumbnail sketches for each two-page spread in the section that has been assigned to you.

✓ As soon as layout sketches have been completed for all pages in your assigned section, review them for consistency of picture sizes, headline sizes, and length of copy.

✓ Discuss the layout sketches with the editor-in-chief, the yearbook adviser, or the designated staff member.

✓ Redo the layout sketches as necessary, transferring approved layout sketches to final layout sheets.

✓ Be exact. When a photograph is to be bled into the margin, the layout *must* so indicate.

✓ Sketch in all headlines exactly as they are worded.

✓ Mark every copy block and picture indicated on the layout. Work with each two-page spread until every element has been located in its desired position.

✓ On the layout, mark the first picture on the left-hand page as "Picture A," the next one as "Picture B," etc. Also mark (or attach) these same identifications on the backs of all pictures. Each block of copy should be similarly marked with a code symbol, letter, or number, both on the page layout and on the copy.

✓ Print the page numbers at the bottoms of all layout pages, keeping a record of all of the materials that have been placed on each of the pages.

✓ Secure final approval for the layouts and send them, with their accompanying pictures, copy, and headlines, to the printer.

Unity

A theme and a consistent style for layouts help a yearbook achieve unity. To further ensure unity, layout editors usually work on facing pages at the same time. They try to use a uniform amount of copy and number of headlines and pictures on each page, to make layouts for each section similar in general style.

To determine the amount of space an article will take when printed and to ensure that all writeups will run about the same length, yearbook staff members might follow this procedure. First, each article should be typed on standard-size paper, 8½ by 11 inches, with a one-inch margin at the left and at the right. After the article has been carefully proofread, the writer counts the number of typewritten lines. If the copy is to be set in an 11-pica measure, the writer divides the number of typewritten lines by *three*. The result indicates the number of inches of space the article will take when printed. If the copy is to be set in a 14-pica

To have unity, layouts should be similar in style.

measure, the writer divides the number of typewritten lines by *four*. If the copy is to be set in a 22-pica measure, the writer divides the number of typewritten lines by *six*. For example, suppose that a yearbook article about the school orchestra takes 28 typewritten lines. If the article is to be set in an 11-pica measure, it will require 9⅓ inches of space. If it is to be set in a 14-pica measure, it will take 7 inches of space. Finally, if it is to be set in a 22-pica measure, it will take 4½ inches of space.

The editor-in-chief can help the yearbook achieve unity by setting up a few general rules, such as the following:

■ Not more than three pictures or six sentences or one headline may be used on any one page.

■ The physical boundaries for photographic layouts, are preset, with the edges of pictures aligned whenever possible.

■ A definite margin should be maintained with at least one photo touching this predetermined margin at least once on each two-page spread. In the style shown in Figure 1 the pictures are squared off with the margins.

■ To bleed pictures (extend the pictures beyond the margins to the edge of the page), photos should not bleed more than once from each edge of a two-page spread, as in Figure 2.

■ Figure 3 shows the variety that can be achieved by using equal-size layout elements in different ways.

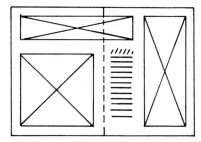

Fig. 1. Layout with photos

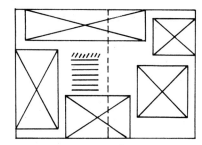

Fig. 2. Layout with bleed photos

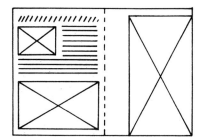

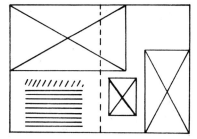

Fig. 3. Two layouts using equal-size elements

The School Yearbook: Copy Editing, Layout, and Design

Coherence

Yearbook page layouts that have coherence also have balance. For example, a skilled layout editor would rarely face a full-page picture with a three-inch-square picture: The pages would not be balanced. Some layout editors think of a two-page spread, imagining that a fulcrum has been placed at the bottom center of the pages; when a layout element is placed on one of the pages, that page will tip down. To equalize the pages, the layout editor places on the opposite page an element having approximately the same "weight." For example, photos with predominantly dark tones have more weight than do lighter pictures having light backgrounds. Consequently, layout editors try to equalize (or anchor) pages by placing the darker pictures on the bottom. They can then locate the "lighter" elements on the page above a heavy, strong element.

Lighter photos should be placed above darker photos.

Emphasis

The most important elements on a page should be the ones to attract immediate attention. Layout editors make the most important elements the largest elements on the page. Photographs can be emphasized by presenting them as strong horizontal and vertical shapes, avoiding square compositions (the least effective shape). Standard size photos (4 by 5, 5 by 7, or 8 by 10 inches) can usually be cropped to make the most important parts of their compositions more forceful.

In order to ensure that the principles of unity, coherence, and emphasis have been followed, yearbook editors-in-chief should go over all page layouts before the layouts are released for printing. Some layouts may have to be redone. When it becomes necessary to redo layouts, the person who did the original should be shown the problem and asked to participate in a good solution.

Formal and Informal Balance

The two basic layout patterns used in most yearbooks are called formal and informal, as in Figures 4 and 5. While both patterns use the same basic layout elements—type, pictures, and white space—each of these patterns is distinctly different from the other. With formal balance, a page looks like a reversed reflection of the page it faces. The advantage to using a formal layout pattern is that such a pattern assures that the yearbook will have unity in visual appearance. The disadvantages to using a formal layout pattern are these: (1) The layouts can often look static and lifeless. (2) The use of photos is limited. (The layout editor may have difficulty finding a suitably shaped photo needed for a page.)

With informal balance, the layout elements for each page (while often retaining similar weights) are not placed in an identical pattern. The major advantage to using an informal layout pattern is flexibility. For example, on a two-page spread the layout editor can better emphasize the most important picture on the spread by making it a completely different size than any other photo on the spread.

Many layout editors prefer allowing the photos to dictate, at least to a degree, the final outcome of the two-page spread, rather

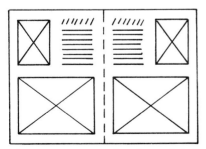

Fig. 4. Layouts using formal balance

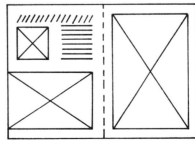

Fig. 5. Layouts using informal balance

This layout shows an effective use of informal balance.

than having a preconceived pattern worked out before seeing the actual pictures. Studying the layouts in professional publications can give layout editors helpful ideas for their yearbook layouts. Many mass media layout editors use more headlines and type on left-hand pages than on right-hand pages because the reader's eye is conditioned to read from left to right.

School yearbooks are the creations of student artists who create with words, cameras, and layouts. A school's yearbook reflects student enthusiasm, talent, creativity, and intelligence. The staff must carefully weigh and consider each step taken to help produce the yearbook, and all members of the yearbook's staff must conscientiously perform to the best of their ability. Then can the yearbook make the school proud.

Activities

1. From the faculty adviser, obtain a copy of an unedited writeup or feature article intended for use in the yearbook.

Using the copyreading symbols given in Appendix VI, copy edit the writeup or the article. Retype the edited copy. With a classmate, exchange original writeups and copy-edited versions. Discuss the reasons for the changes each of you made.

2. From last year's school yearbook, select five headlines that you think could be improved. Rewrite each headline, making sure that it will fit into the available space. Ask a classmate to evaluate your work. Next, select five captions that you think could be improved. Rewrite them as you think they should be. Again, ask a classmate to evaluate your work.

3. Obtain the page size of your yearbook and cut out a piece of white paper with similar dimensions. Then, from colored construction paper, cut out several rectangles and blocks to represent makeup elements (copy and photographs). Arrange the makeup elements on the white paper in as visually pleasing a manner as possible. When you are pleased with the results, paste the makeup elements in place on the white paper. Compare your layouts with those made by your classmates. Select the three best.

4. Try to improve on the layouts of two sections from last year's yearbook by drawing new layout sketches of a two-page spread for each section.

5. Clip a vertical photograph (at least 5 by 7 inches) from a magazine. By proportionately reducing and cropping the picture, give it a horizontal format.

CHAPTER 20

The School Yearbook: Production and Finance

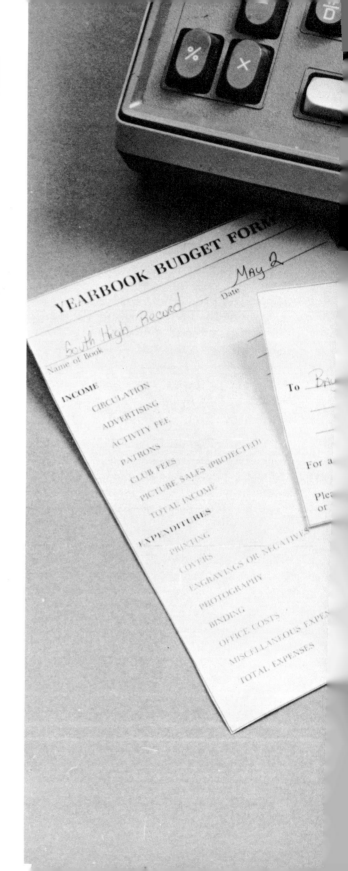

"There it goes again!" Marcie Hoyt, subscription manager for the Lincoln High *Wildcat* pounds the desk in frustration. "This old junk heap of a typewriter has had it! . . . And so have I!"

"Anything wrong, Marcie?" mocks Joel Shomoto, *Wildcat* treasurer. "I used that old heap yesterday. The *e's* wouldn't print. So I just gave up and waited until Scott was through using the literary section typewriter. No problem there."

"Not only don't the *e's* print, but the type goes up and down like the lines on a stock market chart. I can't type out our plans for the follow-up promotion campaign on this relic!" Marcie explodes in disgust. "Say, Joel, how about getting a new typewriter? Will the budget allow it?"

"Better talk to Mac. He's the business manager, and he knows what the budget can stand and what it can't."

"Ok, I will. Hey, Mac . . . ." Marcie heads toward Mac's desk. "Joel, where's Mac?"

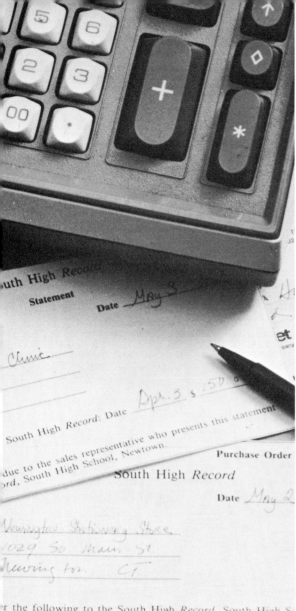

"Oh, he's at a scheduling conference with Jenny and Mr. Taylor. They're trying to work out a plan for getting the *Wildcat* covers printed on time. They've been at it off and on for a couple of days now."

"Well, the period's about over, and I've got to go to chemistry. Tell Mac I want to see him, will you? The sooner, the better. Thanks, Joel."

It's 2:15. Leaving the chemistry lab, Marcie heads toward the yearbook office. As she stops at the water fountain, Mac comes along. He, too, is headed for the *Wildcat* office.

"Hey, Marcie, Joel tells me you wanted to see me."

"I sure do." Marcie gets right to the point. "You know that old typewriter the subscription department inherited? Well, it's falling apart. It's so old Columbus could have charted his course on it. But I sure can't use it to type out our proposal for the follow-up promotion campaign."

"Gee, it's really that bad?"

"Yes, it is. Just ask Joel. But what I want to know is this: Can we buy a new typewriter for the subscription department? Is there enough money in the budget?"

"Yes, there is."

Marcie stops short, staring at Mac in profound disbelief.

Mac chuckles. "You thought I was going to ask you if you were out of your tree, didn't you? Well, luckily, last year's *Wildcat* took in more than anticipated. Tell you what. Why don't you and Joel look into the matter? See how much a new typewriter—or a good used typewriter—will cost. Let me know, and I'll talk with Jenny and Mr. Taylor. I don't think there'll be any problem."

"Super!" exclaims Marcie. "Mac, I love ya!"

Producing the Yearbook

Producing a school yearbook on time requires that schedules must be adhered to strictly. Unless deadlines are met, all the creativity, talent, and intelligence that the yearbook staff reflects will be wasted. Yearbooks that arrive after graduation cannot be greeted with the same degree of student enthusiasm as would those that arrive on time. The final responsibility for the punctual arrival of the yearbook lies with the editor-in-chief.

The Editor-in-Chief

The key to publishing a successful yearbook is the editor-in-chief. The person who fills that position must be a good organizer, capable of working efficiently and harmoniously with everyone on the yearbook staff. The editor-in-chief must be a competent administrator, seeing to it that agreed-on deadlines are met and that materials flow smoothly to and from the printer.

The editor-in-chief makes all of the final decisions concerning the yearbook cover, the theme, the various sections into which the yearbook is to be divided, and the way in which those sections are to be presented. The final decisions regarding budget matters and overall policy are made by the editor-in-chief.

To ensure the effective functioning of the yearbook staff and to ensure steady progress in the production of the yearbook, the editor-in-chief must—as a critical first task—set up a realistic production schedule. Such a schedule might follow these suggestions:

Spring. With the help of the faculty adviser, the person designated to be editor-in-chief for the coming school year should select a printer, a professional photographer, and key yearbook staff members. The editor-in-chief will need at least three key people: a business manager to oversee the advertising and subscription sales, a managing editor to supervise the writing and photographic assignments, and a layout editor to supervise page layouts. Special concern is necessary when choosing photographers: a poorly written news story can usually be successfully edited, but a poorly taken photograph must be discarded.

Summer. The summer—especially the month before the opening of school—is the best time to get as much preliminary planning done as possible. The editor-in-chief should schedule meetings with the yearbook managing editor, layout editor, and business manager. A proposed budget, based on an estimated number of advertisements and subscriptions, should be established. Some picture assignments can be made during the summer. Pictorial shots (of the school campus) and many color pictures can be made at this time. With the layout and art editors, the editor-in-chief should study other school yearbooks to help get ideas for the theme, format, division pages, and opening section. The editor-in-chief may also want to prepare contracts for the printer, photographer, and cover manufacturer or talk with the representatives of the yearbook-printing companies. The managing editor and the business manager should propose the names of their suggested staff members.

September. School begins. Attending classes and doing homework demand much of their time, and yearbook staff members must be careful to plan and schedule the time they will have available to work on the yearbook. Once all of the staff vacancies have been filled, the editor-in-chief should call a staff meeting to discuss the overall plan for the book, and to inspire enthusiasm on the part of the staff members. Each staffer must understand the job he or she has accepted. After reviewing the yearbook's general format, the editor-in-chief should divide the staff into groups to allow the managing editor, layout editor, and business manager to discuss assignments with their staff members.

October. The exact number of pages in the yearbook should be determined. The editor-in-chief and the yearbook staff can arrive at that number by examining yearbooks from previous years and by considering the business manager's estimates of the number of advertisements and subscriptions. Staff members who are not serious about their assignments should be replaced. Preliminary sketches for the cover design should be selected and sent to the cover manufacturer. Photographs showing the opening of school, freshmen, football action, and early fall activities should be submitted. The budget should be reviewed with the business manager and the adviser to see if any item is too high or too low.

November. Subscriptions, advertisements, copy, and pictures should be pouring in by now. November is often the staff's busiest month. The managing editor should be concerned with expediting initial copy and photographs to the printer, being careful not to let yearbook material pile up. As soon as yearbook items have been approved, the managing editor must either deliver them personally or put them in the mail. November is the ideal month in which to take class and organizations section pictures. Seniors should be having their portraits taken at this time. Candid photos of parties, assemblies, and Thanksgiving programs should be taken. The football section can be closed out. The staff should also have ideas about how close they are to achieving the goals of the circulation drive.

December. The yearbook staff must anticipate the reduced activity characteristic of this short school month, or December may throw yearbook production behind schedule. Several sections should be finished prior to the holiday: the opening section, the faculty section, the class section, and the organizations section. Cover and end pages can be released. The fall-sports portion of the sports section can be completed, and more than half of the yearbook should be at the printer. The editor-in-chief should plan a meeting with the art editor, layout editor, managing editor, and business manager before or immediately after the holidays in order to determine what remains to be completed. At this meeting the editor-in-chief should also determine exactly how many subscriptions and advertisements the staff has sold to date.

January. Galley proof for copy, captions, photos, and advertisements should be returned to the printer in January. All material should be proofread carefully and checked for typographical errors. Winter events such as plays, musicals, and social functions can be photographed. The yearbook sales representatives should make final visits to potential advertisers.

February. The advertising sales should be completed. Page numbers should be located at the bottom of each dummy page. Galley proof should be checked, with special attention given to the spelling of names. The sports section can be completed, with exception of one page that can be put aside for inclusion of last-minute sports events (such as the winning of tournament by the basketball team). Spring activity pictures should be sent to the printer. By the end of this month only the remaining few pages of the yearbook should be left to be closed out.

March. Early in March the remaining pages should be released to the printer, who should be asked if everything has been received. Final galley proof must be checked, and final plans for distribution of the book can be made. If the printer suggests a pasteup printer's dummy as a guide, the dummy can be done in March. The dummy can also serve as a check on whether or not the printer has received all of the yearbook material. Spring sport and activity assignments can be made to the photographers of next year's book.

April. Final page proof should be checked to ensure that captions have been placed under the proper pictures and that no picture has been lost. Page proof must be checked for typographical errors and returned early in the month. Subscription sales should be carefully rechecked in order to determine the number of copies to be printed. allowing for extra copies to be printed to be sure to have enough yearbooks to distribute.

May. First copies of the completed yearbook should be available, and the most efficient method of distribution should be decided on. Staff members should be assigned to distribute the copies, making sure that everyone who has paid for a copy receives one. All bills should be checked and paid. A meeting with the staff members of next year's yearbook could be planned in order to discuss with them helpful suggestions and advice.

The Printer

The companies that print school yearbooks can usually be divided into two general groups: local and national.

The major advantage in using a local printer is accessibility. Yearbook materials can be delivered to the local print shop, thus saving mailing time. A local printer, who knows many people in the community, is likely to do the best possible job. Local printers are better able to discuss immediate problems. Deadlines, for example, can usually be more easily extended because materials don't have to be shipped over long distances. Yearbook staffers have an opportunity to learn about the printing process by observing the local printer's work on each section of the yearbook.

The disadvantage in having the yearbook printed locally is cost. The local printer usually charges more than a specialized yearbook-printing company with a nationwide operation. The reason: the local printer is not ordinarily set up to mass-produce yearbooks and may not have new equipment.

Contracting with a specialized yearbook printer with nationwide operations has three advantages. First, production costs are usually lower than those quoted by a local printer. Second, because a national printer can take advantage of the latest printing techniques, the quality of the printing job is likely to be superior. Third, yearbook-printing companies often supply yearbook staffs with kits containing equipment, such as photo croppers, and supplies, such as page-layout sheets. These companies often assign a representative, who will answer questions and handle problems for the yearbook staff.

The yearbook editor-in-chief and faculty adviser should plan to spend some time during the late spring or summer talking to both local printers and to representatives of the national yearbook-printing companies. They should discuss the cost-per-page per 100 books, quality, and deadlines schedules, comparing yearbooks produced by both. It is advisable to talk to editors of other schools to discuss the advantages of choosing one type of printer over the other. When judging sample yearbooks presented by the printer's representative, consider such factors as the following: Are the pictures uniform? Does the ink seem to be darker on some pages than it seems on others? Were parts of pictures at the tops and bottoms of pages cut when the paper was trimmed? Are the captions and headlines set in typefaces that look attractive? The production cost per book may seem high and will, of course, vary considerably, depending on the section of the country in which it is printed. Other considerations that affect cost include the printing process, the current cost of supplies, and the unionization or nonunionization of the printshop. Costs will vary according to the page size of the yearbook. The most common yearbook page size is 8½ by 11 inches. However, both smaller and larger formats are available. When determining page size, one needs to know the total number of pages the yearbook is to have. A 250-page yearbook, for example, with 7¾-by-10½-inch pages will be much too bulky. It would be far better to consider fewer pages and go to a 9-by-12-inch page size. The printer can do much to help the yearbook staff decide on the best page size for the kind of yearbook they want to produce.

Printing Methods

Today, most high school yearbooks are printed by the offset method. Pages 405–407 in Chapter 17, "The School Newspaper: Production, Finance, Public Relations" offer a detailed discussion of both the letterpress and offset printing methods.

Use of Color

The decision to use color in the yearbook will raise costs. Books are printed in sections, called signatures, and careful planning of the color sections will give the most color for the lowest cost. Color printing requires a separate plate for each color to be reproduced. However, in no case need there be more than four plates. Different combinations of red, yellow, blue, and black can produce all secondary colors. A four-color photo is the result of the combination of inks on a red plate, a yellow plate, a blue plate, and a black plate.

Photo is shown reproduced in four different ways. Left is normal halftone. Second left is halftone with color tint. Second right is duotone. Right photo is color halftone.

Yearbook printers can help yearbook staff members decide how most effectively to use black and white, tint blocked, duotoned, and one-color photographs, as in the photos above. Because the process of printing in color is complex, it is an expensive process that should only be considered for yearbooks with large budgets.

Yearbook Covers

The yearbook cover makes the yearbook's first impression, and first impressions can also be lasting impressions. For this reason most yearbook staffers prefer covers that are modern and creative. The three basic types of yearbook covers are these: hard, padded, and paper. Most yearbooks use hard covers because their stiff, fiberboard construction offers durability. The least expensive type of yearbook cover, the paper cover, is used only for books having fewer than 100 pages. Paper covers are manufactured from heavyweight paper stock. Yearbook printers can supply sample books and cover suggestions.

Regardless of the type of material chosen for the cover, a cover layout, prepared by a yearbook staff member, must be submitted to the cover manufacturer or yearbook printer. The layout is then readied for printing by an artist employed by the manufacturer. The yearbook cover design need not be elaborate. Some of the best yearbook covers use only the name of the book and the school seal. Others base a cover idea on the theme of the book.

Local printers usually have covers produced by outside cover manufacturers; most national yearbook-printing companies manufacture their own. These companies usually suggest the use of a standard-type cover that is relatively inexpensive but similar in design to covers used by other schools throughout the country. Standard covers provide blank areas in which are printed the different school seals, titles, and dates.

Costs of covers can range widely. If the yearbook budget permits, embossed, silk-screen, or four-color photographic covers might be considered. These types of covers are considerably more expensive than standard covers.

Financing the Yearbook

Costs for producing the yearbook can vary depending on price fluctuations. So can yearbook income vary, depending on sources of revenue. The staff member responsible for overseeing yearbook financial matters is the business manager.

The Business Manager

The yearbook's business manager's prime responsibility is to ensure that the yearbook is a financial success. First, the amount of revenue to be obtained from subscriptions, advertising, school patrons, and any other sources is estimated. Then the business manager—working with the editor-in-chief and the faculty adviser—sets up a budget for publishing the yearbook. From the budget is determined the approximate overall cost per page, as well as the total number of pages the budget will allow. After establishing projected income, the business manager must carefully estimate the amount of money to be allotted for expenditures— for photography, for covers, for printing, for office supplies, and for miscellaneous expenses.

To ensure that every financial transaction is accurately recorded, the business manager should set up an efficient bookkeeping system if one is not already in use. Staff members who incur expenses that affect the yearbook budget should clear those expenses through the business manager. In fact, the business manager needs to know the exact amount of each expenditure, the resulting balance in the yearbook bank account, and the possibility of situations that might cause expenditures in excess of budget allowances.

In order to keep track of all financial transactions, the business manager should use a budget form. A sample budget form is shown on page 484.

The business manager is the financial watchdog of the yearbook staff. This job includes getting other members of the staff to think of ways to save money, including the following:

Meeting deadlines. Avoid overtime printing charges. Printers operate on tight schedules and must stagger their work loads in order to accomplish work that has been received off-schedule. When the printer's schedule is not met, the printer must double up on the work, often having to charge extra for overtime. Such overtime increases the production costs of the yearbook.

Editing copy correctly the first time. Resetting is costly. If, after copy has been set in type, an editor notices that there are still several misspellings, those misspellings must be corrected. Because copy must then be reset, the printer must charge extra for such alterations. These alterations are called *author's alterations*, and the additional cost is passed on to the yearbook.

Knowing how many photos are needed. Photographic equipment and supplies are expensive. If 300 photos are assigned when only 150 are needed, the overall costs for photography will be higher than necessary.

Being aware of production costs. Original art costs more to produce than photos. Yearbook editors considering using student artwork should be aware that such material usually involves a much greater expense than does the use of photographs. Knowing what the yearbook production costs are and then keeping within those costs are among the important responsibilities of each yearbook staff member.

Finally, the business manager's responsibilities include the supervision and coordination of the work of the yearbook treasurer, the advertising manager, and the subscription manager.

The Treasurer

The yearbook treasurer bills yearbook subscribers and collects payments. The treasurer is responsible for paying bills submitted by suppliers, such as those from photographers and printers.

The treasurer supervises the yearbook bank account, deals directly with the bank, and supervises the yearbook bookkeeping operation. Some yearbook staffs omit the position of treasurer, and the functions are performed by the business manager.

YEARBOOK BUDGET FORM

_____   _____
Name of Book   Date

INCOME

    CIRCULATION   _____

    ADVERTISING   _____

    ACTIVITY FEE   _____

    PATRONS   _____

    CLUB FEES   _____

    PICTURE SALES (PROJECTED)   _____

    TOTAL INCOME   _____

EXPENDITURES

    PRINTING   _____

    COVERS   _____

    ENGRAVINGS OR NEGATIVES   _____

    PHOTOGRAPHY   _____

    BINDING   _____

    OFFICE COSTS   _____

    MISCELLANEOUS EXPENSE   _____

    TOTAL EXPENSES   _____

_____
Business Manager

The Advertising Manager

Most yearbooks pay the greater portion of their expenses through advertising income. In recent years some yearbooks have given up advertising completely, and some have reduced the space allowed for advertising in favor of wider coverage of school activities. Advertisers, in some cases, have felt that yearbook advertising is not as effective as advertising in the school newspaper. Still, advertising constitutes a major source of income for the yearbook. The major goal of the advertising manager is to publish a yearbook with expenses largely paid by advertising.

The primary job of the advertising manager is to see that advertising space is sold. The job includes making sure that the advertisements are in good taste and that advertising copy is received on time and sent promptly to the printer. In addition to supervising the proofreading of advertising copy, the advertising manager sees to it that all advertisements are located effectively on the appropriate pages.

Determining Advertising Rates. The yearbook advertising manager's job is often more difficult than that of the school newspaper's advertising manager. The reason: Advertising rates for yearbook space, which is sold by the page or fraction of the page rather than by the column inch, are often determined by a sliding scale based on the size of the advertisement. One formula is that two thirds of the production costs of the yearbook are paid for out of advertising revenue. The *per-page* advertising rates are determined by dividing two thirds of the estimated production costs by the number of advertising pages desired. (The last third is absorbed by student subscriptions.) This figure is checked against the per-page production costs and then adjusted so that each advertising page pays not only for itself but also for one page without advertising.

Developing Advertising Sales Campaigns.   Another of the advertising manager's important responsibilities is the supervision of yearbook representatives who sell advertising space. These representatives must often face a situation in which some potential advertisers need to be convinced of the value of the yearbook advertising. The advertising manger and the advertising staff must plan their sales campaigns to get commitments from potential advertisers. Ideally, yearbook advertising representatives prepare interesting advertising layouts before calling on potential customers. (Only unimaginative sales representatives suggest that clients run congratulatory advertisements such as "Compliments of Ace Garage.") An advertising layout drawn for a potential customer should address the following needs:

Attention. The advertisement should immediately capture the prospective buyer's attention. The copy and any illustrations should be planned to gain the attention of the intended audience.

Interest. The headline, illustration, and body copy should capture and hold the consumer's interest.

Conviction. The advertisement should convince the consumer that what is being advertised is ideal.

Desire. The advertisement should inspire the desire to purchase the advertised product.

Action. The total effect of the advertisement should be to encourage the consumer to obtain the advertised product as soon as possible.

Yearbook advertising managers should train advertising sales representatives in effective selling techniques. Potential advertisers will be impressed—one way or another—by student sales representatives. These students represent their school and their yearbook, and they should conduct themselves in a professional and businesslike way. Representatives should know what to say to customers, preplanning their sales talks. They should arrive on time for all appointments with potential advertisers.

The School Yearbook: Production and Finance   **485**

The Subscription Manager

The subscription manager has the critical responsibility of selling yearbooks to students, to faculty members, to parents, and to alumni. Although potential buyers are sometimes reluctant to spend the amount charged for the yearbook, the subscription manager should understand that every senior, as well as many other students, will want a copy, and that those who put off buying subscriptions usually want one when the yearbook arrives.

The subscription manager and the subscription staff might post notices in strategic places throughout the school so that each student will know where to reserve and arrange to pay for a subscription to the yearbook. They might design a flier to mail to parents of seniors and to alumni. Although the subscription manager designates staff members as subscription-sales representatives, the subscription manager must assume responsibilty (1) for making sure that all students have an opportunity to subscribe to the yearbook and (2) for recording all subscriptions purchased.

Conducting Subscription Campaigns. A yearbook staff planning to conduct a subscription-sales drive should schedule the drive soon after the beginning of school, with subscription-sales representatives assigned to contact each student organization, teacher, and alumni group. Such a drive must be coordinated with the promotional campaign. Usually the most effective selling tool for a subscription drive is last year's yearbook.

A second major subscription drive can be held early in the spring. The student body should be made aware of the final deadline for ordering yearbook copies. All seniors can be contacted individually by obtaining a list of seniors from the administrative office. A successful subscription sales campaign can often result in an ideal 100 percent sales of yearbooks to the members of the senior class and high sales to the rest of the student body.

The subscription manager might write a promotional article for publication in the school newspaper and might place promotional pictures in the school magazine.

After yearbooks are distributed to students and others who have paid for them, extra copies could be sold in the cafeteria or at a school function or to business people, alumni, or school patrons.

Conducting Promotion Campaigns. An interested person on the subscription manager's staff might be named promotion manager. This person would work closely with the advertising staff and the subscription staff to draw attention to and generate student interest in the school yearbook. The promotion manager supervises creating and placing posters throughout the school to announce subscription drives, and planning yearbook promotional activities such as dances, bake sales, or contests. Yearbook promotion managers supply information about how, when, and where members of the student body may obtain copies of the yearbook.

Promotion managers often use the school newspaper to present news, feature stories, and pictures publicizing the yearbook.

Activities

1. With one or two classmates, draw up a production schedule for your school's yearbook. Organize the schedule by months. For each month, specify the tasks to be completed.

2. With one or two classmates, work out a step-by-step plan for selling advertising space in your school's yearbook. Specify the kinds of layouts you would present to potential advertisers. Also specify the strategy that you think would be successful in selling advertising space to reluctant buyers.

3. a. Having obtained a copy of last year's yearbook, together with the figure showing the final overall production cost involved in publishing the yearbook, calculate the per-page advertising rate.

    b. With a classmate, determine what you consider to be a fair per-page advertising rate for this year's yearbook. From conversations with yearbook staff members, determine the total number of pages to be included. Also find out whether production costs are likely to increase or decrease during the year. Determine, too, the number of pages that are to be allotted to advertising. Present your conclusions to the yearbook editor-in-chief and business manager for their consideration.

4. With a classmate, draw up a plan for an initial promotion campaign for the yearbook. Keep in mind that the plan might involve activities spread over several weeks. Submit your plan to the yearbook editor-in-chief and the subscription manager for their consideration.

5. With a classmate, draw up a plan for a yearbook subscription campaign. Specify how subscriptions are to be contracted for and paid for. Also specify how the subscription-sales staff might avoid errors in recording the subscriptions they obtain.

Subtle winds
content in quiet understanding
whisper through weathered
rooted in the dust of noble
buildings.
Cement chests guard
treasures of life.
Eternal winds speak softly
to those who listen,
with feeling...
a feeling that could have been
and perhaps
in a handful of fleeting moments
was.

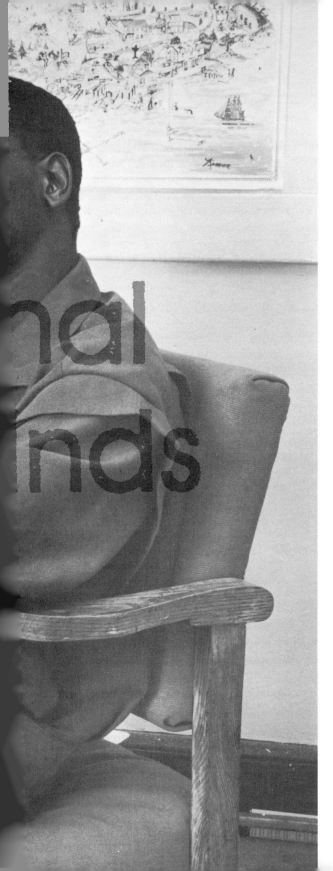

CHAPTER 21

The School Magazine: Organization and Content

Cathy Nolan, a senior at Churchill High, is Fiction Editor of—and sometimes a contributor to—*The Signature*, the school magazine. Today, while eating lunch in the cafeteria, Cathy spots Kent Mazur, a reporter for the Churchill High *Observer*, and waves him over to the table.

"Hi, Kent. Glad you came along. Pull up a chair."

"Thanks, Cath. Don't mind if I do."

"I've been wanting to talk to you about that short, short story you wrote last week for English. 'Alchemy'—wasn't that the title?"

"Yup, that's it." Kent bites into his hamburger.

"Well, when you read it in class the other day, I thought it was great. And so did most of the other kids I've talked to. Even Miss Brooks said that it was well written."

"Well," admits Kent, "I spent lots of time on it. I got the idea from 'Sentry,' one of Frederic Brown's stories."

"Hey, now that you mention it," muses Cathy, "I do see a similarity. Gee, you must have spent quite a while finding just the right words to build the feeling of uneasiness that runs through the story."

"Yeah, I practically lived with the thesaurus for three days."

"And telling the story in a page and a half was really something. How much time did you spend revising and polishing?"

"Hmm. I really don't remember. But I do know that the story I turned in was the fourth rewrite. Quite a bit different from the sports stories I turn in to the *Observer's* sports editor."

"I know," agrees Cathy. "With those stories you're concerned mainly about the five *w's* and the *h*. But with fiction, you're playing in a different ball game. Right?"

"Right!" Kent downs the last spoonful of chocolate pudding.

"Say, Kent, how about letting me publish 'Alchemy' in *The Signature?* The theme of the next issue focuses on the eerie, the unexplainable, the occult. Your story would fit in perfectly. How about it?"

"Well, sure—if you think the story's good enough. That last issue of *The Signature* had some great stuff in it. If you think 'Alchemy' is in that league, sure. Go ahead."

"Super!" exclaims Cathy. "Tell you what. Bring a copy of the story to English class tomorrow. You do have another copy, don't you?"

"Yup. It's sort of rough, but I'll bring it along."

"Fine. I'll take it with me when I go to the magazine office and get it ready to send to the typesetter. Then next week we both can see what 'Alchemy' looks like in print. OK?"

"Sounds OK to me." Kent is beaming. "Thanks, Cath."

"Don't thank me," smiles Cathy. "I thank you. By printing stories like 'Alchemy,' *The Signature* is bound to become a magazine that'll be read by all of the kids at Churchill High. See you tomorrow, Kent."

Purposes and Functions

The rich and noble heritage of literary publications in this country's schools can be traced back to 1777—less than a year after the signing of the Declaration of Independence. Although there are no existing copies of the first issue of our country's earliest school journal, *The Students' Gazette* (dated June, 1777), other copies produced later in the same year have survived. *The Students' Gazette*, handwritten by students at the William Penn Charter School in Philadelphia, was not limited to school news alone. One of its first articles discussed "The many Disturbances which have arisen in this State," thus bringing about the start of our tradition for student comment on social, moral, and political

The Literary Journal.

VOL. I. LATIN SCHOOL, BOSTON, MAY 30, 1829. NO

THE TYROLESE SON.

Continued.

The bereaved bride had been sent home with all the attention due to her rank and delicate situation; and the mourners were left alone to indulge their grief and sooth it by mutual sympathy. We will not attempt to describe the anguish of the despairing fratricide. At one time a vague idea flitted across his sever- so warmly made; but since it is so, shall find, that though you despise alliance, yet you may have cause to the enmity of an injured woman." rose to depart; "Stop, madam, you wr me," said Wallenstein "hear my ex nation and your resentment will turned to pity. Behold in me the willing murderer of an only brother some slight expiation to that broth sacred memory, I made a solemn, i

The Literary Journal was the first printed school publication.

issues. Fifty years after the founding of *The Students' Gazette,* the first printed school publication, *The Literary Journal,* was launched in May, 1829, at the Boston Latin School.

Throughout the country today, hundreds of school magazines are written and published by high school students. Different in purpose from school newspapers and yearbooks, school magazines seek these goals:

1. To identify students with language abilities and interests and to encourage them in the development of their special talents.
2. To present the student body, the faculty, and the community with student writing of quality and literary value.
3. To make possible practical learning situations in which staff members can further develop their technical competency, literary judgment, and good taste.
4. To increase staff members' awareness of the positive effects of the printed word.

In working toward these goals, school magazines perform at least four important functions:

1. They provide a voice for students who are concerned about effective literary expression.
2. They give students an opportunity to develop writing skills and language abilities in an informal atmosphere.

The School Magazine: Organization and Content   491

3. They provide an opportunity for students to read works of literary value written by other students.
4. They provide an opportunity for student contributors and student editors alike to learn to accept and evaluate constructive criticism.

Types of School Magazines

Although the scope of school magazines varies considerably, most school magazines fall under one of the following classifications:

Literary-Art Oriented

Perhaps the majority of school magazines are literary-art oriented. In general, the content includes poetry, plays, short fiction, artwork, and creative photography. In this type of magazine, articles of nonfiction are usually excluded.

Combination Magazine-Newspaper

The content of the combination magazine-newspaper type of school magazine consists principally of interview features, sports features, and feature news stories that are likely to interest students. This type of school magazine might also publish student-written poetry and short fiction. Student magazines of this type often print illustrations of high quality on their covers and may occasionally feature student artwork and photography.

Miscellaneous

Student magazines that fit neither of the categories discussed constitute a "miscellaneous" classification.

At some schools the final issue of the school magazine is published in the spring as a yearbook supplement. In this case, the magazine concentrates on school activities and events that occurred after the printing deadline for the yearbook. Graduation activities, spring sports, and student awards are the subjects most often written about and photographed.

School magazine covers often feature student artwork and photography.

Some school magazines devote complete issues to artwork and photography or to humor or to creative writing projects. For example, one issue of the school magazine produced by the students of Notre Dame High School in West Haven, Connecticut, was titled *53 Voices on Little Red Riding Hood* and consisted of 53 rewritten versions of that classic story. Each version imitated a famous writer or exemplified a distinctive writing style.

Staff Organization

In general, the staff of a school magazine consists of an editor-in-chief, an associate editor, copy editors, layout editor, an editor for each of the sections in the publication (section editors), a business manager, an advertising manager, a circulation manager, a promotion manager, illustrators, proofreaders, and typists. (See the chart on page 495.) The editor-in-chief delegates responsibility for each section to a section editor and is responsible to the magazine's faculty adviser.

Editor-in-Chief

The editor-in-chief has the overall responsibility for the production of the school magazine. He or she works with the faculty adviser, the associate editor, and the business manager, to help establish editorial policy, determine the magazine format, the number of issues to be published, the number of pages per issue, and the price per issue. In conferences with the section editors about each issue of the magazine, the editor-in-chief makes the following decisions:

■ Whether or not each issue will have a theme.

■ The amount of space to be devoted to poetry, to drama, to fiction, to nonfiction, to artwork, and to photography.

■ The specific artwork and photographs to be published in each issue.

Associate Editor and Copy Editors

The associate editor and the copy editors have the responsibility of editing all works printed, for composing titles and captions, and for specifying type faces and sizes for each title and each work published.

Layout Editor

After all of the materials to be printed have been selected and edited, and after the artwork and photographs have been submitted, the layout editor and staff make dummy page layouts. That is, they locate each item to be published on layout sheets. The layout editor and staff indicate the area (width and depth) that each work will occupy when set into type. The exact placement of titles and illustrations accompanying each work must be indicated on the page dummy. To know exactly how long an article will run when set into type, the layout editor must be acquainted with the basics of copyfitting. (See Chapter 22, "The School Magazine: Production and Finance," page 512.) Before cropping a photograph and determining its final size, the layout editor should discuss with the photographer exactly what the photographer's intentions were when taking the picture and what the photograph is

TYPICAL STAFF ORGANIZATION FOR A SCHOOL MAGAZINE

```
                          Adviser
                             |
                       Editor-in-Chief
                             |
        +--------------------+--------------------+
   Associate Editor                        Business Manager
        |                                         |
 +------+------+------+------+          +----------+----------+
Literary  Art  Photo  Copy  Layout    Advertising  Promotion  Subscription
Editor  Editor Editor Editor Editor     Manager     Manager   or Circulation
   |      |      |      |      |            |           |        Manager
 Writers Artists Photo- Copy- Makeup   Advertising                 |
                 graphers readers (Layout) Representatives
                          |      Artists      |
                      Proofreaders            |
   |      |      |      |      |            |           |          |
 Staff  Staff  Staff  Staff  Staff        Staff       Staff      Staff
```

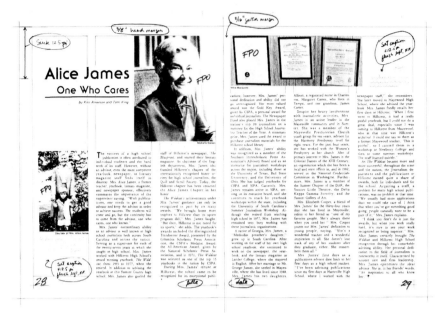

Elements that are to appear on a magazine page must be clearly marked on the page dummy.

intended to express. When picture stories are planned for the school magazine, the layout editor might invite the photographer(s) to help with the layout.

Section Editors

Ideally, the section editors are the best writers on the staff. They are responsible for supplying every work published in each issue of the school magazine. They consult teachers for student-written materials that are worthy of publication. They solicit works from other students, including members of their staff. They may even publish their own writings. Section editors attend all planning meetings and all staff meetings and participate in all editorial discussions concerning magazine content.

Business Manager

The work of the school magazine's business manager is similar to, yet less complex than, the work of the yearbook's business manager. The school magazine business manager must formulate the publication's budget for the year and the budget for each issue. The primary responsibility is to see that the publication is a financial success. In some cases, the functions of the business manager and the advertising manager are combined.

Advertising Manager

Some school magazines carry no advertising; yet many do. Because of the expense involved in producing a school magazine, the advertising manager plays an important role in helping to maintain the publication's financial stability. Ideally, the advertising manager, together with the advertising staff, should contract for enough advertising to fill about 50 percent of the total number of pages in the publication. When advertising revenue doesn't compensate for a substantial portion of the production costs, the price of the publication can become prohibitive for many students. Advertising representatives for the school magazine sometimes canvass alumni to solicit contributions. Additional revenue can sometimes be realized by including the names of donors on pages titled "Patrons."

Circulation Manager

The circulation manager and staff must make sure that all students have the opportunity to purchase each issue of the school magazine. Circulation representatives are often assigned to specific school areas—for example, homerooms, student lounges, and the cafeteria. Tables displaying copies of the magazine are sometimes set up at strategic places throughout the school on the day of publication. The circulation manager might also send representatives into the community to solicit subscriptions from business and professional people and other friends of the school. When advance subscriptions are not sold, the circulation manager, together with the business manager and the editor-in-chief, determines how many copies of each issue are to be printed.

Promotion Manager

Although many school magazine staffs do not provide for the job of promotion manager, the establishing of such a post is strongly recommended. In journalism classes there are often students who are interested in the field of public relations as associated with journalism. Serving as the school magazine's promotion manager offers such students ideal public-relations training and also affords them an opportunity to perform an important function for the school magazine and the school itself. The responsibilities of a promotion manager include the organization of campaigns to make students aware that there is a school magazine and to whet their interest in purchasing and reading each issue.

Major Concerns of the Magazine Staff

Like student journalists working on the school newspaper and the yearbook, the members of the school magazine staff have some special concerns of their own. Two of those concerns will be discussed here.

Publication Deadlines

In most high schools, the school magazine is published less frequently than the school newspaper. In some schools the magazine is published monthly; in some schools, bimonthly or trimonthly; and in a few, only once or twice during the school year.

To make sure that each issue of the magazine comes out on schedule, staff members should plan to allow the printer about a month's time between the receipt of the last piece of copy and the final printing. The exact amount of time, of course, will vary depending on the printer's schedule, the type of material to be printed, the total number of pages in the magazine, and the printing method used. It is always advisable to meet with the printer as early in the school year as possible to agree on specific deadlines and publication dates for all issues of the magazine.

This table of contents is organized by theme.

When the content of the school magazine is organized around a theme, it gains unity and coherence and tends to give the magazine additional appeal. One issue of the school magazine might use "Spring" as the focus for each story, poem, article, photograph, and piece of artwork published. Other issues might then use the remaining seasons for their themes. Another theme frequently used is that of social concern. Such a theme might include the various aspects of urban living or daily life in farm communities or major problems faced by today's young people.

Writing for the School Magazine

Usually the most competent writers for the school magazine are those students who have mastered the basics of journalistic writing discussed in Part II, "Roles of the Journalist in a Democratic Society," pages 140–304. Ideally, these writers will have served their "apprenticeships" as reporters for the school newspaper. But, of course, any student in the school must have the privilege of submitting a written work, a photograph, or a piece of original art to the magazine staff for consideration.

This table of contents is interesting and artistic.

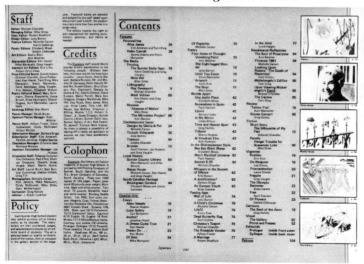

Making Language Work for You

Using Transitions to Unify Your Writing. Very often the prose writing of relatively inexperienced writers lacks unity. That is, succeeding paragraphs in a story or article fail to develop a central idea. To give unity to what you write, you must make sure that each paragraph (and each sentence) builds on the ideas contained in those that precede it. The result, then, is that the entire piece—story or article—focuses on a central idea. One way to ensure unity in what you write is to use *transitional devices* to link paragraphs and sentences. Such devices lead the reader naturally and simply from one thought to another. Some of the more commonly used transitional devices are the following:

1. Structural transitions like *first, second, finally, on the other hand, moreover, however, in the next place.*

> The government of the United States consists of three co-equal branches. The legislative branch, first of all, makes the laws. Second, the executive branch enforces the laws. Third and finally, the judicial branch interprets the laws.

2. A continuation of the same subject from one sentence to the next by repeating the same words or by using a synonym.

> The photographer covering a baseball game might wait at first base and focus the camera on the bag. When runners are on second and/or third base, the photographer might stand halfway between third base and home plate.

3. Pronoun reference to a noun in a preceding sentence.

> The two bands seemed to have caught the spirit of the occasion. Their music was perfect; they executed their formations like drill teams.

4. Sentence construction in which the direct object in one sentence serves as the subject of the succeeding sentence.

> The second batter hit the ball with a whack that resounded throughout the stadium. Up, up soared that ball, finally disappearing behind the bleachers. Home run!

5. Parallel structure.

> Here the milk is tested for acidity and sediment and then sampled and weighed.

> The law not only makes the owner of the land pay a fine for each fire started on his land, but also forces him to pay an extra fee for each acre the fire has burned.

Using Figurative Language. Another way to make language work for you (note the structural transition that begins this sentence) is to use figures of speech appropriately. Effective use of figurative language can help make what you write come alive. The most often used figures of speech are the following:

1. *Simile:* A simile is an expressed comparison of two essentially unlike objects that seem to be alike in a limited way. In an article by Richard Harding Davis, written in 1914, the German army is compared to a river:

> Like a river of steel it flowed, gray and ghostlike.

2. *Metaphor:* A metaphor is an unexpressed comparison between two essentially unlike objects or ideas; one of the objects or ideas replaces another, thus suggesting a likeness or an analogy between them. For example, had Davis used a metaphor, he would have written his comparison like this:

> The army was a river of steel, gray and ghostlike.

In his poem "The Highwayman," Alfred Noyes wrote this now-famous metaphor:

> The road was a ribbon of moonlight over the purple moor.

3. *Hyperbole:* Hyperbole is an exaggeration used for effect.

> I nearly died laughing.

> The mirror fell to the floor and broke into a million pieces.

4. *Personification:* A personification attributes human qualities to nonhuman creatures or things or ideas in order to explain them in human terms.

> Dawn came dancing over the field.

Another example appears in the following paragraph written by Will Irwin for the *New York Sun* following the San Francisco fire of 1906:

> Old San Francisco is dead. The gayest, lightest-hearted, most pleasure-loving city of this continent, and in many ways the most interesting and romantic, is a horde of huddled refugees living among ruins. It may rebuild; it probably will; but those who have known that peculiar city by the Golden Gate and have caught its Flavor of the Arabian Nights feel that it can never be the same.

The following paragraph about the same tragedy was written by Jack London for *Collier's Magazine.* Comparing it with the preceding paragraph will show that without figurative language what one writes—even though the author is well known—can be flat and dull:

<table>
<tr><td>

The earthquake shook down on San Francisco hundreds of thousands of dollars' worth of walls and chimneys. But the conflagration that followed burned up hundreds of millions of dollars' worth of property. There is no estimation within hundreds of millions of the actual damage wrought. Not in history has a modern imperial city been so completely destroyed. San Francisco is gone! Nothing

</td><td>

remains of it but memories and a fringe of dwelling houses on its outskirts. Its industrial section is wiped out. The factories and warehouses, the great stores and newspaper buildings, the hotels and the palaces of the nabobs are all gone. Remains only the fringe of dwelling houses on the outskirts of what was San Francisco.

</td></tr>
</table>

Polishing Your Writing.   To make what you write truly effective, you will undoubtedly need to revise—rewrite if necessary—and polish your work. It has been said that writers, as a group, seem never to be satisfied with their manuscripts. Instead they continually seek out phrases and sentences for revision and polishing. Ernest Hemingway is said to have rewritten one pivotal sentence at least a hundred times. And James Thurber, when asked whether writing was easy for him, replied:

> For me it's mostly a question of rewriting. It's part of a constant attempt on my part to make the finished version smooth, to make it seem effortless. A story I've been working on was rewritten fifteen complete times.

And finally, according to William Faulkner, successful writing requires "ninety-nine percent talent, ninety-nine percent discipline, and ninety-nine percent work."

Writing Interpretive Articles

Because of the time span between the occurrence of a newsworthy event and the deadline established for printing the typical school magazine, some editors like to publish one or more nonfictional interpretive articles in each issue of the magazine. The nonfictional interpretive article makes it possible to say something new about a past event. This kind of article highlights an interesting aspect of the event, giving that aspect added significance.

Writers of nonfictional interpretive articles often use analogies —extended comparisons that imply that if two or more things are alike in some respects, they will probably be alike in others. For example, to give readers a better understanding of the atom, the writer of an interpretive article might make a statement like this:

> The atom has an internal nucleus with a system of electrons traveling around it in much the same way that the sun has planets revolving around it.

Writers of interpretive articles can also capture and hold reader interest by giving specific details and examples. For example, in the following lead from an interpretive article, the writer uses details to point out the reason for the results of the baseball team's poor showing:

> The inability to score runs has cost the hardballers dearly this season. Scoring one run or less in 11 of their 17 games, the team racked up a poor 4-13 record. . . .

Writers of interpretive articles can give their work added impact by using such *reportorial devices* as *anecdotes* and *case studies*. An example of the use of a case study in an interpretive article might be one that documented the events in the life of a school dropout for one year after that person left school.

Using quotations and anecdotes and specific details, the student writer of the following interpretive article won a writing award:

When People Think of Circus—

"When people think of circus, the wherefores and the whys of it, they think of all the adjectives proclaiming the size of it. The most amazing melody of merriment and mirth, the circus is the greatest show on earth."

This has been true from the earliest beginnings of the circus and has kept it alive to the present day Yes, it is alive—at least Mr. Emmett Kelly, Jr., (Clown Prince), and Mr. James Cole, owner-manager of Cole's All Star Indoor Circus have given me definite no's and distasteful looks when I brought up the term "dying institutions." Ringling Brothers and Barnum & Bailey Circus is just beginning its ninety-fourth consecutive season. Think, if you can, of the millions of people, of the wide-opened mouths, and even of the offended noses that have experienced this spectacle.

It has changed: actually there is an entirely new overall concept of the circus. Most of the shows have moved indoors, not because of failure, but because of "class and status improvement." Now you can dress up and watch the thrilling acts from comfortable seats, not planks of wood. One other change, a heartbreaker for those who can say "I remember when," is the elimination of the parade. No more beautiful wagons, prancing horses, and huge elephants to watch as they march down the main street to the circus grounds. Reminiscing, Mr. Kelly told us how this has actually hurt the circus. "In some towns, like Fort Wayne, Indiana, where the coliseum is way out of town, the folks don't even know the circus is in town. They used to follow the parade and then stay to see the show, but not any more." Luckily, this sad state of affairs is not true across the country. The greatest portion of our country knows well when the circus is in town and supports it whole-heartedly. . . .

In the back of my mind, I can hear my mother saying, "If you've seen one, you've seen them all," and it brings me back to the defensive position. At this point, I consider all my readers hostile to the cause of spreading interest in the circus, so may I say that my mother is wrong! The actual turnover and change within acts is tremendous. Many of the acts we see, like the one that was in Rochester—The Rosell Troupe of highwire artistes— are imported from other countries to add variety. This particular troupe is from South America. Three actors are from Colombia, one is from Ecuador, and one is from Santo Domingo. Theirs is only one of hundreds of imports. In addition to variety, I have heard other reasons why acts are brought in. One person said that foreign acts are of a better quality, while another person thinks they are imported because actors are able to do more than one act; that is, one group may appear two or three times in the same show. You can see the resulting conflict: for quality you need specialization, not diversity. In the United States, it is almost impossible to break into the circus from the outside. Naturally, there must be one or two prime exceptions. John Cuneo, one of these exceptions, was born in Chicago. He is the son of a multimillionaire and is a graduate of Georgetown University. Through a hobby, he became an animal trainer. . . .

Perhaps it is circus, perhaps it is the people in it, but something has given the whole of it a rare quality of magic and of longevity. With this, how could it ever die? It will always be the "Greatest Show on Earth"!

The Spectrum

Writing Articles Based on News

Some of the most interesting articles in school magazines are those based on news items. Alert editors keep abreast of general news developments over and beyond the usual school activities, often associating something of local interest with current news events. The result is that the school magazine contains a feature article or two based on the news.

After doing some research on and conducting interviews concerning a power blackout, two student writers produced the following news-based feature article, which was published in the school magazine.

Those Cold Suppers by Candlelight—Remember?

Candlelight, cold suppers, and blazing fires on the hearth—that was the order of the day for many caught in the recent blackout. Mercians, along with all other residents of the area, will long be abuzz about what they did when the power failed.

Debby Oravac heard the doorbell ring.

As she opened the door the lights went out and she greeted a young boy selling light bulbs.

Mary Ann Gould, working downtown at the time, reports jammed cash registers, elevators stuck between floors, and, in general, mass confusion.

Sue Donovan and her family were determined not to go without a hot dinner. Sue's family enjoyed a perfect meal cooked on the barbeque grill by Sue's father. . . .

Dorine MacLauchlan works as a cashier at Loblaw's at Garson and Culver. She says she always has liked her job, but on that day she suffered stiff muscles in her arms by manually cranking the cash register while people shopped.

Mercy volunteers were on the scene at hospitals and rest homes when the lights went out. Maggie O'Dwyer was working at St. Mary's and was forced to trek up the stairs (five flights!) to deliver the patients' trays. Sue Conrad, who works at the Episcopal Home, helped lead the elderly people by flashlight to their rooms. When she was not helping there, she watched the younger children.

On the other side of the city at St. Ann's Home, Mary Ellen LeVan was serving dinner. The lights dimmed for a few minutes but finally went out. Mary Ellen was asked to help the Sisters in a new project. This project was to lead about 100 ambulatory guests up the stairs from the dining room on the ground floor to their rooms on the sixth, seventh, eighth, and ninth floors. Because of recent heart conditions, each guest had to rest at each landing on chairs provided by the residents of the various floors.

Maureen Dever, along with many others, resolved the problem of what to do in a fairly simple way. She went to bed at 7 p.m.—the earliest she's been in bed since she entered Mercy!

The Quill

Writing Articles with a Fictional Approach

Our era might well come to be labeled "The Age of Writers with a Cause," for more and more writers seem to reflect their concern for the human condition. Writers such as William Faulkner, Norman Mailer, Erma Bombeck, Saul Bellow, Flannery O'Connor, Eudora Welty, and John Updike have expressed their concern convincingly through the fictional approach. Student writers concerned about human problems can also express that concern through fiction—as is evidenced by the following:

To Tell—or Not to Tell

The door to the office opened, and Dr. Salter appeared. Dorothy Williams was at his side. Asking her to wait in the reception room for a few minutes, Dr. Salter looked at Walter Williams and said, "Will you come in, please?"

Williams knew instantly that something was wrong, but he didn't say anything as he walked in and sat down in the chair next to the doctor's desk.

Dr. Salter's face was solemn.

"I'm afraid I have bad news for you, Mr. Williams. Your wife has cancer. I believe she has a year or two to live."

Williams blinked, but his voice was unemotional—almost uninterested.

"Wouldn't an operation arrest it? What about chemotherapy?"

Dr. Salter nodded. "You can try them, of course. An exploratory operation should show how bad things are, but I think we already know that. I haven't told Mrs. Williams. I think it would be better not to."

This scene is repeated many times daily across the country, and each time, the script reads much the same.

Some therapists are now suggesting that the patient be told the truth—no matter how distasteful it is. Others—like Dr. Salter—believe that the truth would only make things worse.

Who is right?

Writing Reviews

Many school magazines feature reviews of plays, motion pictures, television shows, and books. Magazine staff members with experience in music, art, or drama are often asked to write such reviews. As a rule, the reviewer composes a lead paragraph (1) that names the book or performance or work under review, (2) that expresses the reviewer's overall appraisal, and (3) that gives a brief synopsis of the work. Specific parts or aspects of the work are then singled out for special comment. Student reviewers should make their reviews constructive as well as informative.

Book Reviews. Even though a book review is often shorter than a review of a play, motion picture, or television presentation, it should still follow a similar format. Book reviews are often preceded by the title of the book, the author's name, the type of book (fiction, nonfiction, bibliography, etc.), the number of pages, and the price. The reviewer's name usually appears at the end of the review. Following is a student example of a book review.

A meaningful book telling of an individual in a collective society, *Anthem*, by Ayn Rand, describes the sin of projecting individuality. The society was one where "I" existed only as a trivial and expendable part of a mighty machine, the whole. People referred to themselves as "We," never "I", for "I" is a strong word. It is a word of vibrant initiative. The unquestioned rule of the society was that each person must be incomplete, totally dependent upon everybody. *Anthem* is particularly intriguing in the era of mass conformity and leisurely individuality.

Horizons

Reviews of Plays, Television Shows, Motion Pictures, Concerts. In some cases, the editorial policy of the school magazine may be to limit reviews of plays to productions given by the school's dramatic club. In other cases, however, the magazine editorial policy is to publish reviews of professionally produced plays, television shows, motion pictures, and concerts. Such reviews, of course, observe the guidelines suggested on page 162.

Writing Poetry for the School Magazine

Students who write for the school magazine often discover that the medium of poetry can be one of the most expressive means available for defining and expressing their innermost feelings. School magazines that are literary-art oriented sometimes devote entire issues to poetry and to artwork. Some of the poems might be quiet and contemplative.

Poems combined with art give impact to the student magazine.

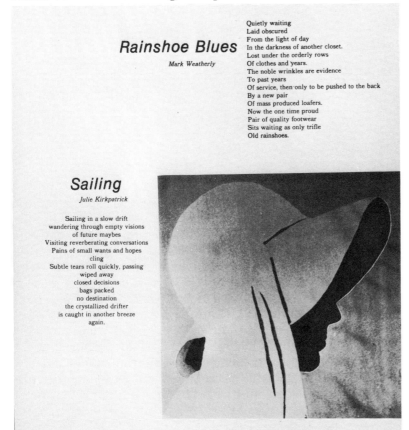

Rainshoe Blues

Mark Weatherly

Quietly waiting
Laid obscured
From the light of day
In the darkness of another closet.
Lost under the orderly rows
Of clothes and years.
The noble wrinkles are evidence
To past years
Of service, then only to be pushed to the back
By a new pair
Of mass produced loafers.
Now the one time proud
Pair of quality footwear
Sits waiting as only trifle
Old rainshoes.

Sailing

Julie Kirkpatrick

Sailing in a slow drift
wandering through empty visions
of future maybes
Visiting reverberating conversations
Pains of small wants and hopes
cling
Subtle tears roll quickly, passing
wiped away
closed decisions
bags packed
no destination
the crystallized drifter
is caught in another breeze
again.

Some of the poems might be humorous and satirical. Such poems can help attract readers to the school magazine. The following student-written poem is a clever parody of a nursery rhyme written in the poetic style of Carl Sandburg.

> Candle Jumper of the world,
> Flame-Leaper, Scorcher of Pants,
> Player with Fire and the Nation's Hot Seat;
>   Nimble, quick, spry
>   Boy of the burned blue jeans;
> They tell me you are inconsistent and I answer:
>   for I have seen you take a running start
>   and sail above the fiery wick.
> They tell me you are inconsistent and I answer:
>   Yes, it is true I have seen you leap up and
>   out and singe your posterior with a frightening
> yelp.
>   Approaching,
>   Springing,
>   Soaring,
>   Screaming,
> Proud to be Candle Jumper of the world, Flame-
>   leaper, Scorcher of Pants, Player with Fire
>   and the Nation's Hot seat.
>
>   *Tam O'Shanter*

Illustrating the School Magazine

The artwork contained in the school magazine can serve one of two purposes: It can be functional, illustrating the editorial content; or it can be decorative, used for ornamental purposes. In either case the artwork in the school magazine is more creative and artistic than that usually published in the school newspaper.

Many school magazines use abstract illustrations and photographs that seek to interpret character and plot and to enhance the tone and mood of the works published. Such illustrations serve a purpose similar to that served by "mood music." They create an atmosphere suitable to the occasion. The student artist illustrating a poem or story or article must do the same thing by translating the writer's words into a visual image that helps the reader visualize a character and sense the mood. Before attempt-

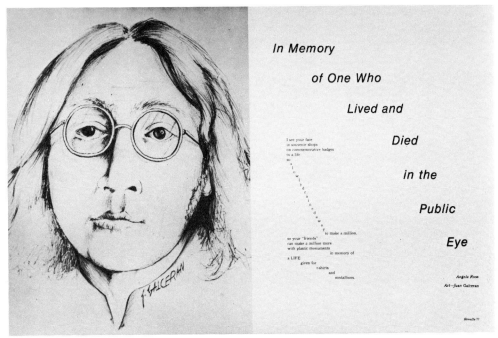

This illustration of John Lennon enhances the tone and mood.

ing to illustrate a literary work, the student artist must read and understand it, consulting with that writer, if possible, in order to understand exactly what he or she had in mind.

In addition to publishing student-created artwork, school magazines publish photographs taken by students. Photographs taken during the summer *can* often fit in various issues of the magazine. Sometimes quality photographs are difficult to come by, and the school magazines can seek the cooperation of the newspaper and yearbook staff photographers. Those photographers are usually happy to work with the school magazine staff—especially when they know that their work will be displayed prominently in the school magazine. Editors should plan carefully for the photographs to appear in each issue and to make photographic assignments well in advance of publication deadlines.

An example of an attention-getting photograph published in a school magazine appears on page 510.

The artwork and the design for the cover of the school magazine deserve brief attention. Both should convey good taste through simplicity. The covers of many school magazines, for example, bear only the title of the publication and the name of the school. Two interesting covers are shown on page 493.

An attention-getting photo adds excitement to a yearbook page.

Masque

Lay down your mask
Young man, don't hide love,
Emotions, and understanding.
You are yourself
And no one else.
Let others play-act
Through life and love
But let yourself live
In reality, not upon
Shakespeare's round.
An actor, a mime,
A soldier poised
And armed with a
New visage for every battle.
A shield of anonymity stands
As protection
As nothing may enter,
Nothing may leave,
Not love,
Not emotions,
And not you!
Lay down your mask;
Make yourself vulnerable,
Open to trust.
Set yourself free.

Andy Vasquez

Photograph—Cathy Lama

Midnight Movie

Angela Ross

We
two
went
tothe
movies
wedrank
Dr.Pepper
ateFritos
andlaughed
atthepeople
turnedaround
wasittoolate
tofaceburnt
bridgesand
highwalls
mirrored
facesof
Memory
Lanes
good
bye
us

Activities

1. a. After examining the latest issue of your school magazine, prepare a critique of that issue:

   (1) Identify the type of magazine it is.

   (2) In your opinion, what are the magazine's strong points? Why?

   (3) In your opinion, what specific improvements could make the magazine more attractive and interesting?

b. If there is no school magazine, consider the possibilities for producing one. Prepare a proposal for starting a school magazine:

   (1) What type of magazine should it be? Why?

   (2) How often should it be published? Why?

   (3) How should it be staffed?

(4) From what subject area should a faculty adviser be selected? Why?

(5) What should the price of the magazine be?

(6) Should that price be added to the student activity fee (if your school has one), or should students buy individual copies of the magazine as they are published? Why?

2. List at least five possible themes for a literary-art-oriented school magazine. Then, in outline form, suggest how each theme might be developed in an issue of the magazine.

3. Write an article of not more than two pages in which you use sensory images that appeal to all of the five senses. Submit your article for publication in the school magazine.

4. a. Write a brief interpretive article on a controversial subject. Be sure to choose your words carefully so as to shed light on the subject instead of generating heat. In your article, make appropriate use of the four figures of speech discussed in this chapter.

b. Rewrite your article, omitting the figures of speech. Which version do you feel is more effective? Why?

c. Submit both versions to the school magazine staff for possible publication.

5. Select a familiar fairy tale, nursery rhyme, or poem. Rewrite it in the style of a poet or writer of fiction whom you admire. Be prepared to read your work to the class, asking them to identify the writer whose style you have imitated. Submit your work to the school magazine for consideration.

6. Write a review of a television documentary you have watched recently or a book you have read. Submit your review for publication in the school magazine.

7. As art editor for your school magazine, you have been given an article based on a popular song (your choice of song), and you need to have it illustrated.

a. Would you have the article illustrated by an artist, or would you have it illustrated with photographs? Why?

b. (1) If you decide on drawings by an artist, what suggestions would you have for the artist?

(2) If you decide on photographs, what suggestions would you have for the photographer?

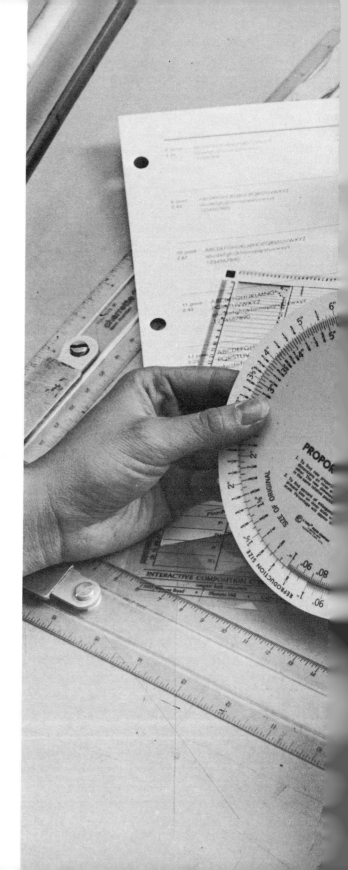

CHAPTER 22

The School Magazine: Production and Finance

Vicki Brown, layout editor for Tuslow High School's magazine, *The Sentinel*, is a designer—although she doesn't realize it. At this particular moment her adviser, Mrs. Burr, has called her up to the desk.

"Vicki, have you ever taken classes in design?"

"No," hesitates Vicki. "Why do you ask?"

"Because your layouts are so artistic," smiles Mrs. Burr. "How do you manage to be so creative?"

"Well, I figure that there are only four elements to consider. So I just juggle the titles, copy, artwork, and white space around until I have what I think is a pleasant arrangement. And then, of course, there's my scrapbook."

"Scrapbook?"

"Yes. When I see a magazine layout that I like, I clip it out and put it in my scrapbook. I also clip advertisements that appeal to me. Then, when I have a page design, I go

through my scrapbook for layout ideas. I hope you don't think that that's cheating."

"Not at all. Many of the top people in magazine staffs refer regularly to good examples of layout and design. And in your case what you're doing works very well. I like your work!"

"Thanks, Mrs. Burr. Thanks for your encouragement."

Some people say that the success of a school magazine depends primarily on the publication's editorial content. Others believe that production techniques emphasizing visual appeal should be the primary concern. It is our view, however, that content of high quality and effective production techniques are both essential. Rather than vying with each other for supremacy, the two are actually complementary—co-equal and vital partners in the publishing of a successful school magazine. Chapter 21, on pages 488–511, focused on editorial content; this chapter focuses on production.

The Importance of Production

All of the production techniques used in the planning, copy editing, designing, and layout of the pages for any school magazine have a major effect on the publication's overall success. Because school magazines have no set format, the role that production techniques can play is well worth some detailed consideration.

Every piece of written material and artwork in a school magazine is, in effect, competing with every other piece for reader attention. Each seeks not only to halt the reader who is browsing through the magazine but also to hold that reader's interest until the entire piece has been read or examined.

Copy Editing the School Magazine

Before being released to the printer, all of the materials making up each issue of a school magazine must be copy edited and proofread. To do an effective job, copy editors and proofreaders follow procedures similar to those used by their counterparts on the school newspaper (pages 360–380) and the yearbook (pages 460–464). Those assigned the tasks of copy editing and proofreading must be especially painstaking and, more often than is the case on the school newspaper and the yearbook, must consult with the contributors to the magazine for approval and verification of proposed changes. The reason: Poets and other writers sometimes use unconventional grammatical and structural forms to produce certain effects. The copy editor or proofreader who is unaware of their intent might easily and unknowingly undo—even destroy—the effects the writers are striving for.

Lemon

RITA URIAS MENDOZA

	The
man I married was a	lemon
picker, and he	was
always smelling	rancid
lemons, and	he
always	had
lots of	lemon
pie and lemon	ade
and he worked	so
hard	he died!

Following Style

"Don't change anything unless you have checked thoroughly and are certain the original will be improved." That's a rule all school magazine copy editors would do well to follow.

It is the copy editor's job to make certain the material is consistent and correct. To do so, the copy editor applies conventional rules of grammar, usage, spelling, capitalization, punctuation, sentence structure, and paragraph organization. However, the copy editor must be aware that our language is continually changing and that conventional rules are sometimes modified to accommodate the unconventional forms educated speakers and writers use on specific occasions.

Preparing a Style Guide.   It is common practice for school magazine editors to set down rules concerning sentence structure, spelling, punctuation, and capitalization. In other words, they prepare a style guide or style sheet that the magazine's copy editors should consult and should follow consistently. See the example on pages 364–365. However, copy editors need to recognize that the goal of the serious writer (and speaker) is to be understood. Rules, if they are to be useful, must allow for variations in formal and informal usage. The appropriateness of one usage over another depends, of course, on the topic, the occasion, and the audience. English is an ever-changing language, and speakers and writers adapt it to their needs in many different ways, none of which is always right or always wrong. In following a style guide for the school magazine, copy editors need to make allowances for such language variations, acknowledging that the style used in any piece of writing will vary from standard usage depending on the writer and that writer's intent. The following anecdote illustrates the point:

> An editor once pointed out to Winston Churchill that the then British Prime Minister had ended a sentence with a preposition. The editor proposed rewriting the sentence to eliminate what he considered a faulty construction. His revision, however, would have resulted in a stilted, pompous sentence. To show the absurdity of the editor's suggestion—and, incidentally, to show the folly of adhering blindly to rules of usage—Churchill objected to the proposed change by indignantly replying: "That is something up with which I will not put!"

Observing Mechanical Requirements.   School magazine editors often specify mechanical requirements for the handling of literary materials. Copy editors need to keep such requirements constantly in mind. (The requirements might be included in the style guide.) If, for example, all poems are to be set in an italic type face and if all short story titles are to be set in a sans serif type face, the copy editor—having consulted the style guide—so indicates on the manuscript that is sent to the typesetter. Once material has been set in type, it should not be changed unless there is very good reason to do so and then only if the magazine staff is prepared to pay the typesetter an extra fee for alterations.

The standard copy-editing symbols appear in Appendix VI. Page 366 shows a copy-edited manuscript.

After a poem, or an article—all of which are referred to as "copy"—has been edited, it must be marked (a) to ensure that it will fit the space planned for it on the layout sheets and (b) to let the typesetter (compositor) know what type faces and type sizes to use. Type is measured in units called points. One point is equal to 1/72 of an inch. Some of the standard type sizes used for the body of stories or articles (not titles) printed in school magazines are the following:

This line is printed in 8-point type.

This line is printed in 9-point type.

This line is printed in 10-point type.

This line is printed in 11-point type.

This line is printed in 12-point type.

There are many different "families," or kinds, of type faces. The face used for the body type on this page, for example, is Zapf Book Light. Most type faces include a roman font, or form, (like the body type of this page), an *italic* font, a **boldface** font, and an ***italic boldface*** font. Some of the type faces most frequently used for works published in school magazines are the following:

This line is printed in 10-point Caslon (roman).

This line is printed in 10-point Caledonia (italic).

This line is printed in 10-point Century Schoolbook (boldface).

This line is printed in 10-point Granjon (roman).

This line is printed in 10-point Times Roman (italic).

This line is printed in 10-point Spartan Light (roman).

This line is printed in 10-pt Spartan (bold italics).

Besides indicating the type face and type size to be used, the copy editor also specifies the amount of leading (lĕd'ing), or white space, to be inserted between the lines of type. An appropriate amount of leading facilitates reading. Like type, leading is measured in points. The amount of leading between the lines of type on this page, for example, is one point. The size of the body type on this page is eleven points. Eleven–point type with one point of leading between the lines is called "eleven on twelve." Here is how a copy editor would mark a manuscript to tell the compositor to set the copy in eleven on twelve Zapf Book Light roman

type using both capital and lowercase letters:

11/12/Zapf rom/ C&lc

After marking the point size and the face of the type to be used, together with the amount of leading to be inserted, the copy editor indicates the width of the type lines. Width is measured in units called picas. One pica consists of 12 points and is ⅙ of an inch. One inch, in other words, contains six picas, or 72 points. To determine the optimum width of a line of type, the copy editor uses a pica ruler (shown at left). For a short story or an article, the copy editor might designate the type-line width at 16 picas or 24 picas, depending on the content and meter of the poem. Suppose, for example, that an article is to be set in ten-point Bodoni roman with two points of leading and that the type line is to be 32 picas wide. The copy editor would mark the manuscript in a manner like the following:

10/12/Bod rom/C&lc x 32

And suppose that a poem is to be set in ten-point Caledonia italics with three points of leading and that the type line is to be 18 picas wide, set flush left. The copy editor would mark the manuscript in a manner like the following:

10/13/Cal ital/C&lc x 18/ fl

Fitting the Copy

Copy editors must know (a) the amount of copy needed to fill each page and (b) the approximate length of each work (story, article, poem) once it has been set in type. The length (column depth) that a story will require when set in type depends on these three factors:

1. The size of the type used;
2. The column width;
3. The amount of leading between lines.

Although there are a number of complicated ways to determine the total length of a work, the most common method used by school magazine copy editors is called the "type-measure" method. To determine the column depth that typed material will take when it is set in type using the "typed-measure" method, take a previous issue of the school magazine and find in it a piece set in the same type size, type face, and column width desired for the material to be printed. Mark off a depth of one inch of printed copy. Then, setting the typewriter margins just as they were when the manuscript was typed, retype the printed sentences (and any parts of sentences) contained in that one inch of material. The result will indicate the number of lines needed to fill a printed space one inch deep. Next, to find out how many inches the entire work will run, divide the number of lines in one inch of printed copy into the total number of typed lines in the manuscript. For example, if you find (a) that five lines of typed copy equal one inch of printed copy when set in ten-point type with two points of leading and in a width of 30 picas, and (b) that the manuscript contains 40 typewritten lines, you know that the printed piece will be eight inches in depth.

Writing Titles

Usually authors of works published in school magazines title their works. If they don't, the copy editor has the task of supplying titles. Every title should have something interesting to say about the work it accompanies and should, when possible, relate to something readers will recognize as worth their attention. No title should promise something that is not fulfilled by the work.

WHICH TITLE INVITES READING?

Summer Vacations   100 Miles—By Canoe!

Handling Artwork

Artwork for the school magazine is usually more artistic than that appearing in the school newspaper and therefore must be handled with special care. All artwork—no matter whether it consists of photographs or illustrations—must be identified both on layout and on the artwork itself. Identification is particularly important with school-magazine artwork because much of it, being interpretive or decorative, will have no accompanying (and thus no identifying) caption. Photo essays, for example, often have only one overall caption for all of the photos making up a two-page spread. To make sure that those photos do indeed appear properly in the essay and not somewhere else, editors must be sure to mark them carefully so that they don't get lost or mixed-up.

Crop marks for artwork are made on the front of each piece of illustrative material; descriptive, locational, and identifying marks are made on the back of each piece.

Below is the layout for a two-page photo essay containing just one caption.

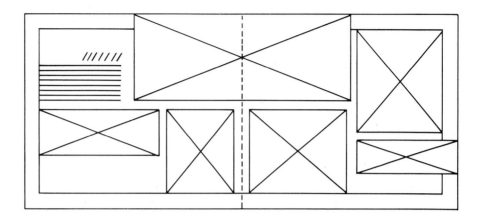

Ensuring Unity, Coherence, and Emphasis

Unity, coherence, and emphasis—the three important elements to be considered in writing and producing the school yearbook (see pages 468–471)—are of equal importance in writing for and producing the school magazine. Unity can be achieved by designating a theme for each issue and by using a consistent style for layouts. Coherence can be achieved through balance in page layouts (see pages 470–472). Emphasis can be achieved by using layouts that focus attention on the most important element on each page.

Designing an Attractive Cover

Many school magazines print attention-getting artwork on their covers; others print only the title of the magazine and the name of the school. Schools that find production costs too high for printing the entire magazine often have only the covers printed commercially.

No matter what their design or how they are printed, the covers of school magazines should be in good taste and should seek to represent—in positive fashion—the content of each issue. As with yearbook covers, the covers of school magazines can be

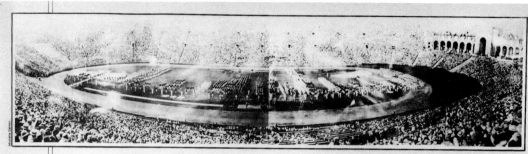

Helen Carroll:

Olympic Views Then and Now

by Dennis Adams and Kevin Manweiler

Mrs. Helen Carroll

The people who know Helen Carroll may not see anything out of the ordinary about her except for her intelligent and outgoing nature. Few people can boast the honor of having an Olympic gold medal and a national championship medal, but Mrs. Carroll won a gold medal for relay swimming during the tenth Olympic Games in 1932.

However, Mrs. Carroll's swimming success occurred almost by accident. Then Helen Johns, she was raised in Medford, Massachusetts, a suburb of Boston. Although she swam a great deal with her father in the ocean surf, "the thought of going into the races" never entered her mind. She did not swim in an indoor pool until her older sister, a physical education teacher at Brookline High School, invited her to bring a friend and come to their pool one afternoon. Thus, as Mrs. Carroll remembers, "I was in the pool having some fun, fooling around. I didn't know that the coach of the women's swimming team of Brookline had come in that afternoon, seen me swimming, and asked what my name was." He told her sister that he had "never seen a girl who could swim like that and later told Edward Johns, her father, that the Olympics were two years away and that he thought she could make the team. Mrs. Carroll adds

that she "does not know what he saw in me, because I didn't know anything about turning, starting, or the strokes."

Soon Helen Johns started training for the Olympics. Her training was not easy; her father had to drive her to Brookline three nights a week when the pool was available to women because Medford lacked indoor pools. Since men were not allowed in the building when the women were using it, Mr. Johns had to occupy himself during her three-hour workouts from 6:00 to 9:00 p.m.

Mrs. Carroll believes in the ancient Greek philosophy of developing both mind and body. Although her Olympic training was very important to her, she notes that her studies came first. "I look back on those years and wonder how I was able to do it all, particularly in my senior year of high school. I simply don't believe how I handled all the homework." At the time, Mrs. Carroll had planned to attend either Harvard or Brown, universities which required both four years of Latin and proficiency in another language. As a senior she

was in her fourth year of Latin and in her sixth year of French. Mrs. Carroll recalls that in her study time she worked first on her Latin and French and that she later worked on her science, math, and English.

Her workouts, studies, and races left Helen Johns with little time for social activity. She spent a large portion of her weekends travelling around New England to participate in swimming events. After gaining her first win as a novice early in competition, Helen Johns advanced to the junior class where she also won her first race rather quickly and graduated into the senior category. In the senior class, Miss Johns competed against the former Olympic champion who was then in college. "She could beat me when I first started, but by the summer she had decided to retire. I won the championship and broke her record," Mrs. Carroll adds. She also won a silver medal in the 1931 Outdoor Nationals.

This would have put her in line for the Olympic team; however, Helen Johns' training suffered a serious setback in her senior year when her

Opening ceremonies of the 1932 Summer Olympic Games were held in the Los Angeles Coliseum.

Mrs. Carroll stands with the rest of her teammates after winning the 400-meter relay in the 1932 Olympics.

Balance gives coherence to a page layout. Emphasis comes from focusing attention on the most important element on the page.

Mayes House Restored to Original Elegance

by Michelle Carson

During Mayesville's more prosperous years, between the early 1900's and World War I, prominent farmers built large homes of the architectural style of the period. The Mayes House, which was entered in the *National Register of Historic Places* in May, 1980, depicts the Southern Classical Greek Revival Architecture that prevailed in that era. Since its restoration, the Mayes House has become the most notable edifice in Mayesville and looks especially impressive when viewed from Highway 76.

The original owners, Mr. and Mrs. R.J. Mayes, built the house about 1910. Their four children were born and reared in the house. After the death of Mr. and Mrs. R.J. Mayes, the house belonged to their son, Mr. W.R. Mayes, who later passed it on to his son, Mr. Bill Mayes. The house remained empty from 1968 until November, 1980, when Mr. Bill Mayes began restoration.

Restoration of the house has taken approximately fifty-five work weeks, in a 15-month period. Mr. Mayes used primarily local labor for the project. The major damage to be repaired was caused by water. Because the house was unoccupied, water collected, rotting the timbers of the wooden structure. Replacing rotten lumber and general modernization became major factors in the restoration.

The exterior of the Mayes House features a portico and fluted columns seventeen feet high with Corinthian capitals. The solid cyprus column

are supported by a tongue-and-groove wooden plug that distributes the weight down through the porch to the concrete foundation. The capitals support no weight and do not even touch the roof of the portico; they merely serve as ornaments. While the house underwent restoration, the columns had to be taken down in order to pour a concrete porch and lay tiles over it. Steel beams supported the portico until two cranes replaced the columns. A majority of the original shutters still exist and have Roman numerals engraved in them. The numerals correspond to the windows so that they could easily be replaced after being removed for cleaning or painting. Leaded glass windows, a common feature of the period according to Mr. Mayes, frame the front door.

Built primarily to be viewed from the outside, the interior of the house has a distinctively simpler style. The main entrance leads into a full-length hallway which contains the original lighting fixtures. The wainscoted dining room, with its high molding, is perhaps the most decorative room in the house. The kitchen has been totally modernized, complete with conveniences unknown to the original owners. There are functional fireplaces in the dining room, library, den, and each of the four bedrooms, all of which have restored mantel pieces. Three of the bedrooms had closets built in, which was unusual in a time when most people used wardrobes. The original brass door knobs and window hardware remain

After reconstruction, the glory of this fine old Southern mansion is evident once again in the beautiful facade.

The original Mayes House stands in its full splendor in the 1930's.

Just inside the main entrance, the stairway parallels a full-length hallway.

padded; they can also have hard covers or paper covers. Paper covers seem to be the kind most frequently used. Made from durable, heavy-weighted stock, paper covers constitute an inexpensive yet wholly satisfactory kind of cover for publications of 100 pages or less.

Methods for Printing School Magazines

Because of high printing costs, many schools have decided not to publish a school magazine or have discontinued such publication. The reason: Offset and letterpress printers' costs often exceed $1.50 per copy to print a 24-page magazine with illustrations. Such high production costs must, of course, be reflected in the per-copy price, thereby putting the purchase of the magazine beyond the reach of many.

But schools and school magazine staffs might consider printing methods other than offset or letterpress. After all, the end result —a medium for publishing student work—is far more important than a high-quality printing job. Here we focus on less expensive printing processes.

Mimeograph Duplication

Some school magazines are mimeographed. The work to be published is typed on an inexpensive, wax coated stencil, the dimensions of which can range from a minimum of 3 by 5 inches to a maximum of 9 by 15 inches. The usual size, however, is the standard 8½ by 11 inches. Each stroke of a typewriter key perforates the stencil to allow ink to be transferred to paper. Typewriter keys must be kept clean, and margins must be carefully observed.

It is also possible to reproduce artwork by this method. The illustrator uses a stylus (a slender metal penlike instrument with a rounded point) to mark the stencil. For the reproduction of black-and-white photographs, the illustrator uses an electronic stylus, as illustrated in Chapter 17, page 409.

When a stencil is ready for printing, it is attached to a circular inked drum. As the drum rotates, the perforated stencil comes into contact with sheets of paper that are automatically fed into the mimeograph machine. As many as 200 sheets can be printed every minute at very low cost. Mimeograph duplication is especially economical when the run amounts to about 5000 copies.

Copier Duplication

Some school magazines are published by means of electronic copiers. As is the case with mimeograph duplication, the material to be published is typed. But instead of using stencils, the typist uses regular white typing paper, 8½ by 11 inches. For best results, the type should be sharp and clear. The typed sheets are then placed on the drum of an electronic copier, which prints and collates as many copies as are desired. Today, electronic copiers can produce materials in color as well as in black. The cost per sheet for electronic duplication runs from two to five cents.

Other Low-Cost Printing Methods

Some school magazines are printed by low-cost offset presses. Such presses—small, do-it-yourself machines—cost under $1000, and the plates for these presses cost only slightly more than do mimeograph stencils. Not only are small offset presses comparatively inexpensive to maintain, they are valuable also because they can reproduce photographs in color and printed materials in many colors.

Small offset presses can print on paper ranging in size from a minimum of 3 by 5 inches to a maximum of 11 by 17 inches. They produce printing of high quality up to 50,000 copies at a very low cost per copy.

Financing the School Magazine

Although business operations for a school magazine are usually much less complicated than those for the school newspaper or yearbook, they are nonetheless important.

One of the questions asked of school magazine editors-in-chief is this: "Why doesn't your magazine come out more often?" The usual reply is that there just isn't enough money in the school's publication budget to permit additional issues.

The job of the school magazine's business manager is similar to that of the business manager on the school newspaper or year-book. He or she is responsible for preparing a budget for each issue of the magazine, as well as an overall budget for the entire school year. In addition, the business manager supervises those in charge of advertising, circulation, and promotion to make sure that the school magazine operates on a profitable basis.

For the most part, the income generated from publishing the school magazine comes from advertising, from patrons, and from sales to individuals—students, faculty, and friends in the community. Printing costs, the purchase of office supplies, and miscellaneous costs constitute the major expenses.

Activities

1. Plan and lay out a two-page spread to appear in a school magazine whose dimensions are 8½ by 11 inches. In your layout, include these elements:

    a. A seven-inch-wide (42 picas) title of a short story.

    b. Two photographs, one measuring 7 by 7 inches, the other measuring 6½ by 4 inches.

    c. A feature article set 18 picas (three inches) wide and ten inches deep.

2. Count the number of lines in three pages of typewritten copy. Using the "typed-measure" method discussed in this chapter, estimate how many inches of printed space the typed material will fill when

    a. it is set in 11-point type in Zapf Book light roman, the face used in this book, with one point of leading, and

    b. it is set in a column 28 picas wide.

3. For a school magazine in which you have used informal balance, explain specifically how you would achieve unity, coherence and emphasis.

4. Prepare a brief (one-page) editorial style guide for a proposed school magazine. Include such items as spelling, punctuation, and capitalization. Give examples of each item you include. For example:

Spelling: Spell compound words as one word *(percent, teenager).*

Punctuation: Use a hyphen between two words that normally are separate but that are used as one modifier *(never-to-be-forgotten* experience, a *two-week* vacation).

Capitalization: Use a capital letter to begin a direct quotation accompanied by an explainer. (He said, "Wait for me." "Don't yell," she shouted).

5. Prepare a brief mechanical style guide for a proposed school magazine. Include guidelines for setting several kinds of material in type—poems, prose, fiction, nonfiction prose, titles, bylines, and captions. For example:

Poetry: Set all poem titles in boldface, flush left.

Bylines: Set all bylines in 8-point roman sans serif, using capitals and lowercase letters. Center the byline under the title of the work.

CHAPTER 23

Photography and School Publications

Graham Claytor, chief photographer for the *South High Record*, is checking the newsroom beatsheet for photo possibilities. Cynthia Cox, editor of the *Record*, calls to him.

"Got something for me?" Graham asks with a smile.

"Sure have," replies Cynthia. "Mr. Rarey—you know, the physics teacher—has a new book out. We're doing a feature on him and would like a photo to go with the story. Any chance of getting more than a head-and-shoulders shot?"

"You mean something that says he's an author as well as a teacher?"

"That's the idea—if it's possible to do both in one photo."

Graham appreciates Cynthia's suggestion, but he's also aware that some picture ideas are impossible to implement satisfactorily.

"What if I arrange several copies of Mr. Rarey's book on a pane of glass and have him look down through the glass? I could lie on the floor, look up through the glass, and take the picture. That'd be a different kind of angle."

"Sounds good. And could you also show that Mr. Rarey is a teacher."

"Well, maybe and maybe not." Graham is hesitant. "But I guess I could ask Mr. Rarey to write some physics equations on the board and try to get them into the picture too."

"That might work, agrees Cynthia.

"I'll try it. But don't be upset if it doesn't work out." As a photographer, Graham is a firm believer in the rule "when in doubt, simplify." He's concerned that the writing on the board may detract from the unity of the picture. And so Graham decides to shoot the picture in two ways—with and without the equations.

Graham stops by Mr. Rarey's office to make an appointment. He also wants to explain a little of what he'd like to do about arranging the set. Mr. Rarey is impressed with Graham's businesslike approach and is happy to cooperate. He likes the idea of using a pane of glass. He even rummages around the physics supply room and comes up with a pane of glass about an inch thick.

"That should hold just about everything," he says with a grin. "See you tomorrow."

Graham knows that Mr. Rarey—like most people who have articles written about them—has many demands on his time. Therefore, the next day Graham arrives a few minutes early. While Mr. Rarey is finishing a conference with a student, Graham gets things ready for taking his pictures. Pulling two chairs fairly close together, he puts the glass on them and then arranges the books on the glass. He then double-checks his camera to make sure that he's inserted the right film, that the shutter is set for the right speed, and that the aperture is properly set. With Mr. Rarey ready, it takes Graham only a few seconds to get himself under the glass plate and take the first picture. Graham then asks Mr. Rarey to write some physics equations on the board behind him. With that done, Graham re-poses Mr. Rarey and, with the new background, takes the second picture.

Graham helps put the chairs back, returns the books to their proper place, and takes the glass back to the supply room. He then thanks Mr. Rarey for his time and cooperation.

"Not at all," smiles Mr. Rarey. "I thank you. You've got a prize-winning photo there, I'm sure. I'm looking forward to seeing the pictures."

"You're not the only one," says Graham to himself as he hurries to the lab to develop and print the pictures. When he sees the negative of the second shot, Graham knows he was right to be skeptical about the equations: They look as if they're coming out of Mr. Rarey's head. And so, Graham decides to use the negative of the first shot. He makes a number of prints until he is satisfied he has the best quality obtainable. He makes an extra print just in case the yearbook editor might want it and still another to give to Mr. Rarey.

He finds Cynthia in the newsroom and hands her one of the prints.

"How's that for one-day service?" he asks.

"Great!" says Cynthia, who calls the other staff members over to share her admiration for Graham's work.

Is the Picture Worth a Thousand Words?

School Photography: General Considerations

In today's age of automatic cameras, almost anyone can take a picture that is satisfactory. But "satisfactory" is not a high enough goal for a school paper's chief photographer to aim for. That goal must be excellence. Other things being equal, the essential difference between a picture taken by a knowledgeable photographer and one taken by an amateur lies in the effective exercise of imagination and creativity—the ability to use that imagination.

A picture, it has been said, is "worth a thousand words." Unfortunately, that's not always the case. Sometimes the photographs in school newspapers are like dictionary definitions: They may be interesting, but they aren't attention-getters. For a news photograph to be worth a thousand words, it must be worth *reading*. That is, not only must it immediately capture and hold reader attention; it must also tell a story. Such a photograph can indeed be worth a thousand words.

Knowledgeable photographers have identified nine factors that combine to make a photograph newsworthy. The school photographer who aims for excellence in the pictures submitted for publication should keep these nine factors constantly in mind.

RESPONSIBILITIES OF THE CHIEF PHOTOGRAPHER FOR SCHOOL PUBLICATIONS

✓ Reports directly to the editor-in-chief and the faculty adviser concerning all photography for the school newspaper and other school publications.

✓ With the help of the editor-in-chief, the managing editor, and the faculty adviser, delegates assignments to other members of the photography staff.

✓ Helps take, develop, and print all photographs for the school paper and other school publications.

✓ Meets all deadlines.

✓ Schedules and supervises the taking of all pictures for the school newspaper and other school publications.

✓ At the beginning of the school year, inventories all equipment and supplies; repeats the inventory at the end of the school year at a time designated by the faculty adviser.

✓ Keeps a book of future photo possibilities and assignments.

✓ Specifies darkroom procedures; cares for all darkroom materials and equipment; keeps the darkroom clean.

✓ Makes out a monthly order for supplies.

✓ Crops all photographs as may be required.

✓ Writes captions as may be required.

✓ Attends all staff meetings.

People. Because the human-interest touch enhances the effectiveness of most photos, people usually make the most successful subjects. Imagine a picture of a chemistry lab that doesn't show any students! On photographic assignments, you may want to take some students with you for inclusion in your pictures.

Action. Whether your subject is at work or at play is unimportant. It is important, however, that your subject be *doing something.* (Most publication judges feel that merely shaking hands does not constitute doing something.) There is no deadlier type of picture than one showing a rigid lineup of people looking directly into the camera.

This photo shows a school activity and tells a story.

Information—Telling the Story. Never be in a hurry to snap your pictures and run. Try to arrive early enough to talk to the subject(s) and solicit advice and ideas about what type of picture will best tell the story. Keep in mind that your subject—like you —wants the best possible picture taken. Photography subjects are usually more than happy to offer suggestions. Also consider using pennants, flags, posters, signs, costumes, or any other available props that will help visually to tell the story.

Closeups. Try to have not more than three or four people in your picture. Suggest that your subjects stand or sit close together to avoid wasting space. You may want to take the picture at the group's left—or right—to avoid other possible waste space. When you print the negative, remember to enlarge it enough to delete unwanted areas around the edges. Crop the picture if necessary.

School Tie-in. Have the pictures show that the persons are from your school. Uniforms and banners can help, and so can the school itself. For example, photograph Student Council officers outdoors, using part of the school building as background.

Technical Quality. A good photographic print consists of solid white areas and solid black areas, together with many shades of gray. Prints with no solid black areas should be reprinted before being submitted for publication. A print that "sparkles" is one that has a range of gray tones. One of the easiest ways to make your prints sparkle is to expose the negative a normal length of time. Don't hesitate to take a number of shots, varying the exposure for each.

Angles. Beginning photographers seem to take most of their pictures from just one angle—head on. You can give your pictures both variety and impact if you take them from high or low angles. A football rally, for example, might best be taken from a third-story window. And a basketball player can often be made to look taller if photographed from a very low angle.

Lighting. In general, basic photography books suggest that beginners take their pictures with the light coming from over the shoulder. But as an advanced photographer, you might have the light source—sun, floodlight, or strobe light—coming from the

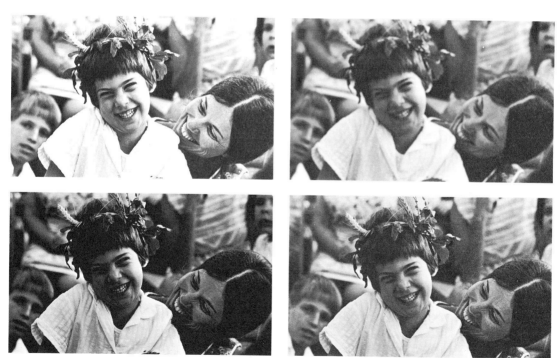

Top left photo is too light. Top right photo is out of focus. Lower left photo is too dark. Lower right photo is correctly exposed and has good technical quality.

Lighting techniques make photos interesting.

side, from above, or even from behind the subject. To achieve a more natural-looking effect, consider using available light. Or you might direct the light source toward the ceiling, from which it can "bounce" down on the subject. This "bounce-light" technique can be effective, but it poses one potential problem—namely, failure to obtain proper exposure. To compensate for the extra distance the "bounce light" has to travel, you need to double the exposure time.

Posing. To get a posed picture to look candid (unposed) is an art. You can get that candid look in your pictures by using your imagination in posing your subjects. Above all, avoid handshaking and presentation shots; they tend to be dull and unimaginative. Think through taking the picture before you actually shoot. First, consider what a head-on shot of your subject would look like. Next, imagine how the subject would appear with head turned and looking over the left—and then the right—shoulder. Then try other appropriate poses. When you find the "right" one, take the picture. Or again, suppose you have an assignment to photograph a Drama Club production. You probably would want to wait until after a dress rehearsal to pose the actors in a way that captures the action and the expressions you want.

School Photography: Makers of Viewer Interest

Besides the nine general considerations discussed above, several "makers of viewer interest" must also concern the school photographer who seeks excellence. These "makers of viewer interest" can be thought of as the characteristics that make a photograph an attention-getter. The knowledgeable photographer gets as many "makers of viewer interest" into the pictures as possible.

Human Interest. Pictures of people in action are almost sure to attract attention. Why? Because people respond to other people. Whenever a poem, story, or photograph concerns human beings and their triumphs and tragedies, we say it has human interest.

Timeliness. To attract reader attention, the news photo or yearbook photo should be timely—up to date. Usually, pictures of people who no longer have any connection with the school or pictures of situations that no longer exist are uninteresting. They have little to attract or hold reader attention.

The Local Angle. The more a picture tells student viewers that it was taken at their school, the more attention it is likely to get. Photographers are often surprised at how many items around the school bear its name—banners, trophies, sports uniforms and equipment, band uniforms, and even the bass drum. Getting one or more of these items—used appropriately, of course—into school pictures will help localize the pictures and help generate a sense of pride in student viewers.

Celebrities. Names make news. Pictures of famous people are sure-fire attention-getters. Suppose, for example, that a graduate of your school has become a movie or television star. If that person has come back to the school for "homecoming" or some other special event, a photographer might take a picture of the star showing Drama Club members how to apply makeup. Or suppose a famous politician is to speak at a school assembly. A photographer could take a picture of him or her chatting with the Student Council president.

Conflict. A sports photo that depicts conflict is relatively easy to get. Other school activities and situations involving conflict seem much more difficult to spot. Yet they do exist. A school election campaign, for example, might present the occasion for a photograph of opposing candidates carrying banners or placards that suggest conflict. A sales campaign to sell the school yearbook might suggest a photograph humorously showing a yearbook salesperson overcoming the resistance of a reluctant buyer.

Emotion. Within the bounds of good taste, pictures that reveal human emotion can be prime "makers of viewer interest." The knowledgeable photographer is ever on the lookout for situations and occasions likely to produce emotional reactions—joy, fear, happiness, sorrow, anger, jealousy, and the like—in human beings. For example, a candid photograph showing the opposing candidates for student office watching ballots being counted could be a real attention-getter. A close-up of a winner's face when election results are announced is likely to be worth a thousand words. Consider carefully whether it would be appropriate to take a photo of the loser's face. It is never appropriate to invade a person's privacy.

Photographs taken at sports events can often reveal emotion. It is said, for example, that the story of the game is told in the losers' locker room. Pictures that reveal frustration and dejection can attract as much attention as those showing joy and victory.

Any photo assignment might call for publishing more than one picture. Staff photographers should take and submit a number of pictures showing a variety of emotions.

Consequence. Sometimes we overlook the conditions, situations, and people that make the school a good place in which to get an education, and we take things for granted. Knowledgeable photographers find ways to help students become aware of and appreciate the advantages of their school. For example, when a new facility—a gymnasium, an auditorium, a computer room, a language laboratory—is added to the school, a photographer can find interesting ways to bring it to the attention of the student body.

Using the Camera

Actually, it doesn't matter what camera a school photographer uses as long as the picture to be printed in the newspaper, yearbook, or school magazine is sharp and clear. School photographers use a variety of cameras. The most commonly used, however, is the 35mm (millimeter) single-lens reflex. Black and white film should be used for pictures intended for publication in the school newspaper; color film is generally not used because of the high cost of processing. But in the yearbook and the school magazine, color pictures contribute variety and attractiveness.

The Lenses

Most 35 mm cameras come equipped with a 50mm lens, which is considered a "normal" lens. The field of view of such a lens is comparable to that of the human eye. For the most part, a 35mm camera equipped with a 50mm lens will suffice for most of the staff photographer's assignments.

Lenses with a focal point of more than 50mm are generally considered to be telephoto lenses, and those with a focal length of less than 50mm are considered wide-angle lenses. Ideally, 35mm cameras can be fitted with interchangeable lenses. In situations where the photographer is unable to stand back far enough to see the entire setting in the viewfinder, he or she should use a 28mm wide-angle lens. To get a closeup of a distant scene, the photographer should use a 135mm telephoto lens. Telephoto lenses compress distance, making the subject and the background seem closer. Wide-angle lenses, on the other hand, push the background even farther back than it seems to the unaided eye.

Efficient Operation

Loading the Film. Film for 35mm cameras is available in either 20- or 36-exposure cassettes. Getting the film into the camera is a simple, yet critical, procedure. If the film is not loaded properly, it will not advance in the camera. Result: no pictures. Follow the directions printed on the film package.

When the film is firmly in place, click the shutter a few times to advance the film and make sure that the film is tightly engaged. Close the back of the camera and snap the shutter three additional times. You are now ready to take your first picture.

Once you have made your last exposure, you must rewind the film into the lightproof cassette. Turn the rewind/advance indicator to "Rewind," and turn the rewind lever until you are sure the film has been completely rewound into the cassette.

Focusing. To focus the 35mm single-lens reflex camera, you turn the focusing ring around the barrel of the lens until the image in the viewfinder is sharply defined. If the image isn't sharp, any picture you take will be blurred. There is usually a vernier scale printed on the focusing ring to help the photographer get the focus that is best for the distance between the camera and subject. Sports photographers must often guess where the action will be and focus their cameras accordingly. When covering a football game, for example, the photographer might focus on a 25-foot distance and wait (and hope) for the action to occur there. In covering a basketball game, the photographer might sit on the floor behind the backboard and focus the camera on the foul line. A photographer covering a baseball game might wait at first base and focus the camera on the bag. With runners on second and/or third base, the photographer might stand halfway between third and home plate in order to focus equally well on both bases.

Checking Light Intensity. Many cameras have a built-in light meter that automatically adjusts the lens opening. If a camera lacks such equipment, you can buy a separate light meter (a photoelectric cell) that accurately measures the intensity of the light. The brighter the light on the subject, the smaller the lens opening needed for proper exposure.

Setting the Shutter Speed. Because camera movement or subject movement can ruin any picture, the photographer must make sure that the shutter speed is fast enough to prevent blurring.

For routine pictures, set the shutter speed at about $1/125$ of a second or faster. For sports action, shoot at the fastest speed possible—$1/500$ of a second or faster. When, because of poor lighting, it is necessary to shoot a picture at a slow speed (under $1/60$ of a second), use a tripod to brace the camera. If no tripod is available or if shooting at a slow speed would blur the picture, shoot at the faster speed and compensate by leaving the film in the developing solution for a longer time.

Taking Pictures

Anyone can take a picture. The difficulty lies in taking a picture that says something. When you have a picture-taking assignment, therefore, first make sure that your camera has been loaded correctly and that the shutter speed has been set properly. You then won't need to be concerned about those essentials while you are arranging the set and posing the people who are to appear in the picture. When you do pose people, eliminate any dead space and have them doing something—even if it's only looking at a piece of paper. Then, looking into the viewfinder, double-check to make sure that the scene you see is the picture you want. Next, check to make sure that you have the proper exposure setting, and then focus the camera. Carefully squeeze the shutter-release mechanism and take the picture.

Take several pictures, varying the exposure and camera angle slightly each time. This technique is called bracketing. At this point, you may want to change the composition of the picture to obtain a different effect. If so, follow the same procedure as suggested above. When you have completed the picture-taking, thank the participants for their time and their cooperation. Finally, make sure that the room (or the place where the pictures were taken) is put back the way you found it.

Preparing the Photograph for Publication

Some school photographers send their exposed films out to be developed by commercial photo-finishing labs. But this arrangment may require several days. That's why school photographers who have the necessary darkroom facilities prefer to do their own developing and printing.

With the exception of self-developing film, all film-developing is carried out in a darkroom. The exposed film is placed on a specially constructed spool, which is then inserted into a small tank (with a diameter of about four inches) filled with a developing solution. The specially constructed spool allows the film to be wound in such a way that the developing solution comes into contact with every part of the film. Because the development time depends on the type of developer used, the photographer must be familiar with the instructions that accompany the developing solution and must follow them carefully.

At the appropriate time, the developer is poured out of the tank and replaced by a stop-bath solution, which remains in the tank for a minute or so. Again, at the appropriate time, the stop-bath solution is poured out and another solution—called an acid fixer, or hypo—is poured into the tank. This solution stops all development and fixes the image on the film. It is at that time that ordinary electric lights can be turned on and the developed negatives taken out of the developing tank.

Once it has been removed from the tank, the developed film should be washed in cold running water for several minutes to remove all chemicals. It is then hung up to dry in a dust-free area. When throughly dry, the developed negatives should immediately be placed in protective envelopes to prevent their being damaged by dust or fingerprints or scratches of any kind.

Because school photographers are often asked to reprint specific photographs, they should set up a filing system that permits the ready retrieval of the negative of any photo taken.

Writing Captions

After taking a picture, the photographer must record the facts needed to distinguish it from other pictures he or she has taken or will take. When taking a picture of a group, the photographer must be careful to take down the names of all persons in that group, listing the name of each in the order in which he or she appears in the picture, starting at the left. Because it is important that all names be spelled correctly, the photographer should print the names instead of writing them.

When photographing a sports event, the photographer should take down the numbers of the players shown, the quarter or period during which the picture was taken, and a brief description of the action portrayed. As soon as possible after taking the picture, he or she should type up this information, supplying whatever additional information is needed to identify that specific picture. For example, if a halfback is shown beginning a run that resulted in a touchdown, a photographer should so indicate in the typed information.

When a photographer is expected to write a caption exactly as it is to appear in print, he or she should be sure the information in the caption includes the five w's, and the h. If the picture is to be published without an accompanying story, the caption must contain even more detail. In such a case, the photographer tells the entire story *briefly* in the caption. If, on the other hand, a picture is to be published with a news story or a feature story, the photographer keeps the caption as brief as possible, describing only what is going on in the picture.

Creating a Picture Story

Sometimes a student newspaper or yearbook will run a picture story. In planning what photographs to take for such a story, the photographer should plan the story to show a beginning, a middle, and an end. So that the story will unfold logically, the photographer must do the research necessary to help him or her decide what pictures will tell the *best* story and what pictures will best tell the *story*.

This picture story shows the action at a track meet.

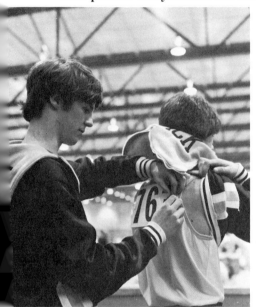

The Establishing Shot. The first picture in a picture story is usually a "distance shot," showing the area or situation to be covered in the story. Such a picture establishes the setting and helps the viewer get his or her "feet on the ground." For example, in a picture story about the school's band director, the establishing shot might show the director and the entire band at marching practice on the football field near the school.

Medium Shots. For the next sequence of pictures, the photographer moves in closer to the main subject of the story for "medium" shots. In the story about the band director, for example, the photographer might take three or four pictures as follows: one showing him or her practicing with the brass section of the band, one showing the band director and a couple of trombone players who have inadequate space to extend their trombone slides fully, and one showing the director with the uniformed drum major about to start off on parade. Pictures like these would help the viewer "see" the subject in specific relationships within the overall story situation.

Closeups. For impact, the picture story should have several closeups that focus on the main subject exclusively. For example, a number of closeups of the band director showing annoyance, satisfaction, doubt, and joy would suggest some of his or her feelings as conductor of the band and would give added impact to the picture story.

The Final Shot. The last picture should seek to give the picture story a feeling of finality. Such a picture could be taken at dusk, suggesting that the day—and the picture story—are at an end. The final shot in the story about the band director, for example, might show him or her in the foreground and the band in the background as they tip their hats to the spectators after their half-time performance at a football game.

Cinematography

Filmmaking is taught in many American high schools. With recent improvements in the manufacture of motion-picture cameras, this once complex and expensive undertaking has become less complicated and less costly. Courses that once taught journalism students how to use a motion-picture camera correctly have developed into detailed courses in filmmaking. Now many journalism students produce their own documentary, educational, and news films for use in journalism laboratory courses.

Making a Motion Picture

Knowing the techniques used by cinematographers in making films for movies and television will help students create films worthy of attention.

An important element that contributes to the success of any filmed presentation is continuity. Like any news story prepared for the print media, the scenes making up a motion picture must proceed in logical sequence from a beginning, through a middle, to an end (conclusion).

As in still photography, the cinematographer must act as the "brain" for the camera. The basic purpose of all filmed material is communication. To communicate successfully, the cinematographer must use imagination and creativity and be able to apply knowledge of photographic techniques to filmmaking.

The Television Camera

The television camera operates on the same principle as does the standard motion-picture camera. But instead of using celluloid film that must be developed in a darkroom, the television camera uses a cathode ray tube, which transmits an image in terms of the brightness of the light on that image. The cathode ray tube in the camera converts shades of brightness into electronic signals that are sent out over the airwaves. The home television set then converts those signals into appropriate shades of light and dark. The picture seen by viewers has 525 lines of different shades of light and dark, and each frame changes at a rate of 30 times per second. Thus, the images appear to move.

Videotape

For many years, scientists had worked at finding a way to put television picture signals on magnetic tape so that the images could be played back on a tape recorder. By the early 1970s such a device was perfected. With the invention of portable television cameras, videotape could be played back almost immediately after the action was completed. Thus was "instant replay" in sports telecasting made possible. Videotape, of course, can also be stored for later telecasts.

Schools have many uses for videotape. For example, a videotape of a football game can be used for instruction or a pep rally. Videotapes can be made of school plays or other school activities.

The Three *C*'s of Photography

Creativity, communication, and craftsmanship are recognized by school and professional photographers alike as the three *C's* of successful photography. By using imagination the school photographer has the opportunity to *create* a work of art with any picture he or she takes. If three imaginative photographers covered the same assignment, the picture that each takes would differ markedly from the pictures taken by the other two.

The imaginative photographer has the ability to *communicate* an idea visually by making sure that every picture taken is based on one or more of the "makers of viewer interest."

Craftsmanship is important for successful photography. Knowledge of and an ability to use the techniques of lighting, composing, focusing, exposing the film, and developing and printing it, will enable the photographer to be creative and to communicate.

Eighteen-year old Monte Paulsen, Kodak-Scholastic Award winner, whose photo appears on pages 526–527 offers the following advice to other school photographers:

"The first thing is to do all of your own darkroom work. I can't stress that enough. If you don't, you're likely to remain confused for a long time about technical things.

"The second thing is this: When you take pictures, think. If you're taking a picture of Martha, think 'What is Martha? Who is Martha? What does Martha do? Where does Martha live?' Try to show these things in your photographs.

"If you're really mad at something or really happy, or if you're bored or excited, take a picture that shows how you feel. It doesn't matter what the picture's about. What you're looking for are symbols—things that will show your mood. That's more like the approach art photographers take.

"So shoot for meaning, or shoot for feeling. Do your own darkroom work. And if you do these things long enough, there's no way you can lose."

1. Select a photograph from a current magazine or newspaper, one that, in your opinion, is an immediate attention-getter or is ineffective. Mount the photograph on an 8½ by 11 sheet of paper. Under the photograph, write or type a brief one-sentence answer to each of the following questions:

    a. What story does the photograph tell (or seek to tell but fail to do so)?

    b. What techniques has the photographer used effectively (or ineffectively)?

    c. Why do you think the photographer chose the camera angle, distance, action, lighting, and setting used?

2. a. From a current magazine or newspaper, select an effective photograph. Mount the photo on an 8½ by 11 sheet of paper. Compose a caption for the photo; type or write it below the photograph.

    b. Near the foot of the paper, write a *brief* explanation of your reasons for liking and choosing the photo.

    c. With other members of the class, prepare a bulletin board display of similarly mounted and captioned photographs submitted by your classmates.

    d. Take an informal poll of the class to determine the three best photos in the display. With the class, discuss the results of the poll. What were the most frequently given reasons for the choices?

3. What action would make suitable subjects for a photograph to be used in big-picture page makeup for the front page of your school newspaper? List at least ten actions that could be photographed and made into attention-getting front-page pictures. Explain briefly the photographic appeal of each.

4. Prepare a list of criteria to govern the selection of student-submitted photographs for the school yearbook. From your list, prepare—in outline form—a photograph-evaluation suggestion sheet for your school's yearbook committee. With your class, consider and discuss all the suggestions. Draw up a *class* photograph-evaluation sheet for the editors of the yearbook.

5. Prepare a list of five future school events that would lend themselves to motion-picture or videotape coverage. For each write a brief paragraph suggesting how that event could best be covered to attract student interest in it.

CHAPTER 24

Advertising and School Publications

Mr. Bert Carlisle is the owner and manager of Music City. To Jim Lally, advertising sales representative for the Meadowbrook High School *Banner*, Mr. Carlisle constitutes a challenge. You see, Mr. Carlisle is the first one on a list of ten businesses Jim will call on to sell advertising space in the *Banner*. But Jim has done his preparation. He knows that Music City has a large clientele among Meadowbrook students. And Jim is confident about the sales approach he has worked out.

"Good afternoon, Mr. Carlisle," Jim begins. I'm Jim Lally and I represent the Meadowbrook High School *Banner*."

Mr. Carlisle nods.

"Mr. Carlisle," Jim continues, "it's good to have Music City so close to the school. Many of our students come here to buy their records and tapes because it's very convenient for them to do so. I've just finished a survey, and I find that about 60 percent of the Meadowbrook population patronize Music City."

Mr. Carlisle nods again.

"Since almost all of our students read the *Banner,* our publication offers a unique opportunity for you to increase that percentage. In fact, I have taken the liberty of developing two sample advertisements that seem to me to be just right for your store."

Mr. Carlisle seems pleased and also seems eager to look at them.

"The first ad," explains Jim as he hands it to the shop owner, "stresses the wide range of music products and services available here at Music City. The second emphasizes the latest record albums and tapes available here."

"Hm," muses Mr. Carlisle as he examines Jim's sample ads. "They're both good." Then after another minute or so, he continues, "But I guess I prefer the second one."

"OK." Jim is hopeful.

"Tell you what," says Mr. Carlisle.

"I'll be glad to take advertising space in each issue of the *Banner* if you can agree to this one condition. Before each issue of the *Banner* goes to press, you'll call me to get the names of the newest albums and tapes that I think Meadowbrook students will go for. Can you do that?"

"You bet I can," smiles Jim. "I certainly appreciate your confidence, Mr. Carlisle. Just give me time to go back to the *Banner* office to write up the terms of our agreement. Then I'll return with a contract. What time tomorrow would be most convenient for you?"

"How about this same time tomorrow afternoon?" Mr. Carlisle is impressed with Jim's serious attention to business.

"Great!" exclaims Jim. "I'll be back tomorrow afternoon at 3:30 sharp. Thank you very much, Mr. Carlisle."

Every day millions of people across the United States read newspapers and magazines, and every day millions of people listen to the radio and watch television. Not only do those millions constitute a vast information-receiving audience; they also make up a vast potential market for those who have goods and services to sell. How can those sellers best bring their goods and services to the attention of potential buyers? Through **advertising**.

Newspapers and magazine print advertisements; radio and television stations broadcast commercials. In doing so, they help to bring buyers and sellers together—which, after all, is the principal function of advertising. Thus they are performing a useful service for which they collect fees from the advertisers. Virtually 100 percent of the income of radio and television stations comes from the commercials they broadcast. And fully 60 percent of the income of professionally produced newspapers and magazines comes from the advertisements they print.

School publications, too, can realize significant revenue from advertising. As we have already pointed out, up to 67 percent of the operating revenue of school publications—the newspaper, the yearbook, and the school magazine—can come from the advertisements they carry.

Two sample ads that high school advertising representatives might draw up use the "unique-selling proposition" and "basic-copy appeals."

The Advertising Staff

Our discussions of the finances of the school newspaper, the yearbook, and the school magazine emphasized the close relationship between financial success and the effectiveness and dedication of the advertising manager and the advertising staff. Besides contributing to a school publication's financial health, a dedicated advertising staff helps increase a publication's usefulness to the community. In their contacts with local business people, advertising staff members bring the school and its program to the attention of many people not directly associated with the school. The chances for good school/community relations are thereby increased.

Advertising Policy

To fulfill their responsibilities, the advertising manager and the advertising staff of any school publication must establish an *advertising policy* designed to create revenue. The development of such a policy requires careful planning. In that planning, at least six key elements demand attention.

Determining Advertising Rates

For the most part, advertising rates for a school publication are determined by the advertising manager, the business manager, and the faculty adviser. The cost of an advertisement depends upon (a) its size, (b) the total cost of the publication in which it is to appear, and (c) the number of subscribers to the publication. Since a school publication ordinarily has two principal sources of revenue—advertising and subscriptions—it is essential that advertising revenue cover publication costs not covered by revenue from subscriptions.

Advertising rates can be established in one of several ways. But the method ordinarily followed by school publications is to base them on *per-page* production costs. Suppose, for example, that the printer charges $200 per page to set type, make the plates for illustrations on the page, and print the publication. And suppose, too, that the editorial staff have endorsed the policy—followed by many professional publications—of having 70 percent of the total space given over to advertising and 30 percent taken up by stories or articles and features. With these assumptions in mind, the advertising manager, together with the business manager and the faculty adviser, would most likely establish the basic rate for a *one-time full-page* ad at $250. They would then set up an *advertising rate schedule* based on the *one-time* printing of an advertisement. Such a schedule might look like this:

- Full-page ad: $250
- Three-quarters-page ad: $190
- One-half-page ad: $160
- Quarter-page ad: $70
- One-eighth-page ad: $40
- One-sixteenth-page ad: $30

To encourage advertisers to contract for advertising space in each issue of a school publication (specifically, the paper and the magazine), the advertising rate card could offer a rate reduction—say 10 percent—for every additional insertion of the advertisement.

Assigning "Sales Beats"

It is the advertising manager's responsibility to assign a "sales beat" to each member of the advertising staff. That is, the advertising manager gives each staff member—who is actually an advertising sales representative—the names and addresses of specific businesses in the community. The sales representative calls on every business listed for the purpose of selling advertising space in the school publication that the student represents.

In some cases, the advertising manager assigns advertising "sales beats" on a random basis. However, careful planning of such assignments can do much to promote harmony among advertising staff members and thus help to increase advertising revenue. For example, a staff member may have a relative who owns or manages a local business. To include that specific business in the "sales beat" of that particular staff member would be wise as well as logical.

Furthermore, in planning advertising "sales beats," the advertising manager should consider the special interests of individual staff members. For example, a sales representative who owns a home computer should probably be assigned to call on businesses that make and/or sell home computers.

Researching the Prospective Advertiser

Once an advertising sales representative has been assigned a "sales beat," it is his or her responsibility to find out as much as possible (a) about each business listed and (b) about the products each sells or the services each offers. To obtain that information, the sales representative should (1) walk through the store to get acquainted with the merchandise carried, and (2) look for the store's advertising in other publications, especially the local newspaper, to get an idea of the style of advertising the store does. The sales representative is also well advised to seek answers to questions like the following:

1. To what extent does the business's product or service appeal to high school students? Does it appeal primarily to persons of high school age, or does it appeal to people in general?
2. To what extent is the product or the service purchased on impulse? To what extent is it a standard or staple item purchased in the course of one's ordinary activities?
3. Is the product or the service expensive or inexpensive?
4. To what extent is the product or the service a seasonal item?
5. To what extent does the product or the service have a long life? To what extent is it expendable—designed specifically for relatively short-term use?
6. To what extent is the product or the service worth what it costs?
7. In what other school publication(s) has the business advertised?
8. How frequently has the business advertised in school publications?

9. What type of advertisement has the business run?
10. If the business has advertised in school publications, what do former student sales representatives report about the kind of business relationship that was developed?

Developing Sample Advertisements

Having thoroughly researched all prospective advertisers on the assigned list, the advertising sales representative has one critical task to complete before calling on any potential customer. That task is to design at least two sample advertisements that can be used to generate the prospect's interest in advertising in the school publication. Each sample advertisement should, of course, have its own individual approach and its own overall character.

Writing Copy. The first step in designing sample advertisements for school publications involves the writing of advertising copy. Such copy must, of course, be directed specifically at high school students. Asking a question like this will help: "What products or services offered by this business is of particular interest to students?" The sales representative/copywriter should then apply (a) the principles of "the unique selling proposition," discussed in Chapter 5 on page 112, and (b) one or more of the "basic copy appeals" discussed in the same chapter on pages 113–119. The sales representative/copywriter should also keep in mind the five criteria that make for successful advertising copy:

1. *Attention.* The advertisement should immediately capture the prospective buyer's attention.
2. *Interest.* The advertising copy should hold the consumer's interest.
3. *Conviction.* The copy should convince the prospective buyer that what is being advertised is ideal.
4. *Desire.* The advertising copy should inspire a desire in the consumer to purchase the advertised product or service.
5. *Action.* The total effect of the advertisement should be to spur the prospective customer to action—to purchase the advertised product or service as soon as possible.

After writing a first draft for each sample advertisement, the sales representative should then look for newspaper and magazine ads with written messages that seem especially effective. Using those professional ads as models, the sales representative/copywriter can then revise the first drafts to improve their appeal to high school students. See the sample ads on page 547.

The sales representative should be aware that advertising works two ways: for the benefit of the advertiser and for the benefit of the consumer. Therefore, copy that says something like "Compliments of a friend" or "Compliments of Howe Hardware" should be avoided. Instead, the sales representative should find out what goods and/or services Howe Hardware can offer high school students and then base the advertising copy on that important information.

Designing the Advertisements. After the copy is written, the sales representative needs to consider the overall design for each of the sample advertisements. There are four elements to keep in mind for any design: headlines, body type, illustrations, and white space. Because only a few ads in high school publications —the large and complex ads—use illustrations, the advertising sales representative will most likely be concerned with headlines, body type, and white space. If, however, it seems desirable to use an illustration or photograph in the sample ads, the sales representative must make sure that whatever is used is of good quality and in good taste. An ideal way to illustrate sample advertisements is to use what professional newspapers use—namely, the so-called "clip art" from Metro Associated Services, Inc. Their publication contains professionally prepared artwork that can be adapted to almost any advertising situation.

When designing an advertisement, the sales representative should keep in mind the principles for designing a newspaper or magazine page. Ordinarily, the headline will appear at the top, followed by the body copy. The name of the advertiser and the logotype (if any) should appear at the foot of the ad. But, of course, this standard format can be modified to gain variety.

To obtain the most pleasing, most effective design for sample advertisements, the sales representative might seek the help of a member of the yearbook's or the school magazine's art staff.

How would you improve this ad?

Conducting the Selling Interview

With at least two sample advertisements available for display at the appropriate time, the advertising sales representative is ready to call on the owner or manager of each business listed on his or her "beat sheet." Should the sales representative simply walk in unannounced or telephone to arrange for an interview? Opinions differ. There are many who feel that telephoning is likely to be ineffective. The student salesperson can too easily be given the brush-off. On the other hand, a student who simply walks in unannounced may find the owner/manager too busy at the moment to discuss advertising. Even so, the unannounced approach seems to have advantages. One is immediacy. The advertising sales representative is right there, ready to talk. And even if the owner/manager cannot do so at the moment, the sales representative can quickly and easily arrange to return at a more convenient time to discuss advertising.

Agreeing on the Size of the Ad. Naturally, the sales representative would like to sell as large an ad as possible. But he or she must be realistic. If the customer has advertised before in school publications, the sales representative should suggest running an ad of the same size or one slightly larger. If the customer has not advertised in school publications, the sales representative might suggest that the advertisement be of moderate size—a sixteenth or an eighth of a page. Finally, if a customer wishes to run an ad using an illustration and a good deal of copy, the sales representative has every right to suggest that the ad take a half-page or even a full page.

Agreeing on the Frequency of the Ad. Once the sales representative and the client have agreed on the general content and the size of the ad, they should also agree on the number of times the ad will be printed in the school publication—newspaper and/or school magazine. Obviously, an advertisement that appears in each issue of the publication means increased revenue for that publication. Therefore, the sales representative—in a businesslike way—should point out the advantages to the advertiser of running the ad in as many issues as seems appropriate. Not only does the repetition of an ad reinforce its impact; the repetition also gives the ad wider exposure. In addition, as was pointed out on page 548, repeating the ad brings the advertiser a rate reduction of as much as 10 percent.

A form such as this one can be used to record ads sold and printed.

Name of Advertiser	Number of Issues per Semester						Sales Rep and Remarks
	1	2	3	4	5	6	
Ambrose Co.	1 Col. x 3" Sold		1 Col. x 3" Sold		1 Col. x 3" Sold		Jackson same copy
Ardan Super Market	2 Col. x 4" Sold	2 Col. x 4" Sold	2 Col. x 4" Sold	2 Col. x 4" Sold	2 Col. x 4" Sold	2 Col. x 4" Sold	Barton new copy each issue
Atkinson Shoes		1 Col. x 5" Sold			1 Col. x 5" Sold		Terrell collect at end of sem.

Signing the Contract. When the sales representative and the advertiser have agreed on the makeup of the ad, on its size, and on the number of times it is to appear in the school publication, one critical action has yet to be taken. That action involves the signing of a contract, a written statement detailing the terms of the agreement. A contract serves as an insurance policy against any misunderstanding or any dissatisfaction on the part of either party to the agreement. An example of the kind of contract many school publications use with advertisers appears on page 554.

When the contract has been completed and examined by the school publication's business manager, the advertising manager, the sales representative, and the advertiser, it must be signed. The client—that is, the advertiser—signs it, and so does an authorized member of the school publication's staff. In some cases, the sales representative is authorized to sign the contract; in other cases, it is the advertising manager or the business manager who signs for the school publication. Copies of the contract are then made, one copy going to the advertiser. The other copy goes to the advertising manager, who keeps it for reference and billing purposes.

CONTRACT FOR ADVERTISING

(Name of School)

(Address of School)

Vol.	Issue	Size	Price
	1		$
	2		
	3		
	4		
	5		
	6		
	7		
	8		
	9		
	10		
	11		
	12		
	13		
	14		
	15		
	16		

Advertiser _____

Address _____

City _____ State _____ Zip ____

Contact _____ Tel. _____

Notes:
(Source, copy, special instructions, etc.)

Signed by _____ Date

Date	Vol.	Issue	Price		Paid		Balance	
			$		$		$	

Keeping a Call-Back List

In some instances, a sales representative may be unsuccessful in persuading a local business to advertise in a school publication. In those cases, the advertising sales representatives submit written reports to the advertising manager, specifying the reasons for each refusal. Perhaps the prospective client preferred to advertise in another of the school's publications. Or perhaps the client preferred to advertise only at a specific time of year.

In any case, the advertising manager files each of the reports, thus making a *call-back list.* Such a list should specify the time when a sales representative can call again on each prospective advertiser. In cases where a client prefers to advertise in other school publications, the advertising manager sends the names and the addresses of such clients to the advertising managers of those publications, together with notes of explanation.

Advertising as a Career

The mass media are interested in the sale of their advertising space or of their broadcast time for financial gain. Inasmuch as advertising specialists are the sales representatives for those mass media, each medium—newspapers, magazines, radio, and television—has its own policy and program for training beginners for its sales department.

In many companies, new product development and product research are areas in which men and women work to create or design products and services better than those of their competitors. Once such a product or service is ready for the public, the company will want to notify as many prospective users as possible. The way to tell the greatest number of people about a product or service in the shortest time at the lowest cost per message has been found to be advertising.

Significant to a student selecting a field for his or her life's work is the great rate of expansion in the field of advertising. The money invested in advertising today—over ten billion dollars a year by national advertisers alone—is more than double the amount spent ten years ago.

Students interested in a career in advertising should have good business sense and should be able to express themselves in clear and effective writing. They should take courses in business, in English, and in journalism. A college degree is an advantage.

Advertising and School Publications   555

Without the proper background, any person will find it difficult to succeed in the advertising business. Initiative and creativity are also critical.

The American Association of Advertising Agencies feels that three qualities are of particular importance in building a successful career in advertising:

> The first is a *belief in advertising*. It is a fact in advertising, as in most business, that it is extremely hard to work contentedly if you don't have a basic belief in what you are doing, that it is worthwhile and important.
>
> The second is the ability to *transmit ideas*. It is essential that the advertising person be able to communicate two ways—from buyer to seller, from seller to buyer—and the translation must be accurate.
>
> The third is the ability to *remain a student life long*. Ours is a society which never stands still; advertising is the ally of change; the advertising man or woman must keep abreast of change.
>
> from *Education for Advertising Careers*

Activities

1. a. What were last year's *per-page* advertising rates for your school's (1) newspaper, (2) yearbook, and (3) magazine? That information is obtainable from records on file in the respective offices of those publications.

   b. With those rates in mind, work with a classmate as follows: Assume an eight percent increase in costs. Then calculate what you recommend as the *per-page* advertising rate for this year's (1) school newspaper, (2) yearbook, and (3) school magazine.

   c. Again working with a classmate, use the per-page advertising rate *for each school publication* to work out what you consider to be a fair and practical schedule of advertising rates for (1) a half-page ad, (2) a quarter-page ad, (3) an ad taking an eighth of a page, and (4) an ad taking a sixteenth of a page.

   d. Submit your three recommended per-page advertising rates and your three advertising rate schedules to the respective school publication advertising managers for their consideration and possible implementation.

2. a. Working alone or with a classmate, develop two sample advertisements that you consider good enough to use in actual selling interviews with local businesses. To write the advertising copy for each ad, you'll want to review the "basic copy appeals" discussed on pages 113–119, as well as the five criteria for successful advertising copy (pages 119–120). To design your advertisements, you may want to use actual advertisements as models—but only as models. You may also want to obtain the help of a member of the art staff of a school publication.

b. Submit your two sample advertisements to the advertising manager of one or more of your school publications. At the same time, arrange to talk with at least one of the advertising managers about the effectiveness of your advertisements.

3. a. What specific features make a contract acceptable to both parties? Design a contract form that includes those features and that can be used by the publication staffs at your school in negotiations with prospective advertisers.

b. Submit your contract form to the business manager of one or more of your school publications for consideration and possible use.

CHAPTER 25

The School Radio/Television Station

*A*nd that wraps up the 8:45 news *on WHS. This is Jan Milliken.*"

"*And this is Roger Brett, inviting you to tune in to 'News at Noon' on WHS at Wallson High.*"

"Good show!" exclaims Anita Lopez, manager of Wallson High's radio station WHS and producer of the station's newscasts. "That story Sid Chang did on the new kids at Wallson was a winner. And you two handled it very smoothly. Good job done by both of you."

"Thanks." Jan, Roger, and Sid are pleased.

"Hey, Anita," breaks in Vince Mayowski, WHS music director, "everything's all set for this afternoon's 'Tune Time'. The Beatles records have come in. Each one takes four and a half minutes. So all time slots are filled, and that's a relief!"

"Super, Vince. See you at 3:30."

"Has anyone seen Joel?" Mac Goldberg runs into the studio, looking as if he had lost his two front teeth. As producer of "WHS Whiz Kids" on WHS-TV, Mac is seldom relaxed. "Joel

took my script for tomorrow's telecast to mark some camera-angle changes. I've got to find him before today's run-through."

"Well, I saw him just before we went on the air at 8:45," says Anita. "He and Carla were headed toward the television studio. They said some-thing about trying out some camera shots. They're probably still there."

"Ok. Thanks." Mac races for the TV studio.

"Here's a tentative script for 'News at Noon'." Anita turns back to Jan and Roger. "See you guys at 11:50 for any last-minute changes."

Years ago the term *journalism* referred exclusively to the print media. But when radio—and later, television—came along, *journalism* took on a broader meaning. Today, *journalism* means the "collecting, writing, editing, and dissemination of news material" by the electronic media, as well as by the print media.

A comprehensive study of secondary school journalism, then, must examine the possible—and probable—involvement of the high school journalist with the electronic media. In the United States today, more than 500 senior high schools operate their own radio stations, and more than 200 operate their own television stations, many of which are equipped for color telecasting. This chapter focuses on the staffing and the operation of school-owned radio and television stations.

Establishing a School Radio or Television Station

At least five major factors must be considered in deciding whether or not to set up a school radio or television station:

1. *Cost* of installation and of on-going operation.
2. *Educational contributions* such a facility can make to the total school program.
3. *Availability of professional personnel* to supervise programming and operation.
4. *Availability of competent technicians* to operate and maintain the physical equipment.
5. *Effect* on the community.

Local conditions and circumstances will influence the last four of these factors in arriving at a final decision. For costs, however, reliable, objective data can help in the decision-making process.

The costs involved in getting a high school radio or television station on the air vary, depending for the most part on the amount of operating power desired. The installation of a one-watt radio station, for example—a station whose signal will carry satisfactorily throughout one school building—can cost as little as $5000. If more power seems desirable, a ten-watt transmitter will be adequate to carry the signal to several buildings on a high school campus. Installation of a ten-watt radio station costs about $5500.

As far as operating costs are concerned, a high school radio station will require a yearly budget of from $1000 to $5000.

A one-watt television station broadcasting programs in black and white will cost about $20,000 to install. To add equipment permitting color telecasts would increase the installation cost to about $200,000. One school, for example, spent $100,000 for color television equipment, $60,000 for closed-circuit equipment, and about $40,000 for equipment such as Portapac and Saticon portable cameras.

Operating costs for a school television station broadcasting in color are budgeted at about $10,000 per year. About half of that figure is earmarked for the maintenance of color equipment.

Government Regulation

The Federal Communications Commission licenses almost all radio and television stations operating in the United States. However, no federal license is required for a station whose broadcast signal is limited to a school building or a campus. Still, students interested in radio and television journalism should file for the Radio-telephone Operator License. No test is required; the applicant has only to fill out the application form.

In some cases, a school radio or television station serves an entire community or a part of it. Such a station can operate only if it employs a full-time radio engineer with a Class II FCC license.

Staffing a School Radio Station

The size of the staff of a school radio station depends on the strength of the station's signal and the extent of its programming.

The staff of a one-watt station, for example, might consist simply of a general manager, a news director, and a music director. For a station with a stronger signal and more extensive programming, however, the staff might be made up of the following members.

The Station Manager

The station manager has the responsibility for overall operation of the station. With the help of the faculty adviser, he or she selects the other members of the staff, oversees station programming, and supervises station operation within agreed-on budget limits. To carry out these responsibilities with maximum efficiency, the station manager consults frequently with the faculty adviser. In addition, the station manager meets regularly with the rest of the staff to help solve problems that may arise and to keep the staff informed on policy matters. The station manager may occasionally write the editorials that are aired on designated broadcasts.

The Assistant Manager

The assistant manager serves as the station manager's principal aide, assuming full responsibility for tasks delegated by the station manager. For example, if a special program has been agreed on, the assistant manager might be made responsible for the planning and the production of that program. If the station operates for more than three or four hours a day, the assistant manager assumes full responsibility for station operation when the station manager is away.

The Public-Relations Director

The public-relations director has the responsibility of informing the listening audience—for the most part, students and faculty—of current and future programs. He or she may publish a weekly or monthly program guide in the school newspaper. Another way to keep the listening audience informed is to duplicate and distribute fliers giving the titles and the broadcast times of upcoming programs.

The public-relations director might have responsibility for the station's fund-raising activities. For example, at one school radio station the public-relations director has full charge of the annual Memorial Day Radiothon. This station operates on a frequency of

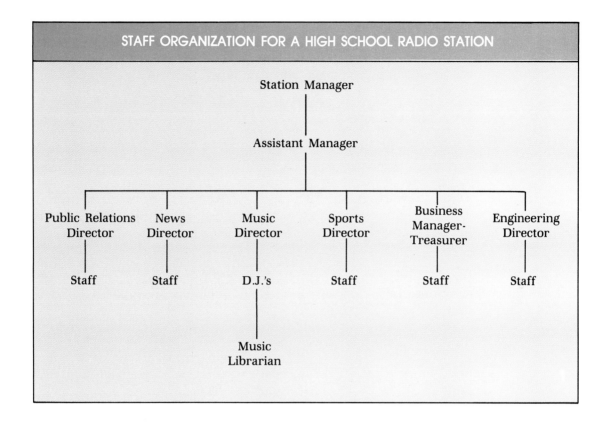

STAFF ORGANIZATION FOR A HIGH SCHOOL RADIO STATION

Station Manager

Assistant Manager

Public Relations Director	News Director	Music Director	Sports Director	Business Manager-Treasurer	Engineering Director
Staff	Staff	D.J.'s	Staff	Staff	Staff

Music Librarian

88 megacycles, and so the Radiothon runs for 88 uninterrupted hours. Local businesses contribute $25 to sponsor one hour of music. Since FCC regulations permit a broadcaster to air a commercial message four times during a one-hour broadcast, the public-relations director sees to it that the name of the sponsor is announced on four separate occasions during each sponsored hour. During the Memorial Day Radiothon, the school radio station raises over $2000 each year.

At another school the radio station's public-relations director arranges for the live broadcast of the school's football and basketball games. To cover the broadcast costs involved—about $85 per game—the public-relations director contracts with local businesses to sponsor all or part of each game.

The Treasurer

The treasurer has full responsibility for collecting and banking all money received by the station, whether from sponsors or from school-appropriated funds or from other donors. The treasurer is responsible for paying bills submitted by suppliers of materials and services for station operation. The treasurer works closely with the station manager and the faculty adviser.

The News Director

In consultation with the station manager and the faculty adviser, the news director decides which of the day's (or week's) news events are of major interest to the listening audience. He or she then indicates which of those news events are to be aired on the station's daily newscasts and the order in which the news stories are to be broadcast.

To carry out these responsibilities, the news director assigns members of the station's news staff to specific "beats" within the school. News staff members must identify and prepare for broadcast those news stories of local, national, and international origin that are considered newsworthy.

Because of the time limitations under which any radio program must operate, broadcast news items cannot be as detailed as those printed in newspapers. The news director must see to it that each news story designated for broadcast focuses immediately and accurately on only the most important facts.

The Music Director

Working closely with the station manager and the faculty adviser, the music director decides which type of music is to be played during each music segment of the broadcast day. Then the music director designates the specific selections to be played during each music broadcast.

The Sports Director

The sports director's responsibility is to keep the student body informed about the school's intramural sports program and about the games to be played by the school's varsity teams. Working from a daily or weekly schedule of sports events, the sports director decides which sports stories are to be aired on each day's news broadcasts. Before any sports story is aired, the sports director edits it for accuracy and succinctness. The sports director draws up a schedule indicating which member of the sports staff is responsible for broadcasting each sports report.

The student engineer is monitoring station equipment.

The Public-Affairs Director

The public-affairs director is responsible for covering and reporting on school affairs. To do so, he or she assigns reporters to cover specific school events—a Latin Club banquet, for example—and specific issues—overcrowding in the cafeteria, for instance. Before any public-affairs story is broadcast, the public-affairs director edits it for accuracy and succinctness.

The public-affairs director is the staff member usually assigned to write the editorials that the radio station airs from time to time.

Staff Reporters

Staff reporters work with the various directors to cover school events and to research and write news stories suitable for broadcast. Their work is much like that performed by reporters for the school newspaper.

Engineers

Students interested in electronics often serve as assistants to the school radio station's professional engineer. Helping to maintain station equipment, student engineers are on call during operating hours. During broadcasts, they often operate the controls.

The School Radio/Television Station

Staffing a School Television Station

A school television station will most likely require a staff like that needed to operate a school radio station. (A possible exception is the position of music director.) In schools that operate both a television station and a radio station, one staff could serve both. But besides the ten positions identified for the operation of a radio station, the efficient operation of a television station requires these additional staff members.

The Producer

The producer is the major creative force behind every television program, for it is he or she who supplies the ideas for a program. The producer helps write the script, casts the program, and has overall direction of the program.

The Camera Director

The camera director's position is in the control room, deciding which one of the pictures being taken by the camera operators will go out on the air. To make these on-the spot decisions, the camera director must judge which picture best serves the overall purposes of the scene that is being televised.

The Floor Director

During a telecast the floor director, who is equipped with earphones, stands beside the camera—or between the cameras. It is the floor director's responsibility to relay the camera director's instructions to the camera operators, to the performers, and to whatever floor assistants are required for the program.

The Lighting Director

The lighting director is responsible for the proper lighting of the set for each televised program. Different programs, of course, require different lighting arrangements, and the lighting director must work closely with the producer and the camera director.

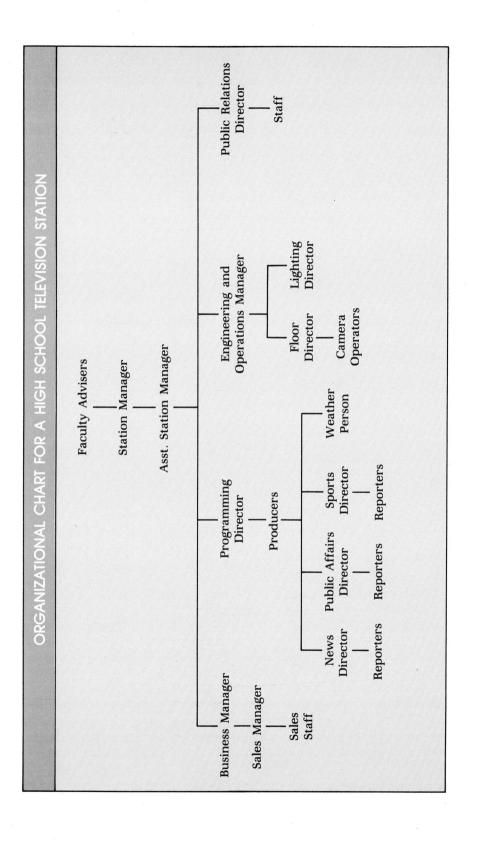

The camera operator (left) is shooting a telecast. Audio and switcher controls are being operated at right.

The Staging Director

The staging director is responsible for arranging the set for every production. If props need to be built or if scenery needs to be painted, the staging director's responsibility is to see that those tasks are completed on time. Of course, the staging director must work closely with the producer.

Camera Operators

Each person operating a television camera must be familiar with proper operating techniques and be responsible for correct camera focus so as to get effective composition of every shot. Camera operators must work closely with the camera director and the floor director in the preproduction planning of appropriate camera positions. During the actual televising of a program, they must be capable of responding immediately to the camera director's on-the-spot instructions.

Airing Radio/Television Programs

Types of Programs

Programs aired by high school radio and television stations are similar to those aired by professionally operated stations. There are news programs that include weather reports, sports reports, and editorials; there are public-affairs programs; there are programs devoted exclusively to music; there are programs offering entertainment; and there are commercials.

News Programs. Radio and television news shows have one important advantage over the print media: They can air important news items on a moment's notice. But radio and television also have one important disadvantage: Because of time constraints, they are limited to surface treatment of the news items aired.

News programs aired by school radio and television stations can vary from one-sentence "news capsules" ("The President today vetoed the tax-credit bill") to 15-minute broadcasts that include editorials, sports items, and weather reports. Station managers and news directors can usually obtain permission from local newspaper editors to air local, national, and international news releases of interest to a school audience. They can obtain weather information from the local office of the Weather Bureau.

News directors and sports directors can air sports items that have been rewritten for broadcast from articles published in school and local newspapers. Station managers and public-affairs directors can air editorials that have been written specifically for designated news programs. But there is a difference: Editorials for radio and television are written to be listened to—not to be read. The editorial aired on a school radio or television station must be shorter than those written for newspaper readers. Unlike printed editorials, radio/TV editorials should conclude with an invitation to students with opposing views to express their points of view on future programs.

Staff members responsible for writing, editing, and broadcasting news on a school radio or television station should review "Newswriting for the Broadcast Media" in Chapter 7, pages 140–165.

Public-Affairs Programs. Public-affairs programs can be produced "live" in the studio at the school, or they can be produced "on location" and taped (by means of a tape recorder and a Portapac camera) for later broadcast.

In getting a story for a public-affairs program, the staff reporter does what any good reporter does—research the topic, talk with key people involved, get all the facts and get them accurately, and keep the interests of listeners/viewers in mind. But because of the time limitations imposed on every program broadcast, the radio/TV reporter must focus the story around its one or two most important points.

Public-affairs programs frequently take the form of question-and-answer interviews. Local leaders and others in the community, as well as visiting celebrities, are often willing to participate in such programs. In conducting interviews, staff reporters/interviewers should follow the suggestions in Chapter 8, "Interviewing," pages 166–189.

Music Programs. School radio stations receive requests for all kinds of music. To meet those requests, the music directors of many stations rotate the types of music they program, playing popular music, for example, one day, soft rock another day, light classics on yet another day, and so on.

Staff members who function as disc jockeys must have a thorough knowledge of each type of music they play. Furthermore, they must develop scripts (comments) that provide their listeners with useful information about the types of music they play.

Before playing the record, the disc jockey reads the script she wrote.

This is the script that the disc jockey reads to introduce the record.

YEARS AFTER HIS DEATH, THERE IS STILL A

SENSE OF SADNESS FOR MILLIONS AT THE MEN-

TION OF THE NAME JOHN LENNON. ONE

REASON THE DEATH STILL SEEMS SO CLOSE TO

US IS THAT THERE ARE REMINDERS ALMOST

DAILY OF LENNON'S IMPRINT ON ROCK. NOT

ONLY ARE LENNON'S BEATLES AND SOLO TUNES

STILL PLAYED REGULARLY ON THE RADIO, BUT

PERFORMERS ALSO CONTINUE TO SALUTE LEN-

NON. BUT THE BEST WAY TO REMEMBER LEN-

NON IS THROUGH HIS MUSIC. YOU MIGHT EVEN

TRY TO PUT TOGETHER YOUR OWN TOP TEN LIST

OF FAVORITE LENNON TRACKS. HERE'S ONE OF

MY FAVORITES, A SONG HE RECORDED IN 1964,

"I WANT TO HOLD YOUR HAND."

END

Entertainment Programs. The entertainment programs aired by school radio and television stations usually consist of short features of from two to 15 minutes in length. Similar to newspaper features, these programs might include quiz shows and audience-participation shows. Others might discuss topics such as how to study for exams, how to succeed as an officer of a school organization, how to try out for a part in a school dramatic or musical production.

Commercials. School radio and television stations that air commercials limit them to public-service announcements. Such announcements can concern the various organizations financed by the United Fund, meetings to be held by various school organizations, and school events and activities. Most school commercials run for 30 or 60 seconds. Staff members who broadcast school commercials should review the suggestions given in Chapter 24, "Advertising and School Publications," pages 545–557.

Script Preparation

Every program aired on a school radio or television program needs to be based on a typed script. Staff members who prepare the scripts must keep in mind that each script will be read aloud. Thus, they should use very few abbreviations. *Mr., Mrs., Ms.,* and *Dr.* are acceptable. Acronyms like *FBI, FCC,* and *SPCA* are also acceptable because they are familiar to most listeners. But symbols —*$,* for example—are not. And so, instead of writing $2000, for instance, the scriptwriter should write *two thousand dollars.*

If a word seems hard to pronounce or if it has an unusual spelling, the scriptwriter needs to help the broadcaster by writing the pronunciation phonetically. For example, suppose that a news bulletin concerns Beirut. After typing the word *Beirut,* the scriptwriter uses parentheses to show its correct pronunciation: *(Bay root').* Thus the script reads "Life in Beirut (Bay root') is returning to normal."

Consider another example. Suppose that the following sentence with the word *mnemonic* appears in the script. The scriptwriter would type the sentence as follows: "To help them remember certain things, people often resort to a mnemonic *(nee mahn'ik)* device like tying a string around a finger."

Before typing a script, the scriptwriter makes sure that the typewriter keys are clean and that the typewriter ribbon is fresh enough to produce sharp, easy-to-read letters. He or she then types the script, using capital letters throughout and triple-spacing between lines.

```
SLUG (name of story)


NAME OF SCRIPTWRITER


DAWN BROKE SHARP AND CLEAR ON THIS THE


FIRST DAY OF THE SCHOOL YEAR. _____


_____


_____

                        END
```

A radio script generally follows this type of format.

When typing a script for either radio or television, the reporter/scriptwriter types the slug (the title of the story) and his or her name in the upper left corner of the page. Only one story should appear on a page. If a story requires more than one page, the reporter/scriptwriter draws an arrow from the last word on the page to the bottom right-hand corner of that page. Then, at the top of the second page, the slug is repeated along with the figure 2. The last line on a page ends the sentence. No page should end in mid-sentence.

Allowing for a one-inch margin at the left and at right, the reporter/scriptwriter typing a radio script uses the full width of the page. A television script, on the other hand, has two columns. Side margins are about one-half inch each. Video instructions—instructions to the camera director and the camera operators—are typed on the left side of the page. The scriptwriter then leaves a one-inch margin of white space in the middle of the page. On the right side of the page, the scriptwriter types the words to be spoken by those participating in the broadcast, together with any instructions to the sound engineer.

```
SLUG


Video →  CAMERA 1: Closeup of        ANNOUNCER: GOOD                The script
instructions   announcer _____
              _____            MORNING TO Y'ALL.
         CAMERA 2: _____
              _____
              _____            TIME FOR THE
              _____
              _____
              _____            9:30 NEWS.
```

A television script combines the audio script with video instructions.

The Broadcast Itself

The Ideal Voice for Broadcasting. The ideal voice for broadcasting is one that sounds natural and uses its full potential. It has a varying cadence, speeding up and slowing down appropriately for emphasis. Its intonation is varied, rising and falling appropriately. The volume is varied appropriately to give effectiveness to what is said.

The speaker with a natural voice enunciates clearly so that listeners can hear and understand each word and yet sounds normal and unaffected.

Suggestions for Broadcasters. Every student who speaks on a school radio or television program has a responsibility to the listening/viewing audience—a responsibility to communicate. This responsibility can be met only if each student speaker keeps these four "rules" in mind:

■ "I must first gain the attention of my audience."

■ "I must hold that attention throughout my participation in the broadcast."

■ "I must speak clearly so that what I have to say will be understood."

■ "I must speak in such a way that each listener will remember the point(s) I make."

Script rehearsals constitute one good way to help student speakers observe those four rules. Students can tape-record what they have to say and then listen to themselves. Repeated listening can help them find the most effective way of speaking their lines. During script rehearsals, speakers can put a slash mark (/) at each place in the script where it is appropriate to take a breath. And they can underline the words that are to be emphasized.

The checklist below will help student broadcasters in their efforts to develop the ideal broadcast voice.

"THE IDEAL VOICE"

✓ *Does my voice sound strained?* The words should come out smoothly and easily.

✓ *Did I run out of breath before finishing?* A full tone comes from deep breathing, making use of your diaphragm.

✓ *Did I drop the endings of my words?* It is not "thinkin." It is "thinking."

✓ *Did I sound sincere?* You are not going to get people to listen until you can speak sincerely.

✓ *Did I speak dully or overdramatically?* One is as bad as the other, unless you are deliberately seeking a certain effect.

✓ *Did I pronounce my words clearly?* Broadcasting is not the place for an announcer who mumbles.

✓ *Did I sound as if I were talking to a friend?* You want to develop a conversational style, for you are talking to friends when you broadcast.

✓ *Did I speak too loudly or too softly?* Volume must be adjusted to the subject and the occasion.

✓ *Did my voice have rhythm?* There is no place for unnecessary speedups and slowdowns, gulps and pauses.

✓ *Did I speak every word in the same tone, or did I stress some words more than others?* Stressing the right words is one way to avoid a monotonous, dull tone.

Timing the Broadcast. On the average, we read aloud at the rate of about 120 words per minute. If we assume that in a line of radio script there are ten words, we know that twelve lines of script can be read in a minute. A radio newscast scheduled to take five minutes requires a total of 60 lines of script.

Different individuals do read at different speeds. Each student announcer or reporter can determine the number of words he or she can read in a minute by following this procedure:

1. Read the script.
2. At the end of 60 seconds, mark your place.
3. Count the number of words read.

An Organization for High School Broadcasters

More than 100 high schools across the country hold memberships in the Intercollegiate Broadcasting System.* In addition to sponsoring regional and national conferences, this organization publishes newsletters and bulletins that advise school radio/television staff members on the efficient operation of their stations. This organization also makes a number of taped programs available for broadcast on school radio and television stations.

Activities

1. **a.** If your school now operates a radio station, draw up a chart showing the organization of its present staff. Then consider these questions:

    (1) What staff positions seem to you to be unnecessary?

    (2) What positions do you think should be added? With those questions in mind, draw up a chart indicating what you think would be an ideal staff organization for the station. Submit your second chart to the station manager for consideration and possible implementation.

    b. If your school does not now operate a radio station, assume that it will do so shortly. Draw up an organiza-

---

*Box 592, Vails Gate, New York 12584

tional chart on which you identify the staff positions you consider essential to efficient station operation.

2. a. If your school now operates a television station, draw up a chart showing the organization of its present staff. Then follow the instructions given in item 1a, above.

   b. If your school does not now operate a television station, assume that it will do so shortly. Then follow the instructions given in item 1b, above.

3. What kind of programming, in your opinion, should a school radio station offer? Assume that the station is on the air for four hours a day—from 8 to 9 a.m., from 12 noon to 1 p.m., and from 3 to 5 p.m. How would you allocate the time during those four hours to include (a) news programs, (b) public-affairs programs, (c) entertainment, and (d) commercials? Draw up a programming chart, indicating the time segments you would give to each kind of program.

4. What kind of programming, in your opinion, would be ideal for a school television station to offer? Assume that the station is on the air for five hours a day—from 8 to 10 a.m., and from 2 to 5 p.m. How would you allocate the time during those five hours to include (a) news programs, (b) public-affairs programs, (c) entertainment, and (d) commercials? Draw up a programing chart, indicating the time segments that you think should be allocated to each kind of program.

APPENDIX I

The Associated Press Managing Editors' (APME) Criteria for a Good Newspaper

A good newspaper prints the important news and provides information, comment, and guidance which are most useful to its readers.

It reports fully and explains the meaning of local, national, and international events which are of major significance in its own community. Its editorial comment provides an informed opinion on matters of vital concern to its readers.

By reflecting the total image of its own community in its news coverage and by providing wise counsel in its editorials, a good newspaper becomes a public conscience. It also must be lively, imaginative, and original; it must have a sense of humor, and the power to arouse keen interest.

To implement these principles of good editing requires a skilled staff, an attractive format, adequate space for news and comment, and a sound business foundation.

The staff must possess the professional pride and competence necessary to breathe life and meaning into the daily record of history. Good writing must be combined with an effective typographical display of copy and pictures to capture the full drama and excitement of the day's news. Good printing is essential.

News and comment of most immediate interest and importance to the local community shall have priority for the available space, which will depend on the size and resources of the newspaper.

To assure a financially strong and independent publication, and one that is competitive with other media, a good newspaper must maintain effective circulation, advertising, and promotion departments.

Criteria of a Good Newspaper

A good newspaper may judge its own performance—and be judged— by the criteria which follow:

Accuracy—The newspaper shall:
1. Exert maximum effort to print the truth in all news statements.
2. Strive for completeness and objectivity.
3. Guard against carelessness, bias or distortion by either emphasis or omission.

Responsibility—The newspaper shall:
1. Use mature and considered judgment in the public interest at all times.

2. Select, edit, and display news on the basis of the significance and its genuine usefulness to the public.
3. Edit news affecting public morals with candor and good taste and avoid an imbalance of sensational, preponderantly negative, or merely trivial news.
4. Accept when possible a reasonable amount of news which illustrates the values of compassion, self-sacrifice, heroism, good citizenship, and patriotism.
5. Clearly define sources of news, and tell the reader when competent sources cannot be identified.
6. Respect rights of privacy.
7. Instruct all staff members to conduct themselves with dignity and decorum.

Integrity—The newspaper shall:
1. Maintain vigorous standards of honesty and fair play in the selection and editing of its contents as well as in all relations with news sources and the public.
2. Deal dispassionately with controversial subjects and treat disputed issues with impartiality.
3. Practice humility and tolerance in the face of honest conflicting opinions or disagreement.
4. Provide a forum for the exchange of pertinent comment and criticism, especially if it is in conflict with the newspaper's editorial point of view.
5. Label its own editorial views or expressions of opinion.

Leadership—The newspaper shall:
1. Act with courage on serving the public.
2. Stimulate and vigorously support public officials, private groups, and individuals in crusades and campaigns to increase the good works and eliminate the bad in the community.
3. Help to protect all rights and privileges guaranteed by law.
4. Serve as a constructive critic of government at all levels, providing leadership for necessary reforms or innovations, and exposing any misfeasance in office, or any misuse of public power.
5. Oppose demagogues and other selfish and unwholesome interests regardless of their size or influence.

Guide for a Good Newspaper

A good newspaper should be guided in the publication of all material by a concern for truth, the hallmark of freedom, by a concern for human decency and human betterment, and by a respect for the accepted standards of its own community.

Preamble to the Television Code of the National Association of Broadcasters

Television is seen and heard in every type of American home. These homes include children and adults of all ages, embrace all races and all varieties of religious faith, and reach those of every educational background. It is the responsibility of television to bear constantly in mind that the audience is primarily a home audience, and consequently that television's relationship to the viewers is that between guest and host.

The revenues from advertising support the free, competitive American system of telecasting, and make available to the eyes and ears of the American people the finest programs of information, education, culture, and entertainment. By law the television broadcaster is responsible for the programming of his station. He is, however, obligated to bring his positive responsibility for excellence and good taste in programming to bear upon all who have a hand in the production of programs, including networks, sponsors, producers of film and of live programs, advertising agencies, and talent agencies.

The American businesses which utilize television for conveying their advertising messages to the home by pictures with sound, seen free-of-charge on the home screen, are reminded that their responsibilities are not limited to the sale of goods and the creation of a favorable attitude toward the sponsor by the presentation of entertainment. They include, as well, responsibility for utilizing television to bring the best programs, regardless of kind, into American homes.

Television and all who participate in it are jointly accountable to the American public for respect for the special needs of children, for community responsibility, for the advancement of education and culture, for the acceptability of the program materials chosen, for decency and decorum in production, and for propriety in advertising. This responsibility cannot be discharged by any given group of programs, but can be discharged only through the highest standards of respect for the American home, applied to every moment of every program presented by television.

In order that television programming may best serve the public interest, viewers should be encouraged to make their criticisms and positive suggestions known to the television broadcasters. Parents in particular should be urged to see to it that out of the richness of television fare, the best programs are brought to the attention of their children.

The Radio Broadcaster's Creed

We believe:

That Radio Broadcasting in the United States of America is a living symbol of democracy; a significant and necessary instrument for maintaining freedom of expression, as established by the First Amendment to the Constitution of the United States;

That its influence in the arts, in science, in education, in commerce, and upon the public welfare is of such magnitude that the only proper measure of its responsibility is the common good of the whole people;

That it is our obligation to serve the people in such manner as to reflect credit upon our profession and to encourage aspiration toward a better estate for all mankind; by making available to every person in America such programs as will perpetuate the traditional leadership in the United States in all phases of the broadcasting art:

That we should make full and ingenious use of man's store of knowledge, his talents, and his skills and exercise critical and discerning judgment concerning all broadcasting operations to the end that we may, intelligently and sympathetically:

Observe the properties and customs of civilized society;

Respect the rights and sensitivities of all people;

Honor the sanctity of marriage and the home;

Protect and uphold the dignity and brotherhood of all mankind;

Enrich the daily life of the people through the factual reporting and analysis of news, and through programs of education, entertainment, and information.

Provide for the fair discussion of matters of general public concern; engage in works directed toward the common good; and volunteer our aid and comfort in times of stress and emergency;

Contribute to the economic welfare of all by expanding the channels of trade, by encouraging the development and conservation of natural resources, and by bringing together the buyer and seller through the broadcasting of information pertaining to goods and services.

APPENDIX IV

The Production Code of the Motion Picture Association of America, Inc.

Motion picture producers recognize the high trust and confidence which have been placed in them by the people of the world and which have made motion pictures a universal form of entertainment.

They recognize their responsibility to the public because of this trust and because entertainment and art are important influences in the life of a nation.

Hence, though regarding motion pictures primarily as entertainment without any explicit purpose of teaching or propaganda, they know that the motion picture within its own field of entertainment may be directly responsible for spiritual or moral progress, for higher types of social life, and for much correct thinking.

On their part, they ask from the public and from public leaders a sympathetic unerstanding of the problems inherent in motion picture production and a spirit of cooperation that will allow the opportunity necessary to bring the motion picture to a still higher level of wholesome entertainment for all concerned.

General Principles

1. No picture shall be produced which will lower the moral standards of those who see it. Hence the sympathy of the audience shall never be thrown to the side of crime, wrong-doing, evil, or sin.
2. Correct standards of life, subject only to the requirements of drama and entertainment, shall be presented.
3. Law—divine, natural or human—shall not be ridiculed, nor shall sympathy be created for its violation.

Proofreading Symbols

In the pages that follow, each black dot (·) preceding a function indicates that the marginal or internal symbol is used in manuscript editing as well as in marking proof.

General Corrections

Function	Marginal Symbol	Internal Symbol	Example
Delete	ℱ	/ OR —	Good𝖽 design is functional. ℱ
Delete & Close up	ℱ	⌐ OR ⊇	Good design is functio𝗈nal. ℱ
· Paragraph	¶ or ℱ	∧	Good design is functional. ⌃Ice ¶ cream melts in hot weather.
· No paragraph	no ¶	[OR ⌐⌐	Functional color is one no ¶ element of good design. ⌐ ⌐It is used to graphically illustrate a pertinent point in the text.
· Spell out	sp	◯	Supplementary publications for textbooks must be available before (Sept.) and as early as possi- sp ble.
· Stet (let it stand)	stet	··············	Good design is ~~functional.~~ stet
· Underscore	u/s	——	Good design is functional. u/s
Designation of a compositor's error	(P.E.) (show correction)	O OR — OR ∧ OR /	Good𝖽 design is functio𝗈nal. (P.E.)

Punctuation and Special Character Corrections

Function	Marginal Symbol	Internal Symbol	Example
Period or decimal point (.)	⊙	∧ or /	Good design is functional. ⊙/· 17 + 4.2 − 5.9 ⊙/
Colon(:)	⊙	∧ or /	Describe these terms: pica, point, ⊙/ spacing and leading.
Semicolon (;)	⊙	∧ or /	Publishing generally involves four major phases: the authoring and editing of a manuscript; the ⊙/ transformation of the manuscript into graphically pleasing forms; ⊙/ the plating, printing and binding of the book; and the distribution and sale of the book.
Hyphen (-)	=	∧ or /	A printbind order must be set = for each new publication based on sales office estimates and related publications.
Comma (,)	⌃		Sharp clean and neat marking ⌃/⌃ of proofs contributes to production efficiency lower costs and ⌃/⌃ greater accuracy.
• En dash (–)	$\frac{1}{N}$	∧ or /	The 1967/1968 football season is $\frac{1}{N}$ underway.
• Em dash (—)	$\frac{1}{M}$	∧ or /	Have the students write $\frac{1}{M}$ seven biographies. three reviews. one thesis.
Quotation mark, single (' ') or double (" ")	✓ or ✓; ✓✓ or ✓✓	∧ or /	Good design is functional. ✓✓ ✓✓
Exclamation mark (!)	!	∧ or /	We got the award !
Interrogation mark (?)	?	∧ or /	Did we get the award. ?
Parentheses ( )	(or)	∧ or /	Publication planning including supplementary titles promotes basic understanding at the time for budget appropriation. ( )
Brackets [ ]	[or]	∧ or /	The Fifty Books of the Year [AIGA is one of the exclusive design award shows.]

Punctuation and Special Character Corrections

Function	Marginal Symbol	Internal Symbol	Example
Virgule (slash) (/)	*shill*	∧ OR /	The designer's choice was limited to 10 points and or 12 *shill* point of a sans serif family.

Typeface Corrections

Function	Marginal Symbol	Internal Symbol	Example
Wrong font	*wf*	/	Good design is functional. *wf*
Broken or smashed type	X	/ OR —	Good design is functional. X
Invert	ℒ	/ OR —	Good design is functional. ℒ
Change to roman basal weight type	*Rom*	⬭	**Good design** is functional. *Rom*
Change to Italic basal weight type	*ital*	⬭	**Good design** is functional. *ital*
Change to roman boldface type	*Rom bf*	⬭	*Good design* is functional. *Rom bf*
Change to Italic boldface type	*ital bf*	⬭	*Good design* is functional. *ital bf*
• Set in roman basal weight capitals	*caps*	≡	Good design is functional. *caps*
• Set in roman basal weight lowercase	*lc*	/////////////	GOOD DESIGN is functional. *lc*
• Set in roman basal weight capitals and lowercase	*cap & lc*	≡ and /// as Required	good design is FUNCTIONAL. *c & lc*
• Set in roman basal weight small capitals	*s. c.*	=	good design is functional *s.c.*
Set in roman basal weight capitals and small capitals	*caps & s.c.*	≡ and = as Required	Good design is functional. *caps & s.c.*
• Set in Italic basal weight capitals	*ital caps*	≡	Good design is functional. *ital caps*
• Set in Italic basal weight lowercase	*ital*	___	Good design is functional. *ital*

Typeface Corrections

Function	Marginal Symbol	Internal Symbol	Example
• Set in Italic basal weight capitals and lowercase	*ital c & lc*	‗	Good design is functional. *ital caps & lc*
Set in roman boldface capitals	*bf caps*	∿∿∿	Good design is functional. *bf caps*
Set in roman boldface lowercase	*bf*	∿	Good design is functional. *bf*

Spacing, Leading, and Positioning Corrections

Function	Marginal Symbol	Internal Symbol	Example
Less space (reduce space)	‿	‿	Good design is functional. ‿
Close up (delete all space)	⊂⊃	⊂⊃	The title was set in italic bold face capitals. ⊂ ⊃
Space	#	∧ OR /	Gooddesign is functional. #
Equal spacing (space evenly)	*eq.* #	∧ ∧ ∧	Gooddesign is functional. *eq.* #
• Transpose (transfer)	*tr*	∪ OR ⊓ OR ↶	functional Good deisgn is. *tr*
Horizontal alignment	⹀	⹀	Good design is functional. ⹀
• Vertical alignment	//	//	Good design is functional, simple and practical //
• Horizontal move of type to the right	⊐	⊐	DESIGN ⊐ ⊐
• Horizontal move of type to the left	⊏	⊏	DESIGN ⊏
• Vertical move of type towards head	⌐	⌐	DESIGN ⌐
• Vertical move of type towards foot	⌊⌋	⌊⌋	DESIGN ⌊⌋
• Center vertically	⌐⌐	⌐⌐	GOOD DESIGN IS FUNCTIONAL ⌐⌐
• Center horizontally	⊐ ⊏	⊐ ⊏	⊐ DESIGN ⊏

Copyreading Symbols

Marked Copy	Meaning	Set Copy
(N.Y.)	Spell out.	New York
(6)	Spell out number.	Six
(Doctor)	Abbreviate.	Dr.
(Fifty)	Write in numerals.	50
write ^the^ letter	Insert a letter or word.	write the letter
walks	Delete letter.	walk
acknowledgement	Delete letter and close up.	acknowledgment
book shelf	Close up space.	bookshelf
book/review	Separate elements.	book review
centre	Transpose letters.	center
park baseball	Transpose words	baseball park
Lim Polymer	Spell as is.	Lim Polymer
the daily newspaper	Delete word and close up.	the newspaper
Dr⊙	Add period.	Dr.
Detroit Mich.	Add comma.	Detroit, Mich.
James house	Add apostrophe.	James' house
Four score and...	Add quotes.	"Four score and..."
boston	Capitalize.	Boston
Presidential race	Change to lowercase.	presidential race
Scholastic Press	Print in small caps.	SCHOLASTIC PRESS
The New York Times	Italicize.	*The New York Times*
The Editor-in-Chief	Set in boldface.	**The Editor-in-Chief**
The Editor in Chief /=/	Insert hyphen.	The Editor-in-Chief
¶ Advertising is growing.	Indent for paragraph.	Advertising is growing.
No ¶ New agencies open...	No paragraph.	New agencies open...
...managers. Executives are...	Bring two sentences together.	...Managers. Executives are...

GLOSSARY OF TERMS

A

Account executive *(Account representative):* member of an advertising agency (or department) responsible for the supervision and management of an advertising client's account.

Action-line column: a newspaper (or magazine) column that receives and investigates readers' questions and complaints, often suggesting solutions.

Advance story: a story that informs the reader about a future event.

Advertisement: a message which has as its goal the transaction of business between a consumer and a supplier.

Advertising agency: a business firm that gives advertising advice and services to clients.

Advertising beat sheet: a listing of advertising sales representatives and of potential advertisers the sales representatives have been assigned to contact.

Advertising contract: written agreement between a customer and an advertising medium or agency concerning advertising space or time.

Affiliate: member of a major national radio or television network system.

Agate: 5½-point type usually used for classified newspaper advertisements.

Anchor story *(bottom anchor story):* story or article, located near the bottom of a page, having enough importance to achieve visual balance in page layout.

Art: photographs or illustrations to be included in an advertisement or in printed material.

Assignment: instructions to a reporter or photographer for covering a specific event.

Assignment sheet: listing of news coverage assignments for reporters and photographers, usually kept by managing editor or news editor.

Audiovisual writer: writer for radio (audio) or television (audiovisual).

Audit Bureau of Circulation: a business agency that monitors and verifies circulation figures of publications, making such information available to clients.

B

Background story: often presented as a sidebar story, supplying the additional background information not contained in a straight news account.

Bank (see *Deck*).

Banner *(Streamer):* headline that extends across the full width of a page.

Beat *(Run):* place or source of news covered regularly by reporters.

Bias: prejudice; opinion of a writer that, when injected into newswriting, destroys the writing's objectivity.

Biased news (See *Slanted*).

Billing copy *(Tear sheet):* printed copy of a page or that part of a page containing an advertisement, usually sent to the advertiser with the bill as proof of publication.

Bleed: any artwork or photo that extends over the edge of the trimmed page.

Blurb (See *Filler*).

Body: all of a news story following the lead.

Body copy: (See *Copy*).

Body type: type, usually 8-point, in which news stories are set (except heads).

Boil down: to reduce a story in size.

Boilerplate (See *Filler*).

Boldface type: type that prints heavier and blacker than regular type. (used for emphasis)

Border *(Box):* metal strips used to box stories, ads, etc.

Break: point in a column at which a story is divided, to be continued in another column or page.

Broadcast: any informative or entertaining presentation made public by means of radio or television.

Buried lead: most important fact in the story, not contained in the opening.

C

Cable television (See *CATV*).

Candid photo: unposed photographs in which subjects are photographed while acting naturally or spontaneously.

Canned material: written or photographed material (usually feature) prepared by news syndicates and sold to the mass media.

Canopy head: headline having a main line of three or more columns in width, with following decks on extreme right and left.

Caps *(Uppercase):* capital letters.

Caps and small caps (also *c & sc*): type matter set in small capital letters, except for first letters of prominent words, which are set in regular capital letters.

Caption *(Cutline, Legend):* descriptive, explanatory material appearing in type above, below, or beside a picture.

Caster: a machine for making type.

Catholic School Press Association: scholastic press association offering services to Catholic high schools and colleges (C.S.P.A., Marquette University, 552 North 13th Street, Milwaukee, Wisconsin 53233).

CATV (Community Antenna Television): television transmitted to areas and communities by means of cable television antennas (usually paid for by consumers).

Censorship: control (usually government or religious) over the communications media in order to prevent certain types of material from being published.

Chain newspapers: groups of newspapers published under the control of one person or organization.

Character: one figure, letter, number, sign, or symbol in a given type face.

Chase: metal frame used to hold a page of type as it is run off on a flat-bed press or before it is stereotyped.

Chronological story: story that presents details in the order that they occurred.

Circulation: average total number of copies of a publication distributed per issue; also, the process of distributing a publication.

Circulation manager: person assigned the over-all responsibility for distributing a publication.

City editor: person assigned to supervise the gathering and preparation of news of the community in which the newspaper is published.

Classified ad: an advertisement for goods or services, usually set in 5½ point type, that appears in the newspaper's classified advertising section.

Classified advertising manager: person assigned the overall responsibility for that section of a newspaper containing classified advertisements.

Cliché: expression that has become trite from overuse.

Clipping service: service set up to cut out and supply materials from many printed sources on any given subject.

Coaxial cable: cable consisting of a tube of electrically conducting material surrounding a central conductor, used to transmit telephone, telegraph, and television signals of high frequency.

Code of ethics: set of principles or standards that determines proper conduct or practice.

Cold type: type used in offset lithography (usually produced by IBM Typewriter, Vari-typer, or Justowriter).

Collate: to put together in specified or chrono-logical order.

Color shot: photograph (or television shot) in color; or a black and white feature picture.

Column: timely and periodically produced presentation of editorial material, giving expression to the writer's own opinion; also, a vertical row of type on a printed page.

Column rule: strips of metal used to produce the vertical rules that divide printed columns on a page.

Combination head: headline that extends across two or more related stories.

Communications satellite: object or vehicle containing transmission apparatus, intended to orbit the earth, receiving and relaying high-speed transmissions.

Community service program (See *Public affairs program*).

Composing room: that part of a printing shop's (or plant's) production department where copy is set into type.

Composite: several parts combined to make a whole; as, a photographic composite, in which several negatives are combined to be printed as one photograph.

Composite news story: news story with more than one main idea or thought; news story combining several stories into one.

Composition: photographic arrangement of subjects to produce an eye-catching, visually pleasing effect.

Continuous tone: photographic image that has not been screened and contains shade tones from black to white.

Copy: any written material ready to be set in type; any photograph or illustration to be made into an engraving.

Copy appeal: ability of copy to catch the reader's eye and hold interest.

Copy blocks: segments of copy used in making up page layouts.

Copy desk: table or desk at which copyreaders work, usually semicircular.

Copyfitting: adjusting or rewriting copy to make it fit alloted space.

Copyholder: person assigned to follow and read aloud original copy while the proofreader checks for errors.

Copyreader: person assigned to correct and improve copy submitted by writers and reporters.

Copyright: author's or artist's right to control publication of his or her original material.

Copywriter: person assigned to write copy, usually for advertisements (advertising copy-writer).

Corantos: first English newspapers of signifi-cance, appearing in the 1620s.

Coverage: obtaining of all available information and facts connected with a news event or story.

Credibility gap: term coined during Johnson administration concerning believability of government-emanated information as reported in the mass media.

Credit line: line of print stating the author's name or source of a story or picture.

Cropper's L's: L-shaped pieces of cardboard used to show how cropping will affect an illustration.

Cropping: marking an illustration or photograph to eliminate unwanted details and indicating for the printer or engraver the part to be used.

Crossline: centered headline deck made up of a single line of type running across a column, not necessarily full-column width.

Crusading newspaper: newspaper that conducts special campaigns to promote worthy causes or to expose unlawful or immoral conditions.

C.S.P.A.: scholastic press association offering services to school publications (Columbia Scholastic Press Association, Columbia University, Box 11, Low Memorial Library, New York, N.Y. 10027).

Cursor: the large blinking symbol that represents the next location on the screen, similar to the striking location on the carriage of a typewriter.

Cut: general term for a halftone, electrotype, stereotype, zinc etching, or any kind of engraving; also, to reduce the length of a story.

Cutline (See *Caption*).

Cut-off rule: printed horizontal rule used to separate stories, advertisements, and other typographical units, usually running from column rule to column rule.

Cut-off test: test applied to news stories to determine if last paragraphs contain essential facts, thus allowing makeup person to delete from end of story when necessary.

D

Dateline: line of type giving date of publication, usually appearing below the nameplate.

Deadline: time limit applied to all copy to be sent to printer.

Deck *(Bank):* secondary headline placed under the main headline; also, table on which typeset copy is stored for future use.

Delete: printer's term for remove or take out.

Disc jockey: person employed by network or local radio stations to play records for broadcast and sometimes to announce news and advertisements.

Display: use of copy, pictures, or headlines in a way designed to make them easy to locate and read.

Display ad: advertisement with large type and usually pictures that is placed in prominent location in a publication.

Display type: large or decorative type used for headlines, titles, or advertising (not body type).

Diurnals: oldest-known regularly published accounts of daily news developed from accounts of English Parliamentary proceedings in 1641.

Division page (yearbook): a page or pages used to separate the major sections in the yearbook.

Documentary: a presentation (filmed or written) providing factual or substantial support for the statements and information contained therein.

Double truck: two facing pages laid out and made up as one double-width page.

Down style: newspaper style for type that capitalizes initial letters of as few words as possible.

Draft: (as in rough draft or first draft) initial manuscript or copy preparation before copyreading and final typing.

Dummy: sketch or layout of the way a page will look, showing makeup person where each makeup element is to be located; also, a blank page or blank book used for planning something to be published.

Duotone: photograph printed in black and one other color.

Duplicated newspaper: newspaper produced by machines using stencils, such as mimeograph.

E

Ear: type composition or design, usually boxed, placed in upper corner of page (to left or right of nameplate).

Editing: checking copy to ensure suitability for publication.

Edition: one issue of a publication.

Editor: person in charge of putting out a publication or section of a publication.

Editorial: type of journalistic writing that interprets the news, often reflecting the writer's or publication's opinions, beliefs, or policy.

Editorial policy: statement of a publication's goal or purpose; a given publication's official attitude toward debatable news topics; a principle followed by a publication in its news presentations.

Editorialize: to inject opinion into straight news presentations.

Education editor: editor assigned to supervise that section of a publication dealing with educational matters.

Educational television: noncommercial or "public" television used (usually on closed-circuit systems) to present educational materials.

Element of news (See *News element*).

Em: unit for measuring a quantity of type, square in shape, with each dimension being the same as the type size it represents; the horizontal space in body type is equal in width to the space occupied by the letter *m*.

En: one-half em.

Endmark: mark written or typed at the end of copy to notify the printer that the story is complete.

Engraving: metal or plastic plates that reproduce illustrations or photos.

Etch: removal of parts of a metallic plate by acid.

Ethnic newspaper: (or publication): newspaper or publication that presents news and information of interest to a specific ethnic group.

Exchange editor: editor assigned the responsibility for the reciprocal exchange of his or her publication for other publications, who usually brings to the attention of other staff members items of note or concern contained in the publications received.

Exchange publications: publications exchanged reciprocally, usually between schools.

Expository feature story: feature story that explains some topic of news value emphasizing the *why* and *how* of the event.

Exposure meter: instrument photographers use to determine correct light exposure.

Extra: special edition of a newspaper.

F

Facing page: opposite page.

Facsimile: process by which printed matter and pictures are electronically transmitted.

Fast film: specially manufactured camera film prepared to allow picture-taking with short exposures.

Feature: news story, written informally, providing information and, sometimes, entertainment.

F.C.C.: Federal Communications Commission—agency of the federal government responsible for licensing and supervising broadcasters.

File: a computer term to describe a story on the disk. This file is referenced by the name that is given during a WRITE operation. For long stories it may be necessary to break the story into several files. These portions of a single long story are called *links*.

Filler *(Boilerplate, Liner):* extra informational material, usually short in length, that can be used at any time, prepared to help fill columns and to relieve monotony of solid columns of type; often supplied by syndicates.

Film holder: device for holding cut film in back of large format camera.

Five "w's" and the "h": the who, what, when, where, why, and how that constitute the basis for news stories.

Flag: nameplate appearing on page one.

Flat-bed press: printing press on which type rests on a flat surface; printing is accomplished by rolling flat pieces of paper across the type.

Flat lighting: results of too much artificial light thrown directly onto subject being photographed.

Flat rate (advertising): fixed advertising rate based on established price per column inch or agate line.

Floating nameplate: publications nameplate, which may appear in different position from issue to issue.

Flush: body type set even with margins.

Flush head: a headline unit having all lines flush with the left-hand rule or margin.

Focus: sharp image obtained by adjusting the distance between camera lens and film, or lens and plate.

Fold: imaginary horizontal line across the center of a newspaper page.

Folio: page number; sheet of paper folded once; book made up from large sheets of paper folded once.

Font: complete set of type of one size and style, including complete alphabets in capitals and lowercase letters plus numerals and special symbols.

Foreign correspondent: news reporter assigned to cover news from areas outside continental limits of the United States.

Form: type composition made up into a specified arrangement and locked into a metal frame (or chase) for printing or stereotyping.

Formal style: composition (writing) that strictly follows traditional rules of grammar and usage.

Format: plan for shape, size, and makeup of a piece of printing or publication.

Free-lance writer: writer having no direct affiliation with any one given publication, enabling him or her to supply materials to several publications.

Free press: a press that is not censored except by itself, that reports the truth as it sees it.

Future book: date book listing story possibilities of future events (usually maintained by city editor).

G

Galley: long, narrow metal or wood tray used to hold type before it is placed in chase.

Galley proof: printed impression or proof of the type contained in galleys, usually printed on long, narrow strips of paper.

Gang: assembling of all similar materials into a single unit, for economy.

Ghost writer: writer who writes materials that are published by or credited to someone else.

Giveaway: commercial publication, distributed free, having little editorial content and much advertising.

Gothic type: sans-serif type faces characterized by unslanted, straight up and down strokes.

Graflex: type of press camera used by news photographers.

Ground-glass plate: plate of glass on some cameras that reflects what will be contained in the picture.

Guideline: printer's instructions, usually written in capital letters above a story.

Gutter: space in a form that produces the inside margins of printed pages.

H

Halftone: cut made from a photograph; engraving that reproduces photographs, made by photographing the original photograph or picture through a fine screen to break the image down into a series (or pattern) of dots.

Hanging indentation: headline deck with first line running from column margin to column margin, succeeding lines indented at left.

Hardcopy: typewritten copy produced on a line printer or typewriter.

Hard news: non-feature and straight news.

Headline schedule: listing of examples of type faces used regularly for a publication's headlines.

Head-shot: photograph (portrait) showing only head and shoulders of subject.

Highlights: those parts of a photograph or picture appearing white or close to white; also, major points in a news story or feature.

Home: most upper left cursor location on the VDT screen.

Horizontal makeup: makeup style using headlines, cuts, and stories that extend across two or more columns.

Hot type: type made from molten metal (usually lead) and set by a linotype machine. (Cold type is set by computer.)

House ad: advertisement in a publication advertising that publication, such as subscription information, feature highlights, etc.

House organ (Company publication, House publication): publication, produced by or for a company, organization, etc., containing information and news of interest to employees or members of that company or organization.

HTK (or HTC): abbreviation for printer's spelling of Head to Kum; incomplete copy awaiting headline.

Human interest: news element designed to stimulate the reader's feelings and emotions by presenting entertaining, interesting news about people and their actions.

I

Immediacy: news element stressing timeliness and freshness of reporting.

Impression: pressure of type, plate, or blanket in contact with paper.

Impulse item: nonessential product marketed by advertisers.

In-depth (coverage, reporting): news presentation emphasizing background, causes, and consequences of events.

Index: alphabetical listing of the contents of a publication.

Interest group (special-interest group): organized individuals using mass media to further their ideas, prestige, and power.

Interpretive journalism: type of journalism in which complex matters are explained and clarified.

Inverted pyramid head: headline in which the lines taper to the bottom, giving the appearance of an upside-down pyramid.

Inverted pyramid structure (or paragraph): newspaper writing style arranging information in order of descending news value.

J

Journalism: all of the activities involved in the gathering, organizing, presenting, and publishing of news.

Journalist: individual connected with gathering, organizing, presenting, and publishing news.

Jump head: line of type preceding continuation of a story that helps identify that story.

Jump line: line of type indicating where a story is continued to or where a story has been continued from.

Justification: making all lines of type in a column exactly the same width.

Justified column (or margin): set type which always fills the line, thus creating uniform margins.

Justowriter: cold type, tape-controlled composing machine that automatically types and justifies a line of copy.

K

Kicker (Astonisher, Read-in, Tagline, Whiplash): short headline above or below main head, usually set in smaller-size type than main head.

Kill: to prevent or prohibit the printing or setting of copy.

Kinetoscope: device invented by Edison for showing pictures that appear to move.

L

Laser: a device that produces a highly concentrated, powerful beam of light. In communications, that beam is used to direct facsimile printing.

Layout (See *Dummy*): finished plan for printed page, showing position and placement of all headlines, copy, photographs, illustrations, and advertisements.

Layout editor: person responsible for planning the location of all items to be printed.

Lead (pronounced *leed*): first section of news story that introduces or summarizes a news event, usually contained in one paragraph.

Lead (pronounced *led*): thin strip of metal used between lines of type to separate and space them vertically.

Legend (See *Caption*).

Letter of query: letter written by free-lance writers to magazine editors, providing details of proposed article.

Letterpress: printing method by which the ink is transferred from the raised surfaces of the printing plate directly onto the paper.

Libel: written statement that attacks or defames a person without just cause.

Light meter: light-sensitive instrument used for measuring light available for photographing.

Line printer: a typewriterlike printer except it does not include a keyboard. The output is controlled by a computer and the line printer can print out stories on paper.

Liner (See *Filler*).

Line cut: engraving made from a drawing rendered in solid black on a white background.

Linotype: hot-metal, typecasting machine which casts a line of type on one piece of metal.

Lithographer: person who prepares an offset plate for printing.

Lithography: process of printing from a plane surface that accepts ink only on the design to be reproduced.

Live coverage: radio and television broadcasting of events simultaneously with their occurrence.

Lock-up: finished form of page, containing all engravings, type, and headlines, ready to be stereotyped.

Log (radio, tv): list of all sales, programming and engineering activities to be forwarded to FCC for review.

Logo *(Logotype):* unique design of cast type used for identifying the name or trademark of a product.

Long-shot *(Establishing shot):* first shot taken by a motion-picture photographer or videotaper when panning the subject.

M

Magazine newspaper supplement: magazine-style publications prepared for weekend newspapers.

Makeup: arrangement of engravings, type, and headlines on a page.

Managing Editor: supervisor of all news-gathering operations on a newspaper.

Marketing research: systematic investigation of consumer needs, attitudes, and habits, usually conducted by an advertising agency.

Mass communication: dissemination of information to large numbers of people.

Mass media: any means of disseminating information or entertainment to large groups of people.

Masthead: statement of ownership and other related facts concerning a publication.

Mat *(Matrix):* mold made by pressing type form against receptive surface; in stereotyping, the paper mold used in printing newspapers.

Measure: width of type, usually expressed in picas.

Mechanical department: division of a newspaper responsible for composition, printing, and production.

Media director: a member of an advertising agency who determines the media an advertisement is to appear in (a decision usually based on which media will give the best return for the most reasonable investment).

Medium: instrument or means for transmitting message between sender and receiver.

Menu: the directory or index of the contents of a computer disk or diskette.

Message: words, pictures, or signs exchanged between sender and receiver.

Modular: type of layout in which every element on the page is squared off, giving the impression of a number of boxes varying in size and shape, some horizontal and others vertical.

Monotype: machine for setting individual characters of type.

Montage: several photographs or illustrations combined to produce one overall photograph or illustration.

More: used at end of page of copy to indicate story is continued.

Morgue: library of files containing background information.

Muckraking: type of journalism dedicated to sensationally exposing problems and wrongdoing.

N

Nameplate: publication's title, usually appearing near the top of the front page or front cover.

National advertising manager: newspaper employee who supervises sales and placement of advertisements for nationally known products.

Network: group of radio stations or television stations that broadcast the same programs.

News: timely information about events that have occurred, are occurring, or will occur.

Newsbook: early forerunner of modern newspaper.

Newscast: any informative presentation (news program, documentary, etc.) made public by means of radio or television.

Newscaster: television or radio announcer who broadcasts news.

News director: individual in charge of the assigning and editing of news stories for the electronic media.

News editor *(Telegraph editor):* journalist who selects wire-service stories for newspaper publication.

News element: one of several qualities that attract reader interest to news presentations.

News interpreter: broadcast commentator who analyzes and interprets news events.

News leak: off-the-record information given to reporters.

Newsprint: inexpensive grade of paper used for printing newspapers.

News release *(Press release, Publicity release):* written information distributed to reporters by news source.

News source: reliable individual or group who supplies information to news reporters.

News story: factual report of news event.

Novelty lead: general term applied to any of several ways for writing an opening paragraph for news stories and feature articles.

N.S.P.A.: scholastic press association offering services to school publications (National Scholastic Press Association, 18 Journalism Building, University of Minnesota, Minneapolis, Minnesota 55455).

N.S.Y.A.: scholastic press association offering services to school publications (National School Yearbook Association, Post Office Box 17344, Memphis, Tennessee 38117).

O

Obituary: news story about a death.

Offset: method of printing from a flat plate.

Optical character reader (OCR): scans copy to drive typesetting machine or to produce tape that drives it. OCR may store story in computer to be called out on a cathode ray tube for editing.

Outline cut: engraving bordered by fine lines on all sides.

Over-banner: banner headline appearing above name of publication.

Overlay: sheet of transparent paper, placed over an illustration, containing instructions for engraver.

Overset: set type not used in a particular edition.

P

Phototypesetting: method for setting type photographically.

Pica: ⅙-inch unit used to measure the size of type.

Pied type: type that is scrambled.

Platen press: flat-bed press used for letterpress plates.

Point: 1/72-inch unit used to measure the size of type.

Policy: editorial views and opinions of a publication.

Positive: photographic image that corresponds to original copy (the reverse of negative).

Prior restraint: an order made to an editor not to print certain material under threat of contempt of court. The order is made by a judge, who warrants that the publication of a fact may be harmful.

Proximity: news element having information about familiar people, places, or situations.

Public-affairs programs: programs in the public interest prepared by radio and television stations.

Pulp magazine: inexpensively produced magazine, often presenting sensational articles.

Pyramided ads: advertisements bulked together on a page to resemble structure of a pyramid so that each ad will be adjacent to news copy.

Q

Quill and Scroll: international honor society of journalism for high schools (School of Journalism, State University of Iowa, Iowa City, Iowa 52240).

R

Reproduction proof *(Repro):* proof (usually on quality stock) of final copy from which offset plates are made.

Retraction: a statement admitting that the publication has made a factual error. A retraction is not a defense in a libel case but may decrease the penalty.

Rotary press: cylinder press used mainly by large newspapers for printing letterpress plates.

Running foot: line of type appearing at bottom of inside pages, giving name, date, and page number.

Running head: line of type appearing at top of inside pages, giving name, date, and page number.

S

Scrolling: the process of running forward or backward through the storage area in the VDT terminal to display the desired lines of text on the screen.

Section editor: editor in charge of a particular section of a yearbook or magazine.

Sensationalism: practice of selecting and treating news in a manner calculated to arouse emotional response.

Silhouette halftone: Halftone in which all of the background material is deleted in order to emphasize only the main subject in the picture.

Slander: false charges made orally or oral misrepresentations that defame or damage a person's character.

Slanted news: news presentations written to reflect an opinion (usually the writer's opinion or the opinion of the medium the material is written for).

Sliding scale of rates: advertising rates that vary according to size, type, and location of advertisement.

Slug: a one-word summary of the topic of an article. This slug is placed in the upper-right corner of the sheet of paper that the reporter is using to write the story; also, a metal bar on which linotype is set.

Spot news: timely news, usually occurring unexpectedly.

Stencil: type of printing plate used on mimeograph machines.

Stereotype: duplicate of a letterpress printing plate.

Stet: printer's term for "leave in" or "let stand."

Stripping: placement of negatives (or positives) in their planned position on a flat before platemaking.

Subhead: small headline within a story, inserted to indicate a subdivision within the story.

Subsidized newspaper: newspaper that is not self-supporting and must depend upon extra financial aid.

Summary lead: opening paragraph of a news story that presents the key facts of the story.

Syndicate: company, organization, or agency that buys and sells newsworthy materials to be used by members of the print media.

T

Tear sheet: a page showing an advertisement in a publication that may be cut (or torn out) and sent to the advertiser as proof that the advertisement did in fact run in that edition.

Theme: general idea expressed throughout a publication's copy and illustrations.

Tombstone: two or more headlines of same size and style placed next to each other on same page.

Type block: page area, exclusive of margins, on which type and illustrations normally appear.

Typo: typographical error made either in typing or setting of copy.

U

Upper and lowercase: type set with first letters of important words capitalized, remaining letters appearing in lowercase.

Uppercase: capital letters.

Up style: newspaper style in which all initial letters of important words are capitalized for emphasis.

V

Varitype: cold-type composing machine that utilizes a wide variety of type sizes, capable of justifying lines of copy.

VDT (*Video display terminal*): the input and editing terminal used in an electronic newsroom system.

Vignette: halftone made so that printed image fades off into white at edges.

W

Web press: term applied to high-speed printing presses that print on a continuous sheet of paper.

Widow: less than a line of type appearing by itself on the top of a page.

Wire service: news-gathering organization that obtains and services news for members of the mass media of communication. *United Press International* (UPI) and the *Associated Press* (AP) are this country's largest wire services; *Reuters* is Great Britain's.

XYZ

Yellow journalism: unethical, sensational news reporting.

Zinc etching: engraving of a line drawing made in zinc.

INDEX

ABCDEFGH   0876543
Printed in the United States of America